AP* Achiever Advanced Placement Economics Exam Preparation Guide

to accompany

Economics: Principles, Problems, and Policies

Eighteenth Edition

Campbell R. McConnell
Stanley L. Brue
Sean Masaki Flynn

Prepared by
Lisa C. Herman Ellison

* Pre-AP, AP, and Advanced Placement program are registered trademarks of the College Entrance Examination Board, which was not involved in the production of and does not endorse these products.

Boston   Burr Ridge, IL   Dubuque, IA   New York   San Francisco   St. Louis
Bangkok   Bogotá   Caracas   Kuala Lumpur   Lisbon   London   Madrid   Mexico City
Milan   Montreal   New Delhi   Santiago   Seoul   Singapore   Sydney   Taipei   Toronto

The **McGraw·Hill** Companies

AP* Achiever Advanced Placement Economics Exam Preparation Guide to accompany
ECONOMICS: PRINCIPLES, PROBLEMS, AND POLICIES, EIGHTEENTH EDITION
CAMPBELL R. MCCONNELL, STANLEY L. BRUE, AND SEAN MASAKI FLYNN

Published by McGraw-Hill Higher Education, an imprint of The McGraw-Hill Companies, Inc., 1221 Avenue of the Americas, New York, NY 10020. Copyright © 2010 by The McGraw-Hill Companies, Inc. All rights reserved.

Printed in the United States of America

3 4 5 6 7 8 9 0 QDB/QDB 15 14 13 12

ISBN: 978-0-07-892841-3

MHID: 0-07-892841-9

www.mhhe.com

* Pre-AP, AP, and Advanced Placement program are registered trademarks of the College Entrance Examination Board, which was not involved in the production of and does not endorse these products.

About the Author

Lisa C. Herman Ellison has taught AP Micro/Macroeconomics at Kokomo High School, in Kokomo, Indiana, since 1988. She also teaches AP U.S. Government and Politics and college-prep Economics. She has served as a reader for AP Economics exams and attended College Board AP summer institutes. She is the teacher representative on the Indiana Council for Economic Education Executive Committee and was a member of the team that wrote the Indiana Economics Standards in 2002 and the Indiana Core-40 Exam in Economics in 2004. Lisa has served as a reviewer for EconEdLink and three high school textbooks, and she has written or co-authored nearly three dozen lessons and articles in publications such as *Social Education*, *EconEdLink*, and *EconExchange*. She was the Midwest award winner and one of five national finalists for the NASDAQ National Teaching Award for Teachers of Excellence and Innovation in 2003. She also won the National Association of Regulatory Utility Commissioners Excellence in Education Award in 1990, as well as 3rd place for the International Paper Company Foundational National Award for the Teaching of Economics in 1993. She is a recipient of the Olin W. Davis Award for Exemplary Teaching of Economics from the Indiana Council for Economic Education, as well as the Jasper P. Baldwin Award for Excellence in Undergraduate Teaching from the University of Oklahoma. Lisa earned her B.A. in Economics and Political Science, her teaching license, and an M.A. in Secondary Education from Ball State University. She also studied in the M.A. in Public Policy program at the University of Oklahoma with a specialty in unemployment policy.

Acknowledgements

This work would not have been possible without the help of several people. First, my deepest gratitude to my husband Brett and our sons Andrew and Cameron for their love, hugs, and willingness to do the extra work required at home so Mom could work on "the book" for the past few months. A family vacation to celebrate is on the way! Deepest thanks and a hug also go to my Mom, Judy Herman, for instilling in me the passion to help kids understand the world around them, and for her faith and constant encouragement throughout this process. I also appreciate the professional advice, personal support, and humor of colleagues and friends Robert McIntire, Tom Richardson, and Mary LaMar. I also want to extend special thanks to Dr. Harlan Day and the entire staff at the Indiana Council for Economic Education for providing so many opportunities for me to grow as a teacher and a writer. And finally, thanks to Mickey Cox, my editor at McGraw-Hill, for her guidance and patience in this project.

Contents

OVERVIEW OF THE AP ECONOMICS COURSE

Economics is much more than a school subject. Economics involves a whole new way of thinking. You will gain insights into the reasoning of consumers and the rationale for decision-makers in firms and governments. Once you understand the principles of economics, you will almost certainly view decision-making, the economy, and the relationships among people, firms, governments, and countries differently.

Economics and the Real World
Economics is about decision making in everyday life. You probably already know a good number of economic principles as a result of your life experiences. If there is a shortage of concert tickets and the official ticket sites sell out, what will happen to the price you have to pay a seller on eBay? If the economy enters a recession and demand falls for a firm's products, will the firm be more likely to hire or lay off workers? The wonderful thing about studying economics is that the question "When will I ever use this?" is unlikely to arise. Economics is about our lives. Consider this subject Life 101.

As you learn the various laws, principles, and models of economic behavior, at some point it will probably strike you that the world doesn't work exactly as the models suggest. For example, if you are deciding whether to buy a glass of orange juice or a cup of coffee, it is unlikely that you will whip out a pencil and paper to analyze the numerical value of the satisfaction you would receive from each of the drinks, calculate that satisfaction received per dollar spent for each of the drinks, and then make your selection based on that result. But you'll *act* as though you did just that. You will learn numeric and graphic representations of economic principles to help you understand why people make the economic decisions they do, but most people make their decisions without such formal analysis. In these situations, think about the smiley face symbol. ☺ We all recognize it as a face, but have you ever met someone whose face really looked exactly like a smiley face? A frightening proposition, indeed! In the same way, you will learn the "behind-the-scenes" rationales for economic decision making, understanding that, while the models may not *exactly* match real-world behaviors, they provide our best understanding of economic relationships, principles, and policies.

The Advanced Placement Program
The Advanced Placement (AP) program was created by the College Board, which also developed the SAT exam. The AP economics course descriptions and exams are written by the AP Economics Development Committee, which consists of college economics professors and high school teachers with experience teaching the AP economics course. This committee has studied the economics course descriptions from hundreds of university professors to determine which concepts to include in the AP economics course descriptions and the focus of the AP economics exams. The College Board requires audits of high school courses with the AP designation to ensure that the high school curriculum meets standards equivalent to the college economics course. From time to time, the College Board asks college students to take the AP exam, so that the College Board may compare scores and ensure that the score distribution for high school test-takers is appropriate.

So...What IS Economics?
Microeconomics and macroeconomics are generally two one-semester courses that explore different aspects of our economy. Because the resources we need to produce the products we want are scarce, we have to make decisions about how to satisfy our unlimited wants with those

limited, scarce resources. While microeconomics focuses on the small picture of decision making by individuals and firms, macroeconomics studies the big picture of national economies, governments, monetary systems, and international trade.

Microeconomics
According to the College Board, the microeconomics course (and by extension, the AP microeconomics exam) consists of the following areas of study, with the approximate percentage of course content involved in each area:

1. Basic economic concepts   (8–14%)
2. Product markets   (55–70%)
    A. Supply and demand   (15–20%)
    B. Consumer choice theory   (5–10%)
    C. The production function and costs   (10–15%)
    D. Profit maximization and market structures   (25–35%)
3. Factor markets   (10–18%)
4. Market failure and the role of government   (12–18%)

Macroeconomics
According to the College Board, the macroeconomics course (and by extension, the AP macroeconomics exam) consists of the following areas of study, with the approximate percentage of course content involved in each area:

1. Basic economic concepts   (8–12%)
2. Measuring economic performance   (12–16%)
3. National equilibrium (aggregate supply and demand)   (10–15%)
4. Money, banking, and finance   (15–20%)
5. Inflation, unemployment, and economic stabilization policies   (20–30%)
6. Growth and productivity   (5–10%)
7. International trade and finance   (10–15%)

Micro or Macro or Both?
You may be preparing for only one of the AP economics exams or both. This book contains the information necessary to prepare for both exams. Further, many economic principles are shared by both disciplines. The basic economic concepts of scarcity, tradeoffs, comparative advantage, voluntary exchange, and supply and demand are found in a variety of concepts in both courses. Changes in interest rates can affect the decision making of the individual firm in microeconomics, and those same changes can be seen in macroeconomics as firms across the nation respond to those interest rate changes. So if you are a student of only one of the AP economics courses, the other half of the economic picture isn't a foreign entity; it's the larger or smaller picture of how our portion of the world economy works. The table of contents, as well as the chapter introductions, identifies the content's relevancy to the AP microeconomics exam, the AP macroeconomics exam, or both.

The AP Economics Exam Prep Guide
In the chapter reviews that follow, you'll find boxes that draw your attention to special issues related to each chapter. The **Taking the EEK! Out of Economics** boxes focus on connections between concepts, confusing concepts, common mistakes made by economics students, and potential solutions and "tricks of the trade" to keep things straight. The **Bear in Mind** boxes highlight the material most likely to appear on the exams and the way in which that material might appear. Keep in mind that such suggestions are based on the items that have appeared on

previous AP economics exams and provide no guarantee about the specific kinds of questions that will appear on future exams.

In the same way, sample multiple-choice and free-response questions are provided at the end of each chapter review to test your understanding of the material in that chapter. The questions are designed to reflect the level of difficulty of actual AP economics exam questions, as well as the types of concepts tested on previous exams. Again, such questions are no guarantee of what types of questions you might encounter on your AP economics exam but will help prepare you for the material you will see on your exam.

OVERVIEW OF THE AP ECONOMICS EXAMS

The Structure of the Exam
Each of the AP economics exams – microeconomics and macroeconomics – is a two-hour and ten-minute exam. The College Board schedules these exams on the same day in May, with one exam in the morning and one in the afternoon. The multiple-choice section accounts for two-thirds of the score, and a free-response section provides the other one-third of the score.

The Multiple-Choice Section
The first portion of the exam consists of sixty multiple-choice questions, which are to be answered within seventy minutes. The multiple-choice questions can include a wide range of information, including definitions and applications of principles, calculations, interpretations of graphs, explanations of the causes or results of an economic action, and choosing an appropriate economic policy to deal with an economic event.

Multiple-Choice Test Tips
Each question has five potential answers. Each correct answer is worth one point, while one-fourth point is subtracted for each incorrect answer to penalize guessing. Questions left blank earn no points. So if you answered forty-five questions correctly, erred on eight questions, and left seven questions blank, your score for the multiple-choice section would be forty-three points. Because the College Board must distinguish among students earning the highest scores, it is likely that you will encounter high-level questions that you cannot answer with complete certainty. If you can eliminate at least one or two of the potential answers, it may be worth it to guess at the correct answer. But if you cannot eliminate any of the potential answers, you are better off to leave the question blank and move on.

It is important to watch your pace, as you have just over one minute to answer each question. Some questions can be answered very quickly, while others will require more complicated analysis, so keep moving.

Be careful, too, not to overanalyze questions. In many cases, a correct answer may appear too simple or straightforward, but beware of second-guessing your answers. Many times on multiple-choice tests, students initially select the correct answer only to return to the question and change the answer. Unless you realize you have misread the question or have missed a better answer among the choices, trust your first decision.

Forbidden Test Items

Calculators are *not* allowed in the AP economics exams. While you will likely be asked to perform calculations for some questions, the math is relatively simple if you understand the principles involved and remember how to set up the equations. In addition, colored pencils and markers are no longer allowed for drawing graphs; all free-response writing must be in blue or black pen.

The Free-Response Section

The second portion of the exam consists of three free-response questions, with half of the score given for the first written response and the other half divided between the other two written responses. The sixty minutes of free-response time begins with a mandatory ten-minute reading period, during which you may begin outlining your answers and sketching graphs. You will then have the remaining fifty minutes to write your answers. The College Board suggests that you spend approximately twenty-five minutes writing the long response and divide the other 25 minutes between the shorter responses. The long response generally involves interconnections among several different concepts central to the course, while the shorter responses generally focus on one specific concept or a pair of related concepts.

Free-Response Writing Tips

AP economics responses are quite different from the formal essays written for some other AP subjects, which require thesis statements and a five-paragraph developmental structure. AP economics free-response questions generally consist of a series of questions and sub-questions which can be answered in several sentences. Responses should *directly* answer the questions asked.

Keep in mind the economic concept of efficiency and apply that to your free-response writing. Be complete but be efficient about it. Directly answer the question asked, and explain why that answer is correct. Don't write as though you've swallowed a dictionary, reaching for complex language and unnecessary difficulty. Some of the best answers use the appropriate terms and the clearest language to explain the situation, causes and effects, and reasoning. The readers want to see a clear analysis and your reasoning.

Over the years, free-response readers have consistently noted that students have problems linking the concepts and explaining why a change in one factor will lead to changes in other factors. For example, if a hurricane wipes out the Florida orange crop, how will the price of apple juice be affected? The price of apple juice will increase. The link is that the lower supply of oranges will increase the cost of producing orange juice, which is a substitute product for apple juice. When consumers see the higher price of orange juice, many will reduce the quantity of orange juice consumed and increase their demand for apple juice, pushing up the price of apple juice. It is important to make those kinds of links clear to demonstrate to the reader that you understand causes and effects.

It is very important to understand what the question is asking you to do. One big clue is to look for the verbs: "define," "identify," "explain," "label," or "using a graph, show." Try to envision what the rubric (answer key) will look like. What are the readers looking for from each part of the question? Then answer each part of the question in the order it was asked. If you refer to a graph in your writing ("As you can see in Graph A"), title that graph clearly ("Graph A") so readers can quickly identify the appropriate graph.

Many of the free-response questions also require you to draw one or more graphs. As the exam directions indicate, it is *very* important that you correctly label your graphs. Your axis labels should be clear (for example, "Price and Quantity," or "Price Level and Real Output"). Every curve should be appropriately labeled. If you want to indicate the shift of a curve, be sure to draw arrows between the curves to show the direction of movement, and label the second curve differently (for example, D1 and D2). Draw equilibrium points where appropriate and indicate those equilibrium prices or quantities on the axes of your graph. Remember that the readers want to award you points for every correct portion of your response, so make their job as easy as possible.

Once you have finished your free-response questions, it is essential that you carefully read your answers again. Have you specifically answered each part of each question? Have you made links to explain why that answer is correct? Have you labeled all axes and curves on each graph, illustrating equilibrium points and showing the directions of shifts in curves? Very often, easy points are lost because of a moment of carelessness in missing a sub-question or drawing an arrow facing the wrong direction. Give yourself credit for your hard work!

And one last note about the actual writing of the free response: for those of you who are "handwriting-challenged" – and you know who you are – take a moment to consider that your reader will be taking a week out of his or her summer vacation to read thousands of free-response answers to the very same question, over and over for eight hours a day. Do you really want to challenge that reader with handwriting that requires use of a magnifying glass? Or a chicken-scratch interpreter? It is in your best interest to make it as easy as possible for the reader to understand what you have to say. If your printing is awful, try cursive. If your cursive is a wreck, try printing. If both are bad, try printing in all capital letters. Making your writing easy to read ensures you the best possible chance that your reader will be able to accurately find your correct answers to grant you the score you deserve.

It is important to note that because the rubrics are so precise, multiple points can be awarded throughout each free response. For example, using the earlier example of the hurricane wiping out the orange crop, if you responded that the apple juice prices would increase but erroneously gave the reason that the hurricane had also wiped out the apple trees, you might receive one point for identifying that the apple juice price increased but not receive the second point for correct reasoning.

It is also important to note that when an answer involves a chain of events, the readers recognize that one error at the beginning of the chain might cause all of the following answers to be wrong, even though your logic is correct. For example, the free-response question could list economic data that indicates the economy is in a recession and then ask you to identify the economic problem and fiscal policy needed to stabilize the economy. A correct answer would be to identify the recession and explain that the government should lower taxes and raise government spending to increase the aggregate demand in the economy. But if you made the mistake of seeing the problem as inflation and therefore reversed your policy answers to raise taxes and lower government spending, your entire answer could be wiped out. In order to more fairly recognize good economic reasoning, sometimes rubrics will be set in such a way that if the initial response is wrong but the rest of the answers flow correctly based on that initial answer, you will lose the point for the initial answer but still receive credit for the rest of your answers. On the free-response questions, there is no penalty for guessing, so it is always in your best interest to make an attempt to answer.

The Free-Response Reading
In June of each year, high school AP economics teachers and college economics instructors gather to score the exams. The chief reader, who directs the reading, is assisted by question leaders, who direct the reading of each free-response question, and table leaders, who lead each table of readers who are focused on a single free-response question. Before the reading begins, the chief reader, the question leaders, and the table leaders, all experienced readers, create the rubric for each free-response question. They determine the correct answers and then consider the many ways a student could express a correct answer, reading several of the student submissions to help develop the most accurate rubric. When other readers arrive, they are taught how to apply the rubric, and they practice grading to identify concerns until all readers of a particular question are comfortable with the rubric. Throughout the reading, table leaders spot check the scores assessed by each reader- in an effort to ensure that all responses will be scored in the same way, regardless of which reader actually scores the response.

Determining the AP Exam Score
The multiple-choice section is scored electronically, while readers grade the free-response sections. The College Board then applies a weighting formula and combines the raw multiple-choice and free-response scores to create a composite score. Finally, a conversion factor is used to award the student one of five final scores:

- *5 – Extremely well qualified*
- *4 – Well qualified*
- *3 – Qualified*
- *2 – Possibly qualified*
- *1 – No recommendation*

AP Scores and College Credit
Because the AP microeconomics and macroeconomics courses are intended to represent the two one-semester college courses, the two AP exams are are scored independently. You may opt to take either exam or to take both exams. A passing score on either exam can provide college credit for institutions that accept AP credit, but colleges and universities differ markedly in requirements and credits offered. Some schools accept a score of 3 for credit, while other schools require a 4 or a 5 in order to receive credit. It is highly recommended that you explore the websites or contact the admissions offices of the colleges or universities you are considering to find out what scores are required for credit at each institution.

CHAPTER 1: LIMITS, ALTERNATIVES, AND CHOICES

Introduction

At the heart of the study of economics is the simple but very real prospect that we cannot have it all. We have too few resources to meet all of our wants and needs, so we are forced to make choices. Chapter 1 identifies the basic problem of economics and introduces the first models of decision making by individuals, firms, governments, and societies. The principle of tradeoffs takes both numeric and graphic form and provides the foundation for the rest of the economics course. Material from Chapter 1 appears in several multiple-choice questions on both the AP microeconomics and macroeconomics exams and occasionally appears in free-response questions.

Scarcity and Economics

Throughout the economics course, you will probably notice terms that are familiar to you from other contexts. But you will find that, very often, economists use those terms in different or more specific ways. Take the word "scarce." In most contexts, the word "scarce" simply means that something is rare or that little of it is available. But economists add a very important second part to the definition, which is that consumers want more of the item than is available. It is an important distinction. There is little polio in the world any more. However, an economist would not say that polio is scarce in the economic sense, because people are not trying to obtain more polio than is available. The competition for products and the resources used to make them is the foundation of the study of economics. In economics, we study how people make choices, using limited resources to satisfy their unlimited wants.

The Economizing Problem

Scarcity of products results from the scarcity of resources used to make them. Land, labor, capital, and entrepreneurship—the factors of production—are all used to produce economic products. The competition for those resources forces us to make choices about what we will produce, how we will produce it, and who will receive the products. Just as individuals have to make choices, firms must choose what to produce and how to produce it. In the same way, whole societies have to make choices about whether to spend more of the federal budget for military or social welfare programs, or whether to use resources to drill for more oil or to invest in alternative forms of energy.

Microeconomics and Macroeconomics

Microeconomics is the study of the small picture—the decision making of individuals, households, and firms. Macroeconomics is the study of the big picture—the decision making of consumers as a group, firms nationwide, governments, and banking systems. It is important to keep in mind that macroeconomic changes are the result of the many decisions made by individual consumers and firms.

Bear in Mind

While the College Board has developed separate AP microeconomics and macroeconomics exams, many concepts are central to both disciplines. The issues of scarcity, the economizing problem, opportunity cost, and production possibilities introduced in Chapter 1 are concepts that will very likely appear on both exams.

Theories, Principles, and Models

Economists use the scientific method to understand economic performance by observing, creating and testing hypotheses, and developing theories. These theories become models that explain and predict the behaviors of people, firms, and governments in our society. While people can make choices contrary to what we might expect, we can recognize generalized patterns of behavior with these principles or laws. During analysis, economists rely on *ceteris paribus*, an assumption that nothing in the world changes during the analysis except the variable(s) being measured. In that way, we can better determine the cause-and-effect relationships between variables. Of course, in the real world there is no way to hold everything else equal, but that assumption is essential for helping to sort out the many variables that can affect economic decision making.

Opportunity Cost

Because we cannot have everything we want, we are forced to make choices which involve opportunity costs—the cost of giving up the next best opportunity when we make a decision. When you buy a hamburger, what is your next best alternative? A fish sandwich? When you go to class, what is your next best alternative? Working? Every decision involves an opportunity cost, because there is always some other alternative that might have been chosen. Some important things to note about opportunity cost:

- The opportunity cost is the other choice, not the price or the resource used to obtain it. If you spend $20 to buy a DVD rather than a T-shirt, your opportunity cost is the T-shirt. It isn't the $20, because you were going to spend that money either way. Your opportunity cost is your next best alternative *use* of that money.
- Opportunity cost is only the *next* best choice, not every available alternative. When you buy the DVD, your opportunity cost isn't the T-shirt and gas for your car and a pizza. It was only the next best choice. Think about the term "opportunity cost." What was the opportunity you gave up?
- Costs that are incurred regardless of which choice you make are not opportunity costs. If you had to choose between going to a school band concert or a home basketball game, you would use the same amount of gas to drive to school, regardless of your decision. Therefore, even though gas does have a monetary cost, it would not be represented as an opportunity cost in that decision. But if you chose between going to the concert or staying home to watch TV, the cost of gas would be involved in that choice, since staying home incurs no cost of gas.
- Opportunity cost only involves costs, not benefits. Consider the expenses you will incur in college: tuition, fees, books, and room and board. The opportunity cost for your college education may be a house or cars. Your opportunity cost also includes the income you could have earned by working full-time during those college years. Despite the opportunity cost, students go to college because the long-term benefits outweigh the initial costs. But it's important to note that the opportunity cost doesn't include those benefits. Opportunity cost only recognizes what was given up, as a way of studying the problem of scarcity.

Taking the EEK! Out of Economics

You must be able to recognize that every choice involves another alternative that was given up, even if the choice made the person better off. Keep in mind that you're looking for what was given up in making the decision, and that will help you to identify what is—and what is not—an opportunity cost.

Chapter 1: Limits, Alternatives, and Choices

Tradeoffs and Budget Constraints
Because our unlimited desires are greater than our limited resources, we are forced to make choices. We can see those choices in a budget constraint, which illustrates the combination of products we can buy with our limited income. If you have $120 to buy DVDs (at $20 each) or books (at $10 each), you could spend all of your money to buy six DVDs or twelve books. You could also buy a different combination such as three DVDs and six books.

One important concept to understand from this model is that the budget constraint line represents the tradeoffs involved in making choices. For each additional DVD you buy, you must give up buying two books, which represent the opportunity cost of your decision. Conversely, for each book you buy, you incur the opportunity cost of one-half DVD.

Another key point is that while points on or below the budget constraint are attainable, points outside the budget constraint are not attainable with your income. You could buy one DVD and one book and save the rest of your money, but you wouldn't maximize your satisfaction. However, buying six DVDs and six books simply isn't an option, because you don't have the income to satisfy your wants. While those with higher incomes are able to buy more DVDs and books, they still face a budget constraint; theirs is simply higher. The budget constraint serves as a limit, illustrating the problem of scarcity.

Utility
When people make choices, economists assume that people will act rationally in their self-interest. Clearly, this isn't always the case. Remember the smiley face symbol (☺)? However, most people make decisions that they believe will be in their self-interest, given the information they have. When people make decisions, they try to increase their satisfaction through the utility of a product or an activity. Because people have determined that a car holds more utility than a can of soda, they are willing to incur a much larger opportunity cost to buy a car than to buy a soda.

The Production Possibilities Curve
The production possibilities curve is a graphic model that can help us visualize the tradeoffs of opportunity cost and the limits of production in society. It is similar to the budget constraint facing the individual, but rather than focusing on what an individual can purchase, the production possibilities curve instead focuses on how many products can be produced by a society. This model starts with the assumptions that only two products can be produced in this society, that resources are fully employed, and that resources and technology are fixed for the period of analysis. Of course, in the real world, economies don't look exactly like this. Remember the smiley (☺)? However, the limitations on resources and technology limit our ability to produce all of the products people want in our society.

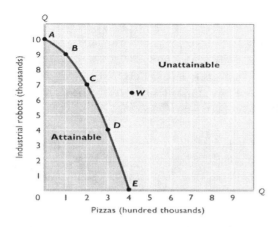

The production possibilities curve

The production possibilities curve shows the maximum combination of goods that can be produced in an economy, given limited resources and technology. Every point on the curve represents full employment of resources. The curve shows the opportunity cost of producing a product. In this example, if we choose to produce ten units of industrial robots, we cannot produce any pizzas. If we then choose to produce our first unit of pizza, we must give up producing one unit of industrial robots. Therefore, our opportunity cost of producing one unit of pizza is one unit of industrial robots. The most important concept the production possibilities curve illustrates is that because of scarce resources, if we produce more of one good, we have to produce less of something else.

Bear in Mind

You must be able to identify opportunity cost in words, numerically, and graphically. Be sure you can read a table that lists combinations of goods that can be produced with available resources. Also be sure you are comfortable interpreting a production possibilities curve with points illustrating those combinations. In either case, to identify the opportunity cost of increasing production of one good, look at how much production of the other good falls.

Points inside the curve are attainable but are not desirable and represent unemployment of resources. In this example, it would be possible to produce three units of robots and two units of pizza, but, because resources are scarce, we want to maximize the use of our resources to make as many products as possible. When we are producing at a point of unemployment, it is possible to increase production of both robots and pizza because we have unused resources available to make both products. Our short-run economic goal is to reach full employment and produce at a point on the production possibilities curve.

Chapter 1: Limits, Alternatives, and Choices

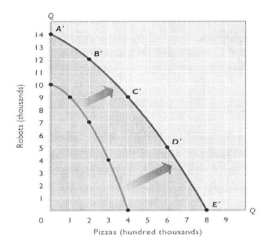

Economic growth and the production possibilities curve

Points outside the curve are unattainable right now, due to limits on resources and technology. Over time, though, we can expand our production possibilities by finding new resources, improving the quality of our resources, and developing new technology. Our long-run goal is to find more resources and improve technology so we can actually shift the production possibilities curve outward–a shift that represents economic growth–to allow us to produce both more robots and more pizza.

One more consideration about production possibilities is the tradeoff between consumer goods for current consumption and capital goods produced for firms. When we produce capital goods like factories and manufacturing equipment, firms can use those capital goods to produce even more goods in the future. If we choose instead to use more of our resources to make consumer goods like televisions, cars, and clothing, that means we have fewer resources available to make capital goods, which can lead to lower long-run output because we have reduced our potential production possibilities. So as a society, it is important for us to find a balance between current consumption and future production.

In later chapters, we will look at the ability of countries to reach beyond their production possibilities by engaging in trade with countries with different production possibilities. When nations and firms specialize to produce goods they are most efficient in producing, consumers can obtain even more goods at lower prices. Even with international trade, though, limitations on resources and technology still limit production possibilities.

Bear in Mind
Previous free-response questions, particularly on the AP macroeconomics exam, have included production possibilities curves illustrating tradeoffs before and after international trade. Other free-response questions have connected increased labor productivity or investments in technology (or lower corporate taxes that would allow firms to invest in technology) to the effect on long-run changes in production possibilities, asking the student to draw a correctly-labeled production possibilities curve to illustrate those changes through shifts in the curve.

Constant Opportunity Costs
Constant opportunity costs occur when the production of one more unit of a good results in the same loss of production of the other good at every point on the production possibilities curve.

Our first production possibilities curve demonstrated that if we chose to produce our first unit of pizza, the opportunity cost would be one unit of industrial robots. If there were a constant opportunity cost in the relationship between pizzas and robots, every unit of pizza produced would cost one more unit of robots. A constant cost relationship between two products results in a straight-line production possibilities curve.

The Law of Increasing Opportunity Costs
Many production possibilities curves do not demonstrate a constant cost relationship between products. At point C in our earlier example, when we produced one more unit of pizza, the opportunity cost increased to two units of robots. When we moved to point D, producing one more unit of pizza, the opportunity cost this time was three units of robots. The opportunity cost increased, since we gave up more and more robots to produce each additional unit of pizza. As a result, the production possibilities curve actually bows out.

The Law of Increasing Opportunity Costs explains that as production of one good increases, the opportunity cost increases. The problem is that resources are not perfectly adaptable in producing different products. Some workers are better at building robots, while other workers are better at making pizzas. When we decide to produce the first units of pizza, we could use the workers who are not very good at building robots; therefore, we wouldn't give up many robots in order to make those pizzas. But as we make more and more pizzas, we begin drawing better and better robot-makers into the pizza-making industry, so our opportunity cost increases, and we give up ever-increasing amounts of robots in order to make each additional unit of pizza. So how many pizzas and robots should our society make? We need to take a look at marginal analysis for that answer.

Marginal Analysis

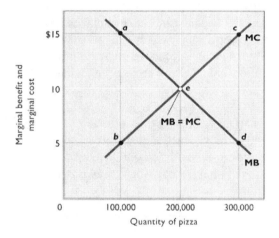

Optimal output: MB = MC

An important economic concept is marginal decision making. When we make decisions, we generally make them at the margin, considering "one more." Should I buy one more car? Should I study for one more hour? When we make rational decisions, we consider the marginal benefit and the marginal cost of that decision. The more of a good you obtain, the less marginal benefit you receive for the next unit. While the first ice cream cone holds a lot of utility, the second one holds somewhat less. By the third or fourth ice cream cone, you may actually be approaching negative utility. So marginal benefit is a downward-sloping curve. At the same time, the

Chapter 1: Limits, Alternatives, and Choices

marginal cost of producing each additional product rises, resulting in an upward-sloping marginal cost curve.

As long as the marginal benefit is greater than the marginal cost, you should undertake an activity and continue until the marginal benefit received from the next unit equals the marginal cost of that unit. That equilibrium point is the optimal output for society. If the marginal benefit from the first unit of pizza is $15 and the marginal cost is $5, it should be produced. The marginal benefit of the second pizza equals the marginal cost at $10. But a third unit of pizza would result in a marginal cost of $15 and marginal benefit of $5, making society worse off. In this case, two units of pizza are optimal.

Once you have determined the optimal output of one product, you can find the optimal output of the other product by looking at the production possibilities curve. Two units of pizza are optimal in this society, and producing on the production possibilities curve is optimal. Therefore, we should produce at point C: two units of pizza and seven units of robots.

Taking the EEK! Out of Economics

If you only have a production possibilities curve or table and no information that allows you to make a marginal analysis, you don't have enough information to determine which point on the production possibilities curve is optimal. While we do not want to produce at any point below the curve (indicating unemployment) and cannot produce anywhere outside the curve (due to limited resources and technology), any point on the curve represents full employment of resources and is equally acceptable.

Multiple-Choice Questions

1. Economics is best defined as the study of
   (A) why people buy products.
   (B) supply and demand.
   (C) how people satisfy unlimited wants with scarce resources.
   (D) who receives the goods produced in an economy.
   (E) how firms maximize profits.

2. Each of the following is a factor of production EXCEPT
   (A) land/natural resources.
   (B) capital.
   (C) labor.
   (D) money.
   (E) entrepreneurial ability.

3. The study of macroeconomics would include
   (A) a consumer's decision whether to buy a car or a motorcycle.
   (B) a grocery store's decision to hire another cashier.
   (C) the federal government's decision to increase military spending.
   (D) a clothing manufacturer's decision to raise the price of jeans.
   (E) a woman's decision to open her own business.

4.   LaKenya's opportunity cost for attending college includes
    I.   other goods that could have been bought with the money spent for tuition.
    II.   clothing LaKenya bought during the four years of college.
    III.   income LaKenya could have earned from work at a full-time job.
    (A)   I only
    (B)   II only
    (C)   II and III only
    (D)   I and III only
    (E)   I, II, and III

Use the production possibilities table below to answer questions 5–7.

	Consumer Goods	Capital Goods
Point A	20	0
Point B	12	1
Point C	6	3
Point D	2	6
Point E	0	10

5.   What is the opportunity cost for moving from point C to point D?
    (A)   four consumer goods
    (B)   two consumer goods
    (C)   six capital goods
    (D)   three capital goods
    (E)   eight economic products

6.   If society chooses to produce at Point D rather than Point B, what will be the long-run effect for this society?
    (A)   Fewer consumer goods will be produced in the future.
    (B)   It will be possible to produce both more consumer and capital goods in the future.
    (C)   Fewer capital goods will be produced in the future.
    (D)   The production of both consumer and capital goods will be lower in the future.
    (E)   The production of consumer goods will increase in the future, but the production of capital goods must fall.

7.   Why does the opportunity cost increase as production of capital goods increases?
    (A)   Capital goods are more expensive to produce than consumer goods.
    (B)   Resources are not perfectly adaptable between producing the two goods.
    (C)   The lower supply of consumer goods causes their price to increase.
    (D)   Capital goods are more useful to society than consumer goods.
    (E)   Buyers are willing to pay more for consumer goods than for capital goods.

Use the production possibilities graph below to answer questions 8–10.

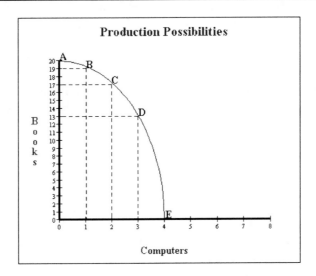

8.   If society is currently producing at Point C, what is the opportunity cost of
     increasing production of computers to Point D?
     (A)   four books
     (B)   seventeen books
     (C)   thirteen books
     (D)   three computers
     (E)   one computer

9.   What would a decision to produce eight books and one computer represent?
     (A)   an unattainable point
     (B)   full employment
     (C)   efficient use of resources
     (D)   economic growth
     (E)   unemployment

10. Society's ability to produce more books and computers is limited by
     (A)   consumer demand for the products.
     (B)   workers' willingness to accept low wages.
     (C)   the wide variety of other products firms could choose to produce.
     (D)   available resources and technology.
     (E)   government quotas and production requirements.

Free-Response Question
Assume the nation of Camandland only produces two products: corn and soybeans.
(a)   Draw a correctly-labeled production possibilities curve to illustrate the relationship
      between these products.
(b)   If all resources are fully employed and society decides to produce more corn,
      (i)   explain what will happen to the production of soybeans.
      (ii) explain why the effect on soybean production occurs.
(c)   Now assume a breakthrough occurs in farming technology. Illustrate the change on your
      production possibilities curve.

Multiple-Choice Explanations

1. (C)   While the other four answers are specific areas within the study of economics, the primary focus of economics is the issue of scarcity.

2. (D)   Money is not a resource used to create products. While money can be used to buy factors of production (such as a piece of equipment), the money itself is not a factor of production.

3. (C)   Macroeconomics is the study of the big picture of the entire national international economy; microeconomics is the study of the small picture of decision making by individuals or specific firms.

4. (D)   Clothing is not part of the opportunity cost, because clothing would have been purchased whether LaKenya went to college or not.

5. (A)   In moving from Point C to Point D, production of consumer goods falls from six products to two. Those four products given up are the opportunity cost.

6. (B)   The current production of capital goods enables firms to expand so they can produce even more goods for consumers and other firms in the future.

7. (B)   Because resources aren't perfectly adaptable, when we make more of one product, we have to give up ever-increasing amounts of the other.

8. (A)   To increase production by one computer, production of books drops from seventeen to thirteen, showing four books were given up to produce the computer.

9. (E)   Unemployment is represented by any point inside the production possibilities curve. It is possible to produce that output, but resources are not being used in a way to maximize possible output.

10. (D)   The production possibilities curve assumes resources and technology are fixed in the short run.

Free-Response Explanation

4 points (1 + 2 + 1)

(a)   1 point:
- 1 point is earned for a correctly labeled production possibilities curve.

(b)   2 points:
- 1 point is earned for correctly stating that the production of soybeans will fall.
- 1 point is earned for correctly stating that resources and technology limit production; producing more corn requires a lower production of soybeans.

(c)   1 point:
- 1 point is earned for correctly illustrating an outward shift of the production possibilities curve.

CHAPTER 2: THE MARKET SYSTEM AND THE CIRCULAR FLOW

Introduction

The problem of scarcity forces societies to make choices about what to produce, how to produce those goods, and who will receive the goods produced. But societies must first decide who will have the power to make those decisions: the government, the people, or both. Chapter 2 examines differences among economic systems and the role of the circular flow model in the market system. The framework of the market system and the role of incentives help to explain how consumers, producers, and governments make decisions. Material from Chapter 2 could appear in a multiple-choice question on either exam, with a question on consumer and firm incentives likely on the AP microeconomics exam and the circular flow model likely to appear on the AP macroeconomics exam.

Economic Systems

Every society must make choices about how to deal with scarcity. Economic systems are institutions and procedures that societies put in place to address the issues raised by unlimited wants and limited resources. Societies make their own choice of economic system by determining who owns and directs the factors of production: the government in the case of command economies or the people and firms in the case of market economies.

Command Economies

A central government makes the decisions in a command economy. The government owns most firms, and a central committee determines the allocation of resources among industries, production quotas for each firm, and prices and the distribution of products to consumers. The government makes production decisions based on long-term goals.

Socialist nations have a significant level of government involvement but not as much as communist nations. Such systems feature government ownership of major industries such as utilities, transportation, and health care but still allow significant private sector decision making. Essential goods may be rationed and incomes redistributed to equalize living conditions, but market forces determine production and prices in private industry.

Command economies have struggled in recent years because of problems coordinating consumer demand with production quotas, firms failing to meet quotas, and increasingly complicated economies overwhelming the ability of government planners to deal with them. In addition, the lack of a profit motive has stifled entrepreneurship, innovation, and capital accumulation, reducing the potential for long-run economic growth.

Market Economies

Market economies rely on markets rather than government to make economic decisions. Markets are mechanisms that bring buyers and sellers together to voluntarily exchange goods or services. Market economies put the decision making power in the hands of consumers and privately owned firms. Owners of firms make decisions based on a profit incentive, and consumers make decisions based on gaining the most satisfaction for the lowest possible price. Output and price decisions are made in markets through the power of supply and demand, eliminating the need for government planning committees.

Taking the EEK! Out of Economics
Markets can occur anywhere buyers and sellers come together. Don't limit your definition of "market" to a store. While stores are markets, they are not the only markets. Markets exist when a Girl Scout sells cookies to her neighbor, a fast food restaurant hires a worker, you buy a ticket to a school dance, or NASA buys rockets.

Mixed Economies

The extreme form of capitalism, *laissez faire*, calls for virtually no government involvement in society other than for the protection of private property and the market system. The form of capitalism used in the United States and other capitalist countries today is known as a mixed economy—free enterprise with some government regulation. While we rely on markets to make most of our economic decisions, our government is instrumental in providing public goods such as national defense and highways, redistributing income through progressive income taxes and supplemental income programs, regulating industry for worker and public safety, and stabilizing the economy through the use of taxes, government spending, and the money supply.

Characteristics of a Market Economy

The primary characteristic of a market economy is the private ownership of the factors of production—land, labor, capital, and entrepreneurial ability. People make their own decisions of whether to open a business and how to run it. The incentive of profit draws firms into industry, and private property protections preventing arbitrary government seizure give entrepreneurs the confidence to take the risk of starting a business. People in a market economy have the freedom to choose their careers and employers and to make decisions about the products they want to buy. Self-interest is the motivating factor for firms, workers, and consumers. Competition among buyers and sellers spreads out market power to keep prices down and provides firms the incentive to improve quality and innovation. Markets provide the mechanism for buyers and sellers to communicate information about tastes, prices, and production output. The market has its own system of rewards for firms that meet consumer demands and punishments for firms that do not.

Technological advance tends to be rapid in market economies because the rewards for invention and innovation go to those responsible for the work. Copyrights and patents guarantee ownership rights to creators, and sales result in monetary rewards, serving as an incentive for further innovation. Technological improvements and capital development increase our long-run production possibilities for future production.

Market economies rely on specialization and the division of labor to increase efficiency. In the same way, nations specialize, basing production on their best local resources and then trading. Because people and firms specialize, modern economies rely on money as a medium of exchange rather than on self-sufficient individuals making everything they need and bartering to get what they want. Money simply makes exchange easier.

Market economies are successful because they promote the most efficient use of resources, provide incentives for producers and workers, and allow producers and consumers the freedom to undertake activities that will best serve their own interests. While market economies focus on private decision making, the government still plays an important role in the economy. In situations where the market fails, government can perform important functions to improve efficiency and effectiveness in the markets.

Five Fundamental Questions

Because all societies face scarcity, every nation must make choices. The McConnell text notes five fundamental questions, while other books may focus on more or fewer.

1. What will be produced? In a market economy, products that result in profit for the producers will be produced. Consumer sovereignty—consumer demand driving the production decisions of firms—is central to a market economy.

2. How will goods be produced? In a market economy, goods are produced in the way that minimizes the cost per unit of production. Firms maximize their profits by finding the right combination of labor and capital and by using technology to lower costs.

3. Who will get the goods? In a market economy, goods go to those who are willing and able to pay for them. Those with higher incomes are able to buy more.

4. How will the system accommodate change? In a market economy, changes in consumer demand affect prices and profits, leading firms to change production. If demand and profits increase, firms produce more; if demand falls, firms produce less.

5. How will the system promote progress? In a market economy, increased profit can be used to invest in the accumulation of capital and development of technology to further increase production possibilities, the profits of firms, and standards of living.

The "Invisible Hand"

Adam Smith, known as the father of economics, explained the operation of market systems in his 1776 book *The Wealth of Nations*. He described how the "invisible hand" of self-interest leads firms and households to act in ways that benefit themselves as well as society. In the quest for profit, firms produce innovative and high-quality products that suit consumer tastes and demands. The quest for profit also leads firms to produce as efficiently as possible, reducing the waste of scarce resources that can be used to produce other goods. The quest for higher income encourages individuals to seek higher education and job training to command that higher wage. That education, in turn, benefits society by improving worker productivity and reducing production costs.

The Circular Flow Model

The circular flow diagram

The circular flow diagram shows how resources and products flow through the economy. In the resource (factor) market, households sell factors of production (land, labor, capital, and entrepreneurial ability) to firms, who use those resources to create products. In the product market, firms sell goods to households. While goods flow one direction, money flows the other way. In the resource (factor) market, workers sell labor to firms in return for a paycheck. Workers use those checks in the product market to buy products from firms. The cycle continues as firms use that revenue to buy more factors of production.

In a market economy, the circular flow model operates without the need for government planning. The "invisible hand" of self-interest serves as the incentive for individuals and firms to act in ways that maximize their incomes and reduce their costs in the economy. The competition for resources and profits promotes productivity and low-cost production, helping us to use our scarce resources in the most efficient manner possible.

Bear in Mind

While few questions on the AP microeconomics and macroeconomics multiple-choice exams are likely to come from this chapter, a good understanding of the incentives and motivations involved in the market system is important to understand the decisions of consumers, workers, firms, and governments explored in later chapters. No free-response questions have been based specifically on material from this chapter.

Multiple-Choice Questions

1.   Economic planning by central government agencies is primarily associated with
        (A)   command economies.
        (B)   market economies.
        (C)   laissez faire economies.
        (D)   mixed economies.
        (E)   traditional economies.

2.   In market economies, the incentive that draws entrepreneurs into industry is
        (A)   government bonuses for meeting production quotas.
        (B)   profit.
        (C)   government assumption of the risk of failure.
        (D)   government assistance with making output and pricing decisions.
        (E)   a guaranteed minimum income level.

3.   In a mixed economy, the economic decisions of what to produce, how to produce, and who will receive products are made by
        (A)   the government.
        (B)   consumers and firms.
        (C)   banks and stock markets.
        (D)   firms, consumers, and government.
        (E)   banks and the government.

4.   Fundamental economic questions that every society must answer include
                I.   What will be produced?
                II.   How will goods be produced?
                III.   How will goods be distributed to consumers?
        (A)   I only
        (B)   III only
        (C)   I and II only
        (D)   II and III only

(E)   I, II, and III

5.   What did economist Adam Smith identify as the "invisible hand" that directs the decision making of firms and households in a market economy?
(A)   government
(B)   product demand
(C)   self-interest
(D)   international trade
(E)   entrepreneurial ability

6.   In the product market of the circular flow model,
(A)   firms buy finished products from households.
(B)   consumers buy factors of production from firms.
(C)   firms sell factors of production to the government.
(D)   consumers buy finished products from firms.
(E)   firms buy factors of production from consumers.

7.   Which of the following activities would occur in the resource (factor) market?
(A)   A teacher buys a new truck from a car dealership.
(B)   The department of defense buys a tank from a weapons manufacturer.
(C)   A farmer buys farmland from a retiring farmer.
(D)   A retirement fund buys stock in a major corporation.
(E)   A welder buys a personal home computer from an electronics store.

8.   While resources and products flow in one direction of the circular flow model, what flows the other direction?
(A)   money
(B)   services
(C)   public goods
(D)   imported goods
(E)   information

Multiple-Choice Explanations
1.   (A)   Government planning is the hallmark of a command economy; in other economies, individuals and firms play the central role in decision making.
2.   (B)   The profit motive draws new firms into industry in market economies, because private property rights allow firms to keep those profits.
3.   (D)   Mixed economies provide for some government intervention, such as regulation and provision of public goods, but primarily rely on the decision making of firms and consumers in markets.
4.   (E)   Scarcity forces societies to answer these and other questions about economic growth and security.
5.   (C)   In *The Wealth of Nations*, Adam Smith recognized that, in market economies, market participants make decisions to benefit themselves.
6.   (D)   In the product market, firms sell products to consumers.
7.   (C)   In the resource (factor) market, firms buy factors of production (land, labor, capital, and entrepreneurial ability) from resource providers.
8.   (A)   Money, in the form of paychecks, profit, and other payments, serves as an incentive for households to provide resources and firms to produce products in a market economy.

CHAPTER 3: DEMAND, SUPPLY, AND MARKET EQUILIBRIUM

Introduction

Supply and demand are mechanisms by which our market economy functions. Changes in supply and demand affect prices and quantities produced, which in turn affect profit, employment, wages, and government revenue. Chapter 3 introduces models explaining the behavior of consumers and producers in markets, as well as the effects of government policies on market activity. The concepts of supply and demand reappear throughout the economics course in discussions of wage determination, interest rates, currency values, and several other concepts. Material from Chapter 3 is heavily covered on the multiple-choice and free-response sections of both AP economics exams, but the macroeconomics questions are more likely to show up in the application of loanable funds, money, currency, or other aggregate markets.

Markets

In market economies, the forces of supply and demand primarily determine the prices and quantities of products produced. Markets occur anywhere buyers and sellers engage in voluntary exchange, from restaurants to electronics stores to websites that sell music downloads. For the purposes of this chapter, we will focus on competitive markets with many buyers and sellers who do not have the market power to control prices or output. In later chapters, you will see how market power affects prices and the output of products.

Demand

Demand is the consumer's willingness and ability to buy a product at a particular price. Both elements must be present because producers do not respond to wish lists; they produce for customers who are actually able to buy the product. Demand is determined first by developing a schedule indicating the quantity the consumer would buy at each potential price. The demand curve is then drawn by graphing those points.

Taking the EEK! Out of Economics

If you have experience with graphs in math or science that place dependent variables on the vertical axis and independent variables on the horizontal axis, the graph setup for economics may look backwards to you. Economists generally develop market graphs with a monetary value on the vertical axis and the quantity of an item on the horizontal axis. This is simply the way economists have developed graphs, and it is important that you learn to follow these conventions to ensure you find the correct results in your analysis of supply and demand.

The Law of Demand

The downward-sloping demand curve illustrates the inverse relationship between the price and quantity sold. According to the Law of Demand, at a lower price, consumers are willing and able to buy more; at a higher price, they buy less. This is something you learned long ago, but now we will explore the reasons for the relationship. It is important to understand that during this analysis, we are making the ceteris paribus assumption—that all other things are equal; nothing else is changing. If the consumer's income changed or the product was no longer desirable, changes in the quantity purchased could result from those changes, rather than from changes in the price of the product itself.

The demand curve slopes downward for three reasons:
- Diminishing marginal utility. The more of a good a person has, the less utility will be gained from each additional unit; therefore, firms must lower the price of the next unit to

entice customers to buy more. Shoe stores run a standard "buy one pair, get the next pair half off" sale for this reason.

- The income effect. When the price falls, consumers have more real income (purchasing power) available to buy more. If you planned to buy a pack of gum for $1.00 and the store had a half-price sale, you could now buy two packs of gum because your dollar stretched further than before the sale.
- The substitution effect. When the price falls, customers buy more as a substitute for other products that now look relatively more expensive. If you had planned to buy a pack of gum and a candy bar for $1.00 each and then noticed the half-price sale on gum, you might choose to spend the entire $2.00 to buy four packs of gum because the gum is now so much less expensive than the candy bar.

Change in Quantity Demanded

The change in quantity demanded refers to a movement from one point to another point on the demand curve. The demand curve did not move. Only a change in the price of the product can cause a change in quantity demanded. Returning to the gum example, you only bought more gum because the price fell. It is very important to keep this definition in mind, because it can be very easily confused with a change in demand.

Market Demand

While study of one consumer's demand can help us understand the principles of demand, producers rarely consider the demand of a single customer. Instead, they focus on market demand—the demand of all customers together. To find the market demand, simply add the quantity demanded by all of the market's individual consumers at each price. By determining the demand of millions of customers, the gum manufacturer can determine how many packs it would need to produce to satisfy market demand at each price.

Change in Demand

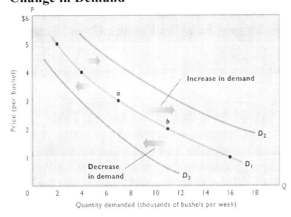

Changes in demand

A number of events can actually shift the demand curve. A change in demand results in consumers buying more (or less) of the product at every possible price. Increases in demand shift the curve to the right, while decreases in demand shift the curve to the left.

One factor that can change demand is a change in consumer taste. Consumer willingness to buy a product is often fueled by advertising, recommendations, or fads. As technology improved, consumer tastes in music changed from cassette tapes to CDs to MP3 files. A change in the number of buyers also affects demand. As more immigrants entered the United States, stores responded to the increased demand by providing more ethnic foods.

Changes in consumer income affect the ability of consumers to buy products as well. But the effects of income depend on the type of product. Most goods are normal goods, for which demand increases when incomes rise and demand falls when incomes fall. Other products known as inferior goods have the reverse relationship to income. When incomes fall, consumers increase demand for inferior goods. If income falls, consumers buy more generic food rather than name-brand food. It is important to understand that consumers aren't actually buying more because their incomes fell; they are buying lower-priced substitutes for the products they would have purchased with a higher income.

Taking the EEK! Out of Economics
It is important to understand the difference between the income effect (which changes the quantity demanded) and a change in income (which shifts the demand curve). The income effect refers to the consumer's reaction to a change in price of the product. If you saw the price of gasoline significantly fall, you might put more in your tank because the $20 you planned to spend for gasoline will now stretch further. Your demand curve for gas didn't move; you just moved from one point to another on your demand curve. However, an increase in your income would allow you to buy more gas at whatever price is being charged, because your demand curve for gas has shifted to the right. The key is to look at whether the price of the specific product changed (so your quantity demanded changed) or your income changed (so your demand for gas at all prices changed).

A change in the price of related products can also shift demand. Substitutes are products that can be used in place of each other. When the price of a good rises, consumers seek lower-priced substitutes. If you normally buy Mountain Dew and the store has a sale on Mello Yello, your demand for Mello Yello may increase. Complements are products that are used together. When the price of a product rises significantly, consumers will buy less of that product and the products that are used with it. When the price of gas rose, the demand for SUVs significantly fell because they just became too expensive to use.

Taking the EEK! Out of Economics
It is important to distinguish between the substitution effect (which changes the quantity demanded) and a change in the price of substitutes (which shifts the demand curve). The substitution effect focuses on the consumer's reaction to the change in price of a product. If you intended to buy chips and found the chips on sale for a lower price, you might buy more chips. Your demand curve for chips didn't shift; you simply responded to the lower price by buying more, which is a movement from one point to another point on your demand curve. However, if the price of a *different* product like pretzels fell, you might buy the pretzels instead of the chips, and your entire demand curve for chips would shift. The key is to look at whether the price of the specific product changed (so your quantity demanded changed) or the price of a different product changed, leading you to buy less of the original product as a result (so your demand for the product at all prices changed).

Consumer expectations also have important effects on the demand for products. If consumers expect the prices of products to increase soon, they will hurry out to buy those products before the price increase. On the other hand, if consumers are worried about the possibility of losing their jobs in a recession, they are less likely to buy new homes and cars, and their demand falls for those products at every price.

Supply

Supply is the quantity of goods producers are willing and able to produce. Just as with demand, a supply schedule is developed by determining how many products the producer will provide at each potential price.

The Law of Supply

The upward-sloping supply curve illustrates the direct relationship between price and quantity sold. According to the Law of Supply, as the price rises, producers increase the quantity supplied; as the price falls, firms produce less. If a firm can make more money from product sales, the profit motive entices the firm to increase output. In addition, after some point, the cost of production begins to increase as the firm hires more workers or buys additional equipment; therefore, a higher price is necessary to cover those increased production costs. The firm can afford to produce more if the revenue it receives from selling the product is higher. In our analysis of supply, we again make the ceteris paribus assumption that nothing else in the world is changing except for the price of the product.

Taking the EEK! Out of Economics

For supply, we are looking at the producer's decision of how many products to produce. It's very important *not* to think about supply as the quantity of products on a shelf. The products on the shelf represent previous output, not current production decisions, and looking at supply that way will cause errors in your analysis. If an increase in consumer demand causes the price of products to increase, that higher price serves as an incentive to produce more products, so the quantity supplied would increase. However, if you look at supply as "products on the shelf," you might see the higher demand resulting in consumers buying those products off the shelf, so you might conclude that the quantity supplied fell. Keep in mind that you're focusing on the producer's decision about production, and you'll be more likely to make the correct decisions in your analysis.

Market Supply

Market supply is the sum of individual firms' supply curves in an industry. The market supply of cars includes the quantity supplied by all of the automakers at each price.

Change in Quantity Supplied

A change in quantity supplied is a movement from one point to another point on the supply curve. When a producer is able to sell the product for a higher price, the quantity supplied by the firm increases; when the price of the product falls, the quantity supplied falls. The curve has not moved; the producer has only responded to a change in the price of the product. It is very important to remember that a change in quantity supplied only occurs when the producer sees a higher or lower price for the product and adjusts the firm's output as a result; nothing has caused the supply curve itself to move.

Change in Supply

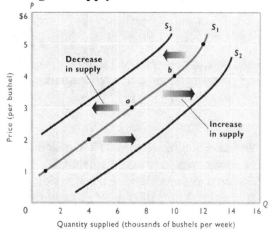

Changes in supply

A change in supply is an actual shift of the supply curve. An increase in supply is shown by a shift of the curve directly to the right, as producers make more of the product at each potential price. A decrease in supply is shown by a shift directly to the left, as producers produce fewer products at each potential price.

Taking the EEK! Out of Economics

It is very important to shift supply and demand curves to the left and right, not up and down. If you try to increase supply by shifting the curve straight up, you will actually create a new supply curve that lies to the left of the original supply curve—and as a result, your answers will all be reversed. Be sure to increase supply or demand by shifting the new curve to the right, and decrease supply or demand by shifting the new curve to the left, and you will be in the right position to continue your analysis.

One factor affecting supply is a change in the cost of resources firms need in order to produce their products. Higher labor, equipment, or utility costs lower profits, so firms produce less at each price; therefore, an increase in the cost of production reduces supply and shifts the curve to the left. On the other hand, if production costs fall, the firm earns additional profit and is willing to produce more at every price, so supply increases.

Changes in technology can also affect supply. When firms adopted the use of computers, automation, and other technologies, the firms were able to produce more products at a lower cost of production, so supply of those products increased.

Taxes and subsidies can also affect product supply. Because taxes are considered a cost of production for the company, higher taxes result in a lower supply of products, while lower taxes can increase product supply. A subsidy is a government payment to a firm to encourage some activity, such as expanding a factory in an urban area. Because the subsidy lowers the cost of production, the firm increases its supply of products.

Changes in the prices of other products can also stimulate changes in supply. If firms discover they can make more profit by producing other products, they may choose to do so. When increased production of ethanol significantly increased demand for corn in commodity markets, the price of corn soared. As a result, many farmers who had previously grown soybeans switched to produce corn, and the supply of soybeans fell.

Producer expectations about the future price of a product can also affect supply, though the producer's reaction may depend on the ability to quickly respond to that price change. If a rice farmer expects rice prices to significantly increase in the next month, there is no time to plant an additional crop; instead, the farmer may reduce the supply of rice for sale right now, waiting for the price to rise before selling it. However, if a carpet producer expects carpet prices to significantly increase in the next month, there is time to make more carpet, and the firm is likely to increase production to earn that higher revenue.

Another factor that changes supply is the number of firms in the industry. In general, the more producers in an industry, the greater supply of products at all prices; with fewer firms, fewer products are produced.

Market Equilibrium

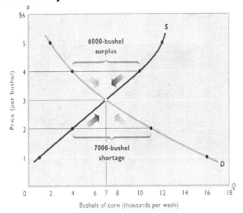

Equilibrium prices and quantity

When supply and demand are put together on a graph, the point of intersection is called equilibrium. At the equilibrium quantity, the quantity demanded by consumers equals the quantity supplied by producers. The equilibrium price is also called the market-clearing price, because at that price, all of the products produced will be bought by consumers; there are no leftovers or shortages. In this graph of the corn market, the equilibrium price is $3 per bushel and the equilibrium quantity is 7,000 bushels of corn sold per week.

Markets seek equilibrium, and in the absence of government intervention or factors that shift either curve, the equilibrium will be found. If corn producers tried to sell corn for $4 per bushel, producers would supply 10,000 bushels, but consumers would only demand 4,000 bushels, leaving a 6,000 bushel surplus. The quantity supplied is greater than the quantity demanded. How can we resolve the surplus? Reduce the price. At a price of $3, the quantity demanded by consumers increases while the quantity supplied by producers falls until equilibrium is reached. If corn producers instead tried to set the price at $2 per bushel, consumers would demand 11,000 bushels, but producers would only produce 4,000 bushels, resulting in a 7,000 bushel shortage— the quantity demanded is greater than the quantity supplied. How do we resolve the shortage? Raise the price. By raising the price to $3, producers are willing to increase the quantity of corn supplied, while consumers reduce the quantity of corn they demand until equilibrium is again reached.

The Efficiency of Markets

Open competition and incentives involved in supply and demand result in the efficient distribution of products and resources to produce them. Effective markets help to achieve two kinds of efficiency: productive and allocative efficiency. Productive efficiency is the production of a good in the lowest-cost way. Competition and consumer pressure for lower prices drive producers to find the lowest-cost methods of production. Productive efficiency is important because we know resources are scarce, and we want to allocate them in ways to produce more products using fewer resources. Allocative efficiency is producing the combination of products that are most valuable to society. When society produces at the point where the marginal benefit to society (represented by demand) equals the marginal cost to society (represented by supply), society has achieved the proper mix of products.

Changes in Supply, Demand, and Equilibrium

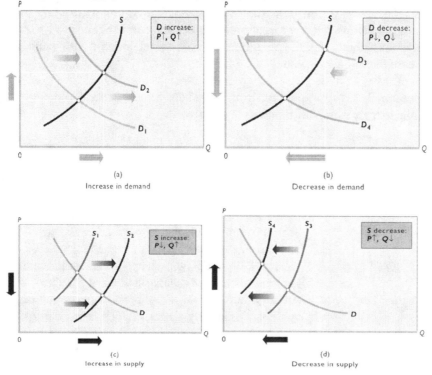

Changes in demand and supply and the effects on price and quantity

---

Bear in Mind

The proper labeling of graphs is *essential* to earn full scores on the free-response portion of the AP economics exams.

- Label each axis (price on the vertical; quantity on the horizontal)
- Label each curve (supply and demand)
- Draw equilibrium lines and label equilibrium price and quantity (such as P and Q)
- Distinguish each curve that shows movement (such as D1 and D2)
- Draw arrows between original and new curves to show the direction of movement
- Draw new equilibrium lines and label your new equilibrium price and quantity to distinguish them from the originals (such as P1 and P2, and Q1 and Q2)

Because scoring rubrics allocate points specifically for correctly labeled graphs, you can earn points just for getting that far—or easily lose points on an otherwise excellent response simply due to sloppy labeling. So maximize your potential score and label carefully!

Shifts in supply and demand curves cause changes in the equilibrium price and quantity of the product sold in the market. When demand increases, the new equilibrium is higher and to the right of the original equilibrium; therefore, increases in demand result in a higher price and higher quantity. On a cold night at a high school football game, you would expect demand for coffee to rise—and entrepreneurs in the concession stand could raise the price and still sell more coffee due to the increased demand. A decrease in demand creates the opposite result, with the new equilibrium showing a lower price and quantity. When consumer demand for SUVs fell because of high gas prices, the quantity sold fell, and dealerships lowered prices in an attempt to draw buyers into the market.

Taking the EEK! Out of Economics

Let the curves tell you what will happen to price and quantity. Students commonly make the mistake of worrying more about the firm's revenue than the market analysis. For example, when demand falls, the quantity sold falls. Many students then make the mistake of thinking that the firm must then raise the price of the product to compensate for the lost sales and to "make up" for the lower revenues. But think about the situation: if consumers are already buying less, and then the firm raises the price, won't consumers buy even less of the product? Keep drawing the graphs for each situation and let the curves illustrate what will happen to price and quantity, so you can avoid such mistakes.

If supply increases, the new equilibrium shows a lower price and a higher quantity sold. If farmers produce a large crop of tomatoes this year, the quantity increases, forcing the price per tomato down. If supply instead decreases, the equilibrium price rises, while the equilibrium quantity falls. When a hurricane damaged oil refineries, the supply of gasoline fell, reducing the quantity of gas in the market and causing the price to increase.

Taking the EEK! Out of Economics

It is at this point that you can begin to understand why the distinction between a change in supply and a change in quantity supplied (or a change in demand and a change in quantity demanded) is so important. Let's take the situation of an increase in demand. The demand curve shifts to the right, causing the price to increase. But did the *supply* increase? No. The *quantity supplied* increased as the producer responded to the higher price by moving to another point higher up the supply curve. Most multiple-choice and free-response questions on the AP economics exams involve the movement of only one curve at a time. Yet one of the most common mistakes students make is to confuse the situation and shift both curves ("Now that the price is higher, the firm will produce more, so I'll shift the supply curve to the right..."). Keep in mind the factors that cause shifts in supply and demand, and determine which factor is at work—a demand factor or a supply factor. Then move only that curve and watch what happens. The other actor (the consumer or producer) will simply react to the change in price by adjusting the quantity bought/sold at that new equilibrium point; a second curve shift doesn't happen!

Double Shifts

In our examples to this point, we have assumed ceteris paribus—nothing else is changing during our analysis. Unfortunately, the models don't always reflect real world conditions where many effects occur at the same time. Remember the smiley (☺)? Double shifts can be complicated, because while we can determine what will happen to either equilibrium price or quantity, we cannot know what will happen to the other. If we start at initial equilibrium, then increase demand and increase supply, then find the new equilibrium from the new supply and demand curves, we know for sure that quantity will increase, because both the increases in supply and demand cause increases in quantity. But we cannot know for sure whether the equilibrium price will rise or fall because that depends on how far the two curves shifted. If supply increased a lot but demand only increased a little, the price would fall; if supply only increased a little but demand increased a lot, the price would rise. If both curves shifted by the same amount, the price would remain the same. If cell phone manufacturers developed new technology allowing them to produce at a lower cost at the same time that consumer incomes significantly fell, supply would increase while demand would fall. Because both curve shifts would result in a lower equilibrium price, we know for sure that the price of phones would fall. But because the higher supply increases the quantity and the lower demand reduces the quantity, the equilibrium quantity is indeterminate; we cannot know what will happen to the quantity.

Bear in Mind

A couple of questions about double shifts have appeared fairly consistently on the multiple-choice portion of the AP microeconomics exam. Double shift questions clearly demonstrate that two separate events are occurring. For example, consumers are buying more iPods due to the new music trend, and workers in iPod-producing plants have gone on strike. The key is to look at each of the shifts independently and then find out what they have in common. An increase in demand causes price and quantity to go up. A decrease in supply causes price to go up and quantity to go down. Since both cause price to go up, we know equilibrium price will rise. Equilibrium quantity is indeterminate; we need more information to know whether it will rise, fall, or remain the same.

Sometimes the exam will pone a double shift question in reverse, with the stem of the question telling you that price and quantity both fell and the question asking which curve(s) must have moved which direction. The process of elimination may be your best tactic to deal with these questions. The key is to look very carefully at the wording of the question. If the question asks which curve shifts would *definitely* lead to a particular result that could be achieved by moving only one of the curves, and that option is one of the answers, that single curve movement is correct. If the question asks which curve shifts *could* lead to a particular result, start the process of elimination. If the result of both shifts is an increase in price, a combination of lower demand and higher supply could not create that result, so rule that answer out. Continue that process until you have only one answer left.

Price Ceilings

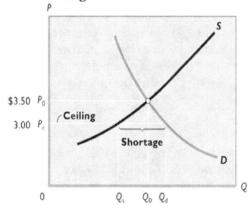

A price ceiling
Sometimes government officials identify goals that are more important than efficiency and create policies to intervene in markets. When a government sets a price ceiling below the equilibrium price, it sets a maximum price firms can charge, helping consumers by lowering the price. In this example, the equilibrium price is $3.50, but the government has set the price ceiling at $3.00. At

the $3.00 price, the quantity demanded is greater than the quantity supplied, so a shortage develops. Because the market cannot efficiently allocate the good, how do we determine who gets the fewer available products? Black markets often develop in such situations, as the market struggles to find equilibrium.

Price Floors

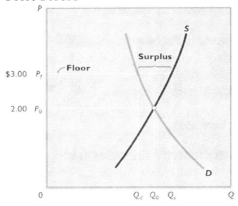

A price floor

A price floor is a minimum price set by a government. An effective price floor, set above the equilibrium price, is intended to help producers by keeping prices higher. In this example, the equilibrium price is $2.00, but the price floor of $3.00 causes firms to increase production while consumers buy less at the higher price, resulting in a surplus. As a consequence, the government must either buy or find other uses for the surplus, and resources that are used to produce this excess cannot be used to produce the other products consumers do want. Because market distortions are caused by price ceilings and floors, American government officials generally allow markets to allocate goods and services.

Taking the EEK! Out of Economics
The placement of the price floor or ceiling in relation to equilibrium may be confusing until you think about what they really mean. A price ceiling *below* equilibrium? Isn't a ceiling high? Think about the market, which always seeks equilibrium. If government imposes a price ceiling below equilibrium, market pressure tries to push prices upward—toward that equilibrium—but the price cannot legally rise. Therefore, it is an effective price ceiling. Now consider what would happen if the equilibrium price of the product were $7, and the government established a price ceiling of $8 on the product. What would happen? Absolutely nothing. A price ceiling higher than equilibrium has no effect because the market rests at equilibrium until something disturbs it. Conversely, if the government places a price floor above equilibrium, market pressure tries to pull the price down to equilibrium, but it cannot go lower because of the floor. If you think about price ceilings and floors as barriers to letting the market go to equilibrium, where it naturally wants to go, it can help you remember where a price floor or ceiling belongs in the graph.

Multiple-Choice Questions

1. Which situation is the best example of the Law of Demand?
   - (A) When the price of books increases, consumers buy fewer books.
   - (B) When wages of auto workers rise, automakers raise the price of cars.
   - (C) When the price of computers falls, demand for computer games increases.
   - (D) When the productivity of bricklayers rises, demand for bricklayers falls.
   - (E) When consumer incomes rise, consumers buy more televisions.

2. Each of the following could result in an increased demand for bicycles EXCEPT
   - (A) The price of gasoline increases significantly.
   - (B) The price of bicycle helmets increases significantly.
   - (C) The local government develops several bicycle trails in the area.
   - (D) Consumer incomes increase.
   - (E) The number of children in the community increases.

3. If demand for Product X decreases when the price of Product Y decreases, then
   - (A) Products X and Y are not related.
   - (B) Products X and Y are both inferior goods.
   - (C) Products X and Y are complements.
   - (D) Products X and Y are substitutes.
   - (E) Product X is a normal good, while Product Y is an inferior good.

4. Steak is a normal good and bologna is an inferior good. If consumer incomes fall,
   - (A) the prices for steak and bologna both will increase.
   - (B) the prices for steak and bologna both will decrease.
   - (C) the price for steak will increase and the price for bologna will decrease.
   - (D) the price for steak will decrease and the price for bologna will increase.
   - (E) the prices for steak and bologna will both remain unchanged.

5. Which of these situations would cause an increase in the supply of jeans?
   - (A) The cost of cotton used to produce jeans increases.
   - (B) The number of firms producing jeans decreases.
   - (C) Producers improve productivity with computerized sewing machines.
   - (D) Consumers increase their demand for jeans.
   - (E) The government imposes a per-unit tax on the production of jeans.

6. A short-run increase in the cost of production will cause
   - (A) the supply curve to shift to the left.
   - (B) the supply curve to shift to the right, while demand will shift to the left.
   - (C) the demand curve to shift to the left, while supply will shift to the right.
   - (D) both the supply and demand curves to shift to the left.
   - (E) the demand curve to shift to the left.

7. What would cause the price of jellybeans to rise in the market?
   - (A) Consumers reduce their demand for jellybeans, so firms must raise their prices to compensate for the lost product sales.
   - (B) The cost of the sugar required to make jellybeans falls.
   - (C) The incomes of jellybean consumers fall.
   - (D) Consumers change their preference to buy healthier foods, so their demand for jellybeans falls.
   - (E) The government imposes a per-unit tax on the sale of jellybeans.

Chapter 3: Demand, Supply, and Market Equilibrium

8.   When ducks are slaughtered for meat, their feathers can be used in the production
        of pillows. Given this relationship, if the demand for duck meat rises,
        (A)   the price of feather pillows falls.
        (B)   the supply of feather pillows falls.
        (C)   the demand for feather pillows rises.
        (D)   the price of duck meat falls.
        (E)   the supply of duck meat rises.

9.   Which of the following curve shifts would definitely cause both the equilibrium price and
        equilibrium quantity to increase?
                Supply   *Demand*
        (A)   Increase   Decrease
        (B)   Decrease   Decrease
        (C)   No change   Decrease
        (D)   Increase   No change
        (E)   No change   Increase

10.   In a competitive shoe market, if consumer incomes rise at the same time that the cost of
        production rises for shoes, one *definite* result would be
        (A)   an increase in the quantity of shoes sold.
        (B)   an increase in the price of shoes.
        (C)   an increase in the profits of shoemakers.
        (D)   a decrease in the demand for slippers (a substitute for shoes).
        (E)   a decrease in the supply of slippers (a substitute for shoes).

11.   The purpose of a price ceiling is to
        (A)   help producers by setting a minimum legal price for a product.
        (B)   raise revenue for the federal government.
        (C)   create a surplus of the product to be saved for future use.
        (D)   help consumers by lowering the legal price of the product.
        (E)   ensure enough of the product is produced to fully meet demand.

12.   An effective price floor for rice will cause
        (A)   a decrease in the quantity of rice supplied.
        (B)   a long-run shortage of rice.
        (C)   a decrease in the quantity of rice demanded.
        (D)   the supply curve for rice to shift to the right.
        (E)   The price of rice to fall.

Free-Response Questions
1.   Farmers sell sweet corn and green beans, which are substitute products, from roadside
        stands in competitive markets. Suppose the surgeon general announces results of a study
        indicating the consumption of corn causes diabetes in humans.
(a)   Using a correctly labeled supply and demand graph for sweet corn, show the effect of the
        announcement on each of the following in the short run.
        (i)   Price
        (ii)   Output
        (iii)   Explain the reason for this effect.

(b)   Using a separate, correctly labeled supply and demand graph for green beans, show the effect of the announcement on each of the following in the short run.
　　　(i)   Price
　　　(ii)   Output
　　　(iii)   Explain the reason for this effect.
(c)   Now assume that butter, a complement of sweet corn, is sold in a competitive market. In a third, correctly labeled supply and demand graph for butter, show the effect of the announcement on each the following in the short run.
　　　(i)   Price
　　　(ii)   Output
　　　(iii)   Explain the reason for this effect.

2.   Assume that milk is sold in a competitive market, which is currently at equilibrium where the store sells 250 gallons of milk per week at a price of $3 per gallon.

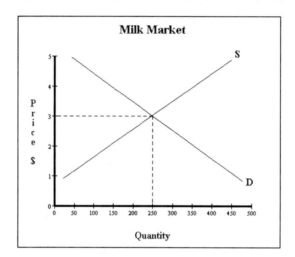

(a)   Redraw the graph above and show how an increase in the cost of cattle feed will affect the equilibrium price and quantity of milk. Explain.
(b)   Now assume the government has imposed an effective price ceiling in the milk market. Redraw the graph above and indicate each of the following.
　　　(i)   The correct position of an effective price ceiling
　　　(ii)   The new quantity demanded as a result of the price ceiling
　　　(iii)   The new quantity supplied as a result of the price ceiling
(c)   What economic problem will result from the price ceiling?

Multiple-Choice Explanations
1.   (A)   The Law of Demand says that at lower prices, people buy more and at higher prices, people buy less. B involves lower supply; C discusses complements; D incorrectly discusses a relationship in the labor market; E involves a change in demand rather than a change in quantity demanded.
2.   (B)   Bicycles and helmets are complements; if the price of helmets increases significantly, demand for bicycles would be expected to fall.
3.   (D)   When the price of substitute Product Y falls, consumers reduce demand for Product X and increase the quantity of Product Y they demand instead.
4.   (D)   When incomes fall, demand for normal goods falls, while demand for inferior goods rises, and prices move with the changes in demand.

5.	(C)	Higher productivity allows firms to produce more at every price. Beware of answers like D; increased demand causes a change in *quantity* supplied (a move along the supply curve) but not a shift in the supply curve.

6.	(A)	A change in the cost of production is one of the factors that can shift the supply curve; it does not cause any change in the demand curve.

7.	(E)	Per-unit taxes raise production costs, lowering supply. Beware of answers like A; if demand falls, firms must lower their prices, not raise them.

8.	(A)	Because duck meat and feathers are harvested together, the increase in the quantity of duck meat supplied will result in a greater supply of feathers, reducing the cost of pillow production; the increase in feather pillow supply lowers the price of feather pillows.

9.	(E)	An increase in demand definitely causes both price and quantity to increase. A is eliminated because both cause price to fall; B is eliminated because both cause quantity to fall. C and D cannot create the result.

10.	(B)	Because the increase in demand (caused by higher incomes) and the decrease in supply (caused by higher costs of production) both result in higher prices, the combination will definitely cause the price to increase.

11.	(D)	A maximum legal price below equilibrium may help some consumers by lowering prices, but the price ceiling results in a shortage.

12.	(C)	A price floor raises the price of rice, and as a result, consumers are not as willing or able to buy as much rice.

Free-Response Explanations
1.	**12 points** (4 + 4 + 4)
(a)	4 points:
* 1 point is earned for a correctly labeled graph with equilibrium price and quantity.
* 1 point is earned for showing a leftward shift of the demand curve.
* 1 point is earned for showing that equilibrium price and quantity decrease.
* 1 point is earned for explaining that consumer tastes changed to no longer desire corn.

(b)	4 points:
* 1 point is earned for a correctly labeled graph with equilibrium price and quantity.
* 1 point is earned for showing a rightward shift of the demand curve.
* 1 point is earned for showing that equilibrium price and quantity increase.
* 1 point is earned for explaining that because demand for corn fell, demand for the corn substitute would increase.

(c)	4 points:
* 1 point is earned for a correctly labeled graph with equilibrium price and quantity.
* 1 point is earned for showing a leftward shift of the demand curve.
* 1 point is earned for showing that equilibrium price and quantity decrease.
* 1 point is earned for explaining that because corn and butter are complements, a decrease in demand for corn also results in a decrease in demand for butter.

2.	**7 points** (3 + 3 + 1)
(a)	3 points:
* 1 point is earned for showing a leftward shift of the supply curve.
* 1 point is earned for showing that price increases and quantity decreases.
* 1 point is earned for explaining that the higher cost of milk production reduces the supply of milk, because some dairy farmers will reduce production or entirely leave the industry.

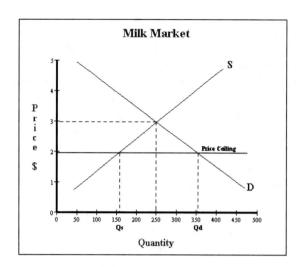

Milk Market

(b)   3 points:
   • 1 point is earned for showing a price ceiling at a price lower than the equilibrium price of $3.
   • 1 point is earned for showing a higher quantity demanded at the price ceiling.
   • 1 point is earned for showing a lower quantity supplied at the price ceiling.

(c)   1 point:
   • 1 point is earned for stating that a shortage is the economic problem.

CHAPTER 4: THE U.S. ECONOMY: PRIVATE AND PUBLIC SECTORS

Introduction
Private sector interaction of firms and households is the foundation of a market system. But in our mixed economy, the government can also shape how those markets work and provide public sector solutions when the market fails. Chapter 4 introduces the roles of government in the market economy, illustrated in the circular flow model and extending to a basic explanation of corrections for market failure. Chapter 4 introduces concepts developed in later chapters. While the material is almost exclusively part of the AP microeconomics exam, national income, consumption and saving, and the circular market flow introduce macroeconomic concepts. Most of the AP economics exam questions are based on the deeper content explanations in later chapters.

Household Income, Spending, and Saving
Households play a pivotal role in the circular market flow, providing resources to firms in the factor market and buying finished products from firms in the product market. Nearly 3/4 of all income in the United States is paid to workers in wages, while smaller amounts of income go to corporate profits, proprietors' income, interest, and rent. In our market economy, household incomes are very unequal, with the wealthiest 20 percent of households receiving more than 50 percent of national income.

Approximately 6/7 of household income is spent for personal consumption, while most of the rest goes to taxes and only 1% or less is saved. Nearly 60 percent of spending is for services rather than goods, which is why the United States is known as a service economy.

Bear in Mind
Questions about specific statistics have not appeared on the AP economics exams. These statistics change from year to year, and exams are written well in advance of the test date. However, it is important to understand basic relationships in the statistics: the vast majority of national income goes to worker wages and salaries; the vast majority of personal income goes to consumption.

Firms
Firms along with households comprise the private sector of the economy. Firms can be organized as sole proprietorships (with one owner), partnerships (with two or more owners), or corporations (owned by stockholders). While nearly 3/4 of firms are sole proprietorships, corporations make nearly 6/7 of sales.

Bear in Mind
While the textbook discusses the organization and legal forms of business, the advantages and disadvantages of corporations, and stocks and corporate bonds, these concepts have not appeared on previous AP economics exams.

The Role of Government
The actions of federal, state, and local governments—the public sector—are vital in our mixed economy. Governments provide the legal structure for market economies, including property rights and the enforcement of contracts. To promote competition, governments limit the formation and power of monopolies and regulate prices charged by natural monopolies. The government redistributes income from the wealthy to the poor through progressive taxes and

transfer payments to ensure that those with low incomes have at least some minimal standard of living. Governments also stabilize the economy through the use of fiscal policy (taxes and government spending) or monetary policy (the money supply and interest rates). Governments also intervene when markets fail to work effectively (in the case of externalities) or fail entirely (in the case of public goods).

Externalities

In the relationship between buyers and sellers in markets, we have made the assumption that all of the costs and benefits involved in the transaction accrue to those buyers and sellers. But with externalities, benefits or costs of economic activity "spill over" onto third parties who are external to the buyer-seller relationship.

A negative externality passes some economic activity costs onto outsiders. The classic example of a negative externality is pollution. If a firm can send its pollution up the smokestack, the lower production cost allows the firm to over-allocate resources and increase production, and the rising supply lowers the product price to consumers. Such decisions impose costs on those who live around the plant, so governments intervene in this market failure. To force firms to absorb all of their costs, governments can prohibit or limit pollution or impose specific taxes on the product. Both actions increase the firm's cost of production and shift supply to the left, returning the market to efficiency.

In the case of a positive externality, outsiders gain benefits from an economic decision. A classic example of a positive externality is vaccinations. When people consider the costs and benefits of a vaccination, they do not take into account others who will benefit by also avoiding disease. As a result, demand is lower than it would be if all benefits were considered, and resources are under-allocated. Governments can intervene in this failed market by subsidizing consumers to increase their demand or subsidizing producers to increase their supply and lower the price, or the government could simply provide the product. With reduced prices, the market can once again be returned to efficiency.

Public Goods

Most products in our economy are considered private goods, which have characteristics of rival consumption and excludability. If you buy an airline ticket, no one else can use your seat at the same time you are using it, and it is easy for the airline to exclude people from the flight if they haven't bought tickets. The market works well for private goods. Public goods, however, are non-rival and non-excludable. Many people can use the same national defense protection at the same time, and if a citizen refuses to pay his taxes, there is no reasonable way to exclude him from protection while still providing national defense to everyone else. Because of these unique characteristics, public goods suffer from a "free rider" problem, with consumers enjoying the benefits without paying for it. Private firms cannot earn a profit in such a market, so the market fails. In these cases, the government intervenes by providing public goods and collecting mandatory taxes to pay for them. Governments also provide quasi-public goods like public education, libraries, and firefighting services. While it would be possible to exclude non-paying customers, the positive externalities involved put provision of these goods in the public interest.

The Circular Market Flow Including the Public Sector

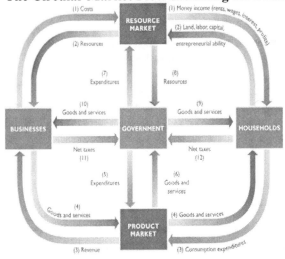

The circular flow and the public sector

In this figure, government has been added to the circular market flow. Like firms, governments buy land, labor, and capital from households in the resource (factor) market. Like households, governments buy products from firms in the product market. Then governments collect tax revenues from households and firms to pay for the provision of public goods. These taxes are noted as "net taxes," recognizing that funds are also flowing back to households and firms in the form of transfer payments and subsidies.

Government Revenues and Spending

The size of the public sector has increased significantly over the past sixty years. Total spending by federal, state, and local governments now accounts for about 1/3 of the total production in our economy. The largest areas of federal spending are pensions and income security, health, national defense, and interest on debt. Federal revenue comes primarily from the individual income tax, payroll tax (for Social Security and Medicare), corporate income tax, and excise taxes on products like cigarettes and gasoline. State and local governments rely on intergovernmental revenues from the federal government to fund substantial portions of their spending. Though states differ, most rely primarily on sales and individual income taxes to provide education, public welfare, health, highways, and public safety. Most local governments rely primarily on property taxes to fund public education, welfare, health, hospitals, and public safety.

Multiple-Choice Questions

1.   Most of the U.S. national income is in the form of
    (A)   rents for natural resource owners.
    (B)   proprietors' income for owning a business.
    (C)   interest on bonds and savings accounts.
    (D)   wages and salaries of workers.
    (E)   corporate profits on product sales.

2. Each of the following is a role of the U.S. government in the economy EXCEPT
    (A)   enforcing property rights and contracts.
    (B)   promoting competition in markets.
    (C)   equalizing incomes among all wage earners.
    (D)   stabilizing the economy through fiscal and monetary policy.
    (E)   providing public goods when markets fail.

3. A spillover cost passed on to a third party is
    (A)   a public good.
    (B)   an externality.
    (C)   a subsidy.
    (D)   an excise tax.
    (E)   a transfer payment.

4. Because polluters do not capture all of their costs of production,
    (A)   resources are over-allocated to this industry and prices are set too low.
    (B)   resources are over-allocated to this industry and prices are set too high.
    (C)   resources are under-allocated to this industry and prices are set too low.
    (D)   resources are under-allocated to this industry and prices are set too high.
    (E)   government must provide the products in order to reduce pollution.

5. An appropriate policy to resolve the positive externality for vaccinations is to
    (A)   place a tax on vaccinations.
    (B)   require pharmaceutical companies to develop free vaccinations.
    (C)   subsidize the consumer price of vaccinations.
    (D)   ration vaccines to ensure there are enough for all consumers.
    (E)   import vaccines to meet the excessive consumer demand.

6. Which of the following products meets the definition of a public good?
    (A)   a car
    (B)   a highway
    (C)   a haircut
    (D)   a vacation
    (E)   a newspaper

7. Why does the market fail for public goods?
    (A)   Public goods generally cost more than consumers are willing to pay.
    (B)   Consumer demand exceeds the supply of public goods.
    (C)   Supply and demand shift so frequently that no price can be set.
    (D)   Consumers gain less utility from public goods than from private goods.
    (E)   Consumers who fail to pay cannot be prevented from using public goods.

8. Each of the following statements correctly describes a role of government in the circular market flow EXCEPT
    (A)   a local government hiring police officers in the resource market.
    (B)   the federal government buying tanks in the product market.
    (C)   a state government collecting tax revenues to provide public education.
    (D)   the federal government selling bonds in order to pay off the national debt.
    (E)   a local government buying a snowplow in the product market.

Multiple-Choice Explanations

1.   (D)   Nearly 3/4 of national income comes from salaries and wages.

2.   (C)   While the federal government uses progressive taxes and transfer payments to redistribute income, it only attempts to raise the standard of living for those with the lowest incomes; equalization of incomes is a goal of socialist, not capitalist, economic systems.

3.   (B)   Negative externalities impose costs on people other than buyers and sellers, while positive externalities result in benefits for outsiders.

4.   (A)   Because the firm avoids some production costs, product supply is too high, which sets the price lower than it would be in an efficient market.

5.   (C)   Positive externalities result in an under-allocation of the product because some of the benefits are not captured; lowering the price to consumers is one way to restore efficiency in the market.

6.   (B)   A public good's characteristics are non-rival consumption and non-excludability of those who do not pay for the good.

7.   (E)   Because non-excludability is characteristic of public goods, firms cannot profit from product sales; therefore, firms will not provide the product.

8.   (D)   Government borrowing through bonds involves an injection of funds into the circular market flow, not an exchange of funds for factors of production or final products.

CHAPTER 5: THE UNITED STATES IN THE GLOBAL ECONOMY

Introduction
Globalization has dramatically changed markets, as producers and consumers around the world are increasingly interconnected through markets. Chapter 5 introduces the global economy by describing the importance of comparative advantage in determining trade patterns, identifying the causes and effects of changing currency values, and explaining the history of government intervention in international trade. Material from Chapter 5 consistently appears on both AP economics exams, with a question or two about comparative advantage and specialization appearing on the multiple-choice portion of the microeconomics exam. Material on comparative advantage, international trade, and currency markets consistently appears on the macroeconomics exam in both multiple-choice and free-response sections. The macroeconomics free-response section, in particular, very often includes a full question or a portion of the larger first question on currency markets or comparative advantage.

U.S. Connections in International Trade
Nations are interconnected through a vast array of markets, including imports and exports of products and resources, migration of workers, information and technology flows, and financial transactions. International trade results from differences in resources and the efficiency with which nations can produce products. International trade has increased significantly since World War II, primarily due to improvements in transportation and communication technology and reduced tariffs and other trade barriers among nations.

The United States is the leading trading nation in both imports and exports, and both have increased significantly over the past several decades. However, the United States now produces a smaller percentage of the world's exports because the exports of other countries have grown more quickly. Leading U.S. exports include chemicals, agricultural goods, and consumer durable goods, while the main U.S. imports include petroleum, autos, and electronics. Canada is our most important trading partner, followed by countries belonging to the European Union, Mexico, China, Japan, and countries belonging to OPEC.

The Balance of Trade
A trade surplus results when a nation exports more than it imports. Trade deficits occur when imports exceed exports. The United States has had trade deficits since the early 1980s.

Bear in Mind
The AP economics exams have not included questions requiring knowledge of specific international trade statistics. It is important, though, to understand trends such as increasing imports and exports and the persistent U.S. trade deficit.

Specialization and Trade
Nations open their economies to trade in order to import products they cannot produce domestically or products they can buy at a lower price than the cost of producing them domestically. Just as individuals specialize in careers and buy other products they need, countries specialize in what they produce most efficiently and then trade for other goods. Economist Adam Smith explained that specialization and trade allow nations to use their resources more efficiently, increasing world output. Economist David Ricardo explained that a nation can benefit from trade, even if that nation has an absolute advantage—the ability to produce more of all products than another country. He said that the focus instead should be on comparative advantage—the ability to produce more efficiently.

Comparative Advantage: The Example of Individuals
Assume Cameron is an architect earning $40 per hour. He wants to develop a website for his business and estimates it would take him 20 hours to bring it online. Andrew is a computer programmer earning $30 per hour. Though he knows computers, he works more slowly and would require 25 hours to do the work. Should Cameron hire Andrew to produce the website or do it himself? We must calculate each of their costs to find out.

If Cameron develops his website, he loses 20 hours of architecture work at $40 per hour, for a cost of $800. Andrew requires 25 hours of work at $30, for a cost of $750. Because Cameron can hire Andrew for less than the value of his lost architecture work, Cameron should hire Andrew and pay him with the money he earns doing architectural work.

Bear in Mind
The AP microeconomics and macroeconomics exams consistently have a multiple-choice question about individual comparative advantage. Even if one person is better at both tasks, one will have the comparative advantage in each task, and each should specialize in that task to maximize production at the lowest cost.

Comparative Advantage: The Example of Nations
To determine comparative advantage between countries, we must assume that these are the only two countries involved in the trade, the countries use equal amounts of resources to make only these two products, the costs of producing both products are constant, and the nations will use barter to trade products rather than use money. Of course, this isn't realistic, but remember the smiley (☺)? You can see the principles of opportunity cost, comparative advantage, and gains from trade in specialization from this scenario.

Assume that Canada could produce 120 tons of wheat or 30 tons of corn. Using an equal amount of resources, Mexico could produce 75 tons of wheat or 25 tons of corn. Canada can produce more wheat and more corn than Mexico, so it holds an absolute advantage in the production of both crops. But that isn't the key to trade—we have to find out who holds the comparative advantage in producing each crop. To do this, set up equations illustrating the productive capacity of each country. For example,

Canada	120 tons of wheat = 30 tons of corn

Reduce the numbers to find Canada's opportunity cost for producing wheat and corn.

Canada	4 tons of wheat = 1 ton of corn
	1 ton of wheat = 1/4 ton of corn

Then do the same for Mexico.

Mexico	75 tons of wheat = 25 tons of corn
	3 tons of wheat = 1 ton of corn
	1 ton of wheat = 1/3 ton of corn

Now we must determine which nation has the lowest opportunity cost to find who has the comparative advantage in each product. To produce 1 ton of corn, Canada's opportunity cost is 4 tons of wheat; Mexico's opportunity cost is 3 tons of wheat. So Mexico has the comparative advantage and should specialize in producing corn. Canada's opportunity cost for producing 1 ton of wheat is 1/4 ton of corn, while Mexico produces 1/3 ton of corn. Therefore, Canada is the lowest-cost producer and should specialize in wheat.

Terms of Trade

Now that we have found that Mexico should produce corn and Canada should produce wheat, we need to determine the terms of trade, or the barter price of corn and wheat. It is important to remember that the terms of trade will *always* fall between the two nations' opportunity costs. Mexico's opportunity cost for 1 ton of corn is 3 tons of wheat, so Mexico will not accept anything less in payment for corn. Canada will not pay more than 4 tons of wheat for 1 ton of corn, because they could produce it domestically at a lower cost. Therefore, the terms of trade for a ton of corn are between 3 and 4 tons of wheat.

Gains from Trade

The terms of trade illustrate how each country will gain from specialization and trade. Let's assume Canada and Mexico agree to a price of 3.5 tons of wheat per ton of corn. At that price, Mexican producers gain because the price they earn for corn is higher than their cost of producing it. At the same time, Canadian consumers gain, because they can buy Mexican corn for a lower price than it would have cost them to produce it at home. Because of specialization and trade, both countries gain from the exchange.

By opening their economies to trade, each country is able to reach beyond its production possibilities curve that limited domestic production. As each country specializes in what it produces more efficiently, resources are allocated to the most efficient producer, output increases, and both nations have more wheat and corn than they could have created alone.

Bear in Mind

Both AP economics exams consistently include questions about comparative advantage, specialization, and trade in the multiple-choice and free-response portions of the exam. Sometimes questions appear in the form of input models rather than output models. In other words, rather than starting with data on the production of final products like corn and wheat, the question will tell you how many hours or resources are needed to produce each product. A quick conversion will calculate the opportunity costs of final products.

Assume these data represent the resources required to produce one product in each country.

	Cars	Motorcycles
Country A	30 resource units	10 resource units
Country B	20 resource units	4 resource units

These are the resources required to *produce* the good, not the number of goods produced. This confusion is one of the most common mistakes students make in this analysis.

To determine comparative advantage, find a common number of resource units within a country. For Country A, assume you have 30 resource units available to produce goods. Country A could produce 1 car or 3 motorcycles. For Country B, start with a total of 20 resource units, which would allow Country B to produce 1 car or 5 motorcycles. After that conversion, you can determine comparative advantage, specialization, and terms of trade in the same way as with the output model. Don't worry about trying to find a common number of resource units between the two countries to determine comparative advantage, because you are only trying to find the opportunity cost of production within each country. That opportunity cost is what will be compared to the other country.

Foreign Exchange Markets

Trade does not rely on barter; money facilitates trade. But firms want to be paid in the currency of their own country in order to pay their production costs. Therefore, in order for a firm to buy a product from another country, it must first purchase that country's currency in the foreign exchange market. The exchange rate is the value of one currency in terms of another. For example, if $1 US = 50 Indian rupees, and you wanted to buy an Indian shawl priced at 1,500 rupees, that price would be the equivalent of $30 US.

Currency values in foreign exchange markets are determined by supply and demand. Remember that the price is expressed in terms of the other currency. In this example, the price of one euro is $1.25 US.

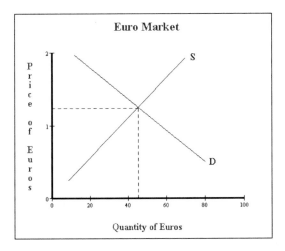

Changes in Currency Values

Changes in the demand for currency can affect the value of that currency in the foreign exchange market. If U.S. consumer incomes increase or consumer tastes change to prefer imported products from Europe, demand for the euro must increase in order to pay for those additional imports. The increased demand pushes up the price of the euro, so the value of the euro appreciates, meaning it increases in value. At this appreciated value, it takes more dollars to pay for each euro. If demand for the euro falls, the euro depreciates, losing value because Americans can buy the euro for fewer dollars.

It is important to understand that in currency exchange, two markets are in motion at the same time—the market for euros and the market for dollars. If an American firm wants to buy a product from Germany, it must buy those euros first. How is the American firm paying for the euros? With U.S. dollars! So we must view effects in both markets at once.

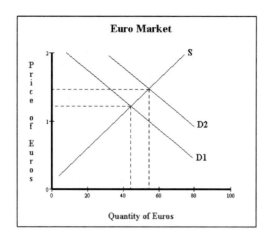

Euro Market

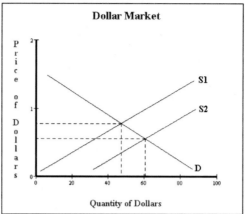

Dollar Market

Our increased demand for euros causes the euro to appreciate in the euro market. When we use dollars to buy euros, the supply of dollars increases in the dollar market, causing the dollar to depreciate in value. It is important to remember that we are looking at a relationship between two currencies. If one appreciates, the other must depreciate. If one currency is getting relatively stronger, the other must be getting relatively weaker.

Taking the EEK! Out of Economics

When drawing side-by-side curves for currencies, it is very important to carefully label each market to avoid confusion. Remember that if demand moves in one graph, supply moves the same direction in the other graph. If American firms buy fewer imports, their demand for the foreign currency falls. Therefore, the supply of dollars to pay for that foreign currency in the foreign exchange market falls, as well.

The Effects of Changes in Currency Values

As the euro appreciates and the dollar depreciates, it takes more dollars to buy each euro. As a result, it costs importers more to buy German products. Although the German firm did not change the product price, because the euro is now more expensive, the product looks more expensive to importers. As a result, the quantity imported begins to fall. At the same time, dollars depreciate and are less expensive for German importers. Although U.S. firms did not change prices, products now look less expensive to German importers. As a result, U.S. exports rise. When the dollar depreciates, U.S. imports fall and exports increase. And when the dollar appreciates, U.S. imports rise and exports decrease.

Barriers to Trade

Although we recognize gains from trade, governments sometimes intervene in markets to erect barriers to trade. Protective tariffs are taxes on imports, while import quotas limit the number of products imported. Both policies are designed to increase the price or limit the quantity of imports to encourage consumers to buy American-made products instead.

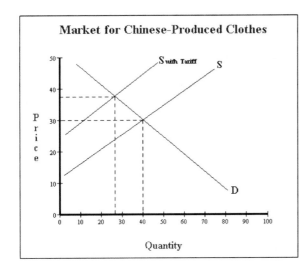

Market for Chinese-Produced Clothes

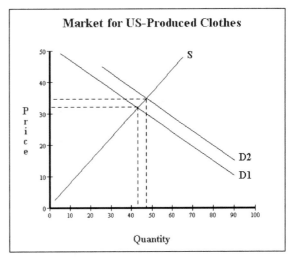

Market for US-Produced Clothes

In this example, $30 Chinese-produced clothes are more attractive to consumers than the $32 clothes produced by American firms. If the U.S. government placed a $7 tariff on Chinese clothes, increasing the price to $37, American consumers would reduce the quantity demanded for imported clothes and instead increase their demand for substitute American clothes. This increase in demand would push the price of U.S.-produced clothes up, but perhaps not as high as the price of the Chinese clothes with the tariff in place.

Countries can use other barriers such as licensing or inspection requirements that make it more difficult and expensive for foreign firms to get their product into the country. Governments can also subsidize American firms, reducing their costs of production to allow them to export their products for lower prices to attract foreign demand.

Reasons for Government Intervention in Trade
Although consumers of imports and producers of exports gain from international trade, domestic producers who must compete with those imports—and the employees who work for those firms—have a strong incentive to support the erection of trade barriers. The benefits of trade barriers are concentrated on domestic producers, and the costs are dispersed among the many consumers of imports who now have to pay higher prices.

Some interpret increased imports as causing a loss of jobs without considering that the increase in exports will create jobs in export industries. Many oppose open trade because it is difficult to transition between careers, sometimes requiring job training, a move, or lower wages. Governments can assist in this transition by providing or subsidizing job training or extending unemployment benefits. It is important, however, to remember that the gains from trade in the form of lower product prices and a wider variety of products help offset some of these transition costs.

World Trade Agreements
Since the 1930s, trade barriers have steadily decreased. The North American Free Trade Agreement (NAFTA) forms a trade bloc among the United States, Canada, and Mexico, eliminating most trade barriers among the countries. The European Union is a similar trade bloc of more than a dozen countries. Production efficiency has improved, and imports and exports have significantly increased among countries involved in trade. The World Trade Organization works to reduce trade barriers and resolve trade disputes on a global scale.

Multiple-Choice Questions

1. The condition in which a country imports more than it exports is a
    (A)   comparative advantage.
    (B)   trade deficit.
    (C)   absolute advantage.
    (D)   exchange rate.
    (E)   trade surplus.

2. Bob is a mechanic who earns $30 per hour repairing farm machinery. He is also an excellent painter who can paint his house twice as quickly as a painter he could hire for $10 per hour. Which of the following is true?
    (A)   Bob has an absolute advantage as both a mechanic and a painter, and he should evenly divide his time between both jobs.
    (B)   Bob has a comparative advantage in painting and should give up his career as a mechanic to become a painter.
    (C)   Bob has a comparative advantage as a mechanic and should hire a painter to paint his house.
    (D)   Bob has an absolute advantage as a mechanic and a comparative advantage in painting, so he should stop working long enough to paint his house, and then return to work as a mechanic.
    (E)   Bob has a comparative advantage in painting and should spend twice as much time painting as he spends working as a mechanic.

Use the production possibilities per week below to answer questions 3–5.

	Cars	Machines
Sweden	100	1,000
France	250	500

3. Which of the following statements is true?
    (A)   Sweden has a comparative advantage in producing cars.
    (B)   France has an absolute advantage in producing both cars and machines.
    (C)   Sweden has an absolute advantage in producing both cars and machines.
    (D)   France has a comparative advantage in producing cars.
    (E)   France has a comparative advantage in producing machines.

4. In order to obtain gains from trade,
    (A)   Sweden should import machines from France.
    (B)   Sweden should import cars from France.
    (C)   Sweden should produce cars and machines and export both.
    (D)   France should produce machines and import cars from Sweden.
    (E)   France should import both cars and machines from Sweden.

5.	Both countries would gain from the trade if the price of one car is
	(A)	750 machines.
	(B)	100 machines.
	(C)	3 machines.
	(D)	11 machines.
	(E)	500 machines.

6.	If U.S. demand for Mexican oil increases,
	(A)	the demand for U.S. dollars increases.
	(B)	the supply of Mexican pesos increases.
	(C)	the price of Mexican oil decreases.
	(D)	the value of Mexican pesos decreases.
	(E)	the demand for Mexican pesos increases.

7.	If the U.S. dollar appreciates in relation to the Japanese yen,
	(A)	U.S. imports from Japan will increase.
	(B)	Japanese products will appear to be more expensive to Americans.
	(C)	U.S. exports to Japan will increase.
	(D)	the U.S. dollar has become relatively less valuable.
	(E)	U.S. exports appear less expensive to Japanese consumers.

8.	If U.S. incomes fall and imported Italian shoes are normal goods,
	(A)	the demand for imported shoes increases.
	(B)	the demand for euros increases.
	(C)	the euro appreciates in value.
	(D)	the supply of U.S. dollars in the foreign exchange market increases.
	(E)	the U.S. dollar appreciates in value.

9.	A tariff is a
	(A)	per-unit tax on imports.
	(B)	limit on the number of imported products.
	(C)	method by which governments support increases in international trade.
	(D)	government subsidy to support exporters.
	(E)	discount in the value of a currency.

10.	The effects of trade barriers include all of the following EXCEPT
	(A)	the prices of imported products increase.
	(B)	efficiency in the market decreases.
	(C)	U.S. exports decrease.
	(D)	employment among producers of exports increases.
	(E)	U.S. imports decrease.

Free-Response Questions

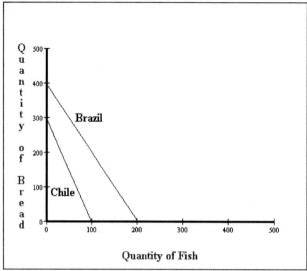

Quantity of Fish

1.   The figure above shows production possibilities for Chile and Brazil. Using all available resources, Chile can produce 300 loaves of bread or 100 fish per day. With the same amount of resources, Brazil can produce 400 loaves of bread or 200 fish per day.

(a)   Calculate the opportunity cost of producing 1 fish in Chile.

(b)   Determine which country has the comparative advantage in the production of fish. Explain how you found your answer.

(c)   Identify which country will import fish.

(d)   If the terms of trade are that 1 fish = 2.5 loaves of bread, will Chile gain from the exchange? Explain why.

2.   Assume there are two competitive markets for beef: a market for beef produced in the United States and a market for beef imported from Canada. U.S. and Canadian beef are substitute products. Now assume Mad Cow Disease has been discovered among Canadian cattle but not among U.S. cattle.

(a)   Using a correctly labeled graph of the market for imported Canadian beef, show the effect of the discovery of Mad Cow Disease on each of the following.
      (i)   The quantity of imported Canadian beef
      (ii)   The price of imported Canadian beef

(b)   Using a correctly labeled graph of the foreign exchange market for Canadian dollars, show how the change in (a) will affect the international value of Canadian dollars.

(c)   How will the change in (b) affect the international value of U.S. dollars? Explain.

Multiple-Choice Explanations

1.   (B)   A trade deficit exists when imports exceed exports.

2.   (C)   Under this scenario, if it takes Bob 50 hours to paint the house, it will take the painter 100 hours to paint the house. Bob's opportunity cost of 50 hours as a mechanic is $1,500 of income, while it would cost him $1,000 to pay the painter for the 100 hours of work. Bob has a comparative advantage as a mechanic and should hire the painter to paint the house.

3   (D)   France's opportunity cost for producing a car is 2 machines, while Sweden's cost is 10 machines; France is the lowest-cost producer.

4.   (B)   Sweden can buy cars cheaper from France than it can produce them, so it will gain from the trade.

5.   (C)   France will not sell a car for any less than its cost of 2 machines, and Sweden will not buy a car for any more than its domestic cost of 10 machines, so any price in that range benefits both countries.

6.   (E)   Importers must buy Mexican pesos in order to pay for Mexican oil.

7.   (A)   A more valuable dollar makes Japanese imports appear cheaper, so U.S. imports from Japan increase.

8.   (E)   The U.S. dollar appreciates, because as demand for euros falls, the value of the euro falls, causing the value of a U.S. dollar to rise relative to the euro.

9.   (A)   A tariff is a tax placed on imports to raise the price of the import.

10.   (D)   Trade barriers limit trade with other countries, reducing U.S. exports, so fewer workers are needed to produce products for export.

Free-Response Explanations

1.   **6 points** (1 + 2 + 1 + 2)

(a)   1 point:
- 1 point is earned for stating that Chile's opportunity cost of 1 fish is 3 loaves of bread.

(b)   2 points:
- 1 point is earned for stating that Brazil has the comparative advantage in fish.
- 1 point is earned for stating that Brazil has a lower opportunity cost for producing fish (2 loaves of bread compared to Chile's 3 loaves of bread).

(c)   1 point:
- 1 point is earned for identifying Chile as the importer of fish.

(d)   2 points:
- 1 point is earned for determining Chile will gain from the trade.
- 1 point is earned for explaining that, at a price of 2.5 loaves of bread per fish, Chile can import fish at a lower cost than it can produce fish.

2.   **9 points** (4 + 3 + 2)

(a)   4 points:
- 1 point is earned for a correctly labeled graph of the Canadian beef market.
- 1 point is earned for illustrating a decrease in demand.
- 1 point is earned for stating that the quantity of imported Canadian beef will fall.
- 1 point is earned for stating that the price of imported Canadian beef will fall.

(b)   3 points:
- 1 point is earned for a correctly labeled graph for Canadian dollars.
- 1 point is earned for illustrating a decrease in demand.
- 1 point is earned for stating that the international value of Canadian dollars falls.

(c)   2 points:
- 1 point is earned for stating that the international value of the U.S. dollar increases.
- 1 point is earned for explaining that, because the supply of dollars in the foreign exchange market decreases, the value of the dollar appreciates.

CHAPTER 6: ELASTICITY, CONSUMER SURPLUS, AND PRODUCER SURPLUS

Introduction
Consumer responses to changes in prices, incomes, and prices of related products can be explained by the concept of elasticity. Firms and governments use knowledge of elasticity to determine how to raise revenue. Chapter 6 introduces formulas to calculate elasticity, interprets the meaning for product demand and supply, and explains consumer and producer surplus and deadweight loss. Material from Chapter 6 consistently appears on the AP microeconomics exam in a couple of multiple-choice questions and occasionally is included as part of a free-response question.

Price Elasticity of Demand
The Law of Demand explains that consumers buy more at lower prices and less at higher prices. But we know that consumers are more responsive to changes in the price of some products and not as responsive to others. Price elasticity of demand measures how sensitive consumers are to price changes by calculating the change in quantity demanded related to price from two points on the demand curve.

The formula to measure the price elasticity coefficient is

$$E = \frac{\text{Percentage change in quantity demanded}}{\text{Percentage change in price}}$$

In order to avoid calculation issues, the midpoint formula is the best and easy to use.

$$E = \frac{\dfrac{\text{Quantity 1} - \text{Quantity 2}}{(\text{Quantity 1} + \text{Quantity 2}) / 2}}{\dfrac{\text{Price 1} - \text{Price 2}}{(\text{Price 1} + \text{Price 2}) / 2}}$$

For example, at a price of $5, a consumer will buy 10 products, and at a price of $3, the consumer will buy 20 products. Using the elasticity formula

$$E = \frac{\dfrac{(10 - 20)}{(10 + 20) / 2}}{\dfrac{(5 - 3)}{(5 + 3) / 2}} = \frac{\dfrac{-10}{15}}{\dfrac{2}{4}} = \frac{-0.67}{0.50} = -1.34$$

Economists use the absolute value of the elasticity coefficient. Because the demand curve is downward sloping, elasticity of demand must be a negative number. But the minus sign is ignored because we are simply looking at the strength of the relationship.

Bear in Mind

While a question on the AP economics exam may ask for the specific coefficient of elasticity or the meaning of a coefficient, it is far more common for questions to deal with applications of elasticity in specific circumstances or to identify whether demand is elastic or inelastic when consumers or total revenues respond in a particular way.

Interpretation of Price Elasticity of Demand

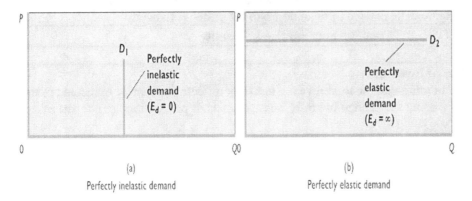

(a)
Perfectly inelastic demand

(b)
Perfectly elastic demand

Perfectly inelastic and elastic demands

If demand is perfectly inelastic, consumers do not change their quantity demanded at all, regardless of price. The result is a vertical demand curve with an elasticity coefficient of zero. It is rare for consumers to buy the same amount at any price, and examples are primarily limited to life-saving medicines and medical procedures.

Demand is inelastic when consumers are not very sensitive to a change in product price. If the elasticity coefficient is less than one, demand is inelastic because even a large change in price causes a relatively small change in quantity demanded. For example, if $E = 0.6$, a 1 percent decrease in price only results in a 0.6 percent increase in the quantity demanded.

A point of unit elasticity is reached when a change in price causes an identical change in the quantity demanded, for an elasticity coefficient of one. If the price decreases by 3 percent, the quantity demanded increases by the same 3 percent.

Demand is elastic if customers are sensitive to a change in product price. If the elasticity coefficient is greater than one, demand is elastic because a small change in price causes a larger change in the quantity demanded. For example, if $E = 5$, a 1 percent decrease in price results in a 5 percent increase in the quantity demanded.

If demand is perfectly elastic, a small price cut causes customers to change from buying zero to buying as many as can be produced. The result is a horizontal demand curve with an elasticity coefficient of infinity. Again, this is rare but can be seen in the case of individual firms selling in perfectly competitive markets, such as agricultural products.

Taking the EEK! Out of Economics

It's easy to mix up elastic and inelastic demand when you're trying to remember the term for a particular situation. One trick to keep them straight is to replace the word "elastic" with the word "sensitive." If demand is inelastic, consumers are insensitive to the price change; when demand is elastic, consumers are sensitive and change the quantity bought when price changes. Another trick is to remember that the perfectly "I"nelastic demand curve is vertical – it looks like the letter I. Perfectly elastic demand is a horizontal curve.

The Total Revenue Test
An easier way to determine the elasticity of demand is the total revenue test. Firms can use the total revenue test to examine the change in revenue when the price is changed.

Total Revenue = Price × Quantity

Taking the EEK! Out of Economics
It is important to keep in mind that the total revenue test only reflects the change in income to the firm. It tells us nothing about the change in profit, because costs of production are not part of the analysis.

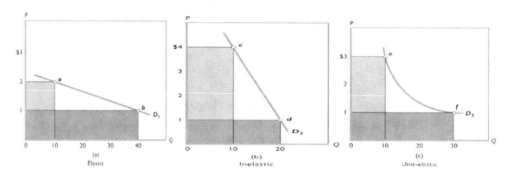

The total-revenue test for price elasticity

When demand is elastic, a decrease in price causes an increase in total revenue. Even though the price is lower, customers respond by buying so many more products that the firm's revenue actually increases. In figure (a), when the price falls, the total revenue rises from $20 to $40. Elasticity is greater than one. Fast food restaurants, for example, can draw in significant numbers of additional customers with a sale or promotional deal.

If demand is inelastic, a decrease in price causes a decrease in total revenue. Consumers respond only slightly to a lower price, so the firm's total revenue declines. In figure (b), when the price falls, the total revenue falls from $40 to $20. Elasticity is less than one. Firms also experience this relationship in reverse; when the price rises, consumers only reduce their purchases by a small amount. When gasoline prices rose significantly in recent years, consumers were unhappy, but cut consumption only slightly in the short run.

When demand is unit elastic, a change in price leaves total revenue exactly the same. In figure (c), at a price of $3 and again at a price of $1, the total revenue is $30. Elasticity equals one. With the total revenue test, watch what happens when product price changes. When the product price falls, if total revenue rises, demand is elastic; if total revenue falls, demand is inelastic; and if total revenue remains the same, demand is unit elastic.

Taking the EEK! Out of Economics
In general, demand tends to be elastic in the higher price ranges and inelastic in the lower price ranges of the curve because of the math involved in the calculation. Therefore, it is important to use two specific points on the curve to determine the elasticity of demand between those two points and not rely on how the slope looks to guess at elasticity.

Determinants of Price Elasticity of Demand

Why do consumers react strongly to price changes of some products but seem oblivious to others? Demand tends to be more elastic if substitutes are available, the product price is high as a proportion of the consumer's income, the product is a luxury, or the consumer has time to make changes in behavior that make the product less necessary. Consumer demand is much more inelastic if there are no substitutes for the product, the product price is a small proportion of the consumer's income, the product is a necessity, or there is little or no time for the consumer to change behaviors to avoid buying the product.

Uses of Elasticity

Elasticity is important because it determines what a firm should do to change revenue. If demand is elastic, the firm can lower its price to increase total revenue. But if demand for the product is inelastic, the firm would instead increase its price to raise total revenue.

Price elasticity of demand is also important to the government. When legislatures raise revenues to pay for public goods, they want to place excise taxes on products customers will continue to buy at the higher price (including the tax). For that reason, governments place taxes on products with inelastic demand, such as cigarettes, gasoline, and liquor.

Price Elasticity of Supply

Elasticity of supply measures how responsive producers are to changes in the price of their products. The formula is the same as for demand, except that it is measuring the percentage change in quantity supplied rather than quantity demanded:

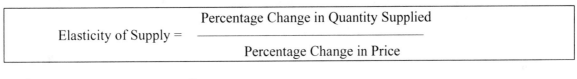

$$\text{Elasticity of Supply} = \frac{\text{Percentage Change in Quantity Supplied}}{\text{Percentage Change in Price}}$$

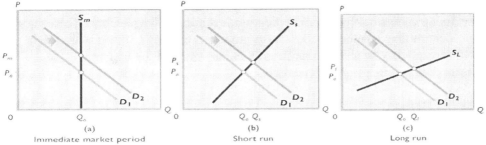

Time and elasticity of supply

Price elasticity of supply relies on how quickly and easily a producer can shift resources to produce more products. In the market period, a firm cannot respond to a price change. If higher demand for apples raised the price, producers could do nothing to immediately increase the quantity of apples because it takes time to grow the trees. In the short run, firms can increase production somewhat but are still constrained by the size of the plant and equipment. If demand for cars significantly increased, producers could add shifts of workers to increase production, but would still be limited by the plant capacity. In the long run, firms can change the size of their plants and other firms can join the industry to produce even more. The more time a firm has, the more responsive it is to price changes.

In some cases, supply remains perfectly inelastic and cannot be increased even with time. A fixed quantity of Van Gogh paintings exists, and with Van Gogh's death, no more can be produced at any price. It is possible that more paintings might be discovered, but Van Gogh cannot respond to a higher price by increasing the quantity supplied.

Cross (Price) Elasticity of Demand

Cross (cross-price) elasticity measures the sensitivity of consumers in buying one product when the price of a related product changes. The formula is similar to the price elasticity of demand, but notice that the products differ in the numerator and denominator.

$$\text{Cross-Price Elasticity} = \frac{\text{Percentage Change in Quantity Demanded for Product X}}{\text{Percentage Change in Price for Product Y}}$$

In addition, cross-price elasticity can be either positive or negative, so don't disregard the negative sign if one appears in this case. If the cross-price elasticity coefficient is zero or near zero, the products are independent and unrelated.

If cross-price elasticity is positive, the products are substitutes. When the price of Häagen Dazs ice cream increases, the quantity demanded of Ben and Jerry's ice cream increases. Because they move the same direction, the elasticity is positive. The larger the cross-price elasticity coefficient, the more substitutable the products are.

If cross-price elasticity is negative, the products are complements. When the price of peanut butter increases, the quantity demanded of jelly falls. Because they move in opposite directions, the elasticity is negative. The larger the cross-price elasticity coefficient, the stronger the complementary relationship between the two products.

Firms use knowledge of cross-price elasticity to determine how seriously consumers will respond to a price increase by switching to a competitor's product – or how easily they can draw consumers away from a competitor by lowering their product price. The government also uses this knowledge in determining whether to allow large producers to merge. Firms with a high cross-elasticity of demand may be able to significantly reduce competition by merging, so the government is more reluctant to allow such mergers.

Income Elasticity of Demand

Income elasticity of demand measures how consumers respond when their incomes change. As with cross-price elasticity, the negative or positive sign is important. The formula is, again, very similar to the price elasticity of demand, but notice this time that the denominator is income, rather than product price.

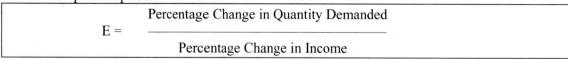

$$E = \frac{\text{Percentage Change in Quantity Demanded}}{\text{Percentage Change in Income}}$$

If income elasticity of demand is positive, the product is a normal good; as income rises, the quantity demanded rises. Most goods are normal goods, as customers buy more when income increases. If the income elasticity is negative, the product is an inferior good. As income increases, the consumer demands a smaller quantity of inferior goods. With higher incomes, consumers buy fewer generic goods in favor of name-brand products.

Knowledge of income elasticity is important to understand which industries will be most strongly affected by economic downturns. Income elasticity is particularly high for new cars, houses, and vacations, so demand for these products falls significantly during times of serious job loss. On the other hand, income elasticity is low for electricity, toilet paper, and milk, which consumers tend to continue to buy even when incomes fall.

Taking the EEK! Out of Economics
Four different elasticity formulas have been introduced in this chapter, but notice that there is very little difference between them. In each case, a change in quantity is in the numerator, because we're looking at the response to a stimulus. The stimulus is in the denominator – the price of the product for price elasticity of demand and supply, the price of a related product for cross-price elasticity of demand, and income for the income elasticity of demand. Keep in mind which relationship you're looking for, and that will help you remember which formula to use.

Bear in Mind
While previous exams have not asked students to calculate cross-price or income elasticities of demand, it is important to be able to explain how changes in incomes and the prices of related products can affect quantity demanded.

Consumer and Producer Surplus

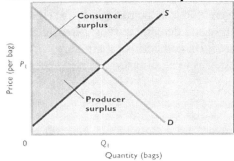

Efficiency: maximum combined consumer and producer surplus

Consumer surplus is the difference between what a consumer was willing to pay for a product and the price that was actually charged. If you ever bought a product for less than you were willing to pay, you enjoyed a consumer surplus. It is represented by the triangle above the price up to the demand curve. If the product price rises, consumer surplus falls. Producer surplus is the difference between the minimum acceptable price to the firm and the price that was actually charged. It is found in the triangle below the price down to the supply curve. If the product price falls, producer surplus falls.

Deadweight Loss
At the point of equilibrium, productive and allocative efficiency are achieved and both producer and consumer surplus are maximized. But in some situations, a product is overproduced or underproduced, and efficiency is lost. This deadweight loss is the reduction in consumer and producer surplus as a result of inefficient production.

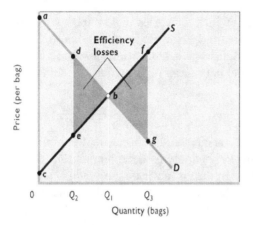

Efficiency losses (or deadweight losses)

If the quantity produced is too low, at Q2 in this figure, the triangle between equilibrium and the quantity produced to the left (between the supply and demand curves) is the deadweight loss. Both consumer and producer surplus are lost. Consumers are willing to pay more than the minimum price firms will accept, but something is reducing output.

If the quantity produced is greater than the equilibrium, at Q3, consumers are not willing to pay the minimum price firms are willing to accept. The deadweight loss is the triangle to the right of equilibrium, out to the quantity produced (between the supply and demand curves). Inefficiency results from using resources to produce these excess products. In competitive markets, inefficiencies generally resolve themselves as the market returns to equilibrium. But in situations we will examine later, inefficiencies sometimes remain.

Multiple-Choice Questions

1. If customers buy a quantity of seven products per week, regardless of the price, the price elasticity of demand for the product is
    (A)   infinity.
    (B)   greater than one.
    (C)   equal to one.
    (D)   less than one.
    (E)   zero.

2. The cable television company increases its monthly price for basic service. The firm's revenues will only increase if
    (A)   demand for cable television is price elastic.
    (B)   demand for cable television is income elastic.
    (C)   supply for cable television is price elastic.
    (D)   demand for cable television is price inelastic.
    (E)   supply for cable television is unit elastic.

3. A local baseball team's concession stand sells hot dogs for $2 and earns $600 in revenue. The next week, the price is raised to $3, and the concession stand still earns $600 in revenue. In this situation, the price elasticity of demand is
    (A)   perfectly elastic.
    (B)   elastic.
    (C)   unit elastic.

(D)   inelastic.

(E)   perfectly inelastic.

4.   In the elastic portion of a firm's demand curve, the firm can raise its revenue by

(A)   reducing the product price.

(B)   hiring additional workers.

(C)   lowering the quantity produced.

(D)   raising the product price.

(E)   increasing its cost of production.

5.   Demand for a product tends to be more price inelastic if

(A)   the consumer can find many available substitutes for the product.

(B)   the product is expensive in relation to the consumer's income.

(C)   the product is a necessity.

(D)   the consumer's income is falling.

(E)   the consumer rarely buys complements for the product.

6.   If golf clubs and golf balls are complementary goods and the price of golf clubs significantly increases,

(A)   the quantity of golf clubs purchased will increase.

(B)   the demand for golf balls will decrease.

(C)   the demand for tee times at golf courses will increase.

(D)   the price of golf balls will increase.

(E)   the quantity of golf balls purchased will increase.

7.   A change in consumer income is least likely to affect the quantity demanded of

(A)   cars.

(B)   DVDs.

(C)   restaurant meals.

(D)   piano lessons.

(E)   toothpaste.

8.   Consumer surplus is the difference between

(A)   the price firms were willing to charge and the equilibrium price.

(B)   the quantity consumers were willing to buy and the quantity firms were willing to sell.

(C)   the quantity consumers were willing to buy before and after a tax increase.

(D)   the price consumers were willing to pay and the equilibrium price.

(E)   the quantities supplied and demanded at a price above equilibrium price.

9.   The loss of producer and consumer surplus resulting from an under-allocation of resources to produce a good is

(A)   deadweight loss.

(B)   diminishing returns.

(C)   scarcity.

(D)   the cross-price coefficient of elasticity.

(E)   a negative externality.

Free-Response Question
Paintings by Pablo Picasso have significantly increased in value since the artist's death in 1973. When a Picasso painting is sold, it is often sold through an auction house, allowing many potential buyers to bid on the painting.

(a)   Using a correctly labeled supply and demand graph, illustrate the market for Picasso paintings.
        (i)   Determine the elasticity of supply for Picasso's paintings.
        (ii)   Explain why that level of elasticity exists for the paintings.

(b)   Now assume incomes significantly increase. Illustrate the effect of the change in incomes on your graph. Explain the effect of higher incomes on
        (i)   The price of Picasso paintings, which are normal goods.
        (ii)   The quantity of Picasso paintings produced.

Multiple-Choice Explanations
1.   (E)   If quantity does not change, the numerator in the formula is zero.
2.   (D)   When demand is price inelastic, consumers are relatively unresponsive and continue to buy at the higher price.
3.   (C)   If the product price changes and total revenue remains the same, demand is unit elastic between those two points.
4.   (A)   When consumers are very sensitive to price changes, a lower price increases the quantity sold so significantly that total revenue rises.
5.   (C)   If the consumer must buy the item regardless of price, demand is inelastic.
6.   (B)   If golf clubs are more expensive, fewer people will buy them, reducing the demand for golf balls to go with the clubs.
7.   (E)   Most consumers will continue to buy toothpaste, even if their income falls.
8.   (D)   Consumers would have been willing to pay more, but the price was lower.
9.   (A)   Deadweight loss illustrates efficiency lost by not producing at equilibrium.

Free-Response Explanation
6 points (3 + 3)
(a)   3 points:
- 1 point is earned for a correctly labeled graph with a vertical supply curve.
- 1 point is earned for stating that supply is perfectly inelastic.
- 1 point is earned for explaining that the producer cannot increase the quantity supplied in response to a higher price because the artist has died.

(b)   3 points:
- 1 point is earned for showing a rightward shift of the demand curve (with higher incomes, consumers buy more normal goods).
- 1 point is earned for stating that the price will increase.
- 1 point is earned for stating that the quantity produced will not change.

CHAPTER 7: CONSUMER BEHAVIOR

Introduction
The consumer is central to a market economy, and understanding how consumers make their purchasing decisions is the key to understanding demand. Chapter 7 explains how consumers maximize their utility through purchases and how that knowledge can be used to determine product demand. The Law of Diminishing Marginal Utility takes numeric and graphic form to illustrate why consumers respond as they do in markets. Material from Chapter 7 consistently appears in a multiple-choice question or two on the AP microeconomics exam and has appeared infrequently as part of a free-response question.

The Law of Diminishing Marginal Utility
The Law of Diminishing Marginal Utility explains that the more of a good a person gets, the less utility he gets from each additional unit. Scarcity still exists, because we want more than resources are available to produce. But at a particular time, our wants for a good can be satisfied and additional consumption can even reduce our well-being. Utility is difficult to quantify, and it differs between people and situations. A blanket holds great utility for someone living in Maine in January but little for a camper in Arizona in July.

Total and Marginal Utility
Economists attempt to quantify utility by measuring the units of satisfaction in terms of "utils." Total utility is the total amount of satisfaction a consumer receives from his total consumption of the product. Marginal utility is the increase in satisfaction (the increase in total utility) the consumer receives from consuming one more unit of the product.

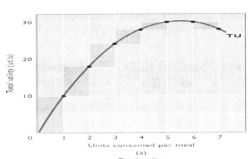

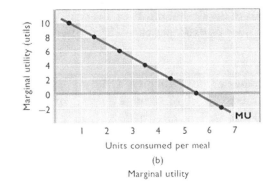

(1) Tacos Consumed per Meal	(2) Total Utility, Utils	(3) Marginal Utility, Utils
0	0	
1	10	10
2	18	8
3	24	6
4	28	4
5	30	2
6	30	0
7	28	-2

Total and marginal utility

It is important to note that marginal utility begins to fall after the very first product consumed. Your first taco holds great utility, and while a second taco is useful, it doesn't bring as much utility as the first one. The third holds even less. At some point, marginal utility becomes negative, as you're worse off by consuming more.

Total utility increases for the first several units consumed. Even though each extra taco brings you less utility than the one before, it still adds to the total utility for all of the tacos together. However, as the marginal utility decreases, the growth of the total utility curve slows, until it peaks at the point where the marginal utility of the next unit is zero. As marginal utility begins to fall into negative utils, the total utility begins to fall, as well.

Marginal Utility and Demand
The Law of Diminishing Marginal Utility is one reason demand slopes downward. If consumers gain less marginal utility from each additional unit, they will only buy more products if the price falls. So at lower prices, consumers buy more—the Law of Demand.

The Utility Maximizing Rule
The theory of consumer behavior begins with the assumptions that people act rationally in their self-interest, have preferences for some products over others, are limited by their budget constraints, and must pay the price of products to obtain goods. Given those assumptions, consumers find the mix of goods and services that bring them the greatest utility within the budget they have available—consumer equilibrium.

Let's assume Brett can choose to buy either orange juice or coffee. He measures his marginal utility for each cup of drink in "utils," or units of utility. Of course people don't sit down to calculate their utils when deciding whether to order juice or coffee. But they act as though they do. Remember the smiley (☺)? Once Brett has found his marginal utility per cup of each drink, he needs to divide that utility by the price per cup to make the units comparable. In this case, orange juice costs $2 per cup, while coffee costs $4 per cup. Therefore, Brett's table looks like this:

Number of Goods	Marginal Utility of Orange Juice	MU per Dollar of Orange Juice	Marginal Utility of Coffee	MU per Dollar of Coffee
First	10	5	24	6
Second	8	4	20	5
Third	6	3	12	3
Fourth	4	2	4	1

If Brett has $18 of income to spend, how much orange juice and coffee should he buy to maximize his utility? According to the utility maximizing rule, consumers maximize their satisfaction by consuming products in a way that the last dollar spent on each of two products brings the consumer the same amount of marginal utility per dollar spent.

Step 1: The first cup of juice brings Brett 5 utils per dollar, while the first cup of coffee yields 6 utils per dollar. Brett is better off buying a cup of coffee first, which earns him 24 utils at a cost of $4.

Step 2: Next, Brett must choose between buying the first cup of juice for 5 utils per dollar or buying a second cup of coffee, which will also bring 5 utils per dollar. Because he is indifferent between them, he will buy one of each. The cup of juice adds 10 utils for a total utility of 34 utils at a total of $6 spent. The second cup of coffee adds 20 utils for a total utility of 54 utils, with the $4 price of the coffee added to total $10 spent.

Step 3: Brett's next choice is between a second cup of juice for 4 utils per dollar or a third cup of coffee for 3 utils per dollar. He is better off buying a second juice for 8 additional utils, bringing total utility to 62 for the $12 spent.

Step 4: Next, Brett must decide between buying a third cup of juice for 3 utils per dollar or a third cup of coffee for 3 utils per dollar. Brett is indifferent between the two choices, so he buys one of each, exhausting his $18. He adds 6 utils from the juice and 12 utils from the coffee to his total. Brett maximizes his utility by buying of 3 cups of juice and 3 cups of coffee for a total utility of 80 utils. He has reached consumer equilibrium.

Taking the EEK! Out of Economics

One common mistake students make is to try to determine whether a consumer should buy a product strictly by comparing the marginal utility of products, rather than comparing the marginal utility *per dollar* of the products. It is crucial that you calculate that column in order to take relative prices into consideration. Another common mistake when calculating the total utility of all of the purchases is to instead add up the marginal utilities *per dollar* rather than the marginal utilities. One way to avoid this mistake is to complete your analysis and determine how many of each product the consumer will buy, and after that, add up the marginal utilities of those purchases to find the total utility.

Bear in Mind

In both multiple-choice and free-response questions, you will need to be able to construct this table. Given the quantities, total utilities, and prices of two products, you must be able to calculate the marginal utilities and MU per dollar. You must also be able to recalculate these numbers if the price of one product changes and to determine how the demand for each product changes as a result of the price change. You will not be allowed to use a calculator on the exam, but the numbers are chosen to keep the math simple.

Mathematical Equation for the Utility Maximizing Rule

Utility-maximizing consumer equilibrium can also be expressed as an equation:

$$\frac{\text{MU of Product A}}{\text{Price of Product A}} = \frac{\text{MU of Product B}}{\text{Price of Product B}}$$

To maximize utility, a consumer should buy Products A and B until the ratios are equal and the consumer's income is spent. If the ratio is unequal, the consumer would be better off reallocating his purchases to increase total utility. In the example above, Brett could have bought 2 juices and 4 cups of coffee, but he would only have gained 78 units of total utility compared to the 80 he received by maximizing his utility. Using the equation, had Brett bought 2 juices and 4 cups of coffee, the equation would have looked like this:

$$\frac{8}{2} > \frac{4}{4}$$

Because the marginal utility per dollar spent for orange juice is clearly larger than the marginal utility per dollar spent for coffee, Brett would be better off buying more orange juice and less coffee until the marginal utilities per dollar become equal.

Utility Maximization and the Demand Curve
The demand curve for orange juice can be calculated by first setting one point where the price of juice is $2 per cup (a quantity of 3). Then change the price of orange juice and develop a new column for MU per dollar at the other price, determine how much juice would be purchased at that price, and then connect the two points into a demand curve.

We can see the income and substitution effects in the downward-sloping demand curve as well. With the income effect, when the price of orange juice lowers, Brett has some income left with which he could buy more juice (or coffee). With the substitution effect, when the price of orange juice falls, Brett buys more juice as a substitute for coffee. In the utility maximization formula, you can see that a lower price reduces the denominator, increasing the marginal utility per dollar and increasing the consumer's utility.

Bear in Mind
While the textbook discusses indifference curve analysis, those concepts are not critical to the AP economics exams and will not be covered here.

Multiple-Choice Questions
1. As DeShawn eats his Halloween treats, he gains less and less satisfaction with each additional treat he eats. This situation can be explained by the
    (A) Law of Supply.
    (B) Law of Diminishing Returns.
    (C) Law of Diminishing Marginal Utility.
    (D) Law of Increasing Opportunity Costs.
    (E) Law of Comparative Advantage.

2. Which of the following statements correctly describes the relationship between marginal utility and total utility?
    (A) When marginal utility is greater than total utility, total utility rises.
    (B) When total utility is greater than marginal utility, marginal utility rises.
    (C) Marginal utility rises with each unit purchased, while total utility falls with each unit purchased.
    (D) Marginal utility falls with each unit purchased, while total utility first rises but begins to fall when marginal utility becomes negative.
    (E) Marginal utility and total utility consistently rise and fall together.

3. When Lauren consumes her third bowl of fried rice, her total utility falls. This can only occur if
    (A) the fried rice is an inferior good.
    (B) the third bowl of fried rice is free.
    (C) Lauren's demand for fried rice is inelastic.
    (D) the marginal utility of her second bowl of fried rice was zero.
    (E) the marginal utility of the third bowl of fried rice is negative.

4.   Because of the Law of Diminishing Marginal Utility,
      (A)   firms must lower prices to sell more products.
      (B)   prices must rise to entice firms to produce more products.
      (C)   government must impose mandatory taxes to avoid the free-rider problem.
      (D)   wages must rise to entice more workers to enter the labor force.
      (E)   consumers tend to buy more inferior goods when wages rise.

5.   The Law of Diminishing Marginal Utility explains why
      (A)   the supply curve is upward-sloping.
      (B)   the demand curve is downward-sloping.
      (C)   a perfectly inelastic demand curve is vertical.
      (D)   the production possibilities curve is downward-sloping.
      (E)   a perfectly elastic demand curve is horizontal.

6.   When Kim owns 3 candles, she has 20 units of total utility. After she purchases another
      candle, she has 24 units of total utility. What is the marginal utility of the fourth candle?
      (A)   1/6 of a unit of utility
      (B)   4 units of utility
      (C)   11 units of utility
      (D)   20 units of utility
      (D)   44 units of utility

7.   Utility-maximizing consumer equilibrium is found where the marginal utility per dollar
      spent for Product A equals
      (A)   the marginal utility for consuming that quantity of Product A.
      (B)   the total utility from consuming units of Product A.
      (C)   zero.
      (D)   the marginal utility per dollar spent for Product B.
      (E)   the total utility from the combined units of Products A and B consumed.

8.   Justin gained 12 units of marginal utility from the last Pepsi he purchased at a price of $2.
      He gained 10 units of marginal utility from the last bottle of water he purchased for $1.
      Which statement most accurately describes Justin's situation?
      (A)   Justin has achieved consumer equilibrium.
      (B)   Justin gains more marginal utility from Pepsi than from water, so he
             should have purchased more Pepsi and less water.
      (C)   Justin gains more marginal utility per dollar from water than from Pepsi,
             so he should have purchased more water and less Pepsi.
      (D)   Justin gains more utility from Pepsi than from water, so he should only
             purchase Pepsi.
      (E)   Water is less expensive than Pepsi, so he should only purchase water.

Free-Response Question

The table below shows the total utility Janet gains from consuming cookies and cupcakes.

Quantity of Cookies	Total Utility of Cookies	Quantity of Cupcakes	Total Utility of Cupcakes
0	0	0	0
1	10	1	26
2	18	2	46
3	24	3	62
4	26	4	66

Assume the price of a cookie is $1 and the price of a cupcake is $2. Janet will spend her entire income of $8 on cookies and cupcakes.
(a)   Determine the marginal utility of the third cookie.
(b)   Using the marginal utility per dollar spent for cookies and cupcakes, identify the utility maximizing quantity of cookies and cupcakes Janet will purchase.
        (i)   Use the mathematical equation for utility maximization to show Janet has maximized her utility by purchasing that combination of goods.
        (ii)   Identify the total utility Janet gains from this total purchase.
(c)   If Janet's income increases by $2, will she purchase one more cupcake or two more cookies to maximize her utility? Explain your reasoning.

Multiple-Choice Explanations
1.   (C)   The marginal utility falls with each product consumed.
2.   (D)   As long as marginal utility is positive, it adds to total utility, but if marginal utility is negative, it subtracts from total utility.
3.   (E)   A negative marginal utility lowers the total utility from consuming goods.
4.   (A)   Because the consumer gains less utility from each additional unit of product, he will only pay a lower price to obtain that next unit.
5.   (B)   Because marginal utility falls, price must fall for consumers to buy more.
6.   (B)   Total utility increased by 4 units, which is the marginal utility.
7.   (D)   MU/P for Product A = MU/P for Product B is the definition of consumer equilibrium.
8.   (C)   Because Justin's MU/P for water is greater than his MU/P for Pepsi, he should have consumed more water and less Pepsi. Both the marginal utility and the price per product must be used to compare products.

Free-Response Explanation
Calculations of marginal utility and MU/P necessary to answer the free response:

Q of Cookies	TU of Cookies	MU of Cookie	MU/Dollar of Cookie	Q of Cupcakes	TU of Cupcakes	MU of Cupcake	MU/Dollar of Cupcake
0	0	—	—	0	0	—	—
1	10	10	10	1	26	26	13
2	18	8	8	2	46	20	10
3	24	6	6	3	62	16	8
4	26	2	2	4	66	4	2

6 points (1 + 3 + 2)

(a)   1 point:
- 1 point is earned for stating that the marginal utility of the third cookie is 6 utils.

(b)   3 points:
- 1 point is earned for stating that Janet will maximize her utility by buying 2 cookies and 3 cupcakes.
- 1 point is earned for showing the mathematical formula 8/1 = 16/2.
- 1 point is earned for stating that Janet's total utility from this purchase is 80 utils.

(c)   2 points:
- 1 point is earned for stating that Janet will buy 2 more cookies.
- 1 point is earned for stating that Janet's total utility will increase by 8 utils if she buys the cookies but only 4 utils if she buys the cupcake.

CHAPTER 8: THE COSTS OF PRODUCTION

Introduction

Now that we have examined consumer behavior in more detail, it is time to look at the decision making of the firm. Costs of production are important to determine points where efficiency and profit are maximized. Chapter 8 introduces the short-run and long-run costs of production, explains their calculation, and graphically illustrates relationships among cost curves. Material from Chapter 8 consistently appears in several multiple-choice questions on the AP microeconomics exam. Concepts from this chapter, along with information in later chapters, form the basis for free-response questions about output and pricing decisions that appear on nearly every AP microeconomics exam.

Economic Costs

Resources are scarce and have alternative uses, so costs are incurred when a resource is used for one product rather than another. Economic costs represent the opportunity cost of using a resource to make a product. Explicit (accounting) costs are money payments for resources we recognize as costs of production labor, materials, utilities, mortgage, equipment, and such. Implicit costs are opportunity costs of resources within the firm that could have gone to other uses. If you are an entrepreneur who used your own savings to start the business and you give up another job to work at your firm, your opportunity cost is the wage you gave up, as well as the interest and dividends you could have earned on the savings you instead invested in this firm. These implicit costs are not captured in accounting costs but nonetheless are still an important cost of business. Normal profit is the payment to the entrepreneur required to keep him or her working for that firm. It equals the cost of the entrepreneur s best alternative choice of career. If the entrepreneur receives no payment, he or she will leave the firm for other opportunities.

Accounting profit is the firm s total revenue minus explicit (accounting) costs. This is the kind of profit we typically hear about in the news. Economists, however, understand the importance of recognizing all of the costs of production, including normal profit and the other implicit costs necessary for production. Economic profit is the total revenue of the firm minus the economic (explicit and implicit) costs. Because accountants don t consider the implicit costs, accounting profit is generally higher than economic profit.

Taking the EEK! Out of Economics

Distinguishing accounting and economic profit will become very important in later chapters, when we consider how economic profits and losses draw firms into and out of industry. We will find that when a firm is making zero economic profit, the industry is in long-run equilibrium, and there is no incentive for firms to enter or leave the industry. At this point, students often ask why a firm would remain in business if it is making no profit. It is important to remember that a firm making zero *economic* profit is still covering all of its explicit costs, as well as paying the entrepreneur a normal profit and paying all other implicit costs. So a firm may show zero economic profit while still showing a substantial accounting profit in the traditional way we ve understood profit.

The Short Run and the Long Run

A firm s ability to respond to a change in demand depends on how much time it has to respond. In the short run, the firm s plant capacity (factory size and large equipment) is fixed, but the firm can somewhat increase production by hiring more workers, increasing work hours, and bringing in new resources to increase production. In the long run, the firm can change the size of its factory and equipment, and other firms can enter the industry. The difference between the short run and the long run is not a calendar time difference as much as it is a difference in the firm s ability to change the plant and equipment.

Diminishing Returns

In the short run, with fixed plant size and equipment, production can be measured in three ways. Total product is the total output from all of the workers together. Average product (productivity) is total product divided by the number of workers, measuring output per worker. Marginal product is the extra output produced when one more worker is hired.

To measure the effect on output as the number of workers increases, we assume that all workers are equal in terms of education, experience, and motivation. One worker is just the same as the next. Of course that isn t realistic. Remember the smiley (☺)? But it will help you understand the effect that occurs with the hiring of additional workers. These models generally focus on labor, but the concepts hold true for any variable resource.

Number of Workers	Total Product	Marginal Product
0	0	
1	10	10
2	25	15
3	45	20
4	60	15
5	70	10
6	75	5
7	75	0
8	70	5

Given total product, you can calculate marginal product by measuring the change in total product from hiring the next worker. The first three workers bring increasing returns, because the next worker adds even more to production than the worker before him due to specialization. Because each worker is more efficient at the one part of production that he s specializing in, and workers save time by not having to switch from task to task, all of the workers become more efficient by virtue of that next worker being there.

Workers 4 7 bring diminishing returns. Each worker adds to total product but less than the worker before him. Specialization wears off until the seventh worker adds no output. After that, each worker actually reduces production. In negative returns, each worker s marginal product is negative as workers overwhelm the fixed capital, so production falls.

Taking the EEK! Out of Economics

It is important to understand that marginal product doesn t change because of the quality of workers. Students commonly make the mistake of thinking the firm hires the highest quality workers first, resulting in high marginal product, but then marginal product starts to drop because the firm begins to hire less and less qualified workers. Remember, we assume all workers are equal. The marginal product falls because more workers are used with a fixed amount of capital, and increases in production will become more limited.

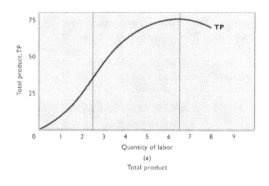

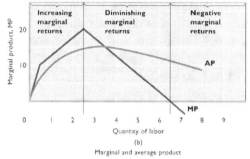

The Law of Diminishing Returns

The Law of Diminishing Returns explains that as more units of a variable resource (like labor) are added to a fixed resource (like capital), marginal product falls. This concept recognizes the limit on production when the plant and equipment are fixed in the short run. Note on the graph that during increasing returns, total product rises quickly. During diminishing returns, total product increases but at a slower rate. In negative returns, total product falls. The relationship between marginal and average product is also important. Whenever the marginal product is higher than the average product, the marginal product pulls up the average, so average product rises. Conversely, if marginal product is lower than average product, average product falls. It is very similar to your grade point average (GPA). If your economics grade is higher than your GPA, that marginal grade will help pull up your GPA; if your econ grade is lower than your GPA, it will pull your GPA down.

Bear in Mind

The Law of Diminishing Returns may sound vaguely familiar. In some ways, it is similar to the Law of Diminishing Marginal Utility. In both cases, the more you have of something, the less you get out of each additional one. It is important to keep these terms straight, as they frequently appear together as options on multiple-choice questions. Diminishing utility measures the utility one gains from consuming one more product. Diminishing returns measures the production a firm gains from hiring one more worker. You must be able to calculate marginal product; identify the ranges of increasing, diminishing, and negative returns; and interpret those portions of the graphs for the exam.

Chapter 8: The Costs of Production

Short-Run Production Costs

	Total-Cost Data			Average-Cost Data			Marginal Cost
(1) Total Product (Q)	(2) Total Fixed Cost (TFC)	(3) Total Variable Cost (TVC)	(4) Total Cost (TC) TC = TFC + TVC	(5) Average Fixed Cost (AFC) $AFC = \frac{TFC}{Q}$	(6) Average Variable Cost (AVC) $AVC = \frac{TVC}{Q}$	(7) Average Total Cost (ATC) $ATC = \frac{TC}{Q}$	(8) Marginal Cost (MC) $MC = \frac{\text{change in TC}}{\text{change in Q}}$
0	$100	$ 0	$100				
							$ 90
1	100	90	190	$100.00	$90.00	$190.00	
							80
2	100	170	270	50.00	85.00	135.00	
							70
3	100	240	340	33.33	80.00	113.33	
							60
4	100	300	400	25.00	75.00	100.00	
							70
5	100	370	470	20.00	74.00	94.00	
							80
6	100	450	550	16.67	75.00	91.67	
							90
7	100	540	640	14.29	77.14	91.43	
							110
8	100	650	750	12.50	81.25	93.75	
							130
9	100	780	880	11.11	86.67	97.78	
							150
10	100	930	1030	10.00	93.00	103.00	

Total-, average-, and marginal-cost schedules for an individual firm in the short run

In the short run, fixed costs are those that do not change with the amount of output, such as the mortgage and equipment bought on contract with monthly payments.

Fixed Cost = Total Cost at Zero Output

Variable costs change with the amount of output, including labor, materials, and utilities. Variable costs increase with output. For the first units of output, the rate of increase in variable cost is small; after some point, variable cost begins to increase at an increasing rate because of diminishing returns. The specialization that occurs with the first few products reduces the amount by which variable cost increases; as specialization wears off and workers begin to overwhelm fixed capital, variable cost increases more quickly.

Variable Cost = Total Cost   Fixed Cost

Total cost is the sum of all production costs. At zero output, total cost is the fixed cost. As production increases, total cost increases by the variable cost at each output.

Total Cost = Fixed Cost + Variable Cost

Average (Per-Unit) Costs

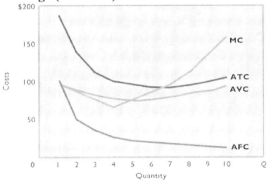

The relationship of the marginal-cost curve to the average-total-cost and average-variable-cost curves

Average costs are calculated by simply dividing the cost by the amount of output.

Average Fixed Cost = Fixed Cost / Output

Remember, the fixed cost did not change with output. Therefore, as that fixed cost is spread over more and more output, the average fixed cost (AFC) continuously falls.

Average variable cost (AVC) is a U-shaped curve because of diminishing returns. As the first workers specialize, the firm increases production using few workers, so variable cost per product falls. But during diminishing returns, more workers and other resources are required to produce each product, so the average variable cost begins to rise again.

Average Variable Cost = Variable Cost / Output

The average total cost (ATC) is found by vertically adding the average fixed cost and average variable cost curves. It is also U-shaped and above both the AFC and AVC. The distance between the ATC and AVC is the AFC, and as more and more units of output are produced, ATC and AVC get closer and closer together as the AFC continues to fall.

Average Total Cost = Total Cost / Output

Marginal Cost
The marginal cost is the extra cost of producing one more unit of output.

Marginal Cost = Change in Total Cost / Change in Output

Marginal cost is the increase in total cost (or variable cost) for producing one more product. Because fixed cost doesn t change, the amounts by which both the total and variable costs change will be identical. The marginal cost curve looks like a checkmark. Marginal cost falls with the first few workers hired because of the Law of Diminishing Returns; as marginal product per worker increases, the marginal cost of producing each additional product actually falls. But as specialization wears off and diminishing returns set in on production, the marginal cost of producing the next unit begins to rise quickly.

Bear in Mind
Given specific data, you must be able to calculate total, fixed, variable, marginal, and average costs in a variety of ways. You may be given total costs and then asked to calculate the marginal cost at a specific output. Or you may be given the fixed and marginal costs and then asked to calculate the total cost at a particular output. Be familiar with different ways to calculate each cost, because such questions have appeared on both the multiple-choice and free-response portions of the AP microeconomics exam.

Relationship of Marginal Cost to Average Variable Cost and Average Total Cost
The marginal cost curve crosses both AVC and ATC at their lowest points. Just as with marginal product and average product, whenever the marginal cost is lower than the AVC or ATC, it will pull down the average; whenever the marginal cost is higher than the AVC or ATC, it will pull up the average. Again, a similar example would be how your marginal grade in economics affects your entire grade point average. Because the fixed cost does not change with the amount of output, the AFC continues to fall as output rises.

Bear in Mind
It is essential that you understand the relationships between the marginal and average cost curves and be able to draw them from memory. Questions about these relationships consistently appear on the multiple-choice portion of the AP microeconomics exam, and almost every AP microeconomics exam contains at least one free-response question that requires you to draw a

graph for a specific type of market and all of t hose markets use cost curves in the relationships shown in this chapter.

Shifts in Cost Curves

Changes in the cost of production shift the cost curves directly up and down (because you are examining the cost at that same level of output). Improvements in technology reduce the cost of production. When a fixed cost such as a property tax increases, the AFC and ATC both increase, but AVC and MC do not change because those costs reflect changes in cost per individual unit produced. If, instead, a variable cost such as the wage for labor increases, the ATC increases along with the MC and AVC, but the AFC does not change.

Bear in Mind

It is vital that you be able to illustrate the shifts in the appropriate curves. Free-response questions frequently ask you to draw the graph for a market, and then present you with a particular scenario and ask you to shift the curves based on that situation. It is very important to know whether that situation shifts the marginal cost curve (if it is a variable cost) or not (if it is a fixed cost), because that decision will determine whether the firm changes the quantity of products it produces to maximize profit.

Long-Run Production Costs

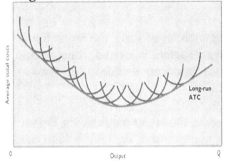

The long-run average-total-cost curve

In the short run, firms are constrained by limitations in plant and equipment, and the fixed costs result from those constraints. But in the long run, all costs are variable. The firm can change its plant size or make significant changes in equipment, and other firms have time to enter or leave the industry. Therefore, the firm s long-run decisions focus on plant size. The long-run average-total-cost curve is U-shaped, made up of the minimum points of the short-run ATC curves for all of the potential quantities of output.

Economies and Diseconomies of Scale

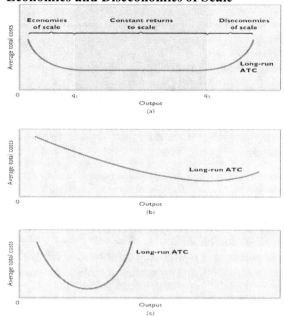

Various possible long-run average-total-cost curves

For the first units of production, long-run ATC falls. With economies of scale, the larger the firm, the lower its ATC. Economies of scale result from factors such as labor and management specialization and the use of more efficient capital. If resource inputs are doubled, the firm s output more than doubles; therefore, the average cost per unit falls.

At some point, long-run ATC rises. With diseconomies of scale, the larger the firm, the higher its ATC. Diseconomies of scale result from significantly larger management, communication issues, and worker alienation reducing productivity. If resource inputs are doubled, the firm s output less than doubles; therefore, average cost per unit rises.

Between economies and diseconomies of scale is a range of production called constant returns to scale. In this range, ATC does not change with the size of the firm. When resource inputs are doubled, the firm s output doubles. The minimum efficient scale is the lowest output at which a firm can minimize its long-run average cost. Because long-run average-total-cost curves vary so much in shape, firms in particular industries can be of very different sizes. Firms with large fixed costs and smaller variable costs, such as automakers and utility companies, tend to become large operations because of the economies of scale. Other kinds of firms with low fixed costs and higher variable costs, such as hot dog vendors, tend to remain smaller operations. Other industries with a wide range of constant returns to scale will tend to develop firms of a variety of sizes.

Multiple-Choice Questions

1. The payment to an entrepreneur to keep him engaged in an enterprise is
   (A) economic profit.
   (B) an explicit cost.
   (C) accounting profit.
   (D) an accounting cost.

(E)   normal profit.

2.   In the short run, output of the firm is limited by
       (A)   quotas set by government.
       (B)   the inability to change the plant and equipment.
       (C)   a significant increase in demand for the product.
       (D)   the number of workers at the plant.
       (E)   the increase in fixed costs.

3.   When the marginal product of the next worker is lower than the average product,
       (A)   average product must be falling.
       (B)   marginal product must be rising.
       (C)   the marginal cost must be falling.
       (D)   wages must be too high.
       (E)   the worker should not be hired.

4.   During diminishing returns, as more workers are hired with fixed capital,
       (A)   production increases at a constant rate.
       (B)   production increases at an increasing rate.
       (C)   production increases at a decreasing rate.
       (D)   production decreases at a constant rate.
       (E)   production remains constant.

5.   Which of the following is an example of a fixed cost?
       (A)   wages paid for labor
       (B)   the rent for the plant
       (C)   the electricity bill
       (D)   the raw materials for production
       (E)   the cost of shipping products

6.   The distance between the average-total-cost and average-variable-cost curves is
       (A)   the average fixed cost.
       (B)   the marginal cost.
       (C)   the average marginal cost.
       (D)   the marginal product.
       (E)   the economic profit.

7.   The cost of producing one more unit of output is
       (A)   the fixed cost.
       (B)   the variable cost.
       (C)   the total cost.
       (D)   the marginal cost.
       (E)   the difference between the total cost and the fixed cost.

8.   An increase in the cost of electricity to produce a product would cause a firm s
       (A)   marginal cost to decrease.
       (B)   average variable cost to increase.
       (C)   economic profit to increase.
       (D)   average fixed cost to increase.
       (E)   average total cost to decrease.

9.   If a firm makes improvements in production technology, average variable cost
     (A)   shifts upward.
     (B)   shifts downward.
     (C)   shifts to the right.
     (D)   shifts to the left.
     (E)   becomes more elastic.

10. Long-run average total cost falls over the range when a firm experiences
     (A)   economic profit.
     (B)   normal profit.
     (C)   economies of scale.
     (D)   constant returns to scale.
     (E)   negative returns.

11. Economies of scale are achieved when a firm doubles its inputs, and as a result
     (A)   output falls to zero.
     (B)   output decreases.
     (C)   output increases, but less than doubles.
     (D)   output exactly doubles.
     (E)   output more than doubles.

Free-Response Questions

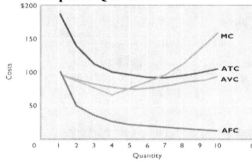

The graph above illustrates the short-run costs of a firm in a competitive industry.
(a)   Explain how the marginal cost is calculated.
(b)   Describe the shape of the marginal cost curve by explaining the following:
      (i)   Explain why marginal cost falls over the first units of output.
      (ii)   Explain why marginal cost eventually increases as output rises.
(c)   Explain why the average-fixed-cost curve continues to fall as output increases.
(d)   Explain the relationship between marginal cost and average total cost below.
      (i)   Describe where the marginal cost crosses the average total cost curve.
      (ii)   Explain why the average total cost curve is downward sloping over the range of
             output when average total cost is higher than marginal cost.

Multiple-Choice Explanations
1.   (E)   Normal profit is an implicit cost included in the economic cost.
2.   (B)   In the short run, the firm cannot make changes in the size of the plant or the
           equipment; in the long run, the firm can make those changes.

3. (A) The lower marginal product causes the average product of all workers together to fall.

4. (C) During diminishing returns, specialization wears off and workers begin to overwhelm capital; production increases but at a slowing rate of growth.

5. (B) Rent is a fixed cost that does not change with the amount of output; all of the other answers are variable costs that increase as production increases.

6. (A) The average total cost equals the average fixed cost plus the average variable cost, so the difference between ATC and AVC must be AFC.

7. (E) Marginal cost is the increase in total product for producing one more unit.

8. (B) Electricity is a variable cost of production; an increase in variable cost also increases the marginal cost and the average total cost.

9. (B) Improved technology lowers the cost of production, so the average variable cost curve shifts downward.

10. (C) Economies of scale occur when the long-run total cost of production falls as plant size increases.

11. (E) With economies of scale, labor specialization and the more efficient use of capital allow firms to increase output at a greater rate than input increases.

Free-Response Explanations
6 points (1 + 2 + 1 + 2)
(a) 1 point:
- 1 point is earned for stating that marginal cost is calculated by the increase in total cost for one more unit of output (or change in total cost / change in output).

(b) 2 points:
- 1 point is earned for stating that marginal cost falls due to increasing returns or increasing marginal product or specialization among employees.
- 1 point is earned for stating that marginal cost rises due to diminishing returns or diminishing marginal product or limitations on productivity with fixed capital.

(c) 1 point:
- 1 point is earned for stating that average fixed cost falls because the fixed cost is divided over larger and larger amounts of output.

(d) 2 points:
- 1 point is earned for stating that the marginal cost curve crosses average total cost at the lowest point on the average total cost curve.
- 1 point is earned for stating that when the marginal cost of producing the next unit of output is lower than the average total cost of producing that output, the marginal cost lowers the average total cost.

CHAPTER 9: PURE COMPETITION

Introduction

In Chapters 9–11, we reach the heart of microeconomics, the concepts which comprise more than a quarter of the AP microeconomics exam. With a fuller understanding of revenues and costs, we bring them together to see how the firm makes profit-maximizing decisions about output and product prices. The firm's ability to control product price highlights the differences among four market models examined over the next three chapters. Chapter 9 describes pure (perfect) competition, explaining how firms make profit-maximizing, loss-minimizing, and shutdown decisions, and how the industry adjusts in the long run. The principles developed in this chapter carry through to decision making by firms in other market structures as well. Material from Chapter 9 appears on the AP microeconomics exam in a large number of multiple-choice questions, and a free-response question about decision making in at least one of the market structures is part of nearly every exam.

Market Structures

Industries are classified by their market structures. Perfect competition involves a large number of firms who produce identical products and can easily enter or exit the industry. The other three market structures are considered imperfect competition. Monopolistic competition is similar to perfect competition in that a large number of firms compete and can easily enter or exit the industry, but the products are slightly different and firms heavily advertise those non-price differences. Only a few firms compete in oligopolies, which experience significant barriers to entry by new firms. Oligopolies are unique in that each firm is affected by its rivals' decisions. In a pure monopoly, one firm is the only producer of a good, and barriers to entry by competitors are complete.

Perfect Competition

Perfectly competitive markets are rare but provide a foundation for understanding profit maximization and efficiency. Remember the smiley (☺)? Four characteristics define a perfectly competitive market. First, a large number of independent sellers produce the product, so decisions of one firm have no effect on competitors. Second, goods produced by all of the firms are identical, so consumers do not care which firm's product they buy. Third, perfectly competitive firms are price takers, meaning they have no control over the product price; they must accept the price set in the market. Fourth, firms can freely enter and exit the industry without significant barriers to entry. Products like corn, wheat, milk, beef, stocks, bonds, and currencies are sold in perfectly competitive markets.

Demand

In a perfectly competitive market, the industry demand curve is downward-sloping. But once the price is set by supply and demand, the firm is a price taker. The demand curve for the individual firm is horizontal, perfectly elastic at that market equilibrium price.

Bear in Mind

Multiple-choice questions asking the difference between the downward-sloping industry demand and the firm's perfectly elastic demand curve are frequently part of the exam.

Revenue

The firm's total revenue is price times quantity sold. Because the firm is a price taker, it sells each product for the same price, so average revenue equals price. Marginal revenue is the change in total revenue from selling one more unit of the product. Because the perfectly competitive firm sells every product for the same price, marginal revenue, price, and the average revenue are all equal, graphed on the horizontal demand curve.

Taking the EEK! Out of Economics
Although the types of revenue are calculated differently, marginal revenue, price, average revenue, and demand are equal for perfectly competitive firms. This is key, because for imperfectly competitive firms, the marginal revenue will separate from the others.

Short-Run Profit Maximization Using Total Revenue and Total Cost
Because the perfectly competitive firm cannot control its price, it must maximize profit based on output. Because the plant and equipment are fixed in the short run, the firm can only change its variable costs and then determine the most profitable output. Firms can determine profit-maximizing output by studying total revenue and total cost or marginal revenue and marginal cost. First, we will look at the total cost and total revenue method.

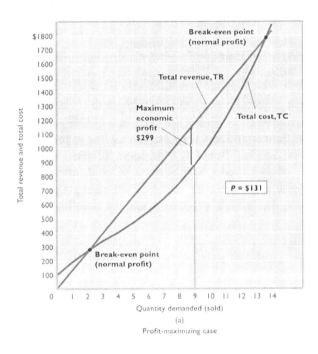

Total-revenue–total-cost approach to profit maximization for a purely competitive firm

Total revenue for the perfectly competitive firm slopes upward at a constant rate because it increases by the product price with each unit sold. In this example, for the first two units of output, total cost exceeds total revenue, so the firm would make a loss by producing at those output levels. After the second unit of output is the break-even point, where total cost equals total revenue and the firm achieves a normal profit, but not economic profit. After the thirteenth unit of output is a second break-even point, and output beyond that point also brings the firm a loss. Between those break-even points, total revenue is greater than the total cost at each output, and the firm earns economic profit. To maximize profit, the firm produces output at the point where total revenue is the greatest vertical distance above the total cost—in this case, at nine units. The distance between the curves is the economic profit per unit. The total economic profit is the profit per unit times the output.

Short-Run Profit Maximization Using Marginal Revenue and Marginal Cost
Firms also find profit-maximizing output by comparing marginal revenue to marginal cost. If marginal revenue is greater than or equal to marginal cost, a firm should produce the unit; if marginal cost is greater than marginal revenue, the firm should not produce it.

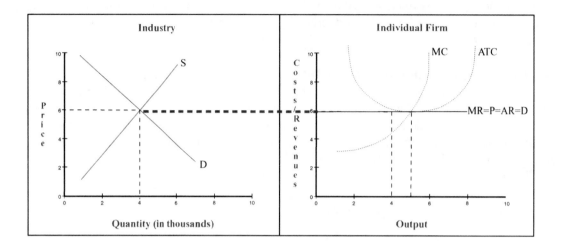

The correct perfectly competitive market graph is actually two side-by-side graphs. On the left is the market for the *industry*, with supply and demand determining the price and quantity. Because the individual firm is a price taker, the price is then connected via a horizontal line to the *individual firm* graph on the right. The Price = Marginal Revenue = Average Revenue = Demand on that horizontal line for the individual firm. Marginal cost crosses the ATC at its minimum point. In long-run equilibrium, marginal revenue, marginal cost, and ATC all meet at the same point. To maximize profit or minimize loss, the firm should produce where the marginal revenue equals the marginal cost.

MR = MC Rule: Firms ALWAYS maximize profit by producing where MR = MC.

Taking the EEK! Out of Economics
Many students look at the graph of the individual firm and wonder why the firm wouldn't maximize profit by producing where MC is at its minimum, as the difference between MR and MC is greatest at that output. But consider what happens when you increase output by one unit. The additional revenue the firm earns from producing that next unit is greater than the cost of producing that unit. It is a smaller difference but still a gain for the firm, and that additional profit is added to the profit earned from earlier units. Remember, the firm is trying to maximize its total profit, not the profit per unit, so if the firm can bring in even a little more profit by producing one more product, it will do so.

The Profit-Maximizing Case
In the long run, the industry and individual firm achieve equilibrium where the firm produces output at the point where MC = MR, and P = ATC, so there is no economic profit. However, in the short run, the firm can earn an economic profit.

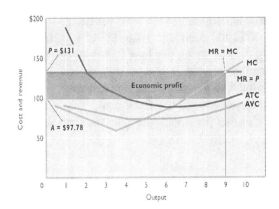

Short-run profit maximization for a purely competitive firm

Remember, the MR = P = AR = D curve for the individual firm is set by supply and demand in the industry. The firm should produce at MC = MR, as always. But notice that this time, the ATC is lower than P. This shows the firm is making an economic profit. The amount of economic profit can be found in two ways:

1.   Total Revenue – Total Cost.
           Total Revenue = Price x Output
           Total Cost = ATC x Output
2.   Profit per Unit x Output.
           Profit per Unit = Price – Average Total Cost

The Loss-Minimizing Case

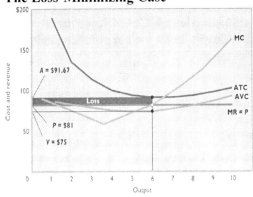

Short-run loss minimization for a purely competitive firm

Again, the MR = P = AR = D curve for the firm results from the price set by industry supply and demand. The firm, as always, should produce where MC = MR. But notice this time, ATC is higher than P, showing the firm is suffering an economic loss. Loss is calculated the same way profit is calculated (P – ATC); it will produce a negative number for a loss. So if the firm is losing money, should it shut down? Not necessarily. Remember, the firm still has fixed costs it must pay in the short run, even if the firm closes. So we need to determine whether the firm will lose more money by shutting down or staying open in the short run. Assume these are the firm's short-run costs at a particular level of output:

           Fixed Cost = $100
           Variable Cost = $150
           Total Cost = $250
           Total Revenue = $200

In this case, the firm has a loss of $50, because the total cost is greater than total revenue. However, if the firm shuts down, it would incur a loss of $100 because it has to cover its fixed costs. Therefore, this firm should remain in business in the short run, because its losses are less if it remains open than if it shuts down. If the firm's marginal revenue is greater than or equal to the average variable cost, the firm should remain in business in the short run, because any additional revenue earned beyond the variable cost can be put toward the fixed cost. You can see this in the loss-minimizing graph. The MR = P curve is above the AVC curve, so the firm should remain in business in the short run.

The Shutdown Case

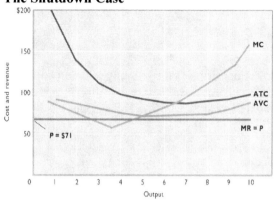

The short-run shutdown case for a purely competitive firm

This market looks very similar to the loss-minimizing case, except that both the ATC and AVC curves are above the MR = P curve. Even if the firm produces where MC = MR, it cannot recover its variable costs. Therefore, the firm should shut down. Let's look at numbers, using the same costs as the loss-minimizing case but lower total revenue:

Fixed Cost = $100
Variable Cost = $150
Total Cost = $250
Total Revenue = $100

In this case, the firm is incurring a loss of $150. Should the firm remain in business in the short run? If it stays in business, it loses $150, but if it shuts down, it loses $100. The firm is better off shutting down. The firm cannot even cover the variable costs of the labor and raw materials to create the output it is selling, so it should shut down.

So we have a series of points to determine production. At the output where MC = MR,
- If the ATC is lower than the MR = P curve, the firm should produce and is earning an economic profit in the short run.
- If the ATC is equal to the MR = P curve, the firm should produce, is earning zero economic profit, and is in long-run equilibrium.
- If the ATC is higher than the MR = P curve, the firm is incurring a loss.
    o If the AVC is lower than or equal to the MR = P curve, the firm should continue to produce to minimize its loss in the short run.
    o If the AVC is higher than the MR = P curve, the firm should shut down.

Marginal Cost and Short-Run Supply

The upward-sloping portion of the marginal cost curve that is above the AVC curve is the firm's
short-run supply curve. The firm will not produce where marginal revenue does not cover the
average variable cost, but from the point where they are equal onward, the firm will produce
where MR = MC to maximize profit (or minimize loss) in the short run.

Short-Run Profit

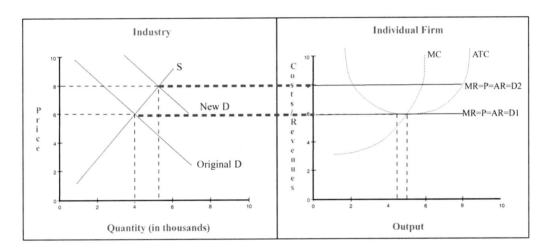

In the short run, if consumer demand for the product increases, the market price increases. The
increase in market price carries over to the individual firm, a price taker that must accept the
market price. Therefore, the marginal revenue curve shifts up from M1 to M2 at the higher price.
At the higher price, the firm has an incentive to increase production to the output where MC =
MR to maximize profit. At this output, the price is higher than the average total cost, so the firm
is earning an economic profit.

Long-Run Equilibrium

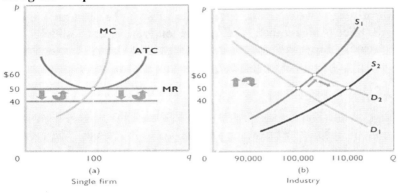

Temporary profits and the reestablishment of long-run equilibrium in (a) a representative firm and (b) the industry

In the short run, perfectly competitive firms may experience economic profit or loss. In this figure, the industry increase in demand raised the market price (marginal revenue to the firm), so the firm increased its production to the output where MC = MR. However, in the long run, the market adjusts as the profit motive entices firms to enter the industry. New firms increase industry supply, lowering the price. The lower price transfers to individual firms in lower marginal revenue, causing the firm to reduce production until once again MC = MR. At that output, MC = ATC, so the firm again returns to zero economic profit, and there is no incentive for other firms to enter the industry.

Short-Run Losses and Long-Run Equilibrium

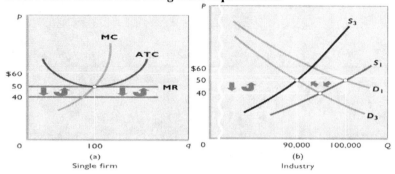

Temporary losses and the reestablishment of long-run equilibrium in (a) a representative firm and (b) the industry

Consider the case of a decrease in consumer demand for the product. Lower demand causes the price to fall, lowering marginal revenue for the individual firm. Because the marginal revenue is lower than ATC, the individual firm suffers a loss. In the short run, firms reduce production to the output where MC = MR to minimize their losses. However, in the long run, some firms that cannot cover their variable costs or are attracted to other profit-making opportunities will exit the industry, reducing industry supply. As the price rises, marginal revenue rises as well, until the firm reaches equilibrium, producing where MC = MR = ATC, and there is no incentive for other firms to exit the industry.

Changes in Per-Unit Production Costs and Subsidies
Changes in production cost can also change the firm's output and cause short-run profits or losses. If the firm's labor cost (a variable cost) increases, the average variable cost, marginal cost, and average total cost all shift upward. Marginal cost crosses marginal revenue to the left of the firm's original output, so the firm reduces its output in the short run to where MC = MR. Because ATC is higher than the price at that output, the firm incurs a loss in the short run but will continue producing as long as the price is higher than ATC. In the long run, industry supply decreases as a result of lower output by firms and some firms exiting the industry. As marginal revenue for each firm rises, the market returns to long-run equilibrium, with firms producing where MC = MR = ATC at the higher price, and the new industry equilibrium shows a higher price and lower quantity.

If the government provides a per-unit subsidy to firms, the process works in reverse. The lower AVC also reduces the ATC and MC for the firm. As a result, the new MC crosses MR further to the right, increasing output. Because the ATC is now lower than the price, the firm experiences a short-run economic profit. In the long run, that profit draws new firms into the industry and supply increases, lowering the product price. The lower price transfers to a lower marginal revenue for the firm, and the firm returns to long-run equilibrium, with the firm producing where MC = MR = ATC with no economic profit.

Changes in Lump-Sum Production Costs and Subsidies

Changes in lump-sum costs, such as property taxes, operating licenses, or rent, affect only average fixed cost and ATC. Because these costs do not affect marginal cost, the marginal cost curve does not shift, and output does not change in the short run. However, the increase in cost causes ATC to shift upward, so the firm incurs a short-run loss. In the long run, industry supply will decrease as firms exit the industry. The market price and thus marginal revenue to the firm will increase, and the firm will again return to long-run equilibrium to produce at the output where MC = MR = ATC.

If the government offers a lump-sum subsidy to firms, AFC and ATC both fall. Because marginal revenue does not move, the firm's output does not change in the short run. Now that the firm is earning economic profit, more firms enter the industry, increasing supply and lowering the price. The lower marginal revenue causes the firm to decrease output, to produce where MC = MR = ATC, and the firm no longer earns an economic profit.

Taking the EEK! Out of Economics

Although firms may make economic profits or suffer losses in the short run, the long-run entry or exit of firms in the industry eventually returns the market to equilibrium, where firms earn zero economic profit. At this point, it is important to remember the difference between normal and economic profit. The firm's accountant is still showing a normal profit, which is paid to the entrepreneur. But beyond that normal profit, there is no economic or excess profit, which would draw other firms into the industry.

Bear in Mind

It is very important to be able to distinguish the effects of changes in per-unit and lump-sum production costs. Changes in per-unit costs affect the variable cost (and therefore average total cost). Changes in these costs also shift the marginal cost curve, so the firm's output will change as the firm produces at MC = MR. Changes in lump-sum costs affect the fixed cost (and therefore average total cost). However, changes in these costs do not affect the firm's marginal cost curve, so the firm's output does not change and the firm continues to produce at the same output in the short run. Questions, particularly those in the free-response portion of the AP microeconomics exam, have asked students to be able to make this distinction to correctly explain the effects of changes in production costs.

Increasing, Constant, and Decreasing Cost Industries

When new firms enter an industry, the additional demand for resources to make products can affect the price of those resources. In increasing-cost industries, the firms' increased demand for resources pushes up the resource cost, causing the firms' ATC curves to shift up. As a result, the industry's long-run supply curve is upward-sloping. In a constant-cost industry, the firms' increased demand for resources has no effect on the cost of those resources. The firms' ATC curves remain in place and the industry's long-run supply curve is horizontal. In decreasing-cost industries, increased demand for resources can lower the cost of resources, so the supply curve would actually be downward-sloping.

Efficiency

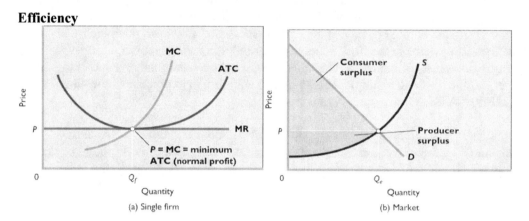

(a) Single firm   (b) Market

Long-run equilibrium: a competitive firm and market

A perfectly competitive industry in long-run equilibrium achieves both productive and allocative efficiency. Productive efficiency occurs when the firm produces at the lowest cost per product. This occurs at the minimum ATC, where MC = ATC. Consumers benefit because the product price is low, and society benefits because scarce resources are used in the most efficient way. The graph on the left illustrates productive efficiency.

Allocative efficiency occurs when resources are divided among goods and services such that society receives the mix of goods and services it wants. Productive efficiency is necessary for an industry to be able to achieve allocative efficiency. Once the firms are producing at lowest cost, allocative efficiency focuses on whether firms are producing the products consumers actually want. This occurs at the output where P = MC. At that point, the value society receives from the last product is equal to the marginal cost of producing it. The graph on the right illustrates allocative efficiency. Notice that these side-by-side graphs are the illustration of long-run equilibrium for the perfectly competitive industry. Consumer and producer surplus are also maximized in a perfectly competitive market.

Economists consider perfect competition to be the perfect model of the "invisible hand" at work. Individual firms are free to enter and exit the industry and produce and set output in ways that maximize profit. Both productive and allocative efficiency are achieved, which help to keep prices down for consumers and ensure that scarce resources are used in the most efficient way to produce the mix of goods society desires. And when changes occur in the market, firms respond to profits and losses in the short run by changing output and the industry changes in the long run as firms enter or exit, until long-run equilibrium and productive and allocative efficiency are once again achieved.

Multiple-Choice Questions

1. Which of the following best describes a perfectly competitive market?
   - I. A large number of firms exist in the industry.
   - II. Products are differentiated.
   - III. Firms can easily enter or exit the industry.
   - (A) I only
   - (B) II only
   - (C) I and III only
   - (D) II and III only
   - (E) I, II, and III

2. Because the perfectly competitive firm is a price-taker, its demand curve is
   - (A) upward sloping.
   - (B) downward sloping.
   - (C) horizontal.
   - (D) vertical.
   - (E) dependent on the marginal cost.

3. In order to maximize profit, the firm should produce where
   - (A) Marginal Revenue = Price.
   - (B) Marginal Cost = Marginal Revenue.
   - (C) Marginal Cost = Average Variable Cost.
   - (D) Price = Average Variable Cost.
   - (E) Average Revenue = Price.

4. At long-run equilibrium for the perfectly competitive firm, the marginal cost is equal to all of the following EXCEPT
   - (A) average total cost.
   - (B) marginal cost.
   - (C) price.
   - (D) marginal revenue.
   - (E) average variable cost.

5. At a particular output, a perfectly competitive firm's price is $10, marginal cost is $11, average total cost is $12, and average variable cost is $8. The firm should
   - (A) increase output to maximize profit.
   - (B) continue production at its current level of output to maximize output.
   - (C) decrease output to minimize loss, but keep producing in the short run.
   - (D) raise the product price to $11 to maximize profit.
   - (E) shut down.

6. If a firm incurs losses, it should continue to produce as long as the price covers the
   - (A) average variable cost.
   - (B) average fixed cost.
   - (C) average total cost.
   - (D) marginal cost.
   - (E) marginal revenue.

7.   If a firm is producing 10 products for a price of $5 per unit, and the marginal cost of producing the 11th product is $3, which of the following statements is true?
(A)   The total cost of producing 11 units is $5 greater than producing 10 units.
(B)   The total revenue of selling 11 units equals the total revenue of selling 10 units.
(C)   The total profit from selling 11 units is $2 more than the total profit from selling 10 units.
(D)   The marginal revenue from selling the 11th unit is $3.
(E)   The marginal cost of producing the 11th unit is greater than the marginal revenue from producing it.

8.   If consumer demand for the product in a perfectly competitive industry increases, which effects will occur for the individual firm in the short run?
            I.   The product price will increase.
            II.   The firm will incur a loss at its current output.
            III.   The firm will increase output.
(A)   I only
(B)   II only
(C)   II and III only
(D)   I and III only
(E)   I, II, and III

9.   If a perfectly competitive firm is initially in long-run equilibrium, and the firm's variable cost increases, all of the following occur in the short run EXCEPT
(A)   the firm's average total cost will increase.
(B)   the firm's marginal cost will increase.
(C)   the firm's average fixed cost will increase.
(D)   the firm's output will decrease.
(E)   the firm will experience a short-run loss.

10.   In a perfectly competitive industry in which firms are achieving short-run economic profit,
(A)   firms will enter the industry.
(B)   firms will increase the product price.
(C)   industry output will decrease.
(D)   firms will exit the industry.
(E)   the government will increase taxes.

11.   Assume a perfectly competitive firm is in long-run equilibrium. If the firm's property tax (a lump-sum cost) increases, in the short run, the firm will
(A)   not change its output.
(B)   increase output to where marginal cost equals the new average total cost.
(C)   reduce output to where marginal cost equals the new average total cost.
(D)   increase output to where the new marginal cost equals marginal revenue.
(E)   reduce output to where the new marginal cost equals marginal revenue.

12.   Assume profit-maximizing firms in a perfectly competitive industry are in long-run equilibrium. In that condition, all of the following are achieved EXCEPT
(A)   firms earn normal profit.
(B)   firms have no incentive to enter or exit the industry.
(C)   both productive and allocative efficiency are achieved.

(D)   consumer and producer surplus are maximized.
(E)   firms earn economic profit.

Free-Response Questions
1.   Assume Joslyn Farm is a profit-maximizing firm in the perfectly competitive corn industry, which is in long-run equilibrium.
(a)   Draw correctly labeled, side-by-side graphs for the corn industry and Joslyn Farm. Show and label each of the following:
    (i)   industry price and output
    (ii)   Joslyn Farm's price and output
(b)   Suppose the government offers a per-unit subsidy to corn farmers. On your graphs from part (a), show the effects of the subsidy on each of the following in the short run:
    (i)   Joslyn Farm's output. Explain the effect.
    (ii)   the area of profit or loss for Joslyn Farm. Explain the effect.
(c)   Explain how the industry will return to long-run equilibrium and why this effect occurs in perfectly competitive markets.

2.   Assume SamKat, Inc., sells lemonade at a county fair, surrounded by dozens of other food stands selling the very same lemonade.
(a)   In what type of market structure is SamKat operating?
(b)   If SamKat increases its product price above the industry equilibrium price, what will happen to its total revenue? Explain.
(c)   Assume the cost of lemons increases for all lemonade stands in the industry.
    (i)   Explain the effect of the cost increase on SamKat's output.
    (ii)   Explain the effect on SamKat's short-run profit or loss.
    (iii) Under what conditions will SamKat continue to produce in the short run?

3.   The table below indicates the short-run costs for Cherryl's Cupcakes, a profit-maximizing firm in a perfectly competitive industry in long-run equilibrium.

Output Produced	Total Cost
0	20
1 box	30
2 boxes	35
3 boxes	38
4 boxes	44
5 boxes	51
6 boxes	60
7 boxes	70
8 boxes	90

(a)   Calculate the marginal cost of producing the second box of cupcakes.
(b)   Calculate the average total cost of producing 4 boxes of cupcakes.
(c)   Cherryl's Cupcakes receives a price of $10 per box of cupcakes. Indicate how many boxes of cupcakes the firm should sell to maximize its profit. Explain how you reached that conclusion.

(d)   If cupcakes are a normal good and consumer incomes decrease, explain
   (i)   the effect on the cupcake industry.
   (ii)   the effect on the price Cherryl's Cupcakes will receive for its product.
   (iii)   the effect on the quantity of cupcakes produced by Cherryl's Cupcakes.
   (iv)   the short-run economic profit or loss incurred by Cherryl's Cupcakes.
   (v)   the industry's long-run adjustment.

Multiple-Choice Explanations

1.   (C)   Products produced in a perfectly competitive industry are identical.
2.   (C)   The industry demand curve is downward-sloping, and the market equilibrium price set in the industry becomes the perfectly elastic demand for the firm. Because the firm has no power to change price in the market, it can sell all of the products it makes at the same price.
3.   (B)   The MC = MR rule is the same for firms in all market structures. The firm should continue to produce as long as the marginal revenue from selling a unit is greater than or equal to the marginal cost of producing that unit.
4.   (E)   For the perfectly competitive firm, marginal revenue and price are equal on the demand curve. The firm maximizes profit where MC = MR, and it reaches productive efficiency by producing where MC = ATC at that same point. The average variable cost curve will be below the ATC, so it is the only curve not equal to all of the others at the profit-maximizing output.
5.   (C)   At that output, marginal cost is greater than marginal revenue, so the firm should decrease output. The firm is incurring a loss because price is lower than the average total cost, but the price is higher than the average variable cost, so the firm should continue to produce in the short run.
6.   (A)   If the firm can recover all of its variable costs, it should continue to produce because it can use any additional revenues toward its fixed costs.
7.   (C)   The marginal revenue of producing the next unit is $5, and the marginal cost of producing the next unit is $3, so the total profit increases by $2.
8.   (D)   Increased industry demand pushes up the price, which causes the firm's marginal revenue curve to shift up. In the short run, the firm increases output to the point where MC = MR again. Because the price is now higher than the ATC, the firm experiences an economic profit in the short run.
9.   (C)   An increase in variable cost increases the firm's average total cost and marginal cost, but it has no effect on average fixed cost. The firm decreases its output to minimize its loss where MC = MR, and the loss is illustrated with the new ATC positioned above the price.
10.   (A)   Economic profit draws firms into the industry. Firms that cannot affect product price are price-takers, and the short-run economic profit would lead firms to increase output rather than reducing it.
11.   (A)   A lump-sum cost only affects average fixed cost and average total cost. Because marginal cost is not affected, the firm's output does not change.
12.   (E)   In long-run equilibrium, firms earn only a normal profit to cover the opportunity cost of the entrepreneur and resources involved in the firm, but there is no economic profit, because the existence of economic profit draws new firms into the industry. While the firm will see an accounting profit, there is no economic profit.

Free-Response Explanations

1.   **10 points** (4 + 4 + 2)
(a)   4 points:

- 1 point is earned for correctly identifying equilibrium price and quantity for the industry.
- 1 point is earned for drawing a horizontal line linking the industry price to Joslyn Farm's marginal revenue curve.
- 1 point is earned for labeling the firm's demand curve as price and showing output where MC = MR.
- 1 point is earned for correctly placing the average total cost curve with its minimum at the output where MC = MR.

(b)   4 points:
- 1 point is earned for showing Joslyn Farm's output will increase.
- 1 point is earned for explaining that the firm produces where MC = MR; because MC shifted downward, they now cross at a greater output.
- 1 point is earned for showing Joslyn Farm's area of profit.
- 1 point is earned for explaining that because the new ATC is below the price (or marginal revenue or average revenue), the firm is earning an economic profit.

(c)   2 points:
- 1 point is earned for explaining that firms enter the industry.
- 1 point is earned for explaining that profits draw the firms into the industry.

2.   **6 points** (1 + 2 + 3)
(a)   1 point:
- 1 point is earned for identifying the market structure as perfect competition.

(b)   2 points:
- 1 point is earned for stating that SamKat's total revenue will fall to zero.
- 1 point is earned for explaining that customers will purchase the substitute product from another firm.

(c)   3 points:
- 1 point is earned for stating that SamKat's output will decrease.
- 1 point is earned for stating that SamKat will incur a short-run loss.
- 1 point is earned for explaining that SamKat will continue to produce in the short run as long as marginal revenue is greater than or equal to average variable cost.

3.   **9 points** (1 + 1 + 2 + 5)
(a)   1 point:
- 1 point is earned for stating that the marginal cost is $5.

(b)   1 point:
- 1 point is earned for stating that the average total cost is $11.

(c)   2 points:
- 1 point is earned for stating that Cherryl's Cupcakes maximizes profit at 7 boxes.
- 1 point is earned for explaining that the marginal revenue equals the marginal cost at that output.

(d)   5 points:
- 1 point is earned for stating that the industry demand decreases.
- 1 point is earned for stating that the price of the product decreases.
- 1 point is earned for stating that the firm's output decreases.
- 1 point is earned for stating that the firm will incur a short-run loss.
- 1 point is earned for explaining that in the long-run, firms will exit the industry.

CHAPTER 10: PURE MONOPOLY

Introduction
While the perfectly competitive firm has no power over prices in the marketplace, the monopoly has the power necessary to determine both the price and output of the product. The monopoly model shows us important differences from perfect competition in terms of efficiency and effects on producer and consumer surplus. Chapter 10 focuses on the ways monopolies develop, output and price determination, the effects of monopoly behavior, and government regulation. The monopoly model is important to understanding the oligopoly and monopolistic competition, which will be covered in Chapter 11. Material from Chapter 10 appears on the AP microeconomics exam in a large number of multiple-choice questions, and a free-response question about decision making in at least one of the market structures is part of nearly every AP microeconomics exam.

Pure Monopoly
A pure monopoly is a market structure with only one producer, no close substitutes, and complete barriers to entry. Unlike a price-taking perfectly competitive firm, the pure monopoly is a price maker, with the firm determining its own output and the price it will charge for its product. Because the monopoly faces a downward-sloping demand curve, it can restrict output in order to raise the product price. Pure monopolies include local natural gas, electricity, and water companies, as well as pharmaceutical companies that hold patents on particular medications. Near monopolies also exist where a single firm provides the vast majority of sales in a particular industry.

Barriers to Entry
Monopolies hold market power, the power to determine prices, because of barriers to entry—factors that prevent competitors from entering the industry. While perfectly competitive firms face no barriers and are free to enter and exit the industry, imperfectly competitive firms must deal with barriers. Monopolies, for a variety of reasons, are able to completely prevent potential competitors from entering the industry.

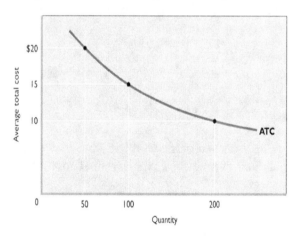

Economies of scale

One important barrier to entry is economies of scale. The larger the firm's output, the more efficient the firm becomes. Natural monopolies achieve economies of scale, with their average total cost curves continuing to fall over a very large range of output. In this example, if one firm produced 200 products, the average total cost would be $10. But if two firms each produced 100 units, the average total cost would be $15; four firms each producing 50 units would lead to an average total cost of $20. Clearly, it is more cost-effective to have one large producer. These economies of scale also serve as a barrier to entry for new firms, which face those higher costs as smaller producers.

The government also creates barriers to entry by granting patents and licenses. The government grants a patent, which protects an inventor's ownership rights, in order to encourage investment in research and development. For the life of the patent, the owner has monopoly control of the product and can use revenues to recoup research and development costs and potentially to support further development of other products. The government can also create a barrier to entry by licensing producers, from taxi drivers and cosmetologists to teachers and electricians.

Other firms create barriers to entry by controlling the resources necessary to produce the product. Monopolists deeply cut their prices to undercut the competition, make deals with retailers to reinforce their monopoly status, or find other ways to make the competitor's product more expensive or less desirable.

Monopoly Demand

Analysis of the pure monopoly assumes no firms can enter the industry, the government does not regulate the firm, and the firm charges the same price for every product. The most important difference between the perfectly competitive firm and the pure monopoly is the demand curve. Remember, the perfectly competitive firm was a price-taker, accepting the price set in the industry. So the individual firm had a perfectly elastic, horizontal demand curve, with the marginal revenue equal to the product price.

Because it is the only firm in the industry, a monopoly has only one graph, unlike the side-by-side graphs for perfect competition. Also, a monopoly faces a different demand curve. Because it is the only producer, industry demand *is* the firm's demand. Therefore, a monopoly faces a downward-sloping demand curve, with quantity demanded increasing as price falls. This difference has important ramifications for price and output decisions.

First, the marginal revenue curve is lower than the price curve. For the firm to sell more products, it must lower the price for *all* the goods it sells, not just the last one. Therefore, the marginal revenue—the change in total revenue from selling one more product—will be lower than the price charged for that product. Say a firm sells 5 T-shirts for $10 each, for total revenue of $50. If the firm wants to sell the 6th T-shirt, it must lower its price of T-shirts to $9—for all of them. Now the firm sells 6 T-shirts for $9 each, for total revenue of $54. So while the price of the T-shirt is $9, the marginal revenue to the firm is just $4 (total revenue increased from $50 to $54). Thus, the marginal revenue is less than the price. Average revenue, price, and demand are all represented on the higher curve.

> **Bear in Mind**
> This concept of marginal revenue being lower than price has frequently appeared on both the multiple-choice and free-response sections of the AP microeconomics exam. It is important to understand and be able to explain the reason for this relationship: in order for the firm to sell more products, it must lower the price on all of the products sold.

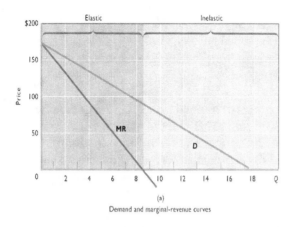

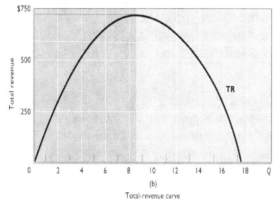

Demand, marginal revenue, and total revenue for a pure monopolist

As the marginal revenue falls, the growth in total revenue slows. As long as the marginal revenue is positive, the sale of additional products adds to the total revenue of the firm, but each additional sale adds less and less revenue. At the point where the marginal revenue of the next product is zero, the total revenue peaks. The total revenue is maximized at the output where the marginal revenue curve crosses through the bottom axis of the graph. After that point, each additional product sold results in a negative marginal revenue. The product price is positive, but the reduction in price for all of the earlier units overwhelms that price, so the marginal revenue curve falls through the bottom of the graph. At the output where marginal revenue becomes negative, total revenue of the firm begins to fall.

A second important implication for a downward-sloping demand curve is that the firm is a price maker. Monopolies control supply and product price through their own output decisions. A third effect of a downward-sloping demand curve is that the firm will set its price in the elastic portion of the demand curve. The firm will never choose to produce where the marginal revenue is negative because that output would result in a lower total revenue for the firm at the same time that total cost is rising; therefore, the firm would experience lower profit in that range of production. Because the monopoly seeks to maximize profit, the firm will set its output in the elastic portion of the demand curve.

Chapter 10: Pure Monopoly

Output and Price Determination for the Monopoly

As was the case for the perfectly competitive model, we assume that the monopoly is in a constant-cost industry. The monopoly firm is such a small part of the market for resources that increased demand will not push up the cost of those resources.

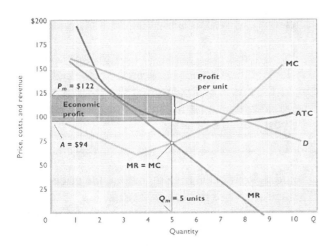

Profit maximization by a pure monopolist

The monopolist maximizes profit at the output where marginal revenue equals marginal cost. As long as the firm receives revenue greater than or equal to the cost of producing the next unit of output, the firm should produce it. If the cost to produce the next unit is greater than the revenue the firm would receive from selling it, the firm should not produce it. In this figure, MR = MC at five units of output, the profit-maximizing output.

To find the monopoly's price, extend the line at the selected output up to the demand curve. Because consumers are willing and able to pay that price, that is the price the firm will charge. In this case, the firm charges a price of $122 for its products.

Taking the EEK! Out of Economics
When determining the price, be very careful to go all the way up to the demand curve. Students often make the mistake of treating the MC = MR point similarly to a supply and demand equilibrium, setting the price at that same point. Consumers are willing and able to pay the higher price, and charging that higher price maximizes the firm's profit.

To calculate the profit the firm earns from the selected output, you must compare the price at that output to the average total cost at that output. Just as was the case for the purely competitive firm, you can calculate the profit two different ways.

1.   Total Revenue—Total Cost.
        Total Revenue = Price × Output
        Total Cost = ATC × Output
2.   Profit per Unit × Output.
        Profit per Unit = Price – Average Total Cost

In this case, profit per unit is $28, so at an output of five units, the firm's profit is $140.

To ensure that you'll show the firm earning an economic profit when drawing the monopoly model, first draw the demand, marginal revenue, and marginal cost curves. Then draw a point on the marginal cost curve between the demand and marginal revenue curves. Make that point the lowest point on your average total cost curve. This tip ensures you'll demonstrate marginal cost crossing ATC at its lowest point (productive efficiency), as well as show that the ATC is lower than the price on the demand curve.

When determining profit, be very careful to only look at the distance between the price and the ATC at the MC = MR output. Students often make the mistake of measuring the distance between the demand curve and the MC = MR point, viewing that difference as the profit per unit. Remember, profit is calculated by subtracting the cost from the revenue.

Bear in Mind
You must be able to draw a monopoly graph, including profit-maximizing output, the price set in the market, and the area of economic profit. The free-response portion of the AP microeconomics exam almost always includes a question requiring you to draw a graph for a firm in one of the four market structures, as well as several multiple-choice questions involving the monopoly. Sketching a graph can help you visualize the market and improve your chance of success in correctly answering those questions.

Remember, the firm is focused on maximizing total profit, not profit per unit. Also, note that the monopoly is limited in the price it can charge. Many people mistakenly believe a monopoly can charge any price it wants, but it is still constrained by the demand curve. The firm will set the price at the point on the demand curve at the output where MC = MR.

Long-Run Economic Profit
The perfectly competitive firm could earn short-run economic profit. But in the long run, the profit motive draws other firms into the industry, lowering the price and the marginal revenue to the firm until economic profit is reduced to zero. The monopolist, however, can sustain economic profit in the long run due to the barriers to entry. Because no new firms are able to enter the industry, no long-run adjustment occurs for monopolies.

Loss Minimization and the Shutdown Decision

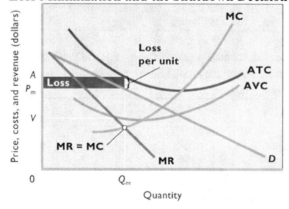

The loss minimizing position of a pure monopolist

While the monopoly can earn a profit, it is also possible for the firm to sustain a loss. A loss occurs when the firm's ATC is greater than the price (on the demand curve) at the MC = MR output. If the firm incurs a loss, should it remain in operation? If the price is greater than the firm's average variable cost, the firm should remain in operation. But if the firm cannot even recover the variable costs to produce the additional output, the firm should shut down. It is important to note that because there is no long-run adjustment of other firms leaving the industry, the firm has to make its own decision of whether to shut down in the long run. If the firm is convinced that losses will persist in the long run, the firm will likely shift its resources to a more profitable opportunity or shut down altogether.

Changes in Production Costs
As with the competitive firm, changes in costs for the monopoly shift the cost curves directly up and down, because the curves represent the costs at each output. If a per-unit (or variable) cost increases, the marginal cost, average variable cost, and average total cost all increase. Because the new marginal cost equals marginal revenue at a lower output, the firm will produce fewer products at the higher cost. The price, set on the demand curve above where MC = MR, will be higher as a result of the lower output. If per-unit costs decrease, such as lower wages or lower-cost resources, the MC, AVC, and ATC all shift downward, the firm increases production, and the price falls.

If a lump-sum (or fixed) cost increases, only the average fixed cost and average total cost increase. Because marginal cost did not change, output and price do not change. With a higher average total cost, the firm's profit is lower but nothing else changes. If a lump-sum cost decreases, such as a firm receiving a subsidy or lower property tax, the AFC and ATC shift down. While the output and price remain the same, the firm's profit increases.

Comparing the Perfectly Competitive and Monopoly Models

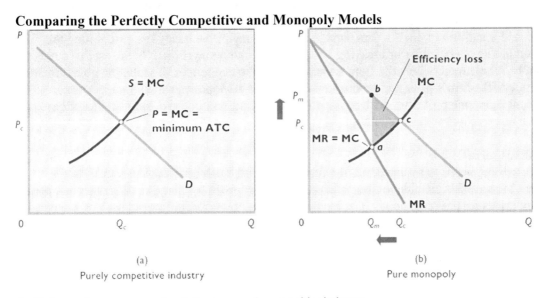

(a)
Purely competitive industry

(b)
Pure monopoly

Inefficiency of a pure monopoly relative to a purely competitive industry

The perfectly competitive model and the monopoly model, the extremes of the four market structures, demonstrate significant differences in efficiency, output, and price.

First, while both productive and allocative efficiency are achieved in the perfectly competitive industry (because firms produce at the lowest cost where MC = ATC and the product's value to society equals the cost of making it where P = MC), neither is achieved for the monopoly. The monopolist produces where MC = MR to maximize profit, at an output lower than that required to achieve productive efficiency. Price exceeds both marginal cost and minimum ATC. Because productive efficiency is not met, allocative efficiency cannot be met by the monopoly. Deadweight loss is illustrated by the triangle to the left of the point where MC = D for the monopoly. This is the loss of efficiency due to monopoly output and represents the loss of consumer and producer surplus.

Second, a monopoly produces fewer products and charges a higher price than a perfectly competitive industry. Monopolists maximize profit at the output where MC = MR, which is less than the allocatively efficient output of MC = D. The monopolist then sets the price on the demand curve, which is higher than the perfectly competitive firm would charge.

Third, a monopoly can sustain long-run profit because the price is higher than ATC and barriers prevent firms from entering to bring the price down. Perfectly competitive firms may enjoy a short-run profit, but in the long run, the entry of new firms lowers the price, translating to lower marginal revenue to the firm, until economic profit returns to zero.

Bear in Mind
Questions comparing the perfectly competitive model and the monopoly model are a standard feature of both the multiple-choice and free-response portions of the AP microeconomics exam. It is important to be able to correctly graph both models, including the area of deadweight loss (loss of efficiency) for the monopoly model.

Government Response to Monopolies
Because of the inefficiency, higher prices, and lower output associated with monopolies, government has an interest in intervening in some monopoly markets. The government can file charges under anti-trust laws if a firm engages in anti-competitive behaviors, prohibiting the firm from continuing the behavior or breaking it into several competing firms. In the case of a natural monopoly, where society benefits from a monopoly due to economies of scale, the government may regulate the firm's price and product quality. Other monopolies which do not cause significant economic problems, such as the only ice skating rink in town, may be allowed to continue in operation without regulation.

Price Discrimination
Up to this point, we have assumed that the firm charges all customers the same price for the product. Monopolists are able to discriminate, increasing profit by charging different customers different prices for the same good. You have likely seen price discrimination, such as a special price for movie tickets for children and senior citizens or discount cards for frequent shoppers at a store. Price-discriminating monopolists charge a lower price for consumers who are more sensitive to price (elastic demand), while customers who are less sensitive to price are charged the full higher price. Price discrimination is common and legal in the United States, as long as it is not used to prevent entry of firms into the industry.

The Regulated Monopoly
Natural monopolies, such as public utilities, are regulated by state and local governments to limit prices and ensure product quality. Because the monopolist reduces output to maximize profit, sets a higher price, and does not achieve productive or allocative efficiency, governments attempt to improve the outcome for society through regulation.

Chapter 10: Pure Monopoly

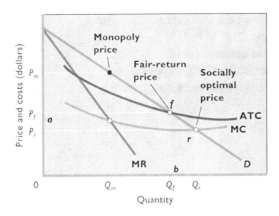

Regulated monopoly

In this figure, the firm maximizes its profit by setting an output of Q_m and a price of P_m. However, in order to achieve allocative efficiency, the government may set a price ceiling at the point where MC = D (= P). At that price ceiling of P_r, the marginal revenue curve becomes the price (as we saw for perfect competition), and the monopoly firm will produce Q_r units of output—where marginal revenue now equals the marginal cost but at a lower price and higher output than it would have produced as an unregulated monopoly. The marginal cost also equals the price at this output, signifying allocative efficiency.

But notice that this arrangement leaves this particular firm producing at a price lower than ATC at this output. The firm incurs a loss and will have to decide whether to even stay in business in the short run. In the long run, if the firm cannot raise its price or lower its costs, it will not remain in business. The government could offer the firm a subsidy to cover those costs, in order to encourage the firm to remain in operation. Or perhaps the government could allow the firm to engage in price discrimination to charge a higher price to those customers with the most inelastic demand for the product.

Often, regulatory commissions instead set the price ceiling at the fair-return price, where ATC = D. At that output, the firm achieves a normal profit but not an economic profit. The price is lower and the output higher than it would be under an unregulated monopoly but not as much as if the regulators set the price ceiling at the socially optimal price of P = MC. But this solution avoids the need for a subsidy to keep the firm in business.

Multiple-Choice Questions
1.   Which of the following characteristics correctly describe a monopoly?
        I.   The firm is the single seller in the industry.
        II.   Barriers to entry exist in the industry.
        III.   Unregulated monopolies are illegal under United States law.
        IV.   The firm determines its own price and output.
    (A)   I and II only
    (B)   I and III only
    (C)   I, II, and III only
    (D)   I, II, and IV only
    (E)   I, II, III, and IV

2. Why are monopoly firms price makers?
    (A) Monopolies produce at a lower cost than perfectly competitive firms.
    (B) Monopoly firms enjoy barriers to entry.
    (C) Monopoly firms face a perfectly elastic demand curve.
    (D) Monopolies are more efficient than perfectly competitive firms.
    (E) Monopolies produce goods that competitive firms cannot produce.

3. The monopolist's demand curve is
    (A) downward-sloping.
    (B) elastic between all points.
    (C) inelastic between all points.
    (D) vertical.
    (E) horizontal.

4. The monopolist's marginal revenue is lower than the product price because the
    (A) firm must accept the price set by the industry.
    (B) firm achieves efficiency when revenues are lower than prices.
    (C) firm must lower the price of all of its products in order to sell more.
    (D) firm becomes less efficient as output increases.
    (E) firm's costs of production constantly increase as output increases.

5. Why do unregulated monopolists not produce in the inelastic portion of the demand curve?
    (A) The marginal revenue is negative, causing total revenue to decrease.
    (B) That output will not bring about allocative efficiency.
    (C) The marginal revenue is lower than the price, causing price to fall.
    (D) The marginal cost is lower than the marginal revenue in that range.
    (E) Inelastic demand indicates consumers will not buy the additional output.

Questions 6–9 refer to the graph below, which shows the costs and revenues for a profit-maximizing monopoly firm.

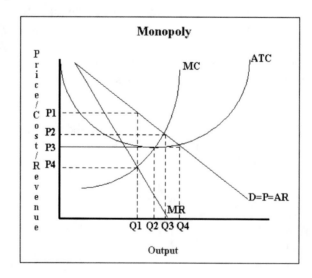

6. This monopoly firm is
    (A)   earning an economic profit.
    (B)   earning a normal profit, but not an economic profit.
    (C)   earning short-run profit but will earn no economic profit in the long run.
    (D)   experiencing a loss but should remain in business in the short run.
    (E)   experiencing a loss and should shut down.

7. The deadweight loss associated with reducing output for the monopoly is the
    (A)   triangle to the left of MC = D, on the Q1 line from P1 to P4.
    (B)   triangle below MC = D, on the P3 line from Q2 to Q4.
    (C)   rectangle between P1 and P3, from the left axis to the Q1 line.
    (D)   rectangle between P1 and P4, from the left axis to the Q1 line.
    (E)   triangle below the demand curve, on the P3 line from Q1 to Q4.

8. To reach allocative efficiency, government would set a price ceiling at
    (A)   P1.
    (B)   P2.
    (C)   P3.
    (D)   P4.
    (E)   MR = ATC.

9. At what output would this firm achieve productive efficiency?
    (A)   Q1
    (B)   Q2
    (C)   Q3
    (D)   Q4
    (E)   Monopolies cannot achieve productive efficiency.

10. Why do monopolies not produce at the point of productive efficiency?
    (A)   The monopoly focuses on achieving allocative efficiency.
    (B)   The firm reduces output in order to raise the price.
    (C)   The firm maximizes profit by producing where ATC = D.
    (D)   The monopoly focuses on minimizing the marginal cost.
    (E)   Monopolies cannot achieve productive efficiency.

11. Which statement is true for a monopoly but not for a perfectly competitive firm?
    (A)   The firm maximizes profit where marginal revenue equals marginal cost.
    (B)   The firm's marginal revenue equals the product price.
    (C)   The firm achieves allocative efficiency where it maximizes profit.
    (D)   The firm produces where MC = MR = ATC.
    (E)   The firm sustains long-run economic profit.

12. Price discrimination occurs when a firm charges different prices based on
    (A)   Changes in the average total cost.
    (B)   Changes in the marginal cost.
    (C)   Changes in the marginal revenue.
    (D)   The excise tax rate the government sets.
    (E)   Customers' sensitivity to the higher price.

Free-Response Questions

1.   Perfectly competitive and monopoly industries differ in several important ways.

(a)   Draw correctly labeled side-by-side graphs for the perfectly competitive industry and a typical firm that is earning short-run economic profit. On your graph, show the following:
   (i)   the price and output for the industry
   (ii)   the price and output for the individual firm
   (iii)   the area of economic profit

(b)   Draw a correctly labeled graph for a profit-maximizing monopoly. On your graph, show the following:
   (i)   the price and output for the firm
   (ii)   the area of economic profit

(c)   Explain this difference between perfectly competitive and monopoly firms.
   (i)   the relationship between price and marginal revenue for the perfectly competitive firm and the reason for that relationship
   (ii)   the relationship between price and marginal revenue for the monopoly firm and the reason for that relationship

(d)   Explain these differences between perfectly competitive and monopoly firms.
   (i)   Explain how and why economic profit is likely to change in the long run for the perfectly competitive firm.
   (ii)   Explain how and why economic profit is likely to change in the long run for the monopoly firm.

2.   Assume Chai Pharmaceuticals holds a patent for an important medication, preventing competing firms from producing that medication. Chai Pharmaceuticals is a profit-maximizing firm earning an economic profit.

(a)   Draw a correctly labeled graph showing the following for Chai Pharmaceuticals:
   (i)   The output
   (ii)   The price
   (iii)   The area of economic profit
   (iv)   The area of deadweight loss

(b)   Explain what deadweight loss represents.
(c)   Is Chai Pharmaceuticals producing at a productively efficient output? Explain.
(d)   Is Chai Pharmaceuticals producing at an allocatively efficient output? Explain.

3.   The graph that follows illustrates the costs and revenues for Cisco's Widgets, a profit-maximizing monopoly that does not price discriminate.

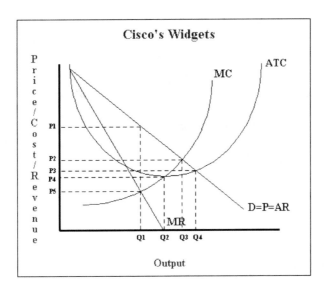

Cisco's Widgets

(a) Using the labeling in the graph, identify each of the following:
  (i) the output at which profit is maximized
  (ii) the output at which total revenue is maximized
  (iii) the output that is socially optimal
(b) Assume the per-unit (variable) cost of materials used to produce Widgets rises.
  (i) What will happen to the price of Widgets?
  (ii) What will happen to the output for Widgets?
  (iii) What will happen to the profit for Cisco's Widgets?
(c) Using the labeling in the graph, assume that the government wants to encourage the firm to produce at the socially optimal output.
  (i) At what price should the government set a price ceiling to encourage socially optimal output?
  (ii) At the socially optimal output, is this firm earning an economic profit or experiencing a loss? Explain.

Multiple-Choice Explanations
1. (D) Unregulated monopolies are allowed to exist under U.S. law and are quite common where demand does not support additional firms.
2. (B) Because a monopoly has no competition, the firm sets its own price.
3. (A) The monopolist faces a downward-sloping demand curve because the firm must lower prices to sell more. Demand is elastic where marginal revenue is positive and inelastic where marginal revenue is negative.
4. (C) Because the monopoly must lower its price to sell more products, it must lower the price for all units, including the first units produced.
5. (A) When marginal revenue is negative, it reduces total revenue, and because marginal cost is increasing, the firm cannot maximize profit in that range.
6. (A) This firm is earning an economic profit because price is higher than ATC.
7. (A) The deadweight loss represents the lost consumer and producer surplus associated with the firm's decision to reduce its output.
8. (B) The firm achieves allocative efficiency where MC = D. If the government sets the price ceiling at that point, the firm's marginal revenue becomes that price, and the firm produces where MC = MR to maximize profit and achieve allocative efficiency at the same point.

9.　　(B)　Productive efficiency is achieved where marginal cost crosses ATC at its lowest point. There, the firm produces at its lowest average cost per unit.

10.　　(B)　The monopoly maximizes profit by reducing output and raising the price, so the firm does not produce at its productively efficient output.

11.　　(E)　The monopoly can earn long-run economic profit because barriers to entry prevent other firms from entering the market.

12.　　(E)　A price discriminating monopolist charges the highest price for customers who are not sensitive to the higher price and lower prices to customers who are sensitive to the price in order to increase its total revenue.

Free-Response Explanations

1.　　**17 points** (5 + 4 + 4 + 4)

(a)　5 points:
- 1 point is earned for correctly identifying industry price and output.
- 1 point is earned for showing a horizontal demand curve for the firm, set at the price determined by the industry.
- 1 point is earned for identifying price on the firm's horizontal demand curve.
- 1 point is earned for setting output where MC = MR.
- 1 point is earned for showing the area of profit.

(b)　4 points:
- 1 point is earned for showing a correctly labeled monopoly with a downward-sloping demand curve and the marginal revenue curve below the demand curve.
- 1 point is earned for setting output where MC = MR.
- 1 point is earned for setting price on the demand curve above where MC = MR.
- 1 point is earned for showing the area of profit.

(c)　4 points:
- 1 point is earned for stating that price and marginal revenue are equal for the perfectly competitive firm.
- 1 point is earned for explaining that in perfect competition every product is sold for the same price, so the increase in revenue for each product sold is the price.
- 1 point is earned for stating that marginal revenue is lower than price for a monopoly.
- 1 point is earned for explaining that the monopoly must lower the price for all of the products in order to sell more.

(d)　4 points:
- 1 point is earned for stating that economic profit falls to zero in the long run for the perfectly competitive firm.
- 1 point is earned for explaining that profit draws new firms into the industry.
- 1 point is earned for stating that long-run economic profit remains for a monopoly.
- 1 point is earned for explaining that barriers to entry prevent firms from entering the industry.

2.　　**10 points** (5 + 1 + 2 + 2)

(a)　5 points:
- 1 point is earned for a correctly labeled graph with a downward-sloping demand curve and marginal revenue lower than demand.
- 1 point is earned for correctly setting output where MC = MR.
- 1 point is earned for setting price on the demand curve above the MC = MR output.
- 1 point is earned for correctly identifying the area of economic profit.

- 1 point is earned for correctly identifying the area of deadweight loss.
(b)   1 point:
- 1 point is earned for stating that deadweight loss represents the area of consumer and producer surplus lost due to the monopoly restricting output.
(c)   2 points:
- 1 point is earned for stating that the firm is not producing at productive efficiency.
- 1 point is earned for explaining that the firm is producing where MC = MR, not where MC = ATC; with the restricted output, ATC is not at its minimum.
(d)   2 points:
- 1 point is earned for stating that the firm is not producing at allocative efficiency.
- 1 point is earned for explaining that the firm is producing where MC = MR, not where MC = P; with the restricted output, price is greater than the marginal cost.

3.   **9 points** (3 + 3 + 3)
(a)   3 points:
- 1 point is earned for stating that profit is maximized at Q1.
- 1 point is earned for stating that total revenue is maximized at Q2.
- 1 point is earned for stating that socially optimal output is at Q3.
(b)   3 points:
- 1 point is earned for stating that the price of Widgets will increase.
- 1 point is earned for stating that the output for Widgets will decrease.
- 1 point is earned for stating that the profit for Cisco's Widgets will decrease.
(c)   3 points:
- 1 point is earned for stating that the government should set the price ceiling at P2.
- 1 point is earned for stating that the firm is earning an economic profit at that output.
- 1 point is earned for explaining that the firm's profit results from the price being higher than the average total cost at that output.

CHAPTER 11: MONOPOLISTIC COMPETITION AND OLIGOPOLY

Introduction

While perfect competition and monopoly represent the extremes of market structures, most American firms are found in the two market structures between those extremes. Monopolistic competition is very similar to perfect competition, though the firm has a small amount of market power. The oligopoly is very similar to the monopoly, though the firm does have a few competitors and the rivalry among those firms leads to an interdependent relationship among firms. Chapter 11 introduces these two models and explains the decision making of firms in these industries. This chapter completes the discussion of the market structures, which constitute the heart of the microeconomics course. Material from Chapter 11 consistently appears on the AP microeconomics exam in a few multiple-choice questions and, in recent years, in free-response questions.

Monopolistic Competition

Monopolistic competition is a market structure in which a large number of firms produce a differentiated product and firms can easily enter or exit the industry. Each firm in the industry sells a very small portion of the market share and has very little market power. Firms act independently, and one firm's actions have little or no effect on the other firms.

In these ways, the monopolistically competitive firm sounds very similar to the perfectly competitive firm. However, the key difference is product differentiation. While products are substantially the same, the firms make slight changes and then heavily advertise those differences in an effort to bring customers to their firm instead of the competing firm. One gas station may offer a car wash, while another may sell food inside the station. One dry cleaner may offer one-hour service, while another offers alterations. One motel may offer convenience to a major highway, while another offers small kitchens in the rooms.

Monopolistically competitive firms are very competitive, so where does the monopoly part of the term come from? Consider how many gas stations are located within a 20-mile radius of your home. Do you tend to use the same station repeatedly? Most people do because of the location, price (including discounts for using the company's card), or another feature. The market is quite competitive, but you act almost as though there's a monopoly because you keep returning to that station. As a result, the monopolistically competitive firm has a little control over the price. Due to customer brand loyalty, the firm can slightly raise the price without losing many customers. However, if the firm significantly raises its price, customers could easily change behavior to buy a substitute.

This brand loyalty also serves as a barrier to entry for new firms. New firms can easily enter a perfectly competitive industry because customers cannot distinguish which firm is producing the identical products. In monopolistic competition, the differences between products matter. So a new firm has to not only introduce its own product but also break customers' brand loyalty to the product they are currently purchasing.

Price and Output Determination for Monopolistic Competition

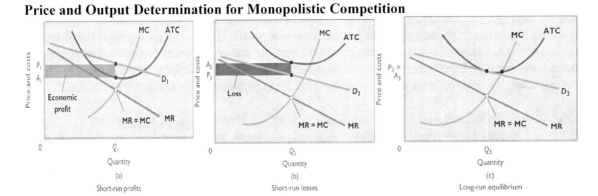

A monopolistically competitive firm: short run and long run

The graph for monopolistic competition is very similar to the monopoly. Demand is downward sloping because the firm must lower its price to sell more. Marginal revenue is below the demand curve, because when the firm reduces its price, it must reduce the price of all of the units of output. As with the monopoly, a monopolistically competitive firm maximizes profit at the output where marginal cost equals marginal revenue and sets the price on the demand curve at the point directly above the point where MC = MR.

As was true for perfectly competitive and monopoly models, changes in costs have effects on the output and profit of the firm. If a *per-unit cost* (a variable cost like labor or resources or a per-unit tax) increases, marginal cost and average total cost both increase for the firm. Because marginal cost shifts up, it now crosses marginal revenue at a lower output. So the firm reduces its output and sells its product at a higher price. But also notice that the higher average total cost shifts up, leaving the firm producing at a loss in the short run until the industry adjusts. If a per-unit cost falls (from lower production costs, lower per-unit taxes, or a per-unit subsidy), the firm increases its output and sells at a lower price. The firm will also enjoy a short-run economic profit until the industry adjusts.

If a *lump sum cost* (a fixed cost such as a property tax or a licensing fee) increases, only the average fixed cost and the average total cost increase. Marginal cost does not change, so output and price do not change. Because ATC increases, the firm will incur a short-run loss until the industry adjusts. Conversely, if a lump sum cost falls (from lower production costs, a lump sum tax cut, or a lump sum subsidy), the firm still will not change output or price, but the firm will enjoy short-run profit until the industry adjusts.

There are important differences between the graphs for monopolistic competition and the monopoly. First, notice that the demand and marginal revenue curves are much flatter for the monopolistic competitor. The demand curve is more elastic in monopolistic competition exactly because there is so much competition. It is easy for consumers to buy a competitor's product if the firm increases the price too much. In this way, the monopolistically competitive firm begins to act more like a perfectly competitive firm.

Second, while the monopolistically competitive firm may earn short-run economic profit or loss, in the long run, the firm will earn zero economic profit. If the price is higher than average total cost at the profit-maximizing output, the firm earns a profit; if average total cost is greater than the price at the profit-maximizing (or loss-minimizing) output, the firm incurs a loss. This is the same method of calculating profit or loss we have used for both the perfectly competitive firm and monopoly. The monopoly establishes complete barriers to entry to prevent competitors from entering the industry; therefore, it can sustain long-run profit. The perfectly competitive firm, on the other hand, has no barriers to entry, so other firms are enticed to enter the market when profits occur, and firms exit the industry in periods of loss. The same is true for monopolistic competition; the ease of entry and exit extends to the monopolistically competitive market.

Short-Run Profit/Loss and Long-Run Equilibrium for Monopolistic Competition
When a monopolistic competitor enjoys a short-run economic profit, new firms are drawn into the industry. As the new firms enter, the demand curve for existing firms shifts to the left and becomes more elastic (flatter). This occurs because the new firms increase the total production of output, and the individual existing firms each provide a smaller portion of the total market output. Demand becomes more elastic because the increased competition allows customers to become even more sensitive to price changes. In long-run equilibrium, after adjustments are complete, the average total cost curve for the monopolistically competitive firm lies above the demand curve and then only tangentially touches the demand curve at the point above MC = MR where the price is set.

When a monopolistic competitor incurs short-run loss, some firms will leave the industry. We use the same formula we used for perfect competition and monopoly to determine whether the firm should remain in business when it incurs a loss. At the loss-minimizing output (MC = MR), if the product price is equal to or higher than the average variable cost, the firm should remain in business in the short run. In that scenario, the firm is receiving enough revenue to cover all of the variable costs of producing the product and can put any additional revenues toward the fixed cost. But if the price is lower than the average variable cost, the firm should shut down. If one firm remains in operation while other firms leave the industry, the firm's demand curve shifts to the right and becomes less elastic. Because customers have fewer firms to choose from, the firm will enjoy a greater piece of the market and will have a little market power to raise the price. In the long run, the exit of firms from the industry reduces the loss to zero (which also means zero economic profit). Firms are no longer enticed to either enter or exit the industry, and ATC is again tangential to the demand curve at the point where price is set above the MC = MR output.

Taking the EEK! Out of Economics
Remember that even though the firm is not earning economic profit, the firm is earning accounting profit and paying normal profit to the entrepreneur in order to keep him/her in the industry. Economic profit is just the excess profit that causes other firms to enter the industry. When economic profit falls to zero in the long run, current producers are covering all of their explicit and implicit costs and will remain in business, but there is no excess profit to draw new firms into the industry.

Efficiency and the Monopolistically Competitive Firm

Monopolistically competitive firms do not achieve productive or allocative efficiency. Productive efficiency occurs when the marginal cost equals the average total cost at its minimum point and the firm is producing at its lowest average cost. In the monopolistic competition model, marginal cost crosses average total cost at a higher output than the point where the firm maximizes profit. Because the firm restricts output in order to raise the price, it produces where the average total cost is a little higher than its minimum.

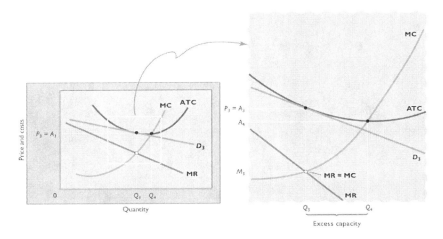

The inefficiency of monopolistic competition

Allocative efficiency is achieved at the point where price (on the demand curve) equals marginal cost. With allocative efficiency, scarce resources are used to produce the products society actually wants. In monopolistic competition, allocative efficiency is also achieved at a higher output than the profit-maximizing output for the firm. The difference in output between the point of allocative efficiency and the point of profit maximization is called excess capacity. Excess capacity is the amount of resources (plant and equipment) that remain unused because the firm has restricted its output from what would be allocatively efficient. Hospitals or hotels that have a number of unused beds or factories that have idle sections are examples of excess capacity that represent inefficiency.

Product Variety Among Monopolistic Competitors

While long-run equilibrium demonstrates that the monopolistically competitive firm will earn no long-run economic profit, such firms certainly have an incentive to be the firm that continues to earn economic profit. These firms have a strong incentive to be innovative and further differentiate their products in order to draw in more customers. This innovation leads to a wide variety of products for consumers. Because of the changes in the product and advertising expenses, production costs can change markedly for the monopolistically competitive firm. While we can demonstrate what long-run equilibrium would look like with this model, in reality, firms struggle to maintain economic profit, and the reality of such markets differs from the model. Remember the smiley (☺)?

Oligopoly

An oligopoly is a market dominated by a few large firms. Products can be standard, such as oil or steel, or differentiated, such as cars or sodas. Using a four-firm concentration ratio, if the four largest firms in the industry control 40 percent of the market, the industry is an oligopoly. "A few" firms could range from two to dozens, but the key is that this small number of firms controls the industry through barriers to entry. Like monopolies, oligopolies use economies of scale, ownership of resources, patents, licensing, strong consumer loyalty, or other means to repel the entry of new competitors into the industry. Oligopolistic firms can develop by differentiating their product enough to attract great numbers of consumers or by merging with other firms to grow significantly larger.

Price and Output Determination for the Oligopoly

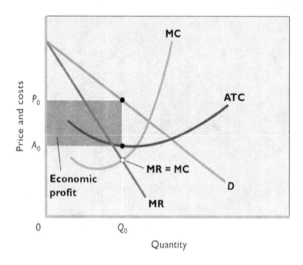

Collusion and the tendency toward joint-profit maximization

The oligopoly graph looks just like the monopoly. The downward-sloping demand curve shows that the firm must lower its price in order to sell more products, though the demand curve is slightly more elastic because there are a few competitors. Marginal revenue falls faster than demand, because when the firm lowers price to sell more, it must lower the price of all of its products. The firm maximizes profit at the point where MC = MR and sets its price on the demand curve directly above that point. Just as with monopoly and monopolistic competition, changes in per-unit costs will change the firm's output, price, and profit/loss, while changes in lump sum costs will only change the level of the firm's profit/loss. The level of economic profit is determined by the distance between the price (on the demand curve) and average total cost. Due to significant barriers to entry into the industry, firms are able to continue economic profit in the long run. If the firm incurs a short-run loss, it remains in business as long as the price is higher than the average variable cost and shuts down if the price is lower than the average variable cost. Just like the monopoly, the oligopoly does not achieve either productive or allocative efficiency.

Bear in Mind
The theory of the kinked demand curve for the oligopoly has not been addressed in questions on the AP microeconomics exam, so it will not be detailed here. When one firm in an oligopoly lowers its price, its rivals will generally lower their prices as well in order to avoid losing customers. If one firm increases its price, however, the other firms are likely not to match the price increase, hoping that customers will leave the high-priced firm and instead buy the rivals' product. It is important to understand that oligopolistic firms will respond to the actions of competitors, but no questions requiring the actual graphing of the oligopoly market have appeared on previous exams.

Mutual Interdependence and Strategic Behavior

While the oligopoly looks like the monopoly, the oligopoly differs from the monopoly in an important way. Firms in an oligopoly are mutually interdependent. When one firm makes a decision about price and output, its profit depends on how its rivals react. So the oligopolist must make strategic decisions by anticipating the reaction of its competitors. This characteristic makes the oligopoly different from the other three market structures.

Game Theory

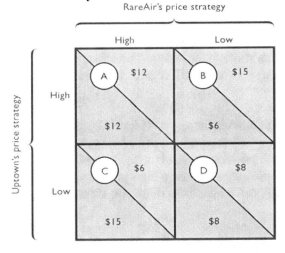

Profit payoff (in millions) for a two-firm oligopoly

The study of these strategic decisions is known as game theory. The payoff matrix in this figure shows the choices available to two firms in an oligopoly. RareAir and Uptown can each choose to set a high or low price for their shoes. But the profit each earns from its decision depends on the decision of the other firm. If both firms set a high price, each firm earns $12 million profit. But if Uptown sells its shoes for a high price and RareAir sells its shoes for a low price, many customers will buy from RareAir instead of Uptown, and RareAir's profit will increase to $15 million while Uptown's profit will fall to $6 million. If Uptown anticipates RareAir's low-price strategy, Uptown could also use a low-price strategy so that both firms would earn $8 million profit. Lower prices and profits are better for consumers, but remember that firms seek to maximize profit.

But there is another solution that would allow both firms to increase profit. If the firms collude, agreeing to set prices and output, RareAir and Uptown could agree to a high-price strategy so that both firms earn the higher $12 million profit. Though both firms are better off colluding rather than settling for the $8 million profit they would each earn alone using a low-price strategy, each firm is still eyeing that higher $15 million profit for taking the low-price strategy alone. If Uptown cheats on the agreement so that RareAir keeps its high-price strategy and Uptown uses the low-price strategy, Uptown's profit will increase from $12 million to $15 million, while RareAir's profit will fall from $12 million to $6 million. Once RareAir figures out that Uptown has cheated, it will use the low-price strategy as well, and both will return to $8 million profit. This incentive to cheat on collusive agreements, as well as differences in costs and demand among firms and the potential entry of new firms, explains why cartels find it so difficult to maintain collusive agreements. The clearest example of a cartel is OPEC, the Organization of Petroleum Exporting Countries. OPEC oil ministers agree to restrict output by each country in order to keep oil prices higher than they would be if the rivals competed. Cartels and their collusive activities are illegal in the United States under antitrust legislation. But because we import products produced by cartels, an understanding of their operation is important.

Dominant Strategy and the Nash Equilibrium

Even when firms do not collude, it is possible they will find long-run equilibrium. Using the example of RareAir and Uptown, each firm needs to determine if it has a dominant strategy—a choice that is better for the firm, regardless of the other firm's decision.

If Uptown chooses a low-price strategy, it would earn $15 million if RareAir chooses a high-price strategy and $8 million if RareAir chooses a low-price strategy. Both of these positions are better off than the profit Uptown would have earned if it had chosen a high-price strategy and RareAir chose a high-price strategy ($15 > $12) or a low-price strategy ($8 > $6). Therefore, Uptown's dominant strategy is to choose a low-price strategy, as it is better off, regardless of what RareAir chooses to do.

At the same time, RareAir must determine if it has a dominant strategy. If RareAir chooses a low-price strategy, it would earn $15 million if Uptown chooses a high-price strategy and $8 million if Uptown chooses a low-price strategy. Both positions result in a higher profit for RareAir than if it had chosen a high-price strategy and Uptown chose a high-price strategy ($15 > $12) or a low-price strategy ($8 > $6). As a result, RareAir also has a dominant strategy to choose a low-price strategy.

In this case, both RareAir and Uptown will choose a low-price strategy, and each firm earns $8 million in profit. Both firms recognize the dominant strategy for their firm, so this arrangement, called Nash Equilibrium, will tend to remain stable and long-lasting. (It is named for John Nash, the Nobel Prize–winning economist whose story is the subject of the film *A Beautiful Mind*). Not all games will have a dominant strategy, and the lack of a dominant strategy can explain the volatility of some oligopolistic markets.

Bear in Mind

Applications of game theory in payoff matrices have appeared consistently in multiple-choice and free-response questions on recent AP microeconomics exams. It is important to understand the mechanics of the matrix, determine whether a dominant strategy exists for either firm or both, and the profit for each firm. A thorough understanding of the one-time game in the Chapter 11 Appendix is essential for success in this portion of the exam.

Price Leadership in the United States

Because cartels and collusion are illegal in the United States, firms instead rely on price leadership. When one major firm in the industry changes its price, the other firms quickly match it. When fuel prices rose significantly in early 2008, one airline began adding a surcharge for each checked suitcase. Other airlines quickly followed suit.

Given the difficulty of predicting how rivals will respond to price changes, oligopolists prefer not to compete with other firms on the basis of price. Instead, these firms focus on product differentiation and heavily advertise those differences. This brand of cereal contains more vitamins and minerals. That brand of tissue is softer. While advertising may provide consumers with important product information to make informed choices, some advertising is also misleading, so consumers must beware of advertising claims.

In review, the most important characteristics of the four market structures are as follows:

	Perfect competition	Monopolistic competition	Oligopoly	Monopoly
Number of firms	Many	Many	Few	One
Firms interdependent?	Independent	Independent	Interdependent	The only firm
Products identical?	Identical	Differentiated	Standardized or differentiated	Only product
Barriers to entry	None	Few	Significant	Complete
Firm's control over price	None	Little	A lot, limited by mutual interdependence	Complete
Demand curve for the firm	Perfectly elastic	Relatively elastic	Relatively inelastic	Relatively inelastic

Multiple-Choice Questions

1. Each of the following is a characteristic of monopolistic competition EXCEPT
   (A) A large number of firms produce in the industry.
   (B) The products produced by the industry are homogeneous (identical).
   (C) Firms can easily enter and exit the industry.
   (D) The firms in the industry act independently.
   (E) Firms rely on advertising the qualities of their product.

2. Why is the monopolistically competitive firm's marginal revenue curve below its demand curve?
   (A) The competition forces the firm to lower its prices.
   (B) To sell more products, the firm must lower the price of all of its products.
   (C) The firm's costs are lower than its revenues at each unit of output.
   (D) The firm has no rivals, so price is significantly higher than marginal cost.
   (E) As output increases, the firm's average total cost of production decreases.

3. If a monopolistically competitive firm is initially in short-run equilibrium and the government places a lump sum tax on production, how would the following change in the short run?

	Output	*Price*	*Short-Run Profit/Loss*
(A)	Increase	Increase	Incur a profit
(B)	Decrease	Increase	Incur a loss
(C)	No change	Increase	No change
(D)	Decrease	No change	Incur a loss
(E)	No change	No change	Incur a loss

4. When the monopolistically competitive industry adjusts to profit in the long run, what happens to the demand curve for the individual firm?
   (A) It shifts inward.
   (B) It becomes vertical.
   (C) It becomes horizontal.
   (D) It shifts outward.
   (E) It does not change.

5. The inefficiency generated by the monopolistically competitive firm results in
   (A) lower prices.
   (B) higher output.
   (C) excess capacity.
   (D) long-run economic profit.
   (E) higher wages.

6. One characteristic that makes oligopolies unique among the market structures is
   (A) long-run economic profit.
   (B) productive and allocative efficiency.
   (C) their role as price-takers.
   (D) product differentiation.
   (E) mutual interdependence among the firms.

7. When oligopolistic firms successfully maintain a long-term collusive agreement,
   (A) in the United States, the government supports the agreement with a subsidy to firms.
   (B) the product price is higher than the marginal cost.
   (C) the output is higher than it would have been under perfect competition.
   (D) the price is lower than it would have been if there was no agreement.
   (E) the long-run economic profit falls to zero.

8. It is difficult for cartels to maintain collusive agreements because
   (A) the agreements are illegal in all countries.
   (B) firms recognize an obligation to their customers to keep prices low.
   (C) competitors can easily enter the industry.
   (D) each firm has an incentive to cheat to increase its own profit.
   (E) the products are so similar that customers cannot distinguish the differences between them.

Questions 9–10 are based on the payoff matrix below.

Robert's Review Producing Strategy

Tom's Times Producing Strategy		Morning Paper	Evening Paper
	Morning Paper	$500, $500	$600, $400
	Evening Paper	$400, $600	$300, $300

The payoff matrix above shows the profits per day that can be earned by two firms producing local newspapers. The first number in each cell shows the profit for *Tom's Times*, and the second number shows the profit for *Robert's Review*.

9. If the two firms do not collude and each uses its best strategy to maximize profit,
   (A) the dominant strategy for *Tom's Times* is to produce a morning paper.
   (B) the dominant strategy for *Robert's Review* is to produce an evening paper.
   (C) each of the firms will earn $300 per day profit in the short run.
   (D) both firms would increase their profits by bringing a third newspaper into the industry.
   (E) if *Tom's Times* produces an evening paper, *Robert's Review* would reap more profit by producing an evening paper rather than a morning paper.

10.   If these two firms make a collusive agreement using their best strategies, then
          I.   each of the firms will earn $500 profit per day.
          II.   both of the firms are following their dominant strategies.
          III.   *Tom's Times* will produce a morning paper.
          IV.   *Robert's Review* will produce an evening paper.
    (A)   I only
    (B)   I and III only
    (C)   II and IV only
    (D)   I, II, and III only
    (E)   I, II, III, and IV

Free-Response Questions

1.   Assume Jenna's Toy Emporium is a retail toy store operating in a monopolistically competitive industry.

(a)   Assume Jenna's Toy Emporium is earning a short-run economic profit. Draw a correctly labeled graph showing each of the following:
          (i)   The profit-maximizing output and price
          (ii)   The area of profit

(b)   Now draw a new graph for Jenna's Toy Emporium maximizing profit in long-run equilibrium, and answer each of the following:
          (i)   Will the firm experience long-run economic profit? Explain.
          (ii)   Given your answer in (b)(i), how does the demand curve for the firm change in the long run? Explain.

(c)   Will the firm achieve productive efficiency in the long run? Explain.

2.   The payoff matrix below shows the profits per year that can be earned by two firms in an oligopolistic industry selling memberships to online political discussion forums. They must determine whether the forum will be strictly moderated or whether members will be free to say anything. Robbie and Dak cannot change that decision during the year due to contracts with the members. The first number in each cell shows Dak's profit; the second number is Robbie's profit.

Robbie's Moderating Strategy

Dak's		Moderators	No Moderators
Moderating	Moderators	$100, $200	$90, $300
Strategy	No Moderators	$80, $100	$60, $250

(a)   What kind of market structure is illustrated in this scenario? Explain.
(b)   Identify the dominant strategy for Dak. Explain.
(c)   If Dak chooses to run a forum with moderators, is a forum with or without moderators the best strategy for Robbie? Explain.
(d)   If both firms use their dominant strategies and do not collude, what is Robbie's annual profit?
(e)   If firms recognize they can increase their profits by collusive arrangements, why are firms in the United States reluctant to collude?

Multiple-Choice Explanations

1.   (B)   In monopolistic competition, products are differentiated.
2.   (B)   Because it must lower the price of all of its products, the marginal revenue earned from selling the next product will be lower than the price.
3.   (E)   A lump sum tax does not affect marginal cost, so output does not change.
4.   (A)   When new firms enter the monopolistically competitive industry, each firm produces a smaller portion of the industry output, so the demand curve for that firm shifts inward to the left.
5.   (C)   Because the firm reduces output to maximize profit, the firm produces less than its allocatively efficient output; excess capacity is available for the firm to produce more output, but it chooses not to do so.
6.   (E)   Mutual interdependence in oligopolies requires each firm to consider its rivals' reactions to pricing and output decisions. Monopolies have no rivals, and perfectly and monopolistically competitive firms are such a small part of the industry, their decisions do not affect other firms.
7.   (B)   Oligopolists produce at an output where the price is higher than the marginal cost of producing the output.
8.   (D)   Because each firm has an incentive to break the agreement in order to increase its own profit, collusive agreements are often unstable.
9.   (A)   The dominant strategy of *Tom's Times* is to produce a morning paper, because it will earn a higher profit from producing a morning paper, regardless of whether *Robert's Review* produces a morning paper or an evening paper.
10.   (D)   Both firms have a dominant strategy of producing a morning paper, because each earns a greater profit doing so than producing an evening paper, regardless of the other firm's decision.

Free-Response Explanations

1.   **11 points (4 + 5 + 2)**
(a)   4 points:
- 1 point is earned for a correctly labeled graph with a downward-sloping demand curve and marginal revenue lower than demand.
- 1 point is earned for showing output where MC = MR.
- 1 point is earned for showing price on the demand curve above where MC = MR.
- 1 point is earned for correctly illustrating the area of profit.

(b)   5 points:
- 1 point is earned for a correctly labeled graph of long-run equilibrium, with the ATC curve above demand, tangential to the demand curve at the price.
- 1 point is earned for stating that the firm will not earn long-run economic profit.
- 1 point is earned for explaining that profit draws firms into the industry.
- 1 point is earned for stating that the firm's demand curve will shift to the left.
- 1 point is earned for explaining that as firms enter the industry, each existing firm produces a smaller portion of the industry's total output.

(c)   2 points:
- 1 point is earned for stating that the firm will not achieve productive efficiency.
- 1 point is earned for explaining that because the firm restricts output in order to maximize profit, it produces where average total cost is higher than its minimum.

2.   **8 points** $(2 + 2 + 2 + 1 + 1)$
(a)   2 points:
- 1 point is earned for stating that this market structure is an oligopoly.
- 1 point is earned for explaining that the firms are mutually interdependent.

(b)   2 points:
- 1 point is earned for stating that Dak's dominant strategy is to have a moderated board.
- 1 point is earned for explaining that Dak's profit is higher when he chooses moderators compared to when he has no moderators, regardless of which option Robbie chooses.

(c)   2 points:
- 1 point is earned for stating that Robbie's best strategy is to have no moderators.
- 1 point is earned for explaining that when Dak chooses moderators, if Robbie chooses no moderators he will earn $300 profit, but if he chooses moderators, he will only earn $200 profit.

(d)   1 point:
- 1 point is earned for stating that Robbie's annual profit is $300.

(e)   1 point:
- 1 point is earned for explaining that collusion is illegal under United States law.

CHAPTER 12: THE DEMAND FOR RESOURCES

Introduction
In terms of the circular flow model, the focus of study thus far has been the product market, where households buy products from firms. This chapter begins a four-chapter study of the factor (resource) market, where firms buy the land, labor, capital, and entrepreneurial resources necessary to produce products. Chapter 12 explains the demand for resources, focusing specifically on the labor market. Principles from this chapter help to explain wage determination and markets for other productive resources. Material from Chapter 12 consistently appears in a few multiple-choice questions and frequently appears as a free-response question on the AP microeconomics exam.

The Perfectly Competitive Resource Market
An understanding of resource markets is important to understanding incomes, costs of production, the allocation of resources to produce goods, and public policy decisions. We begin our analysis with the assumption that the firm is producing in a perfectly competitive market and hires workers from a perfectly competitive labor market. Like the perfectly competitive product market, the individual firm in the perfectly competitive labor market is a wage-taker that must accept the wage set in the industry. The firm can hire as many workers as it needs without affecting the wage (price of workers). We also assume that all workers are equal in terms of ability, motivation, and productivity.

The Demand for Labor
Demand for labor is a derived demand, as the demand for labor is based on demand for labor's product. If a product gains popularity, the firm hires more workers; if consumer incomes fall, firms lay off workers. Due to this derived demand, the demand for labor depends on the productivity of the workers and the market value of the product. Highly productive resources and products with greater value increase the demand for resources.

Productivity is measured by the marginal product, the increase in total product resulting from hiring one more worker. According to the Law of Diminishing Returns, as more workers are hired to work with a fixed amount of other resources, output increases but at a diminishing rate. As each new worker is hired, he adds less and less to total product as specialization wears off and the workers begin to overwhelm the available capital.

But the demand for labor goes one step further, relying on the marginal revenue product for labor—the change in total revenue resulting from hiring one more worker. Marginal revenue product is the firm's demand for labor. The market demand curve for labor in an industry is the sum of all of the individual firms' demand curves.

$$\text{Marginal Revenue Product} = \frac{\text{Change in Total Revenue}}{\text{Change in the Number of Workers}}$$

Profit-Maximizing Labor Hiring
To determine how many workers to hire, the firm also needs to know the marginal resource cost, or the cost of hiring one more unit of labor.

	Change in Total Resource Cost
Marginal Resource Cost =	————————————————
	Change in the Number of Workers

The firm maximizes profit at the quantity of workers where the marginal revenue product from hiring the next worker equals the marginal resource cost of hiring the next worker. If the firm will earn more revenue from hiring the next worker than it will cost to hire that worker, the firm should hire the worker. But if the marginal resource cost is higher than the revenue the worker would bring to the firm, the firm should not hire that worker.

The MRP = MRC Rule: Firms ALWAYS maximize profit by hiring the number of workers where MRP = MRC.

Taking the EEK! Out of Economics

By this point, you should recognize important parallels between the perfectly competitive product market and the perfectly competitive resource market. They are very similar, with most principles transferring between the two markets. The primary difference between them is that the perfectly competitive product market is where consumers are buying finished products from firms, and the perfectly competitive resource market is where firms are buying resources from households in order to create those products.

Labor Hiring in a Perfectly Competitive Product Market

(1) Units of Resource	(2) Total Product (Output)	(3) Marginal Product (MP)	(4) Product Price	(5) Total Revenue, (2) × (4)	(6) Marginal Revenue Product (MRP)
0	0		$2	$ 0	
		7			$14
1	7		2	14	
		6			12
2	13		2	26	
		5			10
3	18		2	36	
		4			8
4	22		2	44	
		3			6
5	25		2	50	
		2			4
6	27		2	54	
		1			2
7	28		2	56	

The demand for labor: pure competition in the sale of the product

In this table, we can see the total product of all of the workers together, the marginal product (the increase in output from hiring one more worker), the total revenue (the total product times the product price), and the marginal revenue product (the increase in total revenue from hiring one more worker). Remember, the firm wants to hire workers where the marginal revenue product is greater than or equal to the marginal cost of the worker. So if the prevailing wage in the industry is $10, the firm would hire three workers. If the wage is $6, the firm will hire five workers. Just like the product market, in the labor market, the quantity of workers demanded increases as the price (wage) falls. What if the wage is $7? No MRP exactly matches. If the firm hires three workers, the MRC (wage) is less than the MRP (the income to the firm for hiring that worker), so the firm wants that worker. But with the fourth worker, MRC > MRP, so the firm should not hire that worker.

> **Bear in Mind**
> Given the total product and product price, you must be able to calculate the marginal product, total revenue, and marginal revenue product in a table. Given the wage, you will also be expected to calculate the number of workers the firm should hire to maximize profit. Questions requiring this specific skill have appeared consistently in both multiple-choice and free-response questions on the AP microeconomics exam.

Profit-Maximizing Hiring in an Imperfectly Competitive Product Market

(1) Units of Resource	(2) Total Product (Output)	(3) Marginal Product (MP)	(4) Product Price	(5) Total Revenue, (2) × (4)	(6) Marginal Revenue Product (MRP)
0	0		$2.80	$ 0	
1	7	7	2.60	18.20	$18.20
2	13	6	2.40	31.20	13.00
3	18	5	2.20	39.60	8.40
4	22	4	2.00	44.00	4.40
5	25	3	1.85	46.25	2.25
6	27	2	1.75	47.25	1.00
7	28	1	1.65	46.20	−1.05

The demand for labor: pure competition in the sale of the product

Labor hiring in an imperfectly competitive product market is very similar, though you'll notice one major difference in the table. In the perfectly competitive product market, the product price remains the same, regardless of how many products are sold, because the firm is a price-taker. In imperfectly competitive product markets (monopolistic competition, oligopoly, or monopoly), price-making firms must lower the price of all of their products in order to sell more. As a result, the price falls, causing the marginal revenue product to fall even more steeply. Therefore, the MRP curve for the firm selling in an imperfectly competitive product market falls for two reasons: diminishing returns and the need to lower prices in order to sell more products. As a result, the labor demand curve for a firm selling in an imperfectly competitive product market is less elastic than the labor demand for a firm selling in a perfectly competitive product market. This can be seen in the firm's decision to restrict output to sell products at a higher price; if the firm produces fewer products, it demands fewer workers to produce those products.

The imperfectly competitive firm also hires where the MRC = MRP. In this example, if the prevailing wage in the industry is $10, the firm would hire two workers. At a wage of $6, the firm would hire three workers. Notice that this imperfectly competitive firm hires fewer workers than the perfectly competitive firm in the previous example.

Determinants of Demand for Resources
The demand for labor relies on a number of factors. First, with derived demand, an increase in demand for the product increases demand for the labor to produce it, so labor demand shifts to the right. The reverse is true when product demand falls. Second, if labor becomes more productive, the demand for labor will increase. When workers can produce more products at a lower cost per unit, the firm has an incentive to increase production in order to gain additional profit. Productivity can be increased through a greater availability of other necessary resources, advances in technology, and increased health, education, and skills of the labor force. High

productivity of the workforce helps to explain why American workers' wages are higher than those in many other nations.

Changes in the price of substitute and complementary resources also affect the demand for labor. Substitute capital takes the place of a worker, such as a fast food restaurant machine that automatically dispenses drinks based on the computerized order. If the cost of the machine falls, the firm can produce at a lower cost, leading the firm to increase the quantity of machines and reduce its demand for workers. Complementary resources, on the other hand, are capital goods that are used together with labor. One ultrasound technician is necessary for each piece of ultrasound equipment. If the price of capital used as a complementary resource falls, the firm buys more capital and the demand for labor will actually rise, as the firm needs more workers to use the additional equipment.

Elasticity of Resource Demand
Elasticity of resource demand refers to the sensitivity of firms to changes in the price of resources; when the price of a resource falls, do firms respond? If the percentage change in the number of workers hired is greater than the percentage change in wage, demand for labor is elastic. If the percentage change in the number of workers hired is less than the percentage change in wage, demand for labor is inelastic. If the percentage change in the number of workers equals the percentage change in wage, labor demand is unit elastic.

One factor affecting resource elasticity is how easily one resource can be substituted for another. It may be relatively easy to find a machine to install headlights on an assembly line, but it is much more difficult to find a machine to provide the services of a physical therapist or financial analyst. A second factor affecting resource elasticity is the elasticity of product demand. The more elastic the demand for the product, the more elastic the demand for labor. If customers significantly reduce the quantity demanded for the product, the firm needs fewer workers to produce those products. Finally, the ratio of the resource cost to the total cost of production affects resource elasticity. If the cost of labor is a large proportion of the cost of production, the demand for labor is more elastic.

Bear in Mind
To determine effects of wages on labor hiring, most questions on the AP microeconomics exam assume labor is the only factor of production, in order to simplify the analysis.

The Least-Cost Rule
The least-cost rule illustrates when a firm is minimizing its costs at a specific output. When the last dollar spent on labor and the last dollar spent on capital both result in the same marginal product, the firm has reached least-cost production.

$$\frac{\text{Marginal Product of Labor}}{\text{Price of Labor}} = \frac{\text{Marginal Product of Capital}}{\text{Price of Capital}}$$

If the last worker hired has a marginal product of six at a price of $1, and the last unit of capital hired has a marginal product of four at a price of $1, the marginal products are not equal. The firm would be better off buying less capital and hiring more workers, because it gains more production for the same cost (which is the same as saying the firm produces the same amount at a lower total cost). The firm will continue to choose among labor or capital, shifting between resources to buy more of the resources that provide a higher marginal product and fewer of the resources that provide a lower marginal product until the marginal products are equal. Then the firm is producing at least cost.

The Profit-Maximizing Rule
While it is important for the firm to minimize costs, doing so will not necessarily maximize profit. As we know, the firm maximizes profit where MC = MR in the product market, and where MRC = MRP in the factor market. In order to maximize profit for the firm in all variable resources, we need to extend the MRC = MRP formula to all resources.

$$\frac{\text{MRP for Labor}}{\text{Price of Labor}} = \frac{\text{MRP for Capital}}{\text{Price of Capital}} = 1$$

The least-cost rule told us which combination of resources—labor or capital—reduced costs. The profit-maximizing rule tells us how many of each resource to buy to maximize profit. We should hire labor until the marginal revenue product equals the price (wage, or marginal resource cost). The numerator and denominator of the fraction should be equal. In the same way, the firm should continue to buy capital as long as the marginal revenue product (additional income the firm earns from products produced by the capital) equals the cost of buying the capital. The profit-maximizing rule includes the least-cost rule within the formula, so the firm maximizing profit is achieving least-cost production. A firm achieving least-cost production, though, may not be maximizing profit. If a firm sells its products for $1 apiece, and the MP for the last unit of labor is nine at a price of $3, and the MP for the last unit of capital is twelve at a price of $4, the firm has achieved least-cost production because both labor and capital produce a marginal product of three units per dollar of cost. However, the firm is not maximizing profit, because the marginal revenue product for each resource is higher than the price of the resource. The firm should continue to hire labor and capital until the MRP of each falls to the price of each.

Multiple-Choice Questions
1.   Which of the following situations illustrates the concept of derived demand?
      (A)   If the price of orange juice increases, the demand for apple juice increases.
      (B)   If demand for shoes increases, the demand for shoelaces increases.
      (C)   If the price of cars increases, the demand for gas decreases.
      (D)   If demand for taxi rides increases, the demand for taxi drivers increases.
      (E)   If the supply of hot dogs increases, the demand for hot dog buns increases.

2.   Each worker hired adds less to total output than the worker before, according to the
      (A)   Law of Demand.
      (B)   Law of Diminishing Returns.
      (C)   Law of Diminishing Marginal Utility.
      (D)   Least-Cost Rule.
      (E)   Principle of Derived Demand.

3.   Marginal revenue product measures the additional
      (A)   output produced from hiring one more worker.
      (B)   income to the firm from producing one more product.
      (C)   cost to the firm for producing one more product.
      (D)   wage required to hire one more worker.
      (E)   income to the firm from hiring one more worker.

4. In order to maximize profit, the firm should hire the number of workers where the
    (A) marginal cost equals the marginal revenue.
    (B) marginal revenue product equals the marginal cost.
    (C) wage equals the product price.
    (D) marginal resource cost equals the marginal revenue product.
    (E) marginal revenue equals the marginal resource cost.

Questions 5–6 refer to the table below, which shows the daily total product of a firm operating in perfectly competitive product and labor markets.

Number of Workers	Total Product
1	25
2	45
3	60
4	70
5	75

5. What is the marginal product of the third worker?
    (A) 15 products
    (B) 60 products
    (C) 35 products
    (D) 20 products
    (E) 30 products

6. If the firm sells its products for $10 each, and the wage the firm must pay workers is $100 per day, how many workers should the firm hire to maximize profit?
    (A) 1 worker
    (B) 2 workers
    (C) 3 workers
    (D) 4 workers
    (E) 5 workers

7. A firm selling products in a monopoly product market finds its marginal revenue product falling much more quickly than a firm selling in a perfectly competitive product market, because in addition to diminishing returns,
    (A) the government is required to regulate the price of the product.
    (B) the firm becomes inefficient by trying to sell too many units of output.
    (C) the firm must lower the price of all products in order to sell more units.
    (D) consumers prefer not to buy from monopolies, so demand falls.
    (E) workers tend to earn higher wages in monopoly product firms.

8. The demand for labor at Tyrone's auto repair shop would increase if
    (A) the cost of complementary capital significantly fell.
    (B) the cost of substitute capital significantly fell.
    (C) wages of auto repair workers significantly increased.
    (D) mild weather resulted in fewer car crashes this winter.
    (E) workers at the auto repair shop became less productive.

9. When the wage increases 5 percent, the quantity of workers hired falls 1 percent, indicating that labor demand is
    (A)   perfectly inelastic.
    (B)   relatively inelastic.
    (C)   unitary elastic.
    (D)   relatively elastic.
    (E)   perfectly elastic.

10. Mary's Noodles is a profit-maximizing firm that specializes in preparing frozen chicken and noodle dinners for sale at local grocery stores. Mary's staff has always prepared the noodles by hand, but recently, a noodle-making machine has been developed which would allow the company to replace some of its staff with the machine. The marginal product of the last worker hired is two pounds of noodles per hour, at a wage of $8. The marginal product of the noodle-making machine is eight pounds of noodles per hour, at a cost of $40. Which of the following statements is true?
    (A)   Mary's Noodles would be better off using labor rather than the machine, because the marginal product per dollar is lower for labor than for the machine.
    (B)   Mary's Noodles would be better off using the machine rather than labor, because the marginal product of the machine is four times as high as the marginal product of the last worker hired.
    (C)   Mary's Noodles has achieved least-cost production.
    (D)   Mary's Noodles maximizes its profit if it buys the machine.
    (E)   Mary's Noodles cannot achieve a profit given these production costs.

11. According to the profit-maximizing rule for hiring resources, the firm should hire labor and capital until the marginal revenue product for each equals the
    (A)   market price of the product.
    (B)   quantity of labor and capital hired.
    (C)   price ceiling for the product.
    (D)   profit per unit for each.
    (E)   marginal resource cost of each.

Free-Response Question
Assume a firm can hire all of the workers it wants at a wage of $60 per day, and the firm can sell all of its products at a price of $10. The firm's production schedule is below.

Number of Workers	Total Product
0	0
1	10
2	19
3	27
4	34
5	40
6	45
7	49

(a)   What kind of market structure does this firm sell its product in? Explain.
(b)   What kind of market structure does this firm hire its workers in? Explain.
(c)   Calculate the marginal revenue product of the fourth worker.

(d)   How many workers should this firm hire to maximize its profit? Explain.

(e)   If the wage fell to $55 per day, how many workers should this firm hire to maximize its profit? Explain.

Multiple-Choice Explanations

1.   (D)   Derived demand is the concept that if the demand for a product increases, the demand for workers to make that product will increase, as well.

2.   (B)   In diminishing returns, each additional worker adds to production, but specialization has worn off, and additional workers begin to overwhelm the fixed capital.

3.   (E)   The marginal revenue product is the marginal product added by one more worker multiplied by the price those additional products can be sold for in the product market.

4.   (D)   The firm maximizes profit where the additional cost to hire one more worker equals the revenue brought into the firm as a result of hiring that worker.

5.   (A)   Marginal product is the increase in total product as a result of hiring one more worker. The third worker increased production from 45 to 60 units, an increase of 15 products.

6.   (D)   The marginal product of the fourth worker is 10 units, which can each be sold for $10, so that worker's marginal revenue product is $100. If the wage is $100, the firm's profit-maximizing output of MRC = MRP is achieved with the fourth worker.

7.   (C)   Imperfectly competitive firms must lower their prices in order to sell more products, so the marginal revenue to the firm falls much more quickly than it does for perfectly competitive firms.

8.   (A)   Complementary capital is a resource that must be used in a fixed amount with a worker (in this case, a paint sprayer and a worker). If the price of the complementary capital falls, the marginal resource cost for the worker and capital together is lower, so that now the marginal revenue product is higher than or equal to that marginal resource cost, and the firm will hire the additional worker.

9.   (B)   When a change in wage causes a relatively smaller percentage change in the quantity of workers hired, demand is relatively inelastic. The firm is not very responsive to the change in wage.

10.   (A)   Least-cost production occurs where the marginal product per dollar of labor equals the marginal product per dollar of capital. In this case, the MP/$ of labor is 0.25 pounds of noodles, and the MP/$ of capital is 0.20 pounds of noodles. Because Mary's Noodles gets a greater marginal product for the cost from labor, the company should continue to use labor rather than the machine.

11.   (E)   The firm maximizes profit when both the labor and capital are hired until the marginal revenue product generated by hiring the next unit equals the marginal resource cost of hiring that unit.

Free-Response Explanation

9 points (2 + 2 + 1 + 2 + 2)

(a)   2 points:

- 1 point is earned for stating that the firm sells its product in a perfectly competitive market.
- 1 point is earned for explaining that the firm does not have to lower its price to sell more units, a characteristic that only occurs in perfectly competitive markets.

(b)   2 points:

- 1 point is earned for stating that the firm hires its workers in a perfectly competitive labor market.

- 1 point is earned for explaining that the firm hires all of its labor for the same wage and does not have to raise its wage to attract more workers.

(c)   1 point:
- 1 point is earned for stating that the marginal revenue product of the fourth worker is $70 (the marginal product of 7 units—the increase from 27 to 34—multiplied by the $10 product price).

(d)   2 points:
- 1 point is earned for stating that this firm should hire five workers.
- 1 point is earned for stating that the fifth worker's MRP = MRC.

(e)   2 points:
- 1 point is earned for stating that the firm still should hire five workers at the lower wage.
- 1 point is earned for explaining that the marginal revenue product of the sixth worker is only $50, so the wage would have to fall to $50 before the firm would hire the sixth worker.

CHAPTER 13: WAGE DETERMINATION

Introduction
The wages earned by workers have broad implications for the profitability of firms as well as the ability of those workers to buy consumer products. Chapter 13 identifies the means by which wages are determined in a variety of labor markets, the causes of wage differentials, and market imperfections. Material from Chapter 13 consistently appears in a few multiple-choice questions and often appears as a free-response question on the AP microeconomics exam. Questions about real and nominal wages, as well as investment in human capital, may also appear on the AP macroeconomics exam.

Labor and Wages
Labor refers to any human work, whether performed by factory workers, agricultural workers, service providers, or management. The wage is the payment firms make to workers for a period of time (per hour or week). Keep in mind that a wage is not only the paycheck the worker receives but includes any benefits such as insurance and vacation time.

An important distinction must be made between the nominal wage and the real wage. The nominal wage is the pay in current dollars—what the worker sees in his or her current paycheck. The real wage is how many goods and services the worker can afford to buy with that paycheck. This distinction is important because, as prices of products rise, the worker's paycheck will not stretch as far. If a worker's nominal wage rises 4 percent this year but prices rise 3 percent in that same time period, the worker's real wage has only risen 1 percent $(4 - 3 = 1)$. For the purposes of this analysis, we will use the real wage.

Real Wages and Productivity
Wages in the United States tend to be higher than those in many countries because of high worker productivity. Demand for labor is strong in advanced economies because large amounts of land, capital, and technology are available to workers and labor quality is high and specialized. In the long run, as productivity increases, real wages also rise.

The Perfectly Competitive Labor Market
In a perfectly competitive labor market, many firms compete to hire labor, and each worker is identical and independent. The market demand for labor consists of all of the demand curves (marginal revenue product curves) for all of the firms in the industry added horizontally. Thus, the demand for labor in the industry is downward-sloping.

Labor supply in the perfectly competitive labor market is represented by an upward-sloping supply curve. Every potential worker has the choice of using his or her time for work or leisure. When wages are low, potential workers see little opportunity cost involved in choosing leisure. But as wages rise, the opportunity cost of remaining idle rises, and more people are enticed to work for the wage. So at a lower wage, the quantity of labor supplied is low, and at a higher wage, the quantity of labor supplied rises. Keep in mind that workers are also free to move between firms and industries, so a higher wage may draw workers from another industry or from serving as a volunteer or homemaker.

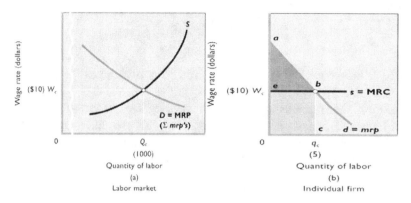

Labor supply and labor demand in (a) a purely competitive labor market and (b) a single competitive firm

The equilibrium wage and quantity of workers hired are found at the point where supply equals the demand for labor. The wage set in the industry then translates to a perfectly elastic (horizontal) supply curve (the marginal resource cost) for the individual firm. The firm is a wage taker, because it must accept the wage set in the industry and it does not change, regardless of how many workers the firm hires. The individual firm maximizes profit (or minimizes loss) at the quantity of labor where the marginal revenue product (the firm's demand curve) equals the marginal resource cost (the firm's supply curve). This is the same MRP = MRC rule we saw in the last chapter and is very similar to the MR = MC rule the perfectly competitive firm uses to determine profit-maximizing output.

Changes in Labor Demand
Because the demand for labor is the workers' marginal revenue product, the demand for labor can change due to a change in the productivity of the workers (marginal product) or a change in the price of the product. If workers become more productive due to better training or improved technology, or if the firm can increase the price of the product it sells, the MRP curve shifts to the right and the firm hires more workers. Because the MRC curve is horizontal, the wage does not change.

It is very important to note that it makes a difference whether the increased labor demand occurs throughout the industry or just for one firm. If one firm can achieve the increased productivity, only that firm will increase its labor demand (shown in the individual firm's graph), but because the firm is such a small part of the industry, it has no effect on the industry graph. However, if the increased MRP occurs throughout the industry, it is shown by increasing the demand for labor in the individual firm as well as the demand in the industry. The increase in industry demand has a second effect, though—with a higher demand for labor, the wage rises, pushing the MRC (wage) for the firm up. The firm will then hire at the point where MRP = MRC at the new equilibrium.

Changes in the wage also affect the firm's decision to hire workers. If the industry wage increases, the MRC shifts upward for the firm, causing the firm to reduce the number of workers it hires in order to maximize profit where MRP = MRC.

Monopsony

A monopsony is a market in which only one firm hires labor. For example, if a coal mine is the only employer in an area, workers only have the option of working for this employer or not working at all, usually because of geographic immobility or limited skills. The firm is a wage maker, as the firm's wage varies with the quantity of workers hired.

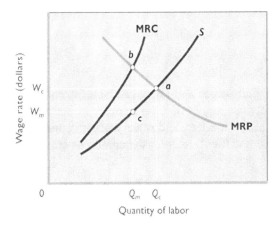

The wage rate and level of employment in a monopsonistic labor market

The monopsony, like a perfectly competitive labor market, has an upward-sloping supply curve, representing the wage. To hire more workers, the firm must raise the wage. The marginal resource cost is higher than the wage, because the firm cannot offer the higher wage only to the next worker hired; it must also raise wages of all of the other workers in order to prevent worker frustration. So if the firm employs four workers at a wage of $10, and it must pay a wage of $11 to hire the fifth worker, the marginal resource cost is actually $15, because the firm must also pay the previous four workers the extra $1 in wage.

The monopolist, like the perfect competitor, maximizes profit at the quantity of workers where MRP = MRC. However, it will only pay the wage on the supply curve at that quantity, because workers are willing to accept that wage. The monopsonist maximizes its profit by hiring fewer workers and paying a lower wage than would occur in the perfectly competitive labor market.

Taking the EEK! Out of Economics
By now, you should recognize parallels between the monopoly selling in the product market and the monopsony hiring in the labor market. The monopsony graph looks like a flipped-over monopoly graph. In both cases, the firm has the market power to restrict its output or hiring in order to raise prices or lower wages. In both cases, society receives fewer products than it would under perfectly competitive conditions. Further, in the case of the monopoly, consumers must pay higher prices, and in the case of the monopsony, workers earn lower wages, than would occur under perfectly competitive conditions.

Labor Unions

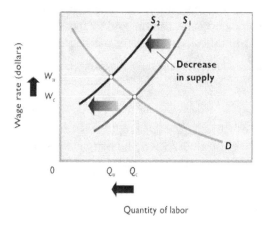

Exclusive or craft unionism

Labor unions use bargaining power to negotiate for higher wages and improved benefits and working conditions. An exclusive (craft) union restricts the supply of labor in order to increase the wage. Doctors, teachers, cosmetologists, electricians, plumbers, and other workers must meet occupational licensing or other requirements that make it difficult to enter the career, so supply is restricted in order to ensure workers higher wages.

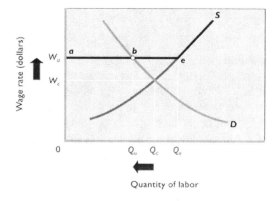

Inclusive or industrial unionism

An inclusive (industrial) union includes all workers in an industry, such as auto and steel workers. Rather than trying to exclude others from entering the industry, inclusive unions use the power of numbers to collectively bargain with management for higher wages. The higher wage (marginal resource cost) must be paid to all workers, and the firm hires where MRC = MRP (demand). At that wage, the quantity of workers supplied is greater than the quantity demanded, resulting in unemployment. Therefore, union members have an incentive to increase demand for their product: to increase the demand for workers and reduce the unemployment associated with the higher wage.

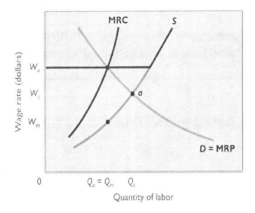

Bilateral monopoly in the labor market

A bilateral monopoly combines a monopsony (a single buyer of labor) with an inclusive labor union (a single seller of labor). An example would be a coal mine that is the only employer in an area combined with workers who are all members of the United Mine Workers union. The firm will hire the quantity of workers where MRC = MRP. But where will the wage be set? The firm wants to set the wage down on the supply curve, but the union wants to set the wage up where MRC = MRP. The final wage will depend on the relative strength of labor and management and will fall somewhere between those two wages.

The Minimum Wage

The federal government and many states set a minimum wage. An effective minimum wage creates a wage floor above the equilibrium wage. The model looks the same as the inclusive union model. If the minimum wage is below or equal to the equilibrium wage, it guarantees workers a minimum income and does not result in unemployment. But if the minimum wage is above the equilibrium wage, unemployment could result.

Wage Differentials

Differences among workers' wages largely result from the effects of supply and demand. Workers in industries with high labor demand or low supply are likely to earn higher wages than workers in industries with low labor demand or high supply. Workers with a high marginal revenue product, such as entertainers and professional athletes, tend to be paid a higher wage than workers with a lower marginal revenue product. Workers who have invested in their human capital (knowledge and skills) through education and training, as well as those with greater ability, are likely to command higher wages. Workers in more difficult, dangerous, and unpleasant jobs also tend to earn higher wages to compensate for the less desirable aspects of the job.

Beyond differences in marginal revenue product, human capital, and compensation for undesirable work, market imperfections also contribute to wage differences. Workers may not have the information that other firms are paying higher wages. Workers may be tied to communities for family reasons and be unwilling or unable to relocate. Unions and government licensing may restrict movement into a different career. Discrimination based on gender, race, age, and disability still result in wage differences that cannot be reasonably explained in other ways. In addition, the models do not take into account salaries of workers paid by the year regardless of daily output or commissions and bonuses that are awarded to employees based on productivity or other factors.

Multiple Choice Questions

1. If Melissa's nominal wage increases 2% this year, and the prices of products she buys increase 3%, Melissa's real wage this year
    (A) increased by 5%.
    (B) increased by 1%.
    (C) increased by 2%.
    (D) decreased by 1%.
    (E) decreased by 5%.

2. The firm's demand curve for labor is its marginal
    (A) resource cost curve.
    (B) cost curve.
    (C) revenue curve.
    (D) product curve.
    (E) revenue product curve.

3. The supply curve for labor represents the worker's choice between
    (A) work and leisure.
    (B) buying American-made products or imports.
    (C) public and private goods.
    (D) wages and benefits.
    (E) real wages and nominal wages.

4. In a perfectly competitive labor market, which is true?
    I.   Firms are wage-takers.
    II. Workers are assumed to have identical skills.
    III. The demand curve for labor is downward-sloping.
    (A) I only
    (B) III only
    (C) I and II only
    (D) II and III only
    (E) I, II, and III

5. Labor is the only resource required for a firm selling its product in a perfectly competitive product market. The marginal revenue product of the next worker is $15 per hour, and the wage of that worker is $13.
    I.   The firm should not hire the worker.
    II. Hiring the worker would increase the firm's profit by $2.
    III. The firm must lower the price to sell that worker's output.
    (A) II only
    (B) III only
    (C) I and III only
    (D) II and III only
    (E) I, II, and III

6. Which of the following would cause the wage for boat makers to decrease?
   (A) The workers' productivity increases.
   (B) The price of boats made by the workers decreases.
   (C) Consumer incomes increase and boats are a normal good.
   (D) The demand for boats increases.
   (E) New technology helps boat makers produce more quickly.

7. If the government sets stricter licensing requirements for electricians, we would expect all of the following to occur in the labor market for electricians EXCEPT for the
   (A) wages of electricians to increase.
   (B) number of people working as electricians to decrease.
   (C) demand for electricians to increase.
   (D) quantity demanded of electricians to fall.
   (E) supply of licensed electricians to fall.

8. An effective minimum wage
   (A) creates a wage ceiling for labor.
   (B) is lower than the equilibrium price for labor.
   (C) results in unemployment.
   (D) increases the quantity of labor demanded.
   (E) reduces the quantity of labor supplied.

Free-Response Questions
1. Maheen's Bakery is a perfectly competitive firm that hires unskilled workers in a perfectly competitive labor market.
(a) Using correctly labeled side-by-side graphs of the labor market for the bakery industry and the labor market for Maheen's Bakery, show each of the following.
   (i) the equilibrium wage in the industry
   (ii) the wage Maheen pays her workers
   (iii) the quantity of workers Maheen hires
(b) Explain how Maheen should determine the profit-maximizing number of workers.
(c) Now assume Maheen discovers a new baking technique that significantly increases the productivity of her workers, but she does not share this information with other firms in the baking industry. Explain the effect on the following.
   (i) the quantity of workers hired by Maheen
   (ii) the wage Maheen pays her workers

2. Susan's Taxi Service operates in a perfectly competitive market and hires drivers in a perfectly competitive labor market. The industry wage for taxi drivers is $8 per hour.
(a) Draw correctly labeled side-by-side labor market graphs for the taxi industry and for Susan's Taxi Service. Show each of the following.
   (i) the equilibrium wage and quantity of drivers hired in the industry
   (ii) the wage paid by Susan's Taxi Service
   (iii) the quantity of drivers hired by Susan's Taxi Service
(b) Now assume the state imposes a minimum wage of $10 per hour.
   (i) What condition will this effective minimum wage create in the industry?
   (ii) What will happen to the wage Susan pays her taxi drivers? Explain.
   (iii) What will happen to the quantity of drivers Susan hires? Explain.

Multiple-Choice Explanations

1.	(D)	The nominal wage increase (2%) minus the inflation increase (3%) leaves a –1% real wage increase.

2.	(E)	The marginal revenue product curve is the firm's income earned from hiring one more worker and represents all of the points where the firm will hire labor, depending on the marginal resource cost.

3.	(A)	At a low wage, people tend to prefer leisure. But at higher wages, the opportunity cost for leisure increases and people prefer to work.

4.	(E)	The firm must accept the wage set in the industry and cannot affect it. Workers are assumed to be interchangeable, and the demand for workers is downward-sloping along the marginal revenue product curve

5.	(A)	Because the MRP > MRC, the firm should hire the worker. The MRP is $2 higher than the MRC, so the firm's profit would increase $2 by hiring that worker. And because the firm is selling in a perfectly competitive product market, it can sell as many products as it can make at the same price.

6.	(B)	A decrease in the product price reduces the marginal revenue product, shifting the industry demand for workers to the left, which lowers the wage.

7.	(C)	Licensing restrictions increase the cost of becoming an electrician, so the supply falls, raising the wage and reducing the quantity demanded.

8.	(C)	Because an effective minimum wage creates a wage floor above the equilibrium wage, the higher quantity of labor supplied and lower quantity of labor demanded combine to create unemployment at the new wage.

Free-Response Explanations

1.	**8 points** (5 + 1 + 2)

(a)	5 points:
  - 1 point is earned for a correctly labeled industry graph with a downward-sloping demand and upward-sloping supply of labor.
  - 1 point is earned for correctly indicating the equilibrium wage in the industry.
  - 1 point is earned for a correctly labeled graph of Maheen's labor market with a horizontal MRC curve at the industry wage and a downward-sloping MRP curve.
  - 1 point is earned for indicating the wage in Maheen's labor market.
  - 1 point is earned for indicating the quantity of workers hired where MRP = MRC.

(b)	1 point:
  - 1 point is earned for stating that the profit-maximizing quantity of workers is found where MRP = MRC (or the wage).

(c)	2 points:
  - 1 point is earned for stating that Maheen will increase the number of workers.
  - 1 point is earned for stating that the wage Maheen pays workers will not change.

2.	**8 points** (3 + 5)

(a)	3 points:
  - 1 point is earned for showing the equilibrium wage at $8 and quantity in the industry.
  - 1 point is earned for correctly linking the industry wage to the wage for the firm.
  - 1 point is earned for indicating the quantity of workers hired at MRC = MRP.

(b)	5 points:
  - 1 point is earned for stating that the minimum wage will create unemployment.
  - 1 point is earned for stating that the wage Susan pays will increase to $10.

- 1 point is earned for explaining that Susan must accept the wage set in the industry (or that she must follow the law).
- 1 point is earned for stating that Susan will hire fewer drivers.
- 1 point is earned for explaining that the increase in the MRC causes the curve to cross the MRP at a lower quantity of workers.

CHAPTER 14: RENT, INTEREST, AND PROFIT

Introduction
Labor resources account for about 70 percent of the national income paid to resource providers, so they receive the focus of attention in resource markets. We now turn to the other resources and the returns that are paid for their use. Chapter 14 discusses land, capital, and entrepreneurial resources and the rent, interest, and profit that accrue to them. Material from Chapter 14 appears in a question or two on the multiple-choice portion of the AP microeconomics exam. A question or two about the loanable funds market, the effects of changes in interest rates, and the distribution of national income also appears on both the multiple-choice and free-response portions of the AP macroeconomics exam.

Distribution of Income
Wages paid for labor services constituted 71 percent of all national income in the United States in 2007. Corporate profits and proprietors' income comprise 23 percent of national income, while interest is 5 percent and rents are 1 percent of national income. The distribution of income has important implications for entrepreneurship, investment in economic growth, and the ability of consumers to buy products and save money for further investment.

Land and Economic Rent

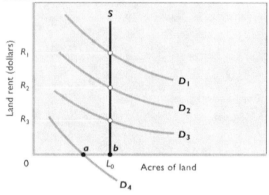

The determination of land rent

We begin our analysis of land with the assumptions that land is fixed in supply, has only one use at a time, is all equal in quality, and is sold in a competitive market with many buyers and sellers who cannot individually affect the price. These assumptions don't completely reflect reality, but remember the smiley (☺)? The distinguishing feature of the land market is that supply is perfectly inelastic. The quantity of land cannot be increased in response to a higher price. Demand (the marginal revenue product for land) is downward-sloping because of diminishing returns and because, as more products produced by the land are sold, the price of those products falls.

Economic rent is the price paid for the use of land (or any other natural resource) that is fixed in supply. This rent is considered a surplus payment, because the same amount of land is available, whether or not anyone is willing to buy it. Because supply is fixed, the economic rent for land is based on the demand for it. The price of goods produced with the land, the productivity of the land, and the costs of other resources (primarily capital) used with the land can all affect the demand for land.

In reality, productivity differs markedly among properties, which explains why farmland in Indiana sells for a much higher price than open land in Wyoming. Greater demand for the land pushes up the price (rent). In addition, land can be used for multiple purposes at once. Farmers can place windmills to produce electricity on farmland or drill for oil or natural gas while still farming the land above the fuel. Such differences in the productivity of the land account for much of the price differential in land.

Capital and Interest

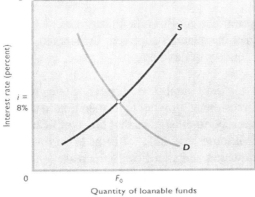

The market for loanable funds

Interest is the price paid for use of borrowed money. Money is not a resource; it is only a means one can use to buy the resources (land, labor, capital, and entrepreneurial ability) necessary to produce goods and services. Interest serves as an incentive for people to forego the present use of money in order to have even more money in the future.

In the loanable funds market, the supply of loanable funds comes from households who have saved money and are willing to loan it to others, often through banks. When interest rates are low, people incur little opportunity cost for holding money in cash, so they have little incentive to put savings in a bank. But as interest rates rise, people are more willing to save and loan that money to others. Therefore, the supply curve for loanable funds is upward-sloping. Because many people save for large purchases, retirement, or economic security regardless of interest rates, the supply curve may be fairly inelastic (vertical).

The demand for loanable funds comes from a number of sources. Consumers borrow to buy houses, cars, and college education. The federal government borrows to finance the national debt. Firms borrow to buy capital, expand factories, and start entirely new businesses. They will only invest if the return on their investment (increased profit) is greater than the interest rate charged for the loan. As a result, at low interest rates, firms are more willing to borrow, and at higher interest rates, firms are less willing to borrow. Therefore, the demand for loanable funds is a downward-sloping curve.

The supply of loanable funds increases if consumers have an incentive to save more, such as a tax break for interest on savings or a concern about rising college costs for kids leading parents to increase their savings to pay those future tuition costs. The supply of loanable funds can decrease if significant numbers of savers lose jobs or real income and households have to dip into their savings for current consumption. In addition to private market actions, the Federal Reserve, the central bank of the United States, can increase or reduce the supply of loanable funds available through banks as a means of stabilizing the economy. An increase in the supply of loanable funds lowers interest rates; a decrease in the supply of loanable funds increases interest rates.

The demand for loanable funds increases if firms find that the productivity of new equipment or increased consumer demand pushing up the product price would result in an increased return on the investment. Conversely, lower productivity or product prices would lead firms to decrease their demand for loanable funds. An increase in the demand for loanable funds increases interest rates; a decrease in demand lowers interest rates.

If the government imposes a ceiling on interest rates below the equilibrium interest rate, the quantity of loanable funds demanded will be greater than the quantity supplied. As a result, though interest rates are lower, a shortage of loanable funds will develop.

Changes in interest rates have implications far beyond the individual firm. If interest rates rise significantly, firms will be less willing to borrow for investment, slowing total spending in the economy and potentially leading to a recession. Conversely, interest rates that fall significantly can create inflation. Further, lower interest rates make it more profitable for firms to borrow to finance research and development, which can spur innovation and significantly increase long-run economic growth. High interest rates can deter that investment or restrict it to only those projects most likely to see a high return on investment.

It is important to make the distinction between nominal and real interest rates in the same way we distinguished nominal and real incomes. The nominal interest rate is the rate expressed in the current value of dollars. The real interest rate is the rate expressed in the purchasing power of dollars—in the value of interest adjusted for expected inflation. When a bank makes a loan, it knows the money repaid by the borrower will be worth less because of inflation. In order to recover the full value of the money loaned, the bank charges the real interest rate plus the expected inflation rate, which equals the nominal interest rate that the borrower sees. So if the bank requires a 4 percent real interest rate and expects 3 percent inflation, it charges the customer 7 percent interest. Because the firm understands it will be repaying the loan with those lower-value dollars, it focuses on the real interest rate in making investment decisions.

Nominal Interest Rate = Real Interest Rate + Expected Inflation Rate

Real Inflation Rate = Nominal Interest Rate – Expected Inflation Rate

Entrepreneurs and Economic Profit
The entrepreneur plays a unique role as a resource for the firm by inventing or innovating or taking a risk and combining the resources necessary to start a business. Normal profit is the minimum payment necessary to keep the entrepreneur in his or her current position. Remember the distinctions we made between accounting, normal, and economic profit when we examined the firm's costs of production? The accounting profit is all of the firm's revenue beyond its explicit costs. But economic profit is the firm's revenue beyond all explicit and implicit costs—which include normal profit.

While we have examined the role of profits in drawing firms into competitive industries, in reality, profits are not stable. Changes in product demand, technology, innovation, resource costs, and government policies all affect the level of profit (if any) for the firm. Monopolies are better able to sustain profits despite these changes because they have the market power to restrict output and raise prices in order to maximize profit under a variety of market conditions.

Profit plays an important role in our market economy. It serves as an incentive for new firms to enter an industry, expanding production and employment and providing more of the products consumers want, while drawing resources away from industries producing products consumers want less. In competitive markets, the entry of new firms can lower prices for consumers. It also spurs firms to invest in research and development, with innovation creating new products and more efficient methods of production, which further improves economic growth.

Multiple-Choice Questions
1. Most of the national income of the United States is in the form of
    (A)   corporate profit.
    (B)   proprietors' income.
    (C)   interest.
    (D)   rent.
    (E)   wages.

2. Because of the unique properties of land as a resource, the price of land is based primarily on
    (A)   the property tax rate.
    (B)   the quantity of land available.
    (C)   government price ceilings on land.
    (D)   the demand for land.
    (E)   a price floor to protect landowners.

3. The supply of loanable funds represents household decisions about
    (A)   saving or consuming.
    (B)   work or leisure.
    (C)   buying imports or domestically-produced goods.
    (D)   buying normal or inferior goods.
    (E)   buying public or private goods.

4. If firms receive a government subsidy for capital investment, what would be the effect in the loanable funds market?

	Loanable Funds	*Real Interest Rate*
(A)	Supply increases	Decreases
(B)	Supply decreases	Decreases
(C)	Demand increases	Increases
(D)	Demand decreases	Decreases
(E)	Supply decreases	Increases

5. An increase in the supply of funds to the loanable funds market
    (A)   increases the real interest rate.
    (B)   occurs when households save less money.
    (C)   results in economic growth.
    (D)   is caused by an increase in government deficits.
    (E)   reduces the profit of firms demanding funds in the market.

6.   When the federal government finances deficits by borrowing from the loanable funds market, which of the following effects occurs?
            I.   The demand for loanable funds increases.
            II.   The supply of loanable funds increases.
            III.   The real interest rate increases.
        (A)   II only
        (B)   III only
        (C)   I and II only
        (D)   I and III only
        (E)   I, II, and III

7.   If the nominal interest rate is 7% based on the expectation of a 4% inflation rate, what is the real interest rate?
        (A)   –4%
        (B)   3%
        (C)   –3%
        (D)   7%
        (E)   11%

8.   In our market economy, profit serves all of the following functions EXCEPT to
        (A)   reward entrepreneurs for taking the risk to start a business.
        (B)   draw firms into competitive industries that achieve short-term profit.
        (C)   redirect resources to their most highly valued use.
        (D)   encourage invention and innovation.
        (E)   allow firms to enter monopoly markets to reduce product prices.

Free-Response Question
Assume the loanable funds market is in equilibrium and the government institutes a tax incentive for households to increase their saving.
(a)   Using a correctly labeled loanable funds market graph, show each of the following effects of the tax incentive:
            (i)   The real interest rate
            (ii)   The quantity of funds available for loans
(b)   How will the change in interest rate you identified in (a)(i) affect firms' investment in plant and equipment? Explain.
(c)   How will the change in investment you identified in (b) affect long-run economic growth? Explain.
(d)   Illustrate the change you identified in (c) on a production possibilities curve.

Multiple-Choice Explanations
1.   (E)   Wages account for approximately 70 percent of national income in the United States.
2.   (D)   The supply of land is perfectly inelastic, and the quantity cannot change in response to a higher price; therefore, changes in the demand for land cause the price to increase or decrease.
3.   (A)   Households supply funds to the loanable funds market through saving. If households consume more of their income, they have less available for saving, and the supply of funds in the loanable funds market falls.
4.   (C)   If the subsidy reduces the cost of capital for the firm, the firm expects a higher percentage return on that now less-expensive investment, so the firm increases its

Chapter 14: Rent, Interest, and Profit

demand for loanable funds to purchase the capital. The increase in demand causes the interest rate to rise.

5.   (C)   When the supply of funds increases, real interest rates fall, enticing firms to increase investment in plant and equipment, which increases long-run economic growth.

6.   (D)   The government's demand for loanable funds increases, causing the real interest rate to increase. This activity does not cause the supply curve for loanable funds to shift, although the higher interest rate will entice some households to save more, which will supply more funds to the loanable funds market. But remember that this is only a response to the change in price (interest rate), so the household is actually moving along the supply curve for loanable funds, an increase in quantity supplied, not an increase in supply.

7.   (B)   The nominal interest rate equals the real interest rate plus expected inflation. In this case: 7% = 3% + 4%.

8.   (E)   Monopolies enjoy long-run economic profit because the barriers to entry prevent other firms from entering the industry, which would reduce profits or prices.

Free-Response Explanation

9 points (4 + 2 + 2 + 1)

(a)   4 points:
- 1 point is earned for a correctly labeled loanable funds market graph.
- 1 point is earned for showing a rightward shift in the supply of loanable funds.
- 1 point is earned for showing a decreasing interest rate.
- 1 point is earned for showing an increase in the quantity of loanable funds.

(b)   2 points:
- 1 point is earned for stating that firms' investment in plant and equipment increases.
- 1 point is earned for explaining that at the lower interest rate, firms are more likely to see a profitable return on investment compared to the cost of the loan.

(c)   2 points:
- 1 point is earned for stating that firms' increased investment will increase long-run economic growth.
- 1 point is earned for explaining that increased investment can improve efficiency and the firm's ability to produce even more in the future.

(d)   1 point:
- 1 point is earned for illustrating an outward shift of the production possibilities curve.

CHAPTER 15: NATURAL RESOURCES AND ENERGY ECONOMICS

Introduction

The information in Chapter 15, while important, is not directly tested on the AP economics exams. The important applications to concepts that may be tested are highlighted below.

- Scarcity exists in every society because the resources needed to produce goods and services are scarce.

- The world demand for resources has grown because the world population has increased and people have increased their consumption per person.

- The increase in the supply of resources has grown even more quickly than the demand for them, causing a decrease in the price of commodities. When both supply and demand increase, quantity definitely increases, but the effect on price depends on whether the change in supply or demand is stronger. In this case, the increase in supply has been stronger, so prices have fallen.

- Increases in productivity and technology allow societies to produce more goods and services from the same number of resources.

- This increased efficiency can also reduce costs of production for firms, leading to lower product prices and higher standards of living for consumers.

- While some forms of energy, such as shale oil and corn-based ethanol, may cost more to produce than the revenue they can be sold for when prices are low, an increase in the price of the product can make it profitable for the firm to produce.

- Energy sources can create negative externalities, transferring part of the costs of production to others so the full costs are not included in the price of the product. Government can play a role in correcting such market imperfections by forcing the firms to reabsorb those production costs and encouraging firms to produce the socially optimal output.

- Inflation reduces the future value of dollars. When decision makers are considering the costs and benefits of current and future decisions, they must consider that the purchasing power of the dollar in the future will be less than it is today because of inflation.

- Governments can create incentives for firms and other resource users to change their production and resource use patterns through clear and enforceable property rights or transferrable quotas and permits.

CHAPTER 16: PUBLIC GOODS AND EXTERNALITIES

Introduction
Markets are central to our form of economy, distributing resources and products to their most highly valued uses. In some circumstances, though, the market fails. Chapter 16 discusses the role of government intervention in firms and industries experiencing market failures of public goods and externalities. The actions of government can help to move markets toward greater efficiency, illustrating the importance of government in our mixed-market economy. Material from Chapter 16 is found in a few multiple-choice questions and very frequently appears as a free-response question on the AP microeconomics exam.

Private and Public Goods
Private goods, which constitute most goods in our economy, exhibit the characteristics of rival consumption and excludability. With rival consumption, once a person consumes a product, no one else can consume the same product. Excludability makes it easy for the firm to prevent those who do not pay from receiving the product. Supply and demand determine the price and quantity sold, and equilibrium exists without shortage or surplus.

Public goods, though, are non-rival. One person's consumption does not prevent another person's consumption of the same product. While you and your friend could not both eat the same slice of pizza, you can both share the same national defense or roadway. Public goods also have the characteristic of non-excludability—it is difficult or impossible to prevent those who did not pay from receiving the good. While it is easy enough for the restaurant to prevent you from receiving a pizza you didn't pay for, it's much more difficult to prevent you from receiving national defense or stop you from using the roads. These two characteristics create a free-rider problem for public goods. Once a public good is provided, it is nearly impossible to keep non-payers from getting it. Knowing this, consumers will prefer to use the product without paying for it—riding along for free. As a result, firms cannot profit from producing and selling the product and will choose not to produce it, even though a clear demand exists in society. The market has failed.

The Role of Government in Providing Public Goods

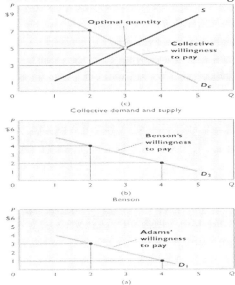

The optimal amount of a public good

Demand for a public good is calculated a little differently from the way market demand is calculated for private goods. For private goods, we horizontally add the demands of all consumers to determine total demand at each price. For public goods, we must determine how much consumers would be willing to pay for each additional unit of a public good, and then vertically add all of those values to determine what everyone together would be willing to pay for each unit of the public good. This curve is the demand for the public good, or the marginal benefit citizens expect to gain from the public good.

Supply of a public good is government's marginal cost of producing each additional unit. As the government adds workers to a fixed amount of capital, diminishing returns occur and marginal cost increases. The optimal quantity of the public good is where marginal benefit (demand) equals marginal cost (supply). With cost-benefit analysis, government provides public goods as long as the marginal benefit of providing the next unit is greater than or equal to the marginal cost of producing that unit of the public good. The optimal quantity of the public good is where marginal benefit equals marginal cost of the last unit.

Externalities

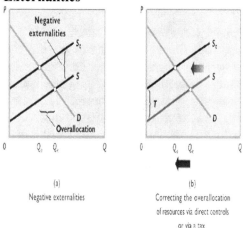

(a)
Negative externalities

(b)
Correcting the overallocation
of resources via direct controls
or via a tax

Correcting for negative externalities

Externalities are spill-over costs or benefits to people who are not involved in the market transaction. With a negative externality such as pollution, a firm passes some of its costs onto society. Therefore, the firm's marginal cost (S) is lower than society's marginal cost (S_t). This distortion causes the firm to over-allocate resources, producing more products and selling them for a lower price than is socially optimal. Governments can resolve the market failure by placing a control on the externality, preventing the firm from imposing the externality and forcing the firm to absorb the full cost of production, so the supply curve shifts back to S_t. A second option is for government to place a tax (amount T) on the product, shifting the firm's supply back to the marginal social cost (S_t). Both options reduce the quantity and raise the price, restoring efficiency. A third potential solution is to create a market for externality rights, allowing firms to buy the right to pollute and sell that right to other firms, as an incentive to reduce pollution and achieve efficiency.

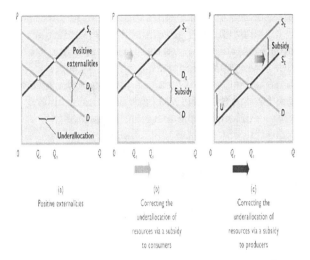

(a)
Positive externalities

(b)
Correcting the
underallocation of
resources via a subsidy
to consumers

(c)
Correcting the
underallocation of
resources via a subsidy
to producers

Correcting for positive externalities

A positive externality, like a vaccination, brings benefits to people who did not purchase the product. Because consumers do not consider all of the benefits of the purchase, the marginal social benefit (D_t) is higher than marginal individual benefit (D). As a result, society under-allocates resources, producing fewer products than is socially optimal. For positive externalities, government has three solutions. First, it can grant subsidies to buyers, increasing their marginal individual benefit (D) to meet marginal social benefit (D_t). Second, government could instead provide subsidies to producers, lowering their cost of production from S_t to S_i. Both solutions correct the under-allocation of resources to production, but the subsidy to consumers does so through demand, while the subsidy to producers does so through supply. A third solution, if the positive externalities are extremely large, is for the government to simply provide the product as a public good.

Clearly defined and enforced property rights can also help to resolve externalities. If firms produce negative externalities that harm property owners, those property owners can sue to protect the value of their properties. In other cases, negotiation between those creating externalities and those affected by those externalities can result in a resolution.

Optimal Externality Reduction

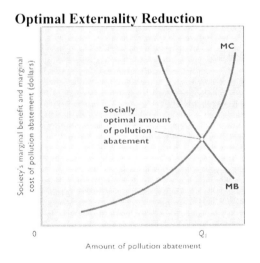

Society's optimal amount of pollution abatement

Although we want to limit negative externalities and support production in the case of positive externalities, as a society we must determine the optimal amount of government intervention in the market. To reduce pollution or subsidize vaccinations, society must use resources that could have been used for other purposes, so every decision involves an opportunity cost. As society performs more clean up, the marginal cost of each additional unit of clean up increases because of diminishing returns. At the same time, the marginal benefit to society of each additional unit of clean up falls because of diminishing marginal utility. As long as the marginal benefit of the clean up is greater than the marginal cost, society should continue to reduce the effects of the externality. The socially optimal amount of externality reduction occurs where the marginal benefit equals the marginal cost of the policy. In reality, determining these costs and benefits is very difficult, so policy decisions are subject to a great deal of debate.

Bear in Mind
Asymmetry of information creates another market failure that requires government intervention for the benefit of consumers, workers, and firms. Because this information is not covered on the AP economics exams, it will not be covered in this text.

Multiple-Choice Questions
1. Public goods have all of the following characteristics EXCEPT
    (A) a free-rider problem develops with public goods.
    (B) those who do not pay cannot be excluded from consuming the good.
    (C) firms find public goods profitable to produce because people value them.
    (D) one person's consumption does not affect another person's consumption.
    (E) tax dollars are used for the provision of public goods.

2. An example of a public good is
    (A) a sailboat.
    (B) a restaurant.
    (C) a doctor's office.
    (D) a road.
    (E) an airplane.

3. If the marginal social cost for a public good increases,
    (A) the marginal social benefit will increase, as well.
    (B) more of the public good will be provided.
    (C) less of the public good will be provided.
    (D) the government can afford more public goods.
    (E) demand for the public good increases.

4. Which of the following is an example of a negative externality?
    (A) a truck dumping trash in a legal landfill
    (B) a college student listening to music through his headphones
    (C) spoiled milk served at a restaurant
    (D) a worker calling in sick to work in order to go to a movie instead
    (E) cigarette smoke in a bowling alley

5. Which of these policies would resolve a negative externality?
    I.   Institute a per-unit tax on production
    II.   Limit the amount of external cost the firm can impose
    III. Fine firms that produce the externality

(A)   I only
(B)   III only
(C)   I and III only
(D)   II and III only
(E)   I, II, and III

6.   If a product creates a positive externality,
    (A)   the firm will tend to overproduce the product.
    (B)   society's marginal benefit is greater than the individual marginal benefit.
    (C)   the firm will produce at an allocatively efficient level of output.
    (D)   the government should establish policies to reduce output of the product.
    (E)   the market will return to long-run equilibrium as firms enter the industry.

7.   If a firm creates a positive externality, government can promote efficiency by
    (A)   increasing taxes on the firm.
    (B)   increasing income taxes for consumers.
    (C)   subsidizing production of the product.
    (D)   putting a limit on the amount of externality produced.
    (E)   requiring the firm to shut down.

8.   If an oil tanker spills oil into sensitive environmental areas, the government, to promote efficiency, should continue to clean up the effects until the
    (A)   marginal benefit of the next unit of clean up equals the marginal cost.
    (B)   firm cannot afford to pay for any more clean up.
    (C)   additional cost of the next unit of clean up would require a tax increase.
    (D)   marginal cost of clean up equals the firm's marginal cost of production.
    (E)   area is returned to the condition it was in before the oil spill.

Free-Response Questions

1.   Chickenpox vaccinations help protect the person who was vaccinated as well as others. Assume the chickenpox vaccine is produced in a competitive market.
(a)   Draw a correctly labeled graph of the vaccine market, showing each of the following:
    (i)   the market equilibrium quantity of vaccines, labeled QM
    (ii)   the market equilibrium price of vaccines, labeled PM
    (iii)   the socially optimal quantity of vaccines, labeled QSO
    (iv)   the socially optimal price of vaccines, labeled PSO
(b)   Identify the area of deadweight loss and explain what deadweight loss represents.
(c)   Identify one policy the government could undertake to correct this market failure.

2.   A nightclub adjacent to a quiet neighborhood has an outdoor pavilion and plays loud rock music late into the night, annoying residents of the neighborhood.
(a)   Name the market failure described above.
(b)   Identify whether the nightclub is producing at its socially optimal output, and explain the reasoning for your answer.
(c)   Explain the relationship between the marginal private cost and the marginal social cost of the nightclub.
(d)   Identify one policy or action the government could take to correct this market failure.

Multiple-Choice Explanations

1.   (C)   The free-rider problem makes it nearly impossible for firms to profit from providing public goods; if people can get them for free, the firm has little revenue. So government provides public goods through tax dollars.

2.   (D)   A road is a public good provided by government and funded through tax dollars. Use of a road is non-rival and non-excludable, so it qualifies as a public good. The other four answers are privately-owned firms and goods.

3.   (C)   The marginal social cost curve (supply) would shift to the left, resulting in a smaller quantity of the public good.

4.   (E)   A negative externality imposes a cost on someone other than the persons involved in the transaction. While the other four situations contain negative aspects, none of them (as defined here) impose costs on others outside of the relationship of the buyer/seller or employer/employee.

5.   (E)   A per-unit tax or fine would force the firm to absorb all of its production costs. A limit on the amount of external cost that can be passed on to others (even zero) will help bring the market closer to efficiency.

6.   (B)   With a positive externality, consumers are not considering the full social benefit of their consumption; therefore, the individual's marginal benefit curve lies below society's marginal benefit curve. The firm produces too little, so the government wants to encourage the firm to produce more.

7.   (C)   Positive externalities benefit society, so the government should subsidize the production, reducing production costs so that the firm produces more.

8.   (A)   Clean up should continue only as long as the marginal benefit is greater than or equal to the marginal cost. If cost outweighs the benefit, resources are wasted that could be used in other pursuits.

Free-Response Explanations

1.   **8 points** (5 + 2 + 1)
(a)   5 points:
  - 1 point is earned for a correctly labeled graph of the market with marginal social benefit higher than marginal private benefit.
  - 1 point is earned for QM where marginal private benefit equals marginal social cost.
  - 1 point is earned for PM where marginal private benefit equals marginal social cost.
  - 1 point is earned for QSO where marginal social benefit equals marginal social cost.
  - 1 point is earned for PSO where marginal social benefit equals marginal social cost.
(b)   2 points:
  - 1 point is earned for identifying the triangle of deadweight loss to the left of MSB = MSC over to the quantity set where MPB = MSC.
  - 1 point is earned for explaining that deadweight loss represents the lost consumer and producer surplus resulting from the externality.
(c)   1 point:
  - 1 point is earned for identifying one correct policy. Examples include the following:
    o A government subsidy or tax cut for consumers getting a vaccination
    o A government subsidy or tax cut for producers selling a vaccination
    o A government mandating vaccinations

2.   **5 points** (1 + 2 + 1 + 1)
(a)   1 point:
  - 1 point is earned for identifying the market failure as a negative externality.

(b)   2 points:
- 1 point is earned for stating that the nightclub is not producing at its socially optimal output.
- 1 point is earned for explaining that it is passing costs onto residents in the neighborhood (or that it is overproducing output or over-allocating resources to production).

(c)   1 point:
- 1 point is earned for explaining that the marginal private cost of the nightclub is lower than the marginal social cost.

(d)   1 point:
- 1 point is earned for identifying one correct policy. Examples include the following:
    o A noise ordinance limiting the sound, so neighbors are not affected
    o An ordinance prohibiting the piping of music outside of business establishments
    o A government subsidy for sound-dampening equipment
    o Fines for firms violating noise ordinances

CHAPTER 17: PUBLIC CHOICE THEORY AND THE ECONOMICS OF TAXATION

Introduction
As we have seen, government plays an important role in addressing market failures. But it also plays a significant role in taxation and redistribution of income, and sometimes policy can create inefficiency. Chapter 17 introduces the types, effects, and efficiency loss of taxation. This begins a series of chapters dealing with specific government policy issues. Material from Chapter 17 consistently appears in a few multiple-choice questions and infrequently in a free-response question on the AP microeconomics exam.

Public Choice Theory and Government Failure
Government has an important responsibility to provide public goods when the market fails, but the dynamics of a democratic system can complicate that effort. Because voters cannot indicate the strength of their desires for public goods, it is difficult for policymakers to determine the appropriate provision of public goods.

Government failure occurs when a government policy creates inefficiency in the market. Special interest effects allow a small, vocal group to obtain policy for their own benefit at the expense of the wider society. Interest groups with an incentive to promote a particular policy outcome lobby strongly, leaving policymakers with a distorted understanding of public positions. Logrolling, or vote trading, can lead to inefficient outcomes, including spending for pork barrel projects, or earmarks—special projects that may benefit a small group or a candidate's reelection but not society in general. And to promote reelection, policymakers prefer programs that bring immediate, clear benefits but that defer or hide costs. Inefficiency within bureaucratic institutions also contributes to government failure.

Bear in Mind
Public choice theory and government failure have not been directly tested on the AP economics exams and are only briefly discussed here.

Apportioning the Tax Burden
Once government determines which public goods will be provided, it must determine who will pay for those public goods through taxes. The benefits-received principle holds that those who receive the most public goods should pay the most in taxes. Gasoline taxes, which are used to fund highway building and maintenance, use this system. However, this principle is clearly ineffective in the case of imposing higher taxes on those who receive food stamps, housing subsidies, and unemployment checks; the low income or unemployment status that qualifies them for the benefits also indicates they are the least able to afford a higher tax rate. Further, how can indirect benefits of public goods be calculated? The ability-to-pay principle instead holds that taxpayers should be charged according to their income; those with higher incomes should pay higher tax rates. Federal income taxes are based on this principle, under the argument that those with higher incomes are more financially able to pay taxes than those with lower incomes. The problem with this principle is the difficulty in determining the relative ability of any particular household to pay a certain tax rate.

Progressive, Regressive, and Proportional Taxes
Under a progressive tax, such as the federal income tax, as income rises, the percentage of income paid in taxes rises. Proportional tax has each taxpayer pay the same percentage of income in taxes, regardless of income. With a regressive tax, those with lower incomes pay a higher

percentage of their income in taxes than those with higher incomes. Sales taxes are regressive taxes, though they may seem to be proportional. Those with lower incomes spend a greater portion of their income on taxable items, while those with higher incomes save and invest part of their income—which is not subject to the sales tax. The lower-income taxpayer may pay 5 percent of his income in sales tax, while the higher-income taxpayer pays only 3 percent of his income in sales tax. Social Security payroll taxes are also regressive, in that only the first $100,000 of income is subject to the payroll tax. Workers earning less than $100,000 pay the payroll tax on their entire income, while those earning higher incomes pay no more payroll tax, and other significant earnings in interest, dividends, and other benefits are not subject to the Social Security payroll tax at all.

Tax Incidence

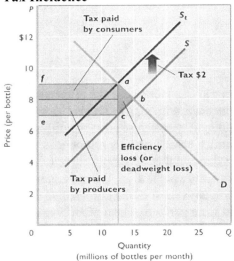

Efficiency loss (or deadweight loss) of a tax

Policymakers must also consider the tax incidence, or who pays the final burden of the tax. Sometimes taxes can be shifted to other people. When graphing a tax increase, the supply curve shifts directly upward by the amount of the tax. Market equilibrium shifts to a lower quantity and a higher price. We then need to determine how the burden of the tax is divided. Is it paid by the firm or by the consumers? In this case, the price to consumers rose from $8 to $9, so consumers paid $1 of the tax. But because the tax is $2, the firm must pay the other $1 of the tax. The firm's revenue at the new equilibrium is $87.5 million ($7 × 12.5 million), while the government's revenue is $25 million ($2 × $12.5 million). A deadweight loss again appears in the triangle *abc*, representing the loss of producer and consumer surplus resulting from the tax. Production and consumption have fallen from the point where marginal benefit equals marginal cost of production (supply equals demand), so we no longer achieve allocative efficiency.

Bear in Mind
It is important to be able to identify producer and consumer surplus, after-tax deadweight loss, the firm's revenue, the tax revenue, and the relative burdens of the tax to consumers and the firm. Previous AP microeconomics free-response questions have asked students to identify such information from a graph presented in the question or from graphs the student has been asked to draw. It is also important to recognize the differences in the tax burden on consumers and the firm based on the elasticity of demand for the product.

Elasticities and the Tax Burden

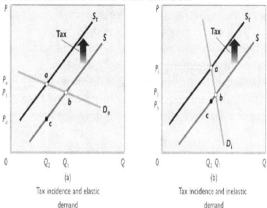

(a) Tax incidence and elastic demand

(b) Tax incidence and inelastic demand

Demand elasticity and the incidence of an excise tax

With elastic demand, consumers are sensitive to price changes. An increase in the price results in a much lower quantity demanded. If we apply the $2 tax increase with elastic demand, quantity shifts significantly to the left. From points above the new output, you can see that the difference between the original price and the new price (*a*), the tax burden passed on to consumers, is very small. At that output, the difference between the original price and the old supply curve (*c*) indicates the burden on the firm. The area *abc* indicates the deadweight loss. When demand is elastic, consumers pay little of the tax burden, while the firm pays most of the burden, and the area of deadweight loss is large. In the extreme, if demand were perfectly elastic (horizontal), any attempt to raise the price of the product through a tax would reduce demand to zero. So if the firm wanted to remain in operation, it would be forced to absorb the entire cost of the tax. The more elastic the demand for the product, the more the firm must absorb the burden of the tax.

When demand is inelastic, consumers are less sensitive to price change, so they only slightly reduce the quantity demanded after the tax. As a result, most of the tax burden is shifted to consumers, while firms pay little of the burden, and the deadweight loss is small. This is why governments tend to place excise taxes on gasoline, cigarettes, alcohol, and other products for which consumer demand is inelastic; consumers will continue to buy the product, generating more government revenue and leaving little burden of the tax on firms. In the extreme situation of a perfectly inelastic (vertical) demand curve, firms would pass the entire tax on to consumers and there would be no deadweight loss because quantity did not change. The more inelastic the demand for the product, the more the tax burden is passed on to consumers.

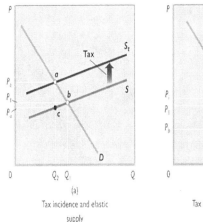
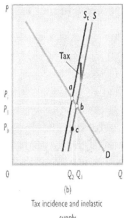

(a)
Tax incidence and elastic
supply

(b)
Tax incidence and inelastic
supply

Supply elasticity and the incidence of an excise tax

Similarly, when supply is more elastic, firms are able to pass more of the tax burden on to consumers. When supply is inelastic, the tax burden primarily falls on the firms.

Bear in Mind
Previous AP microeconomics exam questions have focused on differences in the elasticity of demand for the product, rather than elasticity of supply.

Benefits of Taxes
Because of the free-rider problem, taxes are necessary to raise the funds to pay for public goods. The government also uses taxes to redistribute income. By using progressive income taxes and redistributing those funds to those with lower incomes through safety net programs like TANF, food stamps, and rent subsidies, the government has equalized incomes somewhat. In addition, we have seen that taxes can actually improve efficiency in the case of negative externalities. Government can impose taxes in a way that forces firms to absorb all of their costs and return the market to allocative efficiency.

Multiple-Choice Questions
1. Public policy regarding economic issues can be difficult to develop for all of the following reasons EXCEPT
   (A) special interest effects.
   (B) logrolling.
   (C) pressure in support of pork barrel projects.
   (D) budget surpluses cannot be equally divided among programs.
   (E) policymakers have an incentive to support programs that help their reelection efforts.

2. Which of the following taxes illustrates the benefit principle of taxation?
   (A) regressive payroll taxes used to pay for national defense
   (B) gasoline taxes used to pay for highway building and maintenance
   (C) cigarette taxes used to pay for NASA
   (D) progressive income taxes used to pay for the local police force
   (E) property taxes used to pay for local economic development

3.   A tax which charges those with higher incomes a higher tax rate is
      (A)   progressive.
      (B)   regressive.
      (C)   proportional.
      (D)   excise.
      (E)   efficient.

4.   The federal government primarily redistributes income through
      (A)   regressive Social Security taxes and highway programs.
      (B)   proportional property taxes and education programs.
      (C)   progressive excise taxes and law enforcement programs.
      (D)   regressive sales taxes and national defense programs.
      (E)   progressive income taxes and safety net programs.

5.   If the state places an excise tax on a product with relatively elastic demand, supply,
      equilibrium output, and equilibrium price will change in what ways?

	Supply	Output	Price
(A)	Increase	Increase	Increase
(B)	Decrease	Decrease	Decrease
(C)	Decrease	Decrease	Increase
(D)	Increase	Increase	Decrease
(E)	Increase	Decrease	Increase

6.   If an excise tax is placed on a product with relatively inelastic demand and elastic supply,
      who will pay most of the burden of the tax?
      (A)   the firm
      (B)   consumers
      (C)   the firm and consumers equally
      (D)   the government
      (E)   foreign consumers who purchase those products as exports

7.   The deadweight loss associated with a tax increase is largest when
      (A)   demand is perfectly inelastic.
      (B)   demand is relatively inelastic.
      (C)   demand is unit elastic.
      (D)   demand is relatively elastic.
      (E)   consumers will buy the same quantity, regardless of price.

8.   For what purposes do governments institute taxes?
                 I.   To provide public goods
                 II.   To redistribute incomes
                 III.   To resolve positive externalities
      (A)   I only
      (B)   III only
      (C)   I and II only
      (D)   II and III only
      (E)   I, II, and III

Free-Response Questions

Assume the government imposes a per-unit sales tax in each of the three markets below, all of which have identical upward-sloping supply curves.

(a)   In the pharmaceuticals industry, consumers buy exactly the same amount of heart medicine, regardless of the price.
    (i)   Using a correctly labeled graph, identify each of the following:
        (a)   the equilibrium price and quantity before the tax
        (b)   the equilibrium price and quantity after the tax
    (ii)   Explain how the burden of the tax will be distributed between the consumers and the producers.

(b)   In the food industry, consumer demand for fish sandwiches is relatively elastic.
    (i)   Using a correctly labeled graph, identify each of the following:
        (a)   the equilibrium price and quantity before the tax
        (b)   the equilibrium price and quantity after the tax
    (ii)   Explain how the burden of the tax will be distributed between the consumers and the producers.

(c)   In the fruit industry, consumer demand for apples is perfectly elastic.
    (i)   Using a correctly labeled graph, identify each of the following:
        (a)   the equilibrium price and quantity before the tax
        (b)   the equilibrium price and quantity after the tax
    (ii)   Explain how the burden of the tax will be distributed between the consumers and the producers.

(d)   Is a deadweight loss more likely to develop in the pharmaceuticals industry or in the food industry as a result of the tax? Explain.

(e)   Assume that the quantity of heart medicine and the quantity of fish sandwiches sold per day are equal. If the government imposed a $1 per unit tax on heart medicine and fish sandwiches, which would bring the government more revenue? Explain.

Multiple-Choice Explanations

1.   (D)   The federal government generally runs budget deficits, not surpluses. Decisions on policy often hinge on the interests of those promoting the policy, not an objective consideration of effects and efficiencies involved.

2.   (B)   The benefit principle calls for those who benefit most from a program to pay the most taxes to support it. Those who use highways the most are most likely to buy the gasoline and, therefore, support the highways.

3.   (A)   A progressive tax is based on the ability-to-pay principle, stating that those with the highest incomes are best able to afford the tax.

4.   (E)   The federal government taxes those with the highest incomes at higher tax rates and then redistributes that money to those with lower incomes through TANF, food stamps, rent subsidies, and other income programs.

5.   (C)   The supply curve shifts upward (essentially to the left), decreasing the equilibrium output and increasing the equilibrium price.

6.   (B)   Consumers of the product pay the majority of the tax burden, because with their inelastic demand, the quantity purchased falls very little when the price rises; therefore, the firm can pass the tax increase on to consumers.

7.   (D)   When consumers are sensitive to the change in price due to the tax, the quantity sold drops significantly, causing a greater deadweight loss.

8.   (C)   Taxes are used in the case of negative (not positive) externalities to force firms to absorb all of their costs of production, in order to try to move the market back to allocative efficiency.

Free-Response Explanations

16 points (4 + 4 + 4 + 2 + 2)

(a)   4 points:
  - 1 point is earned for correctly identifying price and quantity before the tax.
  - 1 point is earned for correctly identifying a higher price and no change in quantity.
  - 1 point is earned for stating that consumers will pay the entire tax.
  - 1 point is earned for explaining that because demand is perfectly inelastic, the firm can pass the entire tax on to the consumers.

(b)   4 points:
  - 1 point is earned for correctly identifying price and quantity before the tax.
  - 1 point is earned for correctly identifying a higher price and a lower quantity.
  - 1 point is earned for stating that firms will pay a larger burden of the tax than consumers will.
  - 1 point is earned for explaining that because consumers are so sensitive to the price change, the firm must absorb more of the tax in order to avoid losing sales.

(c)   4 points:
  - 1 point is earned for correctly identifying price and quantity before the tax.
  - 1 point is earned for correctly identifying a lower quantity and no change in price.
  - 1 point is earned for stating that firms will pay the entire tax.
  - 1 point is earned for explaining that because demand is perfectly elastic, the firm must absorb the entire tax or the quantity demanded will fall to zero.

(d)   2 points:
  - 1 point is earned for stating that the deadweight loss will develop in the food industry.
  - 1 point is earned for explaining that the quantity of fish sandwiches demanded fell as a result of the tax, while the quantity of heart medicine demanded did not change.

(e)   2 points:
  - 1 point is earned for stating that the government would earn more revenue from a tax on heart medicine.
  - 1 point is earned for explaining that, with the tax, the same quantity of heart medicine but a lower quantity of fish sandwiches would be sold, which would lower the revenue.

CHAPTER 18: ANTITRUST POLICY AND REGULATION

Introduction

The information in Chapter 18, while important, is only tested on the AP economics exam in the context of monopolies as discussed in Chapter 10. The important applications to concepts that may be tested are highlighted below.

- Antitrust laws limit the formation of monopolies because such firms raise prices, reduce output, prevent competition, and violate allocative efficiency.
- Because the monopoly's price exceeds marginal cost at the profit-maximizing output, society would benefit from the production of additional products.
- Antitrust laws like the Sherman and Clayton Acts limit monopoly formation and outlaw price discrimination and other techniques designed to prevent competition.
- Horizontal mergers of firms making similar products can create monopoly power. Government regulates mergers that would significantly reduce competition.
- Horizontal mergers can be beneficial if they result in economies of scale or if one of the firms has sustained ongoing losses and is in danger of failing.
- Price-fixing and collusion among oligopolists are illegal under U.S. law, and oligopolists are prosecuted and fined for undertaking such activity.
- Natural monopolies result when economies of scale are so strong that allowing one producer to operate is far more efficient than maintaining several firms in the industry; this is most common among utility companies (electricity, natural gas, public water).
- Government ownership and provision of the utility is one way to limit prices.

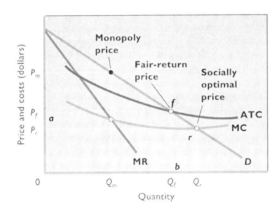

Regulated monopoly

- Government regulation of natural monopolies limits price and increases output, setting the price equal to average total cost where it crosses demand, so the firm still earns a normal profit as a "fair return price."
- Socially optimal price and output are where marginal cost equals demand, a lower price and higher output than where government regulators set the price.
- Social regulation of firms involves rules for worker and consumer safety, investor and environmental protection, and discrimination. It is designed to protect people from decisions of firms focused solely on profit maximization at the expense of other important values.
- Government should regulate until the marginal benefit equals the marginal cost of the regulation. However, such costs and benefits can be difficult to determine.

CHAPTER 19: AGRICULTURE: ECONOMICS AND POLICY

Introduction

The information in Chapter 19, while important, is not directly tested on the AP economics exams. The important applications to concepts that may be tested are highlighted below.

- Because the overall demand for food is relatively inelastic in the United States, changes in supply cause significant changes in the price of food products and the incomes of farmers.
- Major improvements in technology and worker productivity have significantly increased the supply of farm products.
- Because demand for food is income-inelastic and population growth has slowed, supply of agricultural products has increased more than demand, which has lowered prices.
- Lower crop prices, along with the inability of small farms to achieve the economies of scale to reduce production costs, have led to the exit of many family farms from the industry and a large number of consolidations into corporate farms.
- The federal government has granted farmers subsidies to reduce production costs.
- Government sets price floors for some farm products in order to keep prices high enough to support family farms. The price floor causes a surplus of the product, because the quantity supplied at the higher price is greater than the quantity demanded.
- The tax burden of the surplus represents tax dollars transferred to farmers, and allocative inefficiency results because resources are over-allocated to agriculture; *abc* represents the area of deadweight loss.

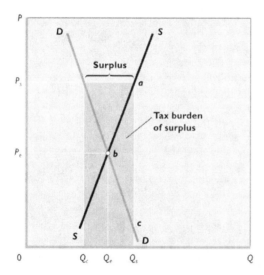

Price supports, agricultural surpluses, and transfers to farmers

- While the higher price helps farmers, it especially hurts those consumers with low incomes; a larger percentage of their income is spent for food, and they cannot easily reduce the quantity of food purchased, so they must give up buying other goods.
- While price supports increase agricultural output, it also increases negative externalities associated with agriculture, including pollution from pesticides and fertilizers, the loss of wildlife habitats, and higher use of water for irrigation.

CHAPTER 20: INCOME INEQUALITY, POVERTY, AND DISCRIMINATION

Introduction
The information in Chapter 20, while important, is only tested on the AP economics exam with regard to the Lorenz curve and causes of income inequality. The important applications to concepts that may be tested are highlighted below.

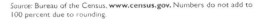

(1) Quintile (2006)	(2) Percentage of Total Income	(3) Upper Income Limit
Lowest 20 percent	3.4	$20,035
Second 20 percent	8.6	37,774
Third 20 percent	14.5	60,000
Fourth 20 percent	22.9	97,032
Highest 20 percent	50.5	No limit
Total	100.0	

Source: Bureau of the Census. **www.census.gov.** Numbers do not add to 100 percent due to rounding.

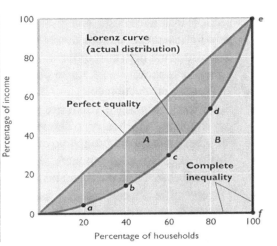

The Lorenz curve and Gini ratio

- The Lorenz curve illustrates the distribution of household incomes in a country.
- The diagonal line illustrates perfect equality of incomes in the country; the further the Lorenz curve is from the equality line, the more unequal are incomes.
- The Gini ratio (or Gini coefficient) numerically measures the area of inequality; the larger the Gini ratio, the more unequal are incomes in the country.
- Income mobility in the United States allows households to move among income groups; households are not permanently members of a single income class over time.
- Government redistributes income through progressive income taxes and transfer payments (safety net or public assistance programs) such as Social Security, unemployment benefits, welfare assistance, food stamps, housing subsidies, and Medicaid.
- The redistribution of income shifts the Lorenz curve inward toward more equality.
- Transfer payments to those with low incomes account for about 80 percent of the reduction in income inequality; progressive taxes account for the other 20 percent.
- Causes of income inequality include differences in ability, education and training, discrimination, preferences for work over leisure, willingness to assume risk, wealth with the opportunity to earn even more income, market power, connections, and luck (or misfortune).
- Since 1970, income inequality has increased due to greater demand for highly skilled workers, increased pay for CEOs and professional athletes and entertainers, demographic changes of divorce and single heads of households, downward pressure on wages of less-skilled workers due to imports, and the decline of union membership leading to lower wages for workers in industry.
- Poverty is a condition in which a household does not have sufficient income to meet its needs for food, shelter, and basic necessities.
- The poverty rate is the percentage of a country's residents living in poverty. The U.S. poverty rate in 2006 was 12.3 percent.

CHAPTER 21: HEALTH CARE

Introduction

The information in Chapter 21, while important, is not directly tested on the AP economics exams. The important applications to concepts that may be tested are highlighted below.

- Workers' increases in total compensation generally match increases in productivity, but because insurance costs have risen much more steeply than productivity, workers have paid for insurance in more slowly rising wages.
- Because of the high cost of insurance, firms have reduced workers to part-time status, turned to temporary workers, or outsourced work to other countries to avoid these costs and reduce production costs.
- Significant increases in Medicare and Medicaid costs expose opportunity costs for governments, which have to choose between limiting medical benefits, reducing spending for other government programs, or raising taxes to pay for the programs.
- Health care, like other products, should be provided until the marginal benefit equals the marginal cost. Such costs and benefits can be difficult to determine.
- The cost of health care has increased rapidly because the demand for health care has increased more strongly than the supply. Increases in both supply and demand raise the price.
- Health care is income elastic; as incomes increase, the quantity of health care demanded increases.
- Health care is price inelastic; even when the price of health care increases, the quantity demanded decreases only slightly.
- Because 80 percent of health care spending comes from insurance companies and government and consumers do not pay all of the costs of their health care, consumers have increased their demand for health care, resulting in an over-allocation of resources toward health care.
- Good health results in positive externalities, as vaccinations and treatment prevent the spread of disease and because a healthy, productive workforce results in greater output at a lower cost for firms. Therefore, the federal government subsidizes this externality by not taxing health care benefits as income.

CHAPTER 22: IMMIGRATION

Introduction

The information in Chapter 22, while important, is not directly tested on the AP economics exams. The important applications to concepts that may be tested are highlighted below.

- Immigrants move to the United States primarily to find jobs with wages that better compensate their investment in human capital than jobs in their native country.
- Larger wage differences, educational opportunities, health care, and government benefits provide an incentive for workers to move between countries to maximize the return on their investment in human capital.

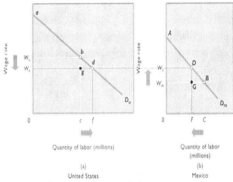

A simple immigration model

- The increase in the supply of workers lowers the equilibrium wage and results in a greater quantity of workers hired and higher output in the United States. At the same time, the lower supply of workers in Mexico raises the wage and reduces the quantity of workers hired and output. As a result, the differential in world incomes decreases.
- Labor migration increases the output of products with available resources, increasing production possibilities and raising the world's standard of living.
- Opponents of immigration argue that lower wages for domestic workers reduce standards of living and the "brain drain" of better-educated, highly productive workers hurts long-run economic growth for the countries losing such workers.
- Immigrants' remittances, sending part of their pay back home to relatives in their native countries, reduce the income gain in the country to which the immigrant has moved and mitigate the loss of workers from their home country.
- While immigration does displace some domestic workers, overall, the number of workers increases as a result of both legal and illegal immigration.
- In cases where illegal immigrants and domestic workers are easily substituted, immigration can lower wages; overall, illegal immigration has had little effect on average wage rates because they are so dependent of labor productivity.
- Because illegal immigrants work for lower wages than domestic workers, prices of products that heavily rely on illegal immigrant labor are lower than they would be if produced by domestic labor; lower prices increase the standard of living.
- State and local governments with large numbers of low-wage immigrants face fiscal strain, because these immigrants pay lower income, sales, and property taxes due to their lower incomes but use public goods such as education and police services and may qualify for income assistance programs.
- Immigration should be increased until the marginal benefit of immigration equals the marginal cost. These numbers, however, can be very difficult to determine.

CHAPTER 23: AN INTRODUCTION TO MACROECONOMICS

Introduction

Macroeconomics is the study of the entire economy, the culmination of all of the forces of individual microeconomic decisions. Macroeconomics explores long-run economic growth, short-run business cycles, and several theories about government intervention to stabilize markets. Chapter 23 introduces the measures of economic growth and performance that provide the foundation for the study of macroeconomic theory in subsequent chapters. Material from Chapter 23 may appear in a question or two on the multiple-choice portion of the AP macroeconomics exam.

Macroeconomics

This study of the entire economy is composed of two separate areas of study. The first is long-run economic growth, which brings increased production and standards of living throughout the economy. The second is the business cycle, which explains short-run rapid increases and declines in production, inflation, and unemployment.

Gross Domestic Product

Gross domestic product (GDP) is the dollar value of all goods and services produced within a country in one year. Nominal GDP measures the output of the economy in current dollars. Because inflation contributes to increases in nominal GDP, it can distort apparent increases in production over time. In order to remove the inflation distortion, real GDP uses constant dollars to measure the actual change in production. Real GDP is our primary measure of economic growth, which is important to us because it allows increased production possibilities for products throughout the economy. GDP per capita is the GDP divided by the population, which measures the average standard of living that would occur if the GDP were equally divided among the citizens of the country. GDP per capita can be used to compare average standards of living among countries.

Unemployment and Inflation

Unemployment is the condition of not having a job but actively seeking one. Unemployment represents lost production, as resources are not fully employed to promote economic growth. Inflation is an increase in the general level of prices. It is important to keep inflation rates low, because if the rate of inflation rises more quickly than wages, standards of living fall, reducing the potential for even greater economic growth. So economists hold simultaneous goals of increasing the real GDP while reducing unemployment and inflation.

Investment

Investment is the foundation of economic growth. Savings occur when consumers choose not to spend all of their income, deciding to forego some current consumption. Investment is the use of resources to increase future output. When firms expand their plants, buy new equipment, or spend for research and development, they are looking toward increasing future production. Savings are used to pay for investment, so the amount of investment and, therefore, future growth is limited by the level of current saving. As we discussed with production possibilities curves, the tradeoff for greater future consumption is less current consumption.

Taking the EEK! Out of Economics

Investment is another term like scarcity that has a more precise meaning in economics than it does in general use. Many people commonly use the term investment to mean financial investment, such as the purchase of stocks or bonds, commodities, an existing home for use as a rental unit, famous paintings, or other items for the purpose of gaining money from them or re-selling them later for a profit. Economic investment specifically refers to firms buying new equipment, expanding factories, and spending in other ways specifically designed to increase future production.

The Role of Financial Institutions

Banks and other financial institutions provide the link between savers and investors. Households provide most of the savings in the economy and are enticed to save by banks and other financial institutions that offer interest. The financial institutions then loan the funds to firms in order to finance their investment in capital. As a result, changes in interest rates can change both the willingness of households to save and the willingness of firms to borrow in order to invest in future economic growth.

Expectations and Shocks

Expectations are important in understanding short-run fluctuations in the macroeconomy. If consumers fear a recession and the possibility of losing their jobs, they reduce their demand for products, which slows economic growth. If firms expect lower returns on their investment, they are less likely to engage in investment spending. Demand shocks also cause short-run economic changes when positive shocks, like a sudden fad, or negative shocks, like a significant drop in incomes, occur. Supply shocks, such as a natural disaster or a significant innovation in technology, can also cause short-run economic volatility. Economists believe that most economic cycles are caused by demand shocks.

"Sticky" Prices

Because prices tend to be "sticky" for many products and change slowly in response to economic forces, most demand shocks instead result in changes in output and employment. Manufacturing firms often create inventories to cushion sudden increases and decreases in demand and smooth the sales process. But if decreases in demand are sustained, the firm decreases output and lays off workers because fewer workers are needed to produce the product. If demand instead increases, output and employment both increase.

Prices of other products such as gasoline, airline tickets, and stocks are very flexible. Such prices often change daily or even within minutes in response to changes in supply and demand. However, most products have relatively stable prices because consumers want predictable prices and because firms must be concerned about the reactions of rivals. If the firm reduces its price, it will only gain additional customers from another firm if that firm does not lower its price as well. But if the other firm matches the price cut, the first firm is left worse off because it not only gained no new customers, it is now selling its normal output at a lower price. This risk leaves most firms hesitant to change their prices.

Prices that are sticky in the short run tend to be much more flexible in the long run. As a result, macroeconomic theories differ in their assumptions about the flexibility of prices. These models allow us to see how the economy behaves at different points in the business cycle and how government policies affect GDP, employment, and prices.

Multiple-Choice Questions

1. Which of these topics would be included in the study of macroeconomics?
    (A)   profit maximization
    (B)   labor hiring
    (C)   marginal utility
    (D)   oligopolistic game theory
    (E)   long-run economic growth

2. Gross domestic product is the measure of
    (A)   the value of all products produced in a country in one year.
    (B)   manufactured products produced in a country in one year.
    (C)   services produced in a country in one year.
    (D)   products produced in a year minus taxes on income and profits.
    (E)   negative externalities produced in a country in one year.

3. In order to compare production from year to year, real GDP is calculated to remove the distortion of
    (A)   unemployment.
    (B)   imports.
    (C)   inflation.
    (D)   taxes.
    (E)   regulation.

4. A measure of the average standard of living that can be used to compare countries is
    (A)   real GDP.
    (B)   government spending.
    (C)   the income tax rate.
    (D)   GDP per capita.
    (E)   welfare spending.

5. Which of these is an example of investment, as economists define the term?
    (A)   An accountant purchases stock to earn money for his son's education.
    (B)   An author purchases a piece of art for her home to impress visitors.
    (C)   A grocery store manager buys more bananas to restock the shelves.
    (D)   Government increases spending for food stamp benefits during a recession.
    (E)   A firm purchases equipment to make production more efficient.

6. Banks and other financial institutions perform an important economic function by
          I.   providing a safe place for households to save money.
          II.   paying interest to give households an incentive to save.
          III. providing loans to firms to invest in capital.
    (A)   I only
    (B)   III only
    (C)   I and II only
    (D)   II and III only
    (E)   I, II, and III

7. When firms expect a lower return on their investment, they
    (A)   try to negotiate a higher interest rate on bank loans.
    (B)   are less likely to invest.

(C)   raise product prices.

(D)   increase hiring.

(E)   continue to invest, focusing on long-run economic growth.

8.   Because prices of most products tend to be "sticky," demand shocks tend to cause changes in

(A)   population.

(B)   employment.

(C)   tax rates.

(D)   the minimum wage.

(E)   production possibilities.

Multiple-Choice Explanations

1.   (E)   Macroeconomics is the study of the entire economy, focusing on long-run economic growth and short-run business cycles. The other four answers are topics of study in microeconomics.

2.   (A)   GDP measures the value of all final products produced in one year, including both goods and services.

3.   (C)   Nominal GDP measures GDP in current dollars, so an increase in GDP may be partially due to increases in production or prices. Real GDP removes the inflation distortion to focus solely on production changes.

4.   (D)   GDP per capita is GDP divided by the population of the country. It is a better measure for comparison than GDP, because it is important to know how many people share the income of the country in order to compare average standards of living.

5.   (E)   Investment is a firm's spending in order to create future economic growth, such as spending for expansion of a plant or new equipment.

6.   (E)   Financial institutions link savers and investors, providing firms the funds they need to pay for capital expansion and long-run economic growth.

7.   (B)   During economic slowdowns, firms tend to reduce investment because of the reduced consumer demand for the product and, therefore, a lower return on the investment.

8.   (B)   If prices are inflexible, changes in output occur instead; as output changes, employment changes as well.

CHAPTER 24: MEASURING DOMESTIC OUTPUT AND NATIONAL INCOME

Introduction
Gross domestic product (GDP) is the primary measure of a nation's macroeconomic performance. So it is important to understand how GDP is calculated and to address cautions in its use. Chapter 24 explains the details of the calculation of GDP, as well as several other measures of national accounts. These measures underlie the discussions of economic performance and economic theories throughout the macroeconomics course. Material from Chapter 24 is very likely to appear in a few multiple-choice questions and has occasionally appeared as a free-response question on the AP macroeconomics exam.

National Income Accounting
National income accounting is a way to measure how well the economy is performing. A variety of statistics are used to evaluate production and income, as well as the relative growth or decline of the economy. Those statistics are then used to determine appropriate policies to stabilize the economy and promote long-run economic growth.

Gross Domestic Product and Gross National Product
GDP is the dollar value of all final goods and services produced in a country in one year. This statistic includes all final products produced in the United States, regardless of the home nation of the company. To calculate GDP, the output of a Honda plant in Indiana would be counted in U.S. GDP, but the output of a Coca-Cola plant in Belgium would not.

Factors Not Counted in GDP
In order to accurately measure production, certain economic activities are not included in GDP. Intermediate goods are used in other goods, such as tires sold to an auto producer. Intermediate goods are not counted, because if the tires were counted when sold to the auto manufacturer, and then the value of the completed car was counted, the value of the tires would have been counted twice. So while sales of final products to consumers, firms, and government are counted in GDP, sales of intermediate products are not.

Purely financial transactions are also not counted as part of GDP. Government transfer payments such as Social Security or unemployment benefits are not counted because households create no production in return for the checks. Further, if transfer payments were counted in GDP, and then households used those checks to purchase consumer goods which were counted as part of GDP, the value of those transfer payments would be counted twice. Private transfer payments such as monetary gifts or sales of stock are also not counted as part of GDP because no output was created as a part of the transaction.

Second-hand sales, or used goods, are also not counted as part of current GDP. The sale of used goods creates no new output in the economy. Further, the product was counted when it was originally produced. By not counting intermediate goods, purely financial transactions, and second-hand sales, economists attempt to increase the accuracy of GDP as a measure of production that can be compared from year to year.

Measuring GDP: Expenditure and Income Approaches
Production in the economy can be measured by spending or income approaches. The expenditure approach adds all of the money spent to purchase final goods in the economy. The income approach adds all of the incomes earned in the economy. Were we able to obtain completely accurate numbers, GDP calculated by the two approaches would be equal, because spending by

one person is income to another. If you bought $20 of gasoline from a gas station, it would contribute $20 toward GDP, whether we counted it from your perspective as spending or from the gas station's perspective as income.

The Expenditure Approach

Calculation of GDP using the expenditure approach calls for adding the spending by the four sectors of the economy with the formula GDP = C + I + G + X, where
- C is personal consumption expenditures,
- I is gross private domestic investment,
- G is government purchases, and
- X is net exports.

Personal consumption expenditures include the spending for consumer items by households. This includes spending for durable goods which last years (such as cars and furniture), nondurable goods (such as food and medicine), and services. Personal consumption is the largest part of the economy, constituting about 70 percent of GDP.

Gross private domestic investment primarily measures spending by firms. It includes firms' purchases of machinery and equipment, construction of homes and businesses, and changes in inventories. Inventories are products produced but not yet sold; because we are measuring total production and not just product sales, we need to include inventories.

Another way to measure investment sector spending is net private domestic investment. Net private domestic investment is gross private domestic investment minus depreciation, or the amount of capital that is used up during a year. Net private domestic investment tries to compensate for the value of capital that is used up and whose replacement does not increase the amount of capital stock. Gross investment is generally greater than depreciation, and the amount of capital increases from year to year. But when the economy is in strong decline, firms may significantly reduce their investment in capital, resulting in negative investment. We will come back to this discussion, but remember that gross private domestic investment is the number used to calculate gross domestic product. Gross private domestic investment accounts for approximately 15 percent of GDP.

Government purchases are the third sector of GDP. Government purchases include spending for goods and services needed to produce public goods, as well as publicly owned capital such as highways. Remember that transfer payments are not counted in the government sector. Government purchases constitute about 19 percent of GDP.

Net exports is spending for exports minus spending for imports. Because we want to measure production within the United States, we must include products that were produced in the U.S. and then exported, while subtracting U.S. spending for products produced elsewhere. Because the U.S. imports significantly more than it exports, the foreign sector actually produces a negative number, reducing the GDP from what it would have been if trade were balanced by approximately 5 percent.

The Income Approach

National income measures incomes distributed to owners of the factors of production. The largest proportion of income is paid to labor in wages and salaries. Rent is the income households and firms receive for supplying property to renters. Interest is the income received for the use of borrowed money. Proprietors' income is the net income of sole proprietorships and partnerships. Although corporate profits are initially earned by firms, the flow of that income is divided among income taxes paid to government, dividends paid to households, and retained earnings held by the corporation. Taxes on production and imports (also called indirect business taxes) account for the tax revenues that are paid to governments through sales taxes, excise taxes, property taxes, and import tariffs. Income earned via wages, rent, interest, proprietors' income, corporate profits, and taxes together are national income. To equate the expenditure and income approaches, economists make additional adjustments to the national income, the most important of which is the consumption of fixed capital, which accounts for the capital that is used up during a year and will eventually have to be replaced (the same idea as depreciation).

Bear in Mind

The relationships between the various types of income and expenditure can be mind-boggling, especially when viewing a flow chart like the one given below. Questions about the calculation of GDP on the AP macroeconomics exam have been much more straightforward. Questions have focused primarily on the expenditure model, such as identifying the sectors or specific types of spending that would be included in the calculation. A multiple-choice question about the income approach is likely to focus on wages, rent, interest, proprietors' income, corporate profit, and taxes.

Other National Accounts

Net domestic product measures new production in the economy minus depreciation. Net domestic product uses the same formula as GDP, except that net private domestic investment is used for the investment sector to include the depreciation. This statistic tells us how much is available for consumption without detracting from our ability to produce more in the future.

Disposable income is the personal income of households minus personal taxes. When we consider all of the kinds of income a household could receive (wages, dividends, interest, government and private transfer payments) and subtract the many personal taxes households pay (income, property, and Social Security taxes), we find the amount households have available for the purchase of goods and services in the economy.

The Circular Market Flow Model

Receipts: Expenditures Approach		Allocations: Income Approach*	
Sum of:		Sum of:	
Personal consumption expenditures (C)	$9734	Compensation of employees	$7874
Gross private domestic investment (I_g)	2125	Rents	65
Government purchases (G)	2690	Interest	603
Net exports (X_n)	−708	Proprietors' income	1043
		Corporate profits	1627
		Taxes on production and imports	1009
		Equals:	
		National income	**$12,221**
		National income	$12,221
		Less: Net foreign factor income	96
		Plus: Statistical discrepancy	29
		Plus: Consumption of fixed capital	1687
Equals:		*Equals:*	
Gross domestic product	**$13,841**	**Gross domestic product**	**$13,841**

*Some of the items in this column combine related categories that appear in the more detailed accounts.

Source: Bureau of Economic Analysis, www.bea.gov.

Accounting statement for the U.S. economy, 2007 (in billions)

Revisiting the circular flow model, you can see that it has grown much more complicated than the basic model introduced in the early chapters of this book. Note that two new sectors—government and foreign—have been added to represent all four sectors of the expenditure model. This model again reinforces the idea that the income and expenditure models of GDP must be equal, because one sector's spending is another sector's income.

Bear in Mind
Questions about the circular flow model on previous AP macroeconomics exams have asked about the basic flow model with households and firms, product and factor markets, not flows as complex as those represented in this model.

Nominal and Real GDP
Nominal GDP is calculated using the current prices of products. In order to compare production over time without the inflation distortion, we must calculate real GDP. In order to do that, we must construct a price index to measure the prices of a market basket of goods and services. The price index used to convert nominal GDP to real GDP is called the GDP price deflator.

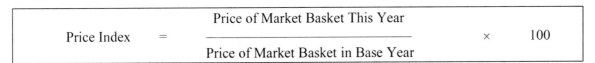

$$\text{Price Index} = \frac{\text{Price of Market Basket This Year}}{\text{Price of Market Basket in Base Year}} \times 100$$

If the total price of a market basket of goods last year was $1,000, and this year that same market basket price total is $1,200, the calculation would be $1,200 / $1,000 = 1.2 × 100 = 120. This number tells us that the price of the market basket this year is 120% of the price of the market basket last year—a 20% increase in prices.

In order to convert nominal GDP to real GDP, we divide inflation out of the equation.

$$\text{Real GDP} = \frac{\text{Nominal GDP}}{\text{Price Index (as a Decimal)}}$$

Using this equation, if nominal GDP for this year is $12,000 and you want to compare this year's GDP to last year's GDP, you must remove the inflation for that time period. Thus, $12,000 / 1.2 = $10,000 is this year's real GDP.

When calculating the percentage change in nominal GDP, it is important to remember that the statistic includes changes in both output and prices.

$$\text{\% Change in Nominal GDP} = \text{\% Change in Real GDP} + \text{\% Change in Prices}$$

If real GDP increased by 3% and prices rose by 2% this year, nominal GDP would increase by 5%. By converting the formula, we can also determine that if the nominal GDP for this year increased by 5% and prices rose 2%, real GDP must have risen by 3%.

Shortcomings of GDP

A measure as broad as GDP, while providing important information about our economy, still has its shortcomings. Nonmarket activities (or home production), such as cooking your own dinner or painting your own house, is also excluded from GDP calculation. It is difficult to get an accurate measure of such production, and money was not exchanged for this economic activity, so official GDP misses a great deal of economic activity.

GDP also cannot measure the value of leisure people have gained as the result of shorter workweeks and labor-saving appliances and services. Further, GDP cannot adequately measure improvements in the quality of life due to higher quality products.

The underground economy is specifically left out of GDP calculations. Although illegal activity is significant, it is very difficult to find reliable figures to quantify the level of activity, so it is left out. In addition, people who work for cash "under the table" or who under-report tips or business incomes in order to avoid taxes also contribute to a lower level of official GDP than the actual level of economic activity.

Further, the GDP cannot measure negative externalities such as pollution and other negative effects of production on the quality of life. GDP says nothing about the mix of goods, making no judgment about whether most of the spending in the country is for government goods or consumer goods. GDP also does not note the distribution of incomes; if 90 percent of national income went to the top 1 percent of citizens, the standard of living for most citizens would be quite low. And while GDP gives us an idea about the economic well-being of a nation's citizens, it cannot measure their feelings of safety and peace, the quality of education, the limitations on government power, or the protection of the nation's natural resources.

The gross domestic product is the most important statistic economists use to measure the state of the economy. But it is important to recognize the limitations on GDP so that you can interpret the data with the understanding that the well-being of a nation's people is based on far more than simply the officially reported GDP.

Multiple-Choice Questions

1.   All of the following products would be included in the calculation of the U.S. GDP EXCEPT
      (A)   Toyota cars produced in Kentucky.
      (B)   haircuts.
      (C)   Starbuck's coffee produced and sold in Canada.

(D)   a firm's purchase of capital equipment produced in Arizona.

(E)   government spending on highways.

2.   Which of the following would be included in the calculation of U.S. GDP?

(A)   a girl mowing her family's yard.

(B)   a student buying a used car.

(C)   a neighbor paying a babysitter with homemade cookies.

(D)   a senior citizen receiving a Social Security check.

(E)   a family buying dinner at a restaurant.

3.   Why are intermediate goods not included in the calculation of GDP?

(A)   They cannot be used by consumers in their unfinished state.

(B)   They are not subject to sales taxes.

(C)   They are imported.

(D)   They would be double-counted when the finished product is counted.

(E)   They require multiple steps of production.

4.   Why are transfer payments not included in the calculation of GDP?

(A)   Recipients have not produced any output in return for the payment.

(B)   The payments generally are made to those with the lowest incomes.

(C)   Government spending is not included in the calculation of GDP.

(D)   Transfer payments are intended to promote economic activity.

(E)   Transfer payments have no impact on the economy.

5.   The largest sector in the expenditure model of GDP is the

(A)   consumer sector.

(B)   investment sector.

(C)   government sector.

(D)   import sector.

(E)   export sector.

6.   The calculation of gross private domestic investment includes

        I.   firms' spending for equipment and machinery.

        II.   all construction.

        III.   depreciation.

        IV.   changes in inventories.

(A)   I only

(B)   II and III only

(C)   III and IV only

(D)   I, II, and IV only

(E)   I, III, III, and IV

7.   Net exports as a factor in U.S. GDP have been negative since the 1980s because

(A)   the federal government has experienced consistent budget deficits.

(B)   the value of imports has exceeded the value of exports.

(C)   the real GDP has been declining throughout this period.

(D)   inflation has reduced the value of the dollar.

(E)   trade barriers have effectively limited the number of imports.

8.   Why must GDP calculated using the expenditure approach equal GDP calculated using the income approach?
        (A)   Income and spending are both reported to government agencies.
        (B)   Spending in the economy must equal the incomes earned in the economy.
        (C)   Taxes must be paid on both income and sales.
        (D)   Both approaches use product sales as their base.
        (E)   Economists add a statistical correction to the expenditure approach C + I + G + X (X as the correction) to ensure that it equals the income approach.

9.   The measure of consumer income after payment of personal taxes is
        (A)   national income.
        (B)   personal income.
        (C)   disposable income.
        (D)   gross domestic product.
        (E)   net domestic product.

10.   Real GDP rather than nominal GDP is used to compare changes in national output over time, because real GDP removes the effects of
        (A)   imports.
        (B)   unemployment.
        (C)   taxes.
        (D)   interest.
        (E)   inflation.

11.   If real GDP increased 2% this year and the price level increased 4% this year, how much did nominal GDP increase this year?
        (A)   –2%
        (B)   2%
        (C)   4%
        (D)   6%
        (E)   8%

12.   The shortcomings of gross domestic product as a measure of all economic activity in a country include all of the following EXCEPT that it
        (A)   does not include home production such as repairing one's own car.
        (B)   cannot measure improvements in the quality of products.
        (C)   does not take into consideration negative externalities such as pollution.
        (D)   does not take into account increased leisure time or quality of life.
        (E)   does not count government spending for public goods.

Free-Response Questions
Econ Island is a very small island that produces a limited amount of products each year. The table below shows this year's prices and purchases of products on the island.

This Year's Output	This Year's Prices
1,000 pounds of hamburger	$2 per pound
2 cars bought from the used car lot	$10,000 per car
10 clothing outfits imported from another island	$20 per outfit
10,000 pounds of rice (8,000 used on the island, 2,000 exported)	$1 per pound

Government spending for workers to clean the beach	$5,000
1 meat processing machine bought from a local producer	$250
Illegal drugs produced and sold on the island	$1,000

(a) Using the data, calculate this year's nominal GDP for Econ Island.

(b) If the price index is 110, calculate this year's real GDP for Econ Island.

(c) Identify the factors in the table that would not be included in GDP using the expenditure model. For each factor, complete the following:
  (i) Identify the factor that would not be included in GDP
  (ii) Explain why that factor would not be included in the GDP calculation

(d) Explain one shortcoming of using GDP as an accurate measure of the standard of living for residents of a country.

Multiple-Choice Explanations

1. (C) Products produced and sold in other countries are counted in that nation's GDP, not ours, even if it is an American company producing the product.

2. (E) (A) and (C) are examples of home production, (B) is the purchase of a used good, and (D) is a purely financial transaction, none of which are counted in GDP.

3. (D) Intermediate goods are sold to other firms to be included in the final product of the other firm. Counting it once when sold to the other firm, and then counting it again in the final product double-counts the product.

4. (A) Because recipients provide no goods or services in return for the transfer payment, GDP does not change as a direct result of the payment. Once households use the transfer payment to buy products in the economy, those purchases would be counted in the consumer sector.

5. (A) Consumers account for more than two-thirds of spending in the U.S. economy.

6. (D) Depreciation is subtracted from gross private domestic investment to calculate net private domestic investment.

7. (B) Net exports are the value of exports minus the value of imports. Because U.S. imports have been greater than U.S. exports since the 1980s, the net exports component of the GDP calculation is negative.

8. (B) As can be seen in the circular market flow, money spent by one market participant is income to another. So if the numbers are accurately compiled, GDP should be the same using either method of calculation.

9. (C) National income is the total income of all resource suppliers plus taxes. Personal income is income before taxes are paid. Gross domestic product is the total economic output. Net domestic product is GDP minus depreciation.

10. (E) Because nominal GDP is calculated using the current value of money, nominal GDP would increase when prices rise, even if the same quantity of products is produced. Real GDP removes that distortion.

11. (D) % Change in Nominal GDP = % Change in Real GDP + % Change in Prices

12. (E) Government spending for public goods is a part of the expenditure formula for GDP: C + I + G + X (G is the government sector).

Free-Response Explanations

7 points (1 + 1 + 4 + 1)

(a) 1 point:
  - 1 point is earned for stating that this year's nominal GDP for Econ Island is $17,050: $(1,000 \times \$2) - (10 \times \$20) + (10,000 \times \$1) + \$5,000 + \$250 = \$17,050$.

(b)   1 point:
- 1 point is earned for stating that this year's real GDP for Econ Island is $15,500: ($17,050 / 1.10) = $15,500.

(c)   4 points:
- 1 point is earned for stating that the used cars are not counted in GDP.
- 1 point is earned for explaining that GDP only measures new output for the year, not used goods.
- 1 point is earned for stating that illegal drug production is not counted in GDP.
- 1 point is earned for stating that illegal activity is not counted because reliable numbers are difficult to calculate.

(d)   1 point:
- 1 point is earned for identifying a shortcoming of GDP. Potential answers include the following:
    o Population (needing to use per capita GDP)
    o Nonmarket activities
    o Bartered goods and services
    o Leisure
    o Quality of life
    o Negative externalities
    o The mix of consumer and government goods
    o Distribution of incomes

CHAPTER 25: ECONOMIC GROWTH

Introduction
With a thorough understanding of how real GDP is calculated, we can explore how it is used to determine economic growth and the importance of economic growth for society. Chapter 25 examines the causes of economic growth, government policies that can promote growth, and the costs and benefits of economic growth. Material from Chapter 25 is likely to appear in one or two multiple-choice questions and occasionally in a free-response question on the AP microeconomics and macroeconomics exams, specifically with reference to the production possibilities curve and the causes of economic growth.

Economic Growth
Economic growth is defined as an increase in real GDP (or real GDP per capita) over time. While real GDP measures the value of the total output of a country, real GDP per capita measures the output per person, taking population changes into account to allow for a more accurate comparison of standards of living. The same formula is used for both, simply using per capita numbers for the per capita calculation.

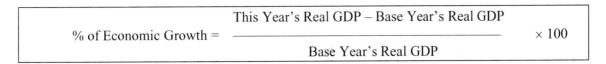

$$\% \text{ of Economic Growth} = \frac{\text{This Year's Real GDP} - \text{Base Year's Real GDP}}{\text{Base Year's Real GDP}} \times 100$$

Economic growth is one of the most important goals for our economy. Scarcity is the fundamental problem of economics, and economic growth helps reduce the burden of scarcity for people. Higher real incomes raise standards of living, reduce poverty, increase investment and the provision of public goods, and allow us to produce more consumer and capital goods at the same time, promoting even more future growth.

The real GDP of the United States has increased by an average of 3.5 percent per year since 1950, while real GDP per capita has grown by an average of 2.3 percent during that same period. It is important to note that this only represents average growth, because short-term fluctuations have brought about faster growth or even declines during recessions. The caveats that we noted in the last chapter for using GDP as a measure of well-being also extend to using GDP as a measure of growth in well-being. GDP cannot account for improvements in product quality, additional leisure time, externalities, or quality of life.

Differences in the levels of GDP growth and the standard of living among countries can result from differences in the amount of technology and innovation, the length of time the nation has engaged in modern economic growth, the labor supply, labor productivity, and government policies that promote economic growth.

Bear in Mind
The history of economic growth over the centuries and information about the economic growth of specific countries have not been the subject of questions on previous AP economics exams and are not covered in detail here.

Institutional Structures that Promote Growth
Economists identify a number of factors that promote economic growth. Strong property rights encourage entrepreneurs to invest in opening businesses with the knowledge that government

cannot take over the business. Patents and copyrights promote invention and innovation by protecting the ownership rights of inventors and allowing them to financially gain from their creations. Efficient financial institutions funnel the savings of households to firms in order to promote investment in capital and economic growth. Literacy and widespread education promote further inventions and implementation of new technologies and increase worker productivity. Free trade promotes growth because countries specialize in what they produce most efficiently, promoting efficient use of resources and allowing growth to spread among countries. A competitive market system allows firms to follow market signals in setting output and prices. Stable political systems, enforcement of contracts, and cultural values with a positive attitude toward work and risk-taking also help to promote economic growth.

Factors Directly Promoting the Rate of Economic Growth

The factors directly increasing the rate of economic growth include the amount and quality of the factors of production—land, labor, and capital—and improvements in technology. Demand must keep pace with the increasing supply of products or firms will respond to increasing inventories by cutting production. Finally, efficiency and full employment are important, as productive efficiency (producing at lowest cost) and allocative efficiency (producing the mix of goods consumers want) ensure that resources are used in ways that maximize well-being.

Economic Growth and Production Possibilities

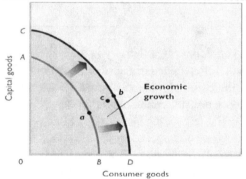

Economic growth and the production possibilities curve

One of the first models we examined was the production possibilities curve, which determines the maximum possible production given current resources and technology. In order to produce more of one product, we have to produce less of another. Our short-run goal is to avoid unemployment and produce at efficiency on the curve. Our long-run goal is to shift out the production possibilities curve, allowing us to produce more of both goods.

Increases in the number and productivity of resources are the primary factors in improving economic growth. The equation below uses another model to calculate GDP.

Real GDP = Hours of Work × Labor Productivity

The labor force participation rate is the percentage of people over age sixteen who are working or seeking work. If a nation can increase the labor force participation rate, or the length of the average workday or workweek, real GDP rises. In addition, productivity can be increased through better technology, increased quality of labor and capital, and better health and education of workers. Improvements in any or a combination of these factors are important for increasing the economic growth of a country.

Factors Increasing Labor Productivity

Increases in labor productivity have accounted for most of the economic growth since the 1950s, largely due to computer and information technology, and economists project it will account for an even larger percentage of economic growth in the future. Five factors contribute to the growth of labor productivity.

Technological advance is the most important factor, responsible for 40 percent of the growth in productivity. Technological advance comes in the form of new production techniques and management methods, capital investment, and innovation. The second major factor in labor productivity is the quantity of capital available to workers, which accounts for 30 percent of the increase in productivity. Improvements in factories and equipment, public infrastructure, and private capital per worker have all increased labor productivity.

A third important factor in improving the productivity of labor is the investment in human capital—the knowledge and skills of workers. Education and training, whether formal or on-the-job, account for approximately 15 percent of the increase in labor productivity. A fourth factor increasing labor productivity is economies of scale, under which larger firms become more efficient. As output increases, the firm can buy more efficient equipment, increase the specialization of labor, and spread research and development costs over more output, increasing productivity. And the final factor is improvements in resource allocation. The movement of workers into higher-productivity jobs, the lessening of discrimination that prevented qualified workers from moving into such jobs, and wider international trade have all helped reallocate workers and other resources into their most productive areas, improving efficiency.

While economic growth can result in negative externalities, higher stress for workers, and the potential to strip the earth of its limited resources, economic growth is essential to increasing standards of living, and proponents argue that government policies and programs can be put in place to correct externalities and address resource issues. Because improvements in education and technology can lead to the more efficient use of resources, economic growth can result in benefits across societies and economic systems.

Multiple-Choice Questions

1.   Why is economic growth an important goal for our society?
    (A)   It reduces the amount of public goods government provides.
    (B)   It results in fewer imports and exports.
    (C)   It reduces the burden of scarcity among people.
    (D)   It reduces the inequality in the distribution of incomes in society.
    (E)   It allows society to focus on the production of goods rather than services.

2.   If the 2009 real GDP of a country is $2.6 billion, and the 2008 real GDP was $2 billion, what was the rate of economic growth for the country in 2009?
    (A)   0.6%
    (B)   1.3%
    (C)   4.6%
    (D)   30%
    (E)   60%

3. Which of the following institutional structures promote economic growth?
    - I. private property rights
    - II. a command economy
    - III. widespread public education
    - IV. strong trade barriers
   - (A) I only
   - (B) I and III only
   - (C) II and IV only
   - (D) II, III, and IV only
   - (E) I, II, III, and IV

4. An increase in each of these factors would increase economic growth EXCEPT an increase in
   - (A) the labor supply.
   - (B) technology.
   - (C) the amount of capital.
   - (D) the quality of workers.
   - (E) the corporate tax rate.

5. Which of these policies would lead to an increase in production possibilities?
   - (A) decreasing government spending for public education
   - (B) government increasing the minimum working age to 18
   - (C) increasing property taxes for business property
   - (D) government granting tax credits to firms that buy new equipment
   - (E) stopping government funding of university research

6. Which factor significantly increased production possibilities in U.S. history?
   - (A) women entering the labor force
   - (B) the provision of Social Security benefits
   - (C) laws prohibiting child labor
   - (D) increases in college tuition
   - (E) increased government safety regulations for industry

7. What do economists credit for most of the economic growth since the 1950s?
   - (A) increases in labor productivity
   - (B) government subsidies of business
   - (C) increases in international trade
   - (D) increases in income tax rates
   - (E) reductions in government spending

8. Economies of scale contribute to economic growth because as firm size increases,
   - (A) wages increase.
   - (B) costs of production decrease.
   - (C) tax burdens decrease.
   - (D) the quantity of workers hired decreases.
   - (E) demand for the product decreases.

Free-Response Question

Increases in labor productivity are central to economic growth.

(a) Identify three ways to increase labor productivity.

(b) Identify one government policy to encourage increases in labor productivity.

(c) Assume a nation's economy can only produce consumer goods and capital goods, and that economy is currently experiencing full employment. Using a correctly labeled production possibilities graph, illustrate the following.

  (i) Label a point at full employment, "F."

  (ii) Show the effect of the government policy you identified in (b).

Multiple-Choice Explanations

1. (C) Scarcity is the fundamental problem of economics, and economic growth increases production of goods, helping to reduce the burden of scarcity.

2. (D) The formula for calculating the percentage change in real GDP is as follows:

$$\frac{\text{This Year's Real GDP} - \text{Base Year's Real GDP}}{\text{Base Year's Real GDP}} \times 100$$

($2.6 billion – $2 billion) / ($2 billion) = 0.3 × 100 = 30

3. (B) Property rights give entrepreneurs confidence that they will keep their firms and profits, while widespread public education provides productive workers. Market economies promote economic growth better than command economies, and trade barriers reduce the efficiencies gained through comparative advantage.

4. (E) If corporations have to pay higher income taxes, they have less money available to purchase additional capital or invest in research.

5. (D) If the cost of buying equipment falls, firms buy more equipment, expanding production possibilities.

6. (A) A significant increase in the quantity of labor resources increased production possibilities and economic growth.

7. (A) Increases in labor productivity have resulted from improvements in education and technology and the quality and quantity of capital.

8. (B) The larger the firm becomes, the more costs of production fall due to more efficient use of capital, the ability to specialize workers, and other factors.

Free-Response Explanation

7 points (3 + 1 + 3)

(a) 3 points:
  - 1 point is earned for each correctly identified cause of an increase in labor productivity. Potential answers include the following.
    - improvements in technology for workers to use
    - an increase in the quantity of capital resources for workers to use
    - an increase in the quality of workers (investment in human capital)
    - economies of scale as a result of increased plant size, equipment, and specialization
    - movement of workers into higher productivity jobs

(b)   1 point:
  • 1 point is earned for correctly identifying one government policy that would promote labor productivity. Potential answers include the following.
    o   tax deductions/credits or subsidization for firms' purchase of equipment
    o   tax deductions/credits or subsidization for research and development
    o   tax deductions/credits, subsidization, or increased government spending for worker education and training

(c)   3 points:
  • 1 point is earned for a correctly labeled production possibilities curve.
  • 1 point is earned for labeling any point on the original (inner) curve "F."
  • 1 point is earned for showing an outward shift in the curve.

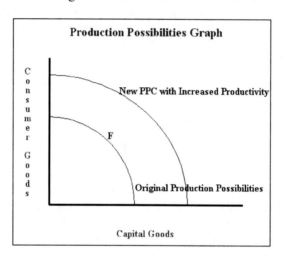

CHAPTER 26: BUSINESS CYCLES, UNEMPLOYMENT, AND INFLATION

Introduction

While long-run economic growth is sustained, short-run economic performance is much more variable. Business cycles commonly result in changes in output, unemployment, and inflation. Chapter 26 explores macroeconomic instability, explaining the phases and causes of business cycles. Discussion continues with the measurement, types, and causes and effects of unemployment and inflation. An understanding of business cycles and their effects lays the foundation for understanding macroeconomic models, competing theories, and government policies to address macroeconomic instability. Material from Chapter 26 is very likely to appear in several multiple-choice questions on the AP macroeconomics exam and occasionally is part of a free-response question as well.

The Business Cycle

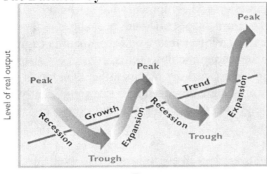

The business cycle

Business cycles are increases and decreases in real GDP over time and composed of four phases. The peak is the highest point of real GDP in the cycle, where the economy experiences full employment, output at or near capacity, and generally rising prices. A recession is a period of decrease in real GDP, generally six months or longer, during which employment and prices tend to fall. The trough is the lowest point of real GDP in the cycle, where output and employment reach their lowest levels. An extended, very deep trough is considered a depression. Expansion, or recovery, is the fourth phase of the business cycle. Real GDP again begins to rise, and employment and prices rise along with it. Business cycles vary in depth and duration.

Taking the EEK! Out of Economics

It is important to remember how GDP, prices, and employment change in each phase of the business cycle. If you keep in mind that all three factors generally move in the same direction, it will help you to keep the effects straight. Some students expect prices to rise during an economic downturn, thinking firms must raise their prices to make up for lost sales. Remember, if demand and production are dropping, firms must lower prices to attract customers back; consumers respond to higher prices by buying even less.

Causes of Business Cycles

Unexpected spending changes in the economy are the primary cause of business cycles. Inventions and innovation lead firms to increase investment spending to adopt new technologies. Changes in labor productivity, the money supply, consumer confidence, and unexpected economic shocks also can affect economic performance.

An increase in investment spending, productivity, consumer confidence, or the money supply results in greater demand. This increased demand raises output, and employment increases as workers are hired to produce that output. The increased demand pushes up the price level, so real GDP, employment, and prices increase together.

If the level of spending in the economy falls due to reduced productivity, consumer confidence, investment spending, money supply or an economic shock, firms reduce output. Fewer workers are needed to produce the reduced output, so employment falls. Prices tend to be sticky downward in the short run but fall if the downturn is sustained. Again, real GDP, employment, and prices move in the same direction.

Business Cycle Impacts on Production
While business cycles impact all sectors of the economy, the strength of impact differs among industries. Producers of capital goods (such as construction and equipment) and consumer durable goods (such as cars and appliances) tend to be more deeply affected by changes in the business cycle. When product demand falls, firms expect a lower return on investment in capital, so they instead produce with existing resources. During economic downturns, consumers also reduce purchases of homes, cars, computers, and appliances, making repairs rather than buying new items. When the economy is strong, consumption of such items tends to rise significantly. Thus, producers of these capital and durable goods tend to sustain strong cyclical swings in economic activity.

Producers of services and non-durable consumer goods are less likely to face strong cyclical changes in demand for their products. During recessions, consumers still tend to purchase food, gasoline, medical care, and haircuts, and demand does not significantly increase during expansions. As a result, output and employment in capital goods and durable goods industries tend to be more strongly affected by economic cycles than in service and non-durable goods industries.

Unemployment
To calculate the unemployment rate, the Bureau of Labor Statistics calls approximately 60,000 households per month. Respondents are placed in two categories. Those who are under sixteen, institutionalized, or not working by choice (for example, retired, students, or homemakers) are outside the labor force. They are not included in unemployment statistics because they are unavailable or unwilling to join the workforce. The second category is the labor force, consisting of people who are willing and able to work. Within the labor force are two groups: the employed and the unemployed. Those who are unemployed are not working but are actively seeking work.

$$\text{Unemployment Rate} = \frac{\text{Unemployed}}{\text{Labor Force}} \times 100$$

It is important to note that the official unemployment rate underestimates unemployment. Because samples are used, many unemployed people may be missed in the sample, such as people without phones or living with others. Underemployed workers work part-time because they cannot find full-time jobs or work in jobs for which they are overqualified because they cannot find appropriate jobs. They are counted as fully employed, though the designation isn't fully accurate. Discouraged workers are also entirely left out of the statistics. Discouraged workers are those who have been unemployed for so long that they have stopped looking for work. They would accept a job if offered, but under the definition of unemployment, they have left the labor force and are not included. Because of the method of gathering data, underemployment, and discouraged workers, the official unemployment rate underestimates the actual level of unemployment in the economy.

Types of Unemployment
People are unemployed for a variety of reasons. One type of unemployment is frictional unemployment, which refers to people temporarily between jobs. People who have been fired, have quit, or are looking for first jobs briefly experience frictional unemployment while they search for new jobs. Frictional unemployment always exists, as there are always people moving between jobs.

A second type of unemployment is seasonal. Lifeguards at outdoor pools in the north, field workers harvesting crops, and commercial fishermen experience unemployment at the same time every year based on seasonal conditions. Workers in these jobs understand the seasonal nature of the work and often seek other jobs during the off-season.

Structural unemployment occurs when a worker's skills do not match the available jobs. Structural unemployment can result from a change in product demand, as when autos replaced horses, reducing demand for blacksmiths to make horseshoes. It also results from industry migration; when steel production grew overseas and mills closed here, U.S. steelworkers lost careers. Automation can also cause structural unemployment when machines replace workers. Structural unemployment is long-term, requiring workers to relocate to where jobs still exist or retrain for new careers where demand is higher.

The fourth type of unemployment, cyclical unemployment, results from swings in the business cycle. You can see the word "cycle" right in the word "cyclical." When total spending in the economy falls and firms reduce output during a recession, they lay off workers. During expansion, cyclical unemployment falls. Cyclical unemployment is generally the target of government policy to stabilize the economy.

Full Employment
It is impossible for an economy to reach zero percent unemployment, because frictional, seasonal, and structural unemployment always exist in a dynamic economy. Full employment is defined as the absence of cyclical unemployment. Full employment is also known as the natural rate of unemployment. At the natural rate of unemployment, the economy is producing at the full potential output; real GDP is at capacity.

The natural rate of unemployment can change over time as demographics and policies change. The natural rate of unemployment rose as women and teenagers joined the labor force in large numbers and as unemployment benefits allowed people to extend their job searches longer. It fell as birth rates fell and fewer people entered the labor force, as the Internet made job searches easier, and as changes in government policy required work for welfare recipients. An unemployment rate of 4 to 5 percent is now considered full employment.

Effects of Unemployment
As we learned in Chapter 1, unemployment is illustrated by a point inside the production possibilities curve. So the cost of unemployment is the forgone output that could have been made by society. The GDP gap is the difference between potential and actual GDP:

$$\boxed{\text{GDP Gap} \;=\; \text{Actual GDP} \;-\; \text{Potential GDP}}$$

Potential GDP increases each year at the expected rate of long-run growth, around 2 to 3 percent. If unemployment is higher than the natural rate, it reduces actual output, resulting in the GDP gap. The higher the unemployment rate, the higher the GDP gap. If unemployment is less than the natural rate of unemployment, actual GDP can exceed the expected potential GDP, resulting in a negative gap—more output than expected. But because rapid expansion causes inflationary pressure, it cannot be sustained long-term.

Okun's Law defines the relationship between unemployment and the GDP gap. Under Okun's Law, for every percentage point the unemployment rate is above the natural rate of unemployment, the GDP gap increases 2 percentage points. So if the natural rate of unemployment is 5 percent and current unemployment is 7 percent, the GDP gap would be 4 percent.

The effects of unemployment are distributed unequally. Workers with less education and low skills, teens, African-Americans, and Hispanics are more likely to be unemployed and unemployed longer than other workers. Deep and sustained unemployment can also lead to poverty, crime, divorce, and even political unrest, if severe enough.

Inflation
Inflation is an increase in the general price level. During a period of inflation, the value or purchasing power of the dollar decreases, and people cannot buy as much as they once could with the same income.

Inflation is primarily measured by the consumer price index (CPI). The Bureau of Labor Statistics creates a "market basket" of hundreds of goods and services that a typical urban consumer would buy in a month. To find the consumer price index, use the formula below:

$$\text{CPI} \;=\; \frac{\text{Total Price of the Market Basket This Year}}{\text{Total Price of the Market Basket in the Base Year}} \;\times\; 100$$

To find the rate of inflation for the year, use this formula:

$$\text{Rate of Inflation} \;=\; \frac{\text{This Year's CPI} - \text{Base Year's CPI}}{\text{Base Year's CPI}} \;\times\; 100$$

Causes of Inflation
Demand-pull inflation, the most common kind of inflation in the United States, is an increase in the price level resulting from demand that is greater than the ability of the economy to produce the output. A significant increase in the money supply can cause such an increase in demand. Because firms are producing at capacity, they cannot increase output, so demand pulls the price up, resulting in inflation.

Cost-push inflation occurs when the cost of production rises, and firms pass the increased cost on to consumers. A supply shock such as a rise in material costs can cause cost-push inflation.

Increased costs reduce the firm's profit, so the firm reduces output and pushes the price upward. As supply falls, output and employment fall while prices rise.

Nominal and Real Income
As we saw with GDP, inflation can distort the value of production. In the same way, inflation can distort the value of income. Nominal income is the income earned in the current value of dollars. Real income is the measure of what one's income will actually buy or, in other words, the purchasing power of a dollar.

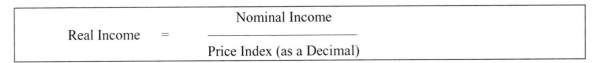

$$\text{Real Income} = \frac{\text{Nominal Income}}{\text{Price Index (as a Decimal)}}$$

If you earned $10,000 this year and the price index is 1.05 (an inflation rate of 5 percent), your real wage for this year is $9,523.81. In other words, it will cost your entire $10,000 income in its current value to buy what $9,523.81 would have bought at its value last year.

This is important when we compare the inflation rate to the change in nominal income to see if nominal income kept up with inflation, rose above inflation, or fell behind.

% Change in Real Income = % Change in Nominal Income – % Change in Price Level

If you received a 3 percent raise at work this year and the inflation rate was 3 percent, you would experience no change in real income; although you would be paid more in current dollars, the value of those dollars fell enough that you could not purchase any more than you did last year. If your nominal income rises more quickly than the price level, your real income increases; if your nominal income rises less quickly than the price level, your real income actually declines. In the latter case, even though the amount on your paycheck has increased, it won't stretch to buy as much as last year's income at its value did.

Unanticipated Inflation
When people do not prepare for inflation, some are hurt, some are helped, and others are unaffected by the inflation. People living on a fixed income, such as retirees on a fixed pension or workers earning the minimum wage, are hurt by inflation. They receive the same dollar amount of income, but it will not buy as much as it once did. Savers are also hurt by inflation, because the interest rate on the savings account or CD does not increase with the inflation rate, so the interest payment will not stretch as far as it once did.

Lenders are also hurt, but borrowers are helped by unanticipated inflation. Inflation erodes the value of money over time, so the money has a greater value at the time it is loaned than when it is repaid. As a result, the money repaid is not worth as much as the money originally borrowed. The lender receives the full amount of the loan back but that money will not buy as much as it would have when the loan was originated.

People who have flexible incomes are less likely to feel the impact of unanticipated inflation. If firms must raise wages to attract workers to meet the increased demand, wages may keep pace or even exceed the inflation rate. If firms are able to raise prices higher than the increase in production costs, profits can increase as well.

Anticipated Inflation

If people are able to anticipate inflation, they can mitigate or eliminate the effects on their real incomes. Social Security benefits automatically adjust with inflation, and some workers have cost-of-living adjustments (COLAs) built into their contracts. Lenders also try to recoup the diminishing value of the dollar over time by building the expected inflation rate into the interest rate they charge customers.

> Nominal Interest Rate = Real Interest Rate + Expected Inflation Rate

If a bank would charge a 4% interest rate for a one-year loan in the absence of inflation and the bank expects a 3% increase in the price level next year, it would charge 7% interest on the loan, so the repaid dollars (with the 3% inflation premium) hold the overall same value as the dollars originally loaned.

Deflation

Deflation is a general decrease in prices, which can occur as the result of a deep, sustained recession. Deflation can help those living on fixed incomes, savers, and lenders, because their fixed incomes now buy more. Borrowers lose from deflation, as the dollars they repay are worth more than the dollars originally borrowed.

Hyperinflation

Hyperinflation is an extreme level of inflation. Prices rise so quickly that wages, profits, and costs of resources become unpredictable. As money essentially becomes worthless, consumers funnel their money into precious metals and other investments that will hold value, but do not produce output in the country. Eventually, many countries experiencing hyperinflation collapse, both economically and politically. Governments can undertake policies to help prevent hyperinflation and other effects of economic instability in order to promote economic growth.

Multiple-Choice Questions

1. A recession is generally characterized by
   - I. a decrease in Real GDP.
   - II. a decrease in employment.
   - III. an increase in price level.
   - (A) I only
   - (B) III only
   - (C) I and II only
   - (D) II and III only
   - (E) I, II, and III

2. Which event could lead to a recessionary phase of the business cycle?
   - (A) an increase in worker productivity
   - (B) firms investing in new technology
   - (C) an increase in consumer confidence
   - (D) a supply shock that reduces the costs of production for firms
   - (E) a reduction in the money supply

3. Which sectors of the economy are most strongly impacted by business cycles?
   - (A) capital goods and consumer durable goods
   - (B) services and consumer non-durable goods
   - (C) public goods and exports

(D)   imports and financial instruments

(E)   tax revenues and energy

4.   Unemployment measures the percentage of people in the labor force who
     (A)   are not working.
     (B)   are not looking for jobs.
     (C)   are actively looking for jobs.
     (D)   have given up looking for jobs.
     (E)   are not working or are only working part-time.

5.   The official unemployment rate is not completely accurate because it leaves out
                 I.   people who have given up looking for work.
                 II.   people who have not filed for unemployment benefits.
                 III.   people who are working part-time but want full-time jobs.
                 IV.   people who do not have phones.
     (A)   I only
     (B)   I and IV only
     (C)   II and III only
     (D)   II, III, and IV only
     (E)   I, III, and IV only

6.   A college graduate searching for her first job is experiencing
     (A)   frictional unemployment.
     (B)   structural unemployment.
     (C)   seasonal unemployment.
     (D)   cyclical unemployment.
     (E)   underemployment.

7.   Full employment is achieved when the economy experiences no
     (A)   frictional unemployment.
     (B)   structural unemployment.
     (C)   seasonal unemployment.
     (D)   cyclical unemployment.
     (E)   underemployment.

8.   If the consumer price index for this year is 240 and the CPI for last year was 200, what is
     the rate of inflation for this year?
     (A)   –40%
     (B)   1.2%
     (C)   20%
     (D)   40%
     (E)   83%

9.   If Don's nominal income increases by 5% and the inflation rate increases by 3%, how did
     Don's real income change?
     (A)   It fell by 8%.
     (B)   It fell by 2%.
     (C)   It rose by 2%.
     (D)   It rose by 5%.
     (E)   It rose by 8%.

10.   Which of the following factors would cause demand-pull inflation?
       (A)   an increase in the cost of raw materials for firms
       (B)   an increase in the money supply
       (C)   a significant decrease in the supply of energy products
       (D)   a serious crop failure
       (E)   a reduction in imports allowed into the country

11.   Which of the following people is least likely to be hurt by unanticipated inflation?
       (A)   retirees living on a fixed pension
       (B)   people who have borrowed money to buy cars
       (C)   savers earning income from interest on savings accounts
       (D)   workers earning the minimum wage
       (E)   creditors who provide loans to customers

12.   If a bank charges customers a nominal interest rate of 12% for car loans and expects a 7% inflation rate over the life of the loan, what is the real interest rate?
       (A)   −5%
       (B)   5%
       (C)   5.8%
       (D)   19%
       (E)   12%

Free-Response Question
In Sereneland, the inflation rate increases by its expected average 2% per year.
(a)   Explain the effect of this inflation on the real income of a worker whose nominal income rises 2% per year.
(b)   Now assume that this year, the inflation rate unexpectedly jumped to 10%. Explain the effect of this increase in inflation on each of the following.
       (i)   the worker whose nominal income rose 2% this year
       (ii)   a retiree living on a fixed pension
       (iii) a senior citizen living on Social Security which is indexed with a COLA
       (iv)   a homeowner paying a 30-year home mortgage with a fixed interest rate

Multiple Choice Explanations
1.   (C)   As real GDP falls, fewer workers are needed to make the diminishing number of products. While prices tend to be sticky downward, at the minimum they would remain the same and would not rise.
2.   (E)   A reduction in the money supply makes it more difficult and expensive for firms and consumers to obtain credit, so demand would fall.
3.   (A)   Capital goods are affected because firms can wait to invest until they expect a profitable return on their investment. Consumer durable goods are strongly affected because they tend to consume a large proportion of the consumer's budget, and consumers can make do with existing goods until the economy improves.
4.   (C)   Unemployment only measures those available for work who want jobs and are actively looking but cannot find one.
5.   (E)   Whether a person has filed for unemployment benefits is irrelevant to the calculation of the official unemployment rate.
6.   (A)   Frictional unemployment is the temporary unemployment that comes with entering the labor force or searching for a new job after losing another.

7.	(D)	Full employment occurs where output is maximized, so firms are not laying off workers due to low product demand.

8.	(C)	Inflation Rate = (This Year's CPI – Last Year's CPI) / Last Year's CPI = (240 – 200) / 200 = 40 / 200 = 0.20 × 100 = 20%

9.	(C)	Don's paycheck rose by 5% but because prices increased by 3%, Don's real income—what he can buy with his paycheck—only rose 2%.

10.	(B)	If too much money chases too few goods, the excess demand pulls prices up. The other four options cause cost-push inflation by reducing supply.

11.	(B)	Borrowers can actually gain from inflation, because the dollars they use to pay back the loan are not worth as much as the dollars they borrowed.

12.	(B)	Real Interest Rate = Nominal Interest Rate – Expected Inflation Rate = 12% – 7% = 5%

Free-Response Explanation

10 points (2 + 8)

(a)	2 points:
- 1 point is earned for stating that the worker's real income would not change.
- 1 point is earned for explaining that the wage increase only equals inflation.

(b)	8 points:
- 1 point is earned for stating that the worker's real income would fall 8%.
- 1 point is earned for explaining that the change in real wage equals the change in nominal wage minus the change in the inflation rate (2% – 10% = –8%).
- 1 point is earned for stating that the retiree's real income would fall.
- 1 point is earned for explaining that prices increased but the retiree's income did not.
- 1 point is earned for stating that the senior citizen's real income did not change.
- 1 point is earned for explaining that the COLA is designed to change the nominal income at the same rate as inflation, to keep real income the same.
- 1 point is earned for stating that the homeowner gains from inflation.
- 1 point is earned for explaining that the money repaid is not worth as much as the money that was borrowed.

CHAPTER 27: BASIC MACROECONOMIC RELATIONSHIPS

Introduction
An understanding of gross domestic product, economic growth, and business cycles lays the foundation for understanding the aggregate expenditure model of macroeconomic analysis. Changes in aggregate (total) spending cause short-run economic instability, and government policies address such instability. Chapter 27 introduces the marginal propensities to consume and save, the relationship between interest rates and investment, and the multiplier effect of spending throughout the economy. These principles provide the basis for understanding the aggregate demand–aggregate supply model in subsequent chapters. Material from Chapter 27 may appear in a few multiple-choice questions on the AP macroeconomics exam.

Income, Consumption, and Saving Relationships
Recall that the definition of disposable income is income after personal taxes are paid. It is the income consumers have available to do one of two things: consume or save.

> Disposable Income = Consumption + Saving
> Consumption = Disposable Income – Saving
> Saving = Disposable Income – Consumption

Americans consume nearly all of their income. The consumption function measures the relationship between income and consumption. As income rises, consumption rises. Those with lower incomes consume a larger percentage of their incomes (save less) than those with higher incomes. In fact, those with low incomes may dissave, spending more than their current income by borrowing, spending previous savings, or selling assets.

Taking the EEK! Out of Economics
You may notice a subtle difference between the word "saving" and the word "savings." This difference is important. Saving is an action, a choice to not spend a stream of income. Savings is a quantity of past income that has been set aside and not spent. Saving is a flow, while savings is a stock, or a set amount. Pay careful attention to which word is used, and you'll be able to discern whether we're talking about a person's current decision about whether to save or the amount of savings previously set aside.

Bear in Mind
The 45-degree line and consumption and savings graphs in Chapter 27 provide the basis for an aggregate expenditure model known as the Keynesian Cross, explained in detail in Chapter 28. The Keynesian Cross is no longer tested as part of the AP macroeconomics exam. The concepts are important and can help you to understand macroeconomic relationships, but specific Keynesian Cross concepts will not be covered here.

Average Propensities to Consume and Save
Average propensities to consume and save measure what consumers do with their entire incomes. Average propensity to consume (APC) is the percentage of total income spent.

$$APC = \frac{Consumption}{Income}$$

If you earn $10,000 of total income this year and spend $9,000, your APC is 0.90 (90 percent).

The average propensity to save (APS) is the percentage of total income that is saved.

$$APS = \frac{Saving}{Income}$$

If you earn $10,000 of total income this year and save $1,000, your APS is 0.10 (10 percent).

Because income can only be consumed or saved, the percentage consumed plus the percentage saved must equal 100 percent of income.

$$APC + APS = 1$$

With these relationships, we can determine either consumption or saving by knowing the other. If the APC is 0.75, the APS must be 0.25. If APS is 0.01, APC is 0.99.

Marginal Propensities to Consume and Save

Marginal propensities to consume and save measure what consumers do with changes in income. If a household normally saves 5 percent of its income but then gains an additional $1,000 of income from overtime work, a tax cut, a gift, or a winning lottery ticket, what will it do with the additional income? Some households will spend all of the additional income as a bonus to themselves, while others will save all of it for future spending, and other households will choose every combination between those extremes. The formulas for the marginal propensities to save and consume look the same as the formulas for the average propensities to save and consume, but the marginal formulas only deal with the *change* in income and spending or saving, rather than the total income.

Marginal propensity to consume (MPC) is the percentage of the change in income that is consumed.

$$MPC = \frac{Change\ in\ Consumption}{Change\ in\ Income}$$

If you earn $1,000 of additional income and spend $600, your MPC is 0.60 (60 percent).

Marginal propensity to save (MPS) is the percentage of change in income that is saved.

$$MPS = \frac{Change\ in\ Saving}{Change\ in\ Income}$$

If you earn $1,000 of additional income and save $400, your MPS is 0.40 (40 percent).

Just as with average propensities, because the additional income can only be consumed or saved, the percentage consumed plus the percentage saved must equal 100 percent of income.

MPC + MPS = 1

Given these formulas and data, answer this: Assume Deb's income is $20,000 and her APC is 0.75. She works overtime hours and earns an additional $2,000. Her MPC is 0.60. How much of Deb's overall income will she spend? How much will she save?

Deb spends 75% of her original $20,000 ($15,000) plus 60% of her additional $2,000 ($1,200), so she spends a total of $16,200. Remember that what isn't spent must be saved. So Deb must have saved 25% of her original $20,000 ($5,000) plus 40% of her additional $2,000 ($800), so she saves a total of $5,800.

Bear in Mind
Once you have found the total consumption of income, it may be tempting to take the shortcut of just subtracting the consumption from total income to determine the total saving. But it is in your best interest to take the extra time to separately calculate the saving using the formula, because you can then compare that answer to the shortcut answer to make sure your math is correct. Don't lose points for a silly math error!

Non-Income Determinants of Consumption and Saving
While a household's disposable income is the primary factor in determining the relative amounts the household will choose to consume or save, other factors also help to make that determination.

Wealth is the value of assets owned by the household minus the debts owed. According to the wealth effect, when wealth increases, households tend to increase consumption and reduce saving; reductions in wealth lead to reductions in consumption and increases in saving. In late 2008, when the price of stock and home values fell significantly, consumer demand for products dramatically dropped.

Borrowing also has an effect on consumption, because if households can borrow money to spend beyond their disposable incomes, consumption increases. It is important to keep in mind that although consumption increases in the short-term, consumption must decrease later in order for the household to repay the debt.

Expectations about future prices and income also affect consumption and saving decisions. If consumers expect prices to rise in the near future, they may increase consumption now, in order to buy before the price rises. The reverse is also true. If consumers are concerned about the possibility of losing their jobs during a recession, they are likely to reduce spending and increase saving to prepare for that possibility.

Changes in real interest rates (those adjusted for inflation) can also affect consumption and saving. If interest rates fall, consumers tend to consume more because of the lower cost of borrowing. At the same time, they tend to save less because the interest they earn on savings is lower. The same effects work in reverse for higher interest rates. This effect tends to be weaker than the wealth, borrowing, and expectation effects, because interest rates tend to only affect products bought with credit, and the interest rate is not the primary determination of whether consumers save. Saving as a long-term investment for retirement, education, or emergencies seems to be a more powerful consideration.

Taxes can also affect consumption and saving. Remember, disposable income is the income households have available after taxes. If taxes rise, less disposable income is available for both consumption and saving. If taxes fall, both consumption and saving tend to increase.

The Relationship Between Interest Rates and Investment

Remember that economists consider investment to be firms' spending for plants, capital equipment, and other factors that help to increase future production. If the marginal benefit (the expected return for the firm, which is the expected additional profit divided by the cost of the investment) is greater than the marginal cost (the interest rate to pay for borrowing), the firm will make the investment. But if the interest rate the firm must pay is greater than the expected return on the investment, the firm will not make the investment. These same conditions are met if the firm is using savings to invest, because in that situation, the interest rate represents forgone interest the firm could have earned on the savings. At lower real interest rates, firms are more willing to invest; at higher interest rates, firms are less willing to invest.

It is important to note that the firm is using the real interest rate, rather than the nominal interest rate, in its investment decisions. The nominal interest rate includes an extra factor to compensate for the expected rate of inflation. But because the firm would repay the loan with those inflated dollars, the inflation factor in the nominal interest rate is not necessary. So the firm only considers real interest rates in making investment decisions.

Shifts in the Investment Demand Curve

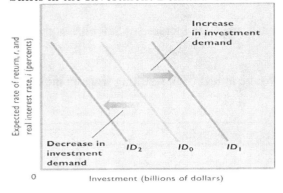

Shifts of the investment demand curve

If firms expect a larger return on their investment, their investment demand increases, shifting to the right. If firms expect lower returns on investment, their investment demand decreases and shifts to the left.

The costs of capital and its operation and maintenance are central to the investment decision. If these costs rise, the firm's expected return on investment will fall and the firm will be less willing to make the investment. Increased taxes on firms also reduce expected return on investment, lowering investment demand. If firms have excess capacity (unused plant and equipment) or large unplanned inventories, the firm will expect little return on investment and be less willing to invest in even more plant and equipment. On the other hand, firms increase investment if they expect to make additional returns from planned inventories. Technological progress increases investment, as the firm expects to increase profit or at least keep up with competitors it expects to also adopt the new technology. Finally, expectations affect investment. If firms are optimistic about the economy and their expected return on investment, they will increase investment demand; if they are pessimistic, their investment demand falls.

Investment spending is the most volatile sector of the economy, and most of the business cycle effects on output and employment can be traced to changes in investment. Part of the instability is due to the durability of capital goods. They are built for longer-term use, and firms can make repairs to keep older capital functioning instead of purchasing new capital. Innovation also occurs irregularly, and investment tends to increase significantly when it is released. Changes in actual profits also affect investment in terms of providing funds to finance the investment and changing expectations about future profit. Quickly changing expectations about future sales, consumer confidence, the stock market, political events, and economic shocks can also increase the variability of investment.

The Multiplier Effect

Increased spending in the economy causes an increase in the real GDP, but the effects reach beyond the initial change in spending. With the multiplier effect, an initial change in spending leads to an even larger change in real GDP. To determine how large the effect will be, we must calculate the spending multiplier:

$$\text{Multiplier} = \frac{\text{Change in Real GDP}}{\text{Initial Change in Spending}}$$

If investment spending rises by $5 billion, resulting in a real GDP increase of $20 billion, the spending multiplier is 4.

Converting the formula, we can also calculate the change in real GDP resulting from an initial change in spending:

$$\text{Change in GDP} = \text{Multiplier} \times \text{Initial Change in Spending}$$

If investment spending increases by $2 million and the spending multiplier is 3, real GDP will increase by $6 million.

While initial changes in spending are often attributed to the investment sector because spending in that sector is so volatile, it is important to remember that changes in spending can also originate in the consumer, government, and net export sectors. It is also important to note that decreases in spending also result in multiplied effects on GDP.

The spending multiplier results from the fact that one factor's spending is another factor's income. When spending increases, part of the income is saved and the rest is spent. Those who receive that second round of spending again spend part of that income and save the rest. The initial spending is multiplied as it goes through round after round of spending in the economy, until there is no more income left to spend. The Council of Economic Advisers estimates the actual U.S. spending multiplier is about 2.

The Spending Multiplier and Marginal Propensities

We can also calculate the specific changes in GDP resulting from the change in spending by using the marginal propensities to consume and save.

$$\text{Multiplier} = \frac{1}{\text{MPS}} \qquad \text{or} \qquad \text{Multiplier} = \frac{1}{1 - \text{MPC}}$$

If the marginal propensity to save is 0.2, the spending multiplier is 5, whether you divide directly by MPS or subtract the MPC (which must be 0.8) from 1 (the 100 percent of income).

The smaller the percentage of income consumed, the smaller the spending multiplier. If a smaller percentage of income is actually spent in each round of spending, even less money is available for the next round of spending, and this continues round after round.

For example, if the initial change in spending is $1,000 and MPC is 0.9, people spend 90 percent of the change in income. In the first round of spending, $900 of additional spending occurs ($1,000 × 0.9). In the second round, $810 of additional spending occurs ($900 × 0.9). The multiplier for this change in spending is 10 (1 / 0.1). Therefore, the change in GDP resulting from this $1,000 initial change in spending is $10,000 ($1,000 × 10).

If, instead, the MPC were 0.5, people would only spend 50 percent of the change in income. In the first round of spending, $500 of additional spending occurs ($1,000 × 0.5), and round two brings only $250 of additional spending ($500 × 0.5). The spending multiplier for this lower MPC is only 2 (1 / 0.5), so the change in GDP resulting from this $1,000 initial change in spending is only $2,000 ($1,000 × 2). Therefore, the larger the marginal propensity to consume, the larger the multiplier, and the larger the effect on GDP when a change in spending occurs.

Bear in Mind
It is important to know how to use both the MPS and MPC formulas to calculate the multiplier, because AP macroeconomics exam questions may only provide you the MPC or MPS, and you must be able to convert information from one measure to the other.

Multiple-Choice Questions
1. According to the consumption function, if income increases by $100,
    (A) saving increases by $100.
    (B) saving increases by more than $100.
    (C) saving increases by less than $100.
    (D) spending increases by $100.
    (E) spending increases by more than $100.

2. When the average propensity to consume is 0.8, if income is
    (A) $1,000, consumption is $80.
    (B) $500, saving is $100.
    (C) $200, consumption is $250.
    (D) $100, saving is $80.
    (E) $600, consumption is $120.

3.   Assume Rivka's income is $10,000 and she spends $9,000 of it. Then she receives a bonus of $500 at work and spends $200 of the bonus. What is Rivka's marginal propensity to save?
(A)   0.9
(B)   0.88
(C)   0.6
(D)   0.4
(E)   0.1

4.   Assume Teng's income is $20,000 and his average propensity to consume is 0.9. Then he receives a $100 gift and his marginal propensity to consume is 0.1. How much of his total income did Teng save?
(A) $20,100
(B) $18,100
(C) $18,010
(D) $2,100
(E) $2,090

5.   Which of the following situations would be most likely to result in increased consumer spending?
(A)   Wealth is reduced by a significant drop in stock values.
(B)   Interest rates for loans increase.
(C)   Income taxes increase.
(D)   Consumers expect significant price increases in the near future.
(E)   Consumers believe the economy is moving into recession.

6.   Firms will invest in capital as long as the real interest rate is less than or equal to
(A)   the firm's expected rate of return on the investment.
(B)   the cost of the capital investment.
(C)   the increase in the quantity of products sold.
(D)   the change in the firm's cost of production.
(E)   the total profit of the firm.

7.   Firms are more likely to increase investment when
(A)   the cost of capital increases.
(B)   corporate income taxes increase.
(C)   there is excess capacity in the plant.
(D)   attitudes are pessimistic about future economic performance.
(E)   technological progress occurs.

8.   The most volatile sector of the economy is the
(A)   consumer sector.
(B)   investment sector.
(C)   government sector.
(D)   import sector.
(E)   export sector.

9.   If firms increase investment by $5 million and the marginal propensity to consume is 0.8, by how much will real GDP change?
        (A) $40 million
        (B) $3 million
        (C) $2 million
        (D) $10 million
        (E) $25 million

10.   The spending multiplier increases as a result of an increase in
        (A)   the marginal propensity to consume.
        (B)   the average propensity to save.
        (C)   investment spending.
        (D)   government spending.
        (E)   the marginal propensity to save.

Multiple-Choice Explanations
1.   (C)   Saving increases by less than the amount of the change in income because consumers spend part of their income.
2.   (B)   If APC is 0.8, 80% of income is consumed, meaning the APS is 0.2, with 20% of income saved. 20% of $500 is $100.
3.   (C)   Her spending from total income is not relevant to the question. Her MPC is 0.4 ($200 / $500), so her MPS must be 0.6 (1 – 0.4).
4.   (E)   Teng saved $2,000 of his original income ($20,000 × 0.1) and $90 of his increased income ($100 × 0.9), resulting in $2,090 of total saving.
5.   (D)   If consumers expect prices to rise significantly, they will increase spending before the prices can increase.
6.   (A)   If the firm expects to earn a greater percentage return than the interest rate cost of making the investment, the firm's profit will increase.
7.   (E)   Firms tend to increase investment to take advantage of new technology in order to reduce production costs or increase output.
8.   (B)   Investment is volatile due to the ability to extend the life of durable goods, the irregular timing of innovation, and economic shocks.
9.   (E)   The multiplier is 1 / MPS or 1 / (1 – MPC), which is 5 (1 / 0.2). The increase in real GDP equals the increase in investment multiplied by the multiplier, which is $25 million ($5 million × 5).
10.   (A)   If the MPC is higher, a higher proportion of the new income is spent in each round, increasing the spending multiplier. Because the spending multiplier is 1 / (1 – MPC), a higher MPC results in a higher multiplier.

CHAPTER 28: THE AGGREGATE EXPENDITURES MODEL

Introduction

Now that you have a basic understanding of how changes in disposable income, investment, and decisions about consumption and saving affect real GDP, we will bring the aspects of the Keynesian aggregate expenditures model together. Chapter 28 begins with a closed private sector economy and then adds international trade and government into the model. This model explains the effects of changes in spending in each sector on real GDP and recessionary and inflationary gaps, as well as the role of government in reducing such gaps. Material from Chapter 28 may appear in several multiple-choice questions on the AP macroeconomics exam, and free-response questions frequently focus on the appropriate fiscal policy measures taken to address recessionary and inflationary gaps.

Bear in Mind

The graphs developed throughout Chapter 28, known as the Keynesian Cross, are no longer tested as part of the AP macroeconomics exam. The concepts are important and can help you to understand macroeconomic relationships, but specific Keynesian Cross graphic concepts will not be covered here.

Classical Theory

Classical theory was the first modern economic theory. It was developed by economists such as Adam Smith, David Ricardo, John Stuart Mill, Thomas Malthus, and Jean Baptiste Say. Classical theorists believed that a market economy would maintain full-employment output in the long run. According to classical theorists, wages and prices were flexible, but output and employment were not. They theorized that even if an economy experienced a short-run shock like a crop failure, a war, or a discovery of new resources, market forces would automatically adjust. If spending fell in the economy, prices and wages would fall in response, enticing consumers to increase their spending again and restoring the economy to full-employment output. They were also convinced that supply would create its own demand, because the spending for resources to produce the output would create income for the resource owners to buy that output. Because they believed that a laissez-faire economy experiencing instability would self-correct, they argued that no government intervention was necessary.

Keynesian Theory

Classical theory was the dominant theory for well over a century—until the Great Depression. The Great Depression dragged on for years, with an extreme drop in GDP and a dramatic rise in unemployment, and the economy did not self-adjust. With the failure of the classical model to explain the Great Depression, British economist John Maynard Keynes brought about a whole new way of thinking about the economy.

According to Keynes, who built his model on Depression-era economic conditions, output and employment were flexible, but prices and wages were not. As a result, it was possible for aggregate spending to remain lower than full-employment output. Prices were so sticky downward that they would not change in response to changes in demand. Millions of workers were unemployed, so if demand increased for products, firms could hire workers without having to raise wages to attract them. Therefore, prices need not rise. Firms had excess production capacity and unplanned inventories, so that if demand increased, a reduction in those inventories would signal to firms to increase production. The economy just needed a stimulus to bring aggregate demand back up. Keynes called for the government to take an instrumental role in correcting economic instability.

To begin this analysis of the Keynesian model, we make several simplifying assumptions. We begin with only households and firms—no government or international sectors. We also assume that because there are no taxes, real GDP equals disposable income. Remember, GDP can be calculated using either the expenditure or income approaches, because one factor's spending is another factor's income. We also assume the excess plant capacity and high unemployment conditions of the Depression, so that increases in output and employment will not put upward pressure on the price level.

Equilibrium GDP

In a closed (no international trade) private sector (no government) economy, consumption spending by households plus planned investment spending by firms equals the aggregate (total) spending in the economy. Equilibrium output is the quantity of output at which the quantity produced (GDP) equals the quantity bought (aggregate spending), and there are no unplanned inventories.

If current spending is less than production, unplanned inventories begin to rise and firms reduce production until the market returns to equilibrium. If current spending is greater than production, inventories begin to decline and firms increase output until the market returns to equilibrium.

At equilibrium GDP, saving equals planned investment. In the circular flow model, saving is considered a "leakage" from the flow of income, because that income is not immediately spent for goods or services. However, firms also do not sell their entire production to households, because capital equipment sold to other firms is investment. This investment is considered an "injection" of spending back into the circular flow model. If saving is greater than investment, the leakage is greater than the injection and real GDP falls. Conversely, if investment is greater than saving, the injection is greater than the leakage and real GDP increases.

Changes in Equilibrium GDP and the Multiplier

Equilibrium GDP is affected by changes in consumer or investment spending, but investment is the more volatile sector. If the real interest rate increases and firms expect their rate of return on investment to be lower than the new interest rate, they reduce their investment spending. Real GDP falls as firms reduce output and employment. But the reduction in GDP doesn't just end with the initial decrease in investment. Remember, the decrease in spending rumbles through the economy over and over, and the multiplier is needed to calculate the total effect on GDP. If the initial reduction in investment is $1 million and the multiplier is 5, that initial reduction in investment will result in a $5 million reduction in real GDP.

International Trade

Releasing one of our beginning assumptions, we now open the economy and include net exports (exports minus imports). If exports exceed imports, net exports are positive. They increase aggregate spending and the real GDP to a higher level than they would have been in a closed economy or if trade were balanced. If imports are greater than exports, the negative net exports lower the aggregate spending and real GDP from what they would have been in a closed economy or if trade were balanced.

A number of factors affect imports and exports. If real incomes abroad increase, consumers in those countries are better able to afford U.S. exports and exports rise. The resulting income from the exports also allows Americans to increase their imports from other countries. A second factor affecting international trade is the use of trade barriers. If another country imposes tariffs on imports, consumers in that country buy fewer American exports, reducing our net exports. If we retaliate by imposing our own tariffs on imports from that country, our imports fall as well, so the relative effect on net exports depends on the relative strength of the trade barriers. A third factor affecting net exports is the exchange rate. If the dollar appreciates, imports appear to be less expensive because their currency is less expensive, so imports increase. At the same time, the relative price of American goods to foreign consumers seems to have increased, so they buy less, reducing our exports. Because exports fall and imports increase, net exports fall and real GDP decreases. Were the value of the dollar to depreciate, the effects would be reversed.

The Public Sector
Releasing another beginning assumption, we now add government revenues and spending to the economy in order to see the full picture of the mixed-market economy. Remember the GDP formula $C + I + G + (X - M)$; the government sector completes the formula. In this analysis, we assume that government spending does not affect the other sectors and that government collects the same amount of tax revenue, no matter what happens to GDP.

Increases in government spending increase aggregate spending and the real GDP. Just as with consumption and investment spending, government spending is affected by the multiplier. If government spending increases by $10 million and the multiplier is 5, the real GDP would increase by $50 million. If government spending decreased, the real GDP would decrease as well.

Taxes also affect real GDP. A lump-sum tax is a tax that brings in the same amount of revenue to the government, regardless of the level of GDP. When a tax is instituted, consumers pay part of the tax from savings and the other part from reduced consumption. We know the percentages from the marginal propensities to consume and save. If the MPC is 0.8, a $10 million tax will reduce consumption by $8 million; the other $2 million of tax revenue will come from reduced saving. Therefore, the increase in tax lowers the real GDP by the amount that consumption falls—by $8 million, not the entire $10 million. Conversely, a reduction in taxes will lead to a higher real GDP.

It is very important to note that changes in government spending and changes in taxes have different effects on real GDP. Changes in government spending have a full impact on real GDP, because the spending goes right out into the economy. However, when taxes are changed, this action has less than a full impact on the economy, because due to the MPC and MPS, part of the impact is on consumption and part is on saving. For example, if the government increases spending by $50 million, the real GDP initially increases by $50 million. If taxes decrease by $50 million and the MPC is 0.8, the real GDP initially only increases by $40 million because the other $10 million is an increase in saving.

Bear in Mind

It is important to keep in mind the differences between the effects of taxation and spending; spending has a fuller effect on GDP than taxes because consumers save some of tax cuts and use savings to pay part of tax increases. Questions about this particular concept commonly appear on the AP macroeconomics exam.

Leakages and Injections

Now that we have included all four sectors of spending into the circular market flow, we must address the leakages and injections in the model, recognizing that the leakages from the flow must equal the injections into the flow. Saving, imports, and taxes are all leakages from the circular flow, because they represent income that was not spent to purchase output in the domestic economy. Investment, exports, and government spending are all injections into the circular flow, because they represent additional spending beyond current income to purchase output in the domestic economy. At the equilibrium GDP, the sum of the leakages must equal the sum of the injections. If the leakages and injections differ, GDP is not at equilibrium.

The Recessionary Expenditure Gap

In the Keynesian model, current spending and full-employment GDP need not be at the same output. In fact, Keynesian analysis, developed during the Great Depression, illustrated GDP output at a rate well below potential GDP output and full employment.

A recessionary expenditure gap is the amount by which current aggregate spending is less than the spending necessary to reach full-employment GDP. An initial decrease in spending is then subject to the multiplier, so a $3 billion recessionary expenditure gap with a multiplier of 5 will eventually create a current GDP of $15 billion less than full-employment GDP.

Keynes advocated government action, or fiscal policy, to correct the economic instability that led to less than full-employment GDP. If government increases spending or lowers taxes, each policy will increase aggregate spending and help restore full-employment GDP. In the case of the $3 billion recessionary expenditure gap discussed above, government need only increase its spending by that same amount to fill the entire $15 billion negative GDP gap between current GDP and full-employment output, because the same multiplier that affects the initial decrease in spending also works to multiply the increase in government spending and return the economy to full employment.

$$\text{Spending Multiplier} = \frac{1}{\text{MPS}}$$

$$\text{Change in Real GDP} = \text{Spending Multiplier} \times \text{Change in Government Spending}$$

The second tool of fiscal policy is to lower taxes. In the case of the $3 billion recessionary expenditure gap, government must reduce taxes by enough to eventually fill the $15 billion difference between current GDP and full-employment GDP. But remember that taxes are not as effective as government spending in changing GDP, because with tax changes, only a fraction of consumption will be affected; the rest of the effect is in saving. So if government reduced taxes by $3 billion, it would not create the full $15 billion. A multiplier of 5 indicates the marginal propensity to save is 0.2, so consumers would actually save 20 percent of their tax cut ($0.6 billion) and spend the other $2.4 billion. Therefore, tax changes must be larger than government spending changes to achieve the same result.

How large must a tax change be to make up for the recessionary expenditure gap?

$$\text{Amount by Which Tax Must Be Decreased} = \frac{1}{\text{MPC}} \times \text{Recessionary Gap}$$

If the recessionary expenditure gap is $3 billion and the MPC is 0.8, government must reduce taxes by $3 billion multiplied by 1 / MPC (1 / 0.8 = 1.25), or $3.75 billion, in order to completely fill the gap. If the government reduces taxes by $3.75 billion, the MPS of 0.2 indicates that consumers will save $0.75 billion and spend the other $3 billion, returning GDP to full-employment GDP over time.

$$\text{Tax Multiplier} = \text{MPC} \times \frac{1}{\text{MPS}}$$

$$\text{Change in Real GDP} = \text{Tax Multiplier} \times \text{Change in Taxes}$$

The Inflationary Expenditure Gap
An inflationary expenditure gap occurs when the aggregate expenditures in the economy are greater than what is necessary to produce full-employment output. While an economy may be able to temporarily produce an output greater than full-employment level via employees working overtime and the heavier use of other resources, such an output cannot be sustained in the long term. Therefore, any increased spending beyond full-employment can only cause demand-pull inflation, raising prices. An inflationary expenditure gap can be reduced by fiscal policy: by increasing taxes or reducing government spending. Government spending has the stronger effect because it receives the full effect of the multiplier, while changes in taxes are less effective because consumers will reduce saving to pay for some amount of the tax. Therefore, taxes must be increased by a larger amount than the spending would be reduced in order to obtain the same effect.

Multiple-Choice Questions
1. Classical theorists believed that if total spending in the economy fell below full-employment output,
    (A)   the economy would self-correct through lower wages and prices.
    (B)   government should intervene by raising spending.
    (C)   government should correct the problem by raising taxes.
    (D)   the economy would tend to remain below full employment for months.
    (E)   lower imports and increased exports would correct the imbalance.

2. An unexpected increase in inventories would signal firms to
    (A)   hire more workers.
    (B)   raise wages.
    (C)   decrease output.
    (D)   raise product prices.
    (E)   increase the cost of production.

3. Which of the following is a leakage from the circular market flow?
    (A)   investment
    (B)   exports

(C)   government spending

(D)   consumer spending

(E)   saving

4.   According to Keynesian theory, an increase in investment spending causes

      (A)   a decrease in the national debt.

      (B)   a decrease in the price level.

      (C)   an increase in tax revenues.

      (D)   an increase in output.

      (E)   a decrease in imports.

5.   At equilibrium GDP,

      (A)   unplanned inventories are greater than planned inventories.

      (B)   there are no unplanned inventories.

      (C)   planned inventories are greater than saving.

      (D)   unplanned inventories are increasing.

      (E)   planned inventories are zero.

6.   All of the following factors would increase equilibrium GDP EXCEPT

      (A)   incomes abroad increasing.

      (B)   the value of the dollar depreciating.

      (C)   foreign countries increasing trade barriers on U.S. products.

      (D)   tax rates increasing.

      (E)   government spending decreasing.

7.   If government wants to change both spending and taxes in a way that has no effect on real GDP, it must

      (A)   increase spending by more than it increases taxes.

      (B)   decrease spending by more than it decreases taxes.

      (C)   increase spending by more than it decreases taxes.

      (D)   decrease spending by less than it increases taxes.

      (E)   decrease spending by more than it increases taxes.

8.   If the economy experiences a recession with a current spending gap $1,000 below full-employment output and the marginal propensity to consume is 0.8, how much must government increase spending to restore the economy to full-employment GDP?

      (A) $500

      (B) $200

      (C) $800

      (D) $5

      (E) $20

Free-Response Questions

1.   Assume the United States economy is producing at full-employment output, the government has a balanced budget, and imports and exports are balanced.

(a)   Now assume that, because of a significant increase in interest rates, firms change their level of investment.

      (i)   Explain whether investment will increase or decrease.

      (ii)   Explain how the change in investment will affect real GDP.

      (iii)   Explain how the change in real GDP will affect employment.

(b)   Identify one fiscal policy action the government could take to restore the economy to full-employment GDP.

2.   Assume the United States economy is producing at full-employment output, the government has a balanced budget, and imports and exports are balanced.

(a)   Now assume that Canada, a major buyer of U.S. exports, goes into a recession. As a result, current GDP falls to $100 billion less than full-employment GDP and the marginal propensity to consume is 0.6.

      (i)   Explain the reason for the effect of Canada's recession on U.S. GDP.
      (ii)   Identify the formula for the spending multiplier.
      (iii)   Calculate the spending multiplier.
      (iv)   Calculate the amount by which government spending must increase to return current GDP to full-employment GDP.

(b)   Would an increase in government spending or a decrease in taxes have a larger impact on real GDP? Explain.

Multiple-Choice Explanations

1.   (A)   Classical economists believed the economy would correct itself, because lower demand would lead to lower prices and wages, which would lead to higher spending again, correcting to full employment automatically.

2.   (C)   An unexpected increase in inventories indicates that consumer demand for products has decreased and firms should reduce production.

3.   (E)   Saving represents income not spent in the circular flow and a leakage from the amount of spending in the economy.

4.   (D)   Increased investment spending increases the real GDP, which increases output and employment.

5.   (B)   At equilibrium GDP, there are no unplanned inventories; firms sell what they produce, though some planned inventories may exist.

6.   (C)   Trade barriers cause less foreign spending for U.S. products, reducing equilibrium GDP.

7.   (D)   Government spending changes have a full effect on the economy, but because tax changes partly affect saving for consumers, tax changes are less effective and must be greater.

8.   (B)   If MPC = 0.8, the multiplier is 5 (1 / MPS = 1 / 0.2 = 5). To increase GDP by a $1,000 recessionary gap, the government must increase spending by $200, which is subject to the multiplier ($200 × 5), to create the $1,000.

Free-Response Explanations

1.   **7 points** (6 + 1)

(a)   6 points:
- 1 point is earned for stating that investment will decrease.
- 1 point is earned for explaining that because of the higher interest rate, the cost of the investment is now greater than the expected return from the investment.
- 1 point is earned for stating that real GDP will decrease.
- 1 point is earned for stating that investment is one of the components of real GDP (C + I + G + X – M), so if investment falls, real GDP falls.
- 1 point is earned for stating that employment will decrease.
- 1 point is earned for explaining that as output falls, fewer workers are needed to produce that output, so employment falls.

(b)   1 point:
- 1 point is earned for identifying either an increase in government spending or a decrease in taxes.

2.   **6 points** (4 + 2)
(a)   4 points:
- 1 point is earned for explaining that as Canadian incomes fall, their demand for U.S. exports falls, reducing U.S. real GDP.
- 1 point is earned for identifying the U.S. spending multiplier as 1 / MPS.
- 1 point is earned for calculating the spending multiplier as 2.5 (1 / 0.4).
- 1 point is earned for calculating the minimum increase in government spending as $40 billion ($100 billion / 2.5).

(b)   2 points:
- 1 point is earned for stating that an increase in government spending has a larger impact on real GDP.
- 1 point is earned for explaining that if taxes are reduced, consumers will save part of the tax reduction rather than spending all of it in the economy.

CHAPTER 29: AGGREGATE DEMAND AND AGGREGATE SUPPLY

Introduction

The aggregate demand–aggregate supply (AD–AS) model provides the primary graphic depiction of changes in the macroeconomy. Shifts in aggregate supply and aggregate demand explain changes in real output, employment, and price levels in the economy. Chapter 29 introduces the AD–AS model, bringing together the concepts of GDP, inflation, unemployment, and recessionary and inflationary gaps that have been introduced throughout the macroeconomics chapters. Material from Chapter 29 is very likely to appear in a large number of multiple-choice questions and appears as part of a free-response question on nearly every AP macroeconomics exam.

Aggregate Demand

Aggregate demand is a curve showing the amount of GDP (output) demanded at each price level. When the price level rises, fewer products are purchased; when the price level falls, more products are purchased. Therefore, aggregate demand is a downward-sloping curve, with the negative slope resulting from three effects: the real balances effect, the interest rate effect, and the foreign purchases effect.

The real balances effect focuses on the value of consumers' wealth. At a higher price level, the real value of a consumer's savings (homes, stocks, savings accounts) falls. With less wealth in real terms, consumers in the economy are less likely to buy products. At lower price levels, consumers buy more because they have more real wealth.

The second reason for the downward slope of the aggregate demand curve is the interest rate effect. When prices rise, consumers and firms must borrow more money to make the same purchases. That increased demand for money pushes up the interest rate (the price of borrowing money), which discourages consumer borrowing to buy products. It also causes firms to reduce spending for capital, because the higher interest rate can exceed the expected return on the investment. At lower prices, less borrowing is necessary, so interest rates fall and the quantity of products demanded in the economy increases.

Taking the EEK! Out of Economics

Although the curves look similar, it is important to recognize the differences between the demand curve for a specific product and the aggregate demand curve for the macroeconomy. Notice the differences in the axis labels. For individual product demand, the label for the vertical axis is price; for aggregate demand, the label is price level. This is because, when we're dealing with the demand for all of the products in the economy, there is no one "price" for everything—and an "average" price makes little sense if we're talking about the average price of a home and a toothpick. So instead we talk about a price level, which can show us increases and decreases in prices, but not precise prices for products. The horizontal axis, which is labeled "quantity" for the individual product, is labeled "real GDP" or "real output" for macroeconomic analysis, because we're looking at all of the spending in the economy together. So while the demand curve for specific products could help us to identify the specific price of the product and the specific quantity sold, the aggregate demand curve shows much more general information about the economic performance of the entire economy.

The third cause of the downward slope in aggregate demand is the foreign purchases effect. When the U.S. price level increases and if exchange rates do not change, Americans buy more imports and foreigners buy fewer U.S. exports. As a result, quantity demanded for U.S. goods falls at higher prices, and at lower prices, the quantity demanded is higher.

> **Bear in Mind**
> The aggregate demand–aggregate supply model is part of a free-response question on almost every AP macroeconomics exam. As part of the question, you are asked to draw a correctly labeled graph. It is very important that you use the correct labeling to distinguish macroeconomic graphs from microeconomic graphs. Price is not sufficient; the label must be "price level." Rather than "quantity," the label should be "real output" or "GDP." "Supply" and "demand" curve labels are not enough; they must be "aggregate supply" and "aggregate demand." Careful labeling will help you earn the points you deserve.

Changes in Aggregate Demand

While the real balances, interest rate, and foreign purchases effects can cause movement along the aggregate demand curve, a number of factors can actually cause the aggregate demand curve to shift. As was true for the individual product demand curve, increases in aggregate demand shift the curve to the right, while decreases shift it to the left. Changes in aggregate demand can result from changes in all four sectors in the macroeconomy.

Consumer sector demand can shift due to changes in wealth, borrowing, expectations, and taxes. If consumer wealth significantly rises, such as by receiving an inheritance or from increasing stock values, consumers gain confidence and increase their demand for products at all prices. If consumers borrow money, their demand for products increases. If consumers expect their real future incomes to increase, or if they fear inflation in the near future, they increase demand for products ahead of the price increase. And if personal taxes decline, consumers have more disposable income to spend, so aggregate demand increases. If consumer wealth falls, consumers borrow less, they are concerned about a decrease in real income, or their personal taxes increase, aggregate demand falls.

The investment sector's investment spending for capital goods depends on the interest rate and expected return on investment. If interest rates fall, aggregate demand increases because costs are now lower than expected return on the investment. Firms also increase investment if the expected returns increase due to optimism about future business conditions, improvements in technology, production at capacity, or a reduction in business taxes. Higher interest rates or lower expected returns on investment reduce aggregate demand through investment. Because interest rates and expectations can change so quickly and often, the investment sector is the most volatile of the four sectors.

The third sector, government spending, is straightforward. If government spending increases (and taxes and interest rates do not change), aggregate demand increases. Decreases in government spending reduce aggregate demand.

Finally, changes in net exports can also change aggregate demand. If exports increase due to higher foreign incomes, U.S. aggregate demand increases and the curve shifts to the right. If the value of the U.S. dollar depreciates in foreign exchange markets, foreign currency gets stronger, and so it appears that U.S. products are cheaper. In this case, demand for U.S. exports increases. At the same time, because the U.S. dollar is weaker, imports look more expensive, and so imports decrease. Because exports increase while imports decrease, net exports increase, increasing aggregate demand. If foreign incomes decline or the U.S. dollar appreciates in currency markets, U.S. aggregate demand falls.

Taking the EEK! Out of Economics

Causes of the downward slope of aggregate demand may seem very similar to the causes of shifts in the aggregate demand curve. The real balances effect looks like the wealth effect, and the interest rate and foreign purchases effects look very similar to causes of change in aggregate demand. A way to keep them straight is to look at the cause of each effect. For the three factors that explain the downward slope, a higher price level is the root cause of each effect. The rise in price level *causes* a decline in the value of wealth, a higher interest rate for borrowing, and a shift toward buying relatively lower-priced imports. At higher prices, people buy fewer products. But for the causes of change in aggregate demand, shifts in the curve result from causes *other* than a change in the prices of products in the economy. Changes in expectations for economic performance, tax rates, incomes, and currency values are among the reasons the entire curve would shift.

Aggregate Supply

Aggregate supply is the quantity of goods produced in an economy at all price levels. The shape of the aggregate supply curve varies depending on the time period discussed. The costs of inputs (resources) and prices of outputs to consumers tend to be sticky or unchangeable in the short run but more flexible in the long run.

In the immediate short run (or immediate period), both the costs of resources and the prices charged to customers are fixed. As a result, the aggregate supply curve is horizontal in the immediate period. If aggregate demand increases in this time period, output increases, but the price level does not change.

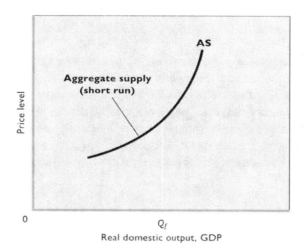

The aggregate supply curve (short run)

In the short run, output prices are flexible, but resource costs are either fixed or very sticky. The stickiness is primarily due to wages, because so many workers are paid via a contract whose terms cannot be changed quickly. As a result, the short-run aggregate supply curve is upward-sloping. Producers provide more products as the price level rises and fewer products as the price level falls. When current output is significantly lower than the firm's capacity, firms can increase output with little increase in production cost. But as production approaches or even passes full-employment output, the per-unit cost of production increases much more quickly. As a result, the short-run aggregate supply curve slopes upward, becoming steeper as output increases.

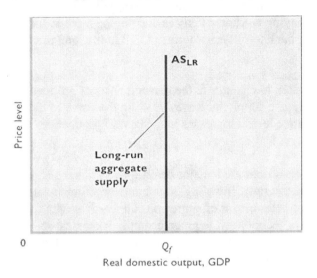

Aggregate supply in the long run

Bear in Mind

The aggregate supply curve can also be presented as representing Keynesian, intermediate, and classical ranges.

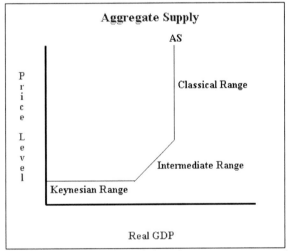

Remember, classical economists were convinced that the economy naturally produced at full-employment output. While prices and wages were flexible, output was not. This theory is represented in the vertical range of the aggregate supply curve. Keynesian theory held the opposite assumptions, with flexible output and employment but fixed prices and wages. These assumptions are found in the horizontal section of the aggregate supply curve. The intermediate range of the aggregate supply curve corresponds with the short-run aggregate supply curve discussed in the text. AP macroeconomics exam questions about short-run aggregate supply generally refer to this upward-sloping aggregate supply curve unless they specifically note they are discussing a vertical or horizontal aggregate supply curve. If you see a question referring to the intermediate range of the aggregate supply curve, it is referring to the upward-sloping section.

In the long run, the costs of inputs, including labor, as well as the prices charged to customers, are flexible. Long-run aggregate supply is a vertical curve, located at full-employment output. Although increases in aggregate demand may cause short-run increases in production beyond full-employment GDP, the additional costs of paying workers overtime and paying a premium for resources will cause firms to reduce production back to full-employment GDP in the long run.

Changes in Aggregate Supply

Changes in aggregate supply are directly connected to changes in the per-unit costs of production faced by firms. If costs of production fall, aggregate supply increases, shifting the curve to the right so that more output is produced at every price level. Increases in the cost of production reduce aggregate supply, shifting the curve leftward.

Changes in the costs of land, labor, and capital resources are a major determinant of changes in aggregate supply. As costs increase, firms reduce supply, lowering output and employment and raising prices. Productivity is another important determinant of aggregate supply. If productivity increases as a result of better worker education or technology, aggregate supply increases, so firms increase output and employment while lowering prices. Changes in government policy can also affect aggregate supply. If business taxes are increased or the government institutes regulations, the increased costs of production reduce aggregate supply. If business taxes are reduced, the government grants firms a subsidy, or if regulation is reduced, the lower per-unit costs of production lead firms to increase production, and aggregate supply increases.

Equilibrium GDP

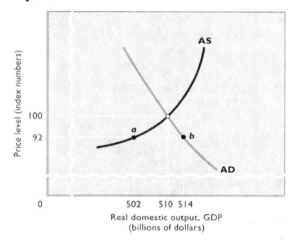

Equilibrium price level and equilibrium real GDP

Equilibrium GDP occurs at the point where aggregate demand equals aggregate supply. This equilibrium establishes price level and real GDP for the economy. In this figure, equilibrium occurs at a real GDP of $510 billion in output and a price level of 100. At price level 92, firms would only produce $502 billion of output while aggregate demand at that price level is $514 billion in output. Given the shortage of goods at that price, consumers would bid up the price. The higher price leads firms to increase production and consumers to reduce quantity demanded until equilibrium is again reached.

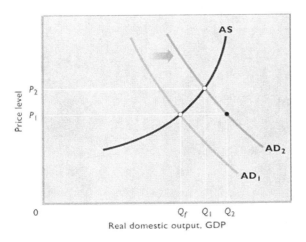

An increase in aggregate demand that causes demand-pull inflation

If the economy is in equilibrium at full-employment output, an increase in aggregate demand causes demand-pull inflation—an inflationary gap. Prices increase as well as real GDP. It is important to note that because the price increased, the full multiplier effect did not occur. The full multiplier requires a horizontal aggregate supply curve so that the full multiplier effect goes to output, rather than being partially absorbed by a price increase.

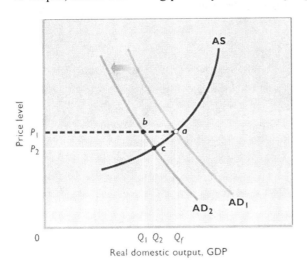

A decrease in aggregate demand that causes a recession

A decrease in aggregate demand causes a decrease in production—a recessionary gap. Employment falls and cyclical unemployment rises as a result, because firms do not need as many workers to produce fewer products. The effect on prices can be harder to determine. With the lower demand, disinflation (a reduction in the rate of inflation) tends to occur. But do prices actually fall—deflation? Wages and prices are sticky downward, so in many recessions, aggregate demand fully impacts output but does not cause a change in price level. As illustrated in this figure, when the price does not change, the full effect of the multiplier occurs in the changing real GDP. If prices do actually fall, part of the multiplier effect is absorbed by the falling price, and teal GDP does not fall by the full amount of the change in aggregate demand.

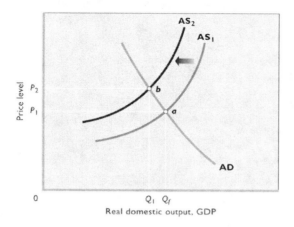

A decrease in aggregate supply that causes cost-push inflation

A reduction in aggregate supply causes cost-push inflation. As the cost of production increases, firms reduce output and raise prices. A sustained decrease in aggregate supply is known as stagflation—a stagnant economy, high inflation (thus the name stagflation), and high unemployment all at the same time. High oil prices in the 1970s sent the U.S. economy into its most significant period of stagflation in history. An increase in aggregate supply resulting from increased productivity and technology shifts the aggregate supply curve to the right. Real GDP and employment increase and prices can fall as a result of the lower per-unit costs of production.

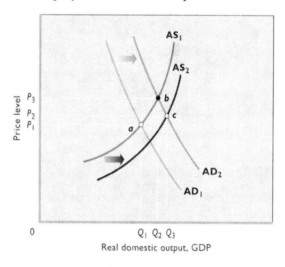

Growth, full employment, and relative price stability

It is possible for both aggregate demand and aggregate supply to shift at the same time, as multiple factors affect the economy. In the late 1990s, full employment, higher incomes, and high consumer confidence led to higher aggregate demand. At the same time, increases in technology and productivity via computers increased aggregate supply. Increases in both curves significantly increased real GDP, while the price level only moderately increased because the curve shifts had contradictory effects on prices.

Changes in aggregate supply and aggregate demand cause recessionary and inflationary gaps and affect real GDP, employment, and prices. In subsequent chapters, we will examine the tools policymakers have available to mitigate—and potentially reverse—the effects of such curve shifts.

Multiple-Choice Questions

1. The aggregate demand curve slopes downward because as the price level rises,
    (A) the real value of consumers' wealth increases
    (B) interest rates decrease.
    (C) consumers purchase more imports.
    (D) the unemployment rate decreases.
    (E) real output increases.

2. Consumer spending as a component of aggregate demand increases when
    I.   consumer wealth increases.
    II. consumer borrowing decreases.
    III. consumer expectations about the economy are optimistic.
    IV. personal taxes increase.
    (A) I only
    (B) II and IV only
    (C) I and III only
    (D) II, III, and IV only
    (E) I, II, III, and IV

3. Each of the following would result in an increase in aggregate demand EXCEPT an increase in
    (A) interest rates.
    (B) exports.
    (C) government spending.
    (D) firms' expected return on investment.
    (E) incomes in countries buying U.S. exports.

4. Aggregate supply increases as the result of an increase in
    (A) the cost of production.
    (B) worker productivity.
    (C) business taxes.
    (D) government regulation of business.
    (E) the price of oil.

5. Stagflation is caused by
    (A) an increase in aggregate demand.
    (B) a decrease in aggregate demand.
    (C) an increase in aggregate supply.
    (D) a decrease in aggregate supply.
    (E) a simultaneous increase in aggregate supply and aggregate demand.

6. The equilibrium point of aggregate supply and aggregate demand determines
    (A) wages and spending.
    (B) saving and investment.
    (C) taxes and government spending.
    (D) profit and saving.
    (E) real GDP and price level.

7.   Which of the following situations would most likely result in a decrease in the price level and a decrease in real GDP?
        (A)   a decrease in consumer confidence
        (B)   an increase in wages
        (C)   a decrease in interest rates
        (D)   an increase in productivity
        (E)   an increase in exports

8.   An increase in aggregate supply causes which of the following output and price level effects?

	Output	Price Level
(A)	Increase	Increase
(B)	Decrease	No change
(C)	No change	Decrease
(D)	Increase	Decrease
(E)	Decrease	Increase

9.   If the aggregate supply curve is horizontal and government spending increases, how will price level, output, and employment be affected?

	Price Level	Output	Employment
(A)	Increase	Increase	Increase
(B)	Decrease	Decrease	Decrease
(C)	No change	Increase	Increase
(D)	Decrease	No change	No change
(E)	Increase	Decrease	Decrease

10.   If equilibrium GDP is in the intermediate range of aggregate supply and interest rates increase, how will price level, output, and unemployment be affected?

	Price Level	Output	Unemployment
(A)	Increase	Increase	Increase
(B)	Decrease	Decrease	Decrease
(C)	Increase	Decrease	Decrease
(D)	Decrease	Decrease	Increase
(E)	Increase	Increase	Decrease

Free-Response Questions
1.   Assume the United States economy is currently operating at equilibrium.
(a)   Draw a correctly labeled aggregate supply and aggregate demand graph, and show each of the following.
        (i)   real output
        (ii)   price level
(b)   Now assume the price of oil, an important resource for U.S. production, increases significantly. Illustrate the effect of the oil price increase on the AD–AS graph.
(c)   Identify and explain the effect of the increase in oil price on each of the following.
        (i)   real output
        (ii)   price level
        (iii)   employment

2.   Assume the United States economy is currently operating at equilibrium.
(a)   Now assume interest rates for investment loans increase.
      (i)   Use a correctly labeled aggregate supply and aggregate demand graph to
             illustrate the effect of the increased interest rate.
      (ii)   Explain the mechanism that causes this change in the curve.
(b)   Explain the effect of the change in investment spending on each of the following.
      (i)   real output
      (ii)   price level
      (iii) employment
(c)   Identify one fiscal policy government could implement to reverse the change in
      investment spending.

Multiple-Choice Explanations
1.   (C)   When domestic prices rise, consumers buy relatively lower-priced imports,
             reducing the quantity demanded of domestic goods. Higher prices reduce the value of
             wealth and result in higher interest rates, which both reduce quantities demanded. With
             the lower quantity demanded, real output is lower, leading to reduced employment.
2.   (C)   Increases in wealth and optimism about economic performance lead consumers
             to increase their demand for products at all prices. An increase in consumer borrowing
             and a reduction in personal taxes would also leave consumers with more available
             income to increase aggregate demand.
3.   (A)   An increase in interest rates makes it more expensive for consumers and firms to
             borrow, so their demand for products would decrease.
4.   (B)   Increases in productivity lower per-unit costs of production, causing an increase
             in aggregate supply. The other options increase costs.
5.   (D)   A decrease in aggregate supply increases prices and unemployment at the same
             time, which is characteristic of stagflation.
6.   (E)   Real GDP and price level are the axes of the aggregate expenditures model
             graph, and each is determined by the level of aggregate supply and aggregate demand in
             the economy.
7.   (A)   If consumers lose confidence in future economic performance, they reduce
             aggregate demand out of concern for a potential loss of a job.
8.   (D)   An increase in aggregate supply shifts the curve to the right.
9.   (C)   An increase in government spending raises output, so employment rises to make
             those products. Because price is inflexible, it does not change.
10.   (D)   Higher interest rates reduce aggregate demand, so price level and output fall.
             Fewer workers are needed to produce output, so unemployment rises.

Free-Response Explanations
1.   **10 points** (3 + 1 + 6)
(a)   3 points:
      • 1 point is earned for a correctly labeled AD–AS graph.
      • 1 point is earned for identifying real output from the equilibrium point.
      • 1 point is earned for identifying price level from the equilibrium point.
(b)   1 point:
      • 1 point is earned for shifting the aggregate supply curve to the left.
(c)   6 points:
      • 1 point is earned for stating that real output will decrease.
      • 1 point is earned for explaining that with a higher cost of production, firms produce less.

- 1 point is earned for stating that the price level will increase.
- 1 point is earned for explaining that with a higher cost of production and lower output, firms increase prices.
- 1 point is earned for stating that employment will fall.
- 1 point is earned for explaining that because firms are producing less, they need fewer workers to create the output.

2. **7 points** (3 + 3 + 1)
(a)   3 points:
   - 1 point is earned for a correctly labeled AD–AS graph.
   - 1 point is earned for shifting aggregate demand to the left.
   - 1 point is earned for explaining that because the higher interest rate increases the cost of investment, firms reduce investment spending.
(b)   3 points:
   - 1 point is earned for explaining that real output decreases because of reduced investment spending.
   - 1 point is earned for explaining that the price level decreases because of reduced aggregate demand or that prices remain the same if the answer specifically explains that prices and wages are sticky downward.
   - 1 point is earned for explaining that employment decreases because fewer workers are needed to produce the reduced output.
(c)   1 point:
   - 1 point is earned for identifying either an increase in government spending or a decrease in taxes as an appropriate fiscal policy to increase aggregate demand.

CHAPTER 30: FISCAL POLICY, DEFICITS, AND DEBT

Introduction

Changes in aggregate supply and demand affect output, employment, and price level in the economy. But as a result of Keynesian theory, government now has tools it can use to reduce inflationary gaps or close recessionary gaps, all with the goal of returning the economy to full-employment output. Use of these policy tools, though, can also result in budget surpluses or deficits, which can affect the national debt. Material from Chapter 30 is included in several multiple-choice questions and commonly appears as part of a free-response question on the AP macroeconomics exam.

Expansionary Fiscal Policy

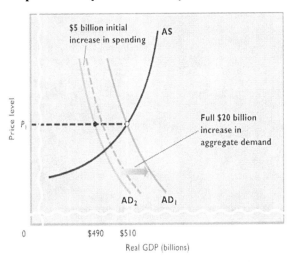

Expansionary fiscal policy

Fiscal policy is the use of discretionary government spending or taxes in order to stabilize the economy. If aggregate demand falls, output falls and cyclical unemployment rises. If prices are sticky, the full effect of the decrease in aggregate demand accrues in lower output. Government can use expansionary fiscal policy to shift aggregate demand to the right by increasing government spending, reducing taxes, or both. Precisely how much of a change in taxes or spending is required depends on the marginal propensity to consume and the related multiplier. If the MPC is 0.75, the MPS is 0.25, and the multiplier is 4 (1 / 0.25). If the negative GDP gap is $20 billion, government spending would only have to increase by $5 billion, because the multiplier would continue to fill the rest of the gap.

However, we know that a reduction in taxes is not as effective as an increase in government spending, because consumers will save some of the tax cut. In this case, consumers would only spend 75% of a tax cut, so taxes would have to be reduced by $6.67 billion to achieve the same $20 billion increase in aggregate demand that was achieved by a $5 billion increase in government spending.

Expansionary fiscal policy also has ramifications for the federal budget. Assume the United States begins with a balanced budget. If the government lowers taxes or increases spending as a part of expansionary fiscal policy, it will create a budget deficit—spending more than its revenues in a year. Government must borrow money through the sale of government securities (bonds, bills, and notes) in order to finance that deficit. A deficit also adds to the national debt, the total amount the government has borrowed over the years.

Contractionary Fiscal Policy

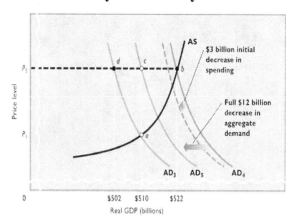

Contractionary fiscal policy under the ratchet effect

Contractionary fiscal policy is the use of a tax increase or a reduction in government spending in order to reduce a demand-pull inflationary gap. If aggregate demand rises, part of the inflationary gap increases prices, while the other part increases output. To correct an inflationary gap, the government uses contractionary fiscal policy: increasing taxes, reducing government spending, or both. A reduction in spending directly affects aggregate demand. But in determining how far to lower spending, it is important to keep the ratchet effect in mind. A ratchet is a tool that turns a screw or bolt in one direction but not the other. With the ratchet effect, once the price level ratchets up, it tends not to come back down—the sticky wages and prices we discussed earlier. So when the government decides how much to reduce spending, it must take this ratchet effect into account. In this figure, if the increase in real output is $12 billion with a multiplier of 4, the government should reduce spending by $3 billion to bring aggregate demand back down to full employment GDP at point C. Notice, however, that the price remains at the higher level. The contractionary fiscal policy is able to stop the escalation of the inflation rate but generally is not effective in reducing prices to their former levels.

The government also has the option of closing an inflationary gap by increasing taxes. As we have noted, changes in taxes are not as effective as spending changes, because part of the increase in the tax rate will be paid from savings, rather than reducing consumption by the full amount of the tax. If the MPC is 0.75, consumers will use savings to pay a quarter of their tax increases. So in order to fill the gap, government must increase taxes by $4 billion in order to reduce consumption by $3 billion. The multiplier of 4 will then continue to reduce consumption by the entire $12 billion negative GDP gap.

Contractionary fiscal policy also has ramifications for the national budget. If government begins with a balanced budget, the increase in taxes or reduction in government spending to address the inflationary gap will result in a budget surplus—tax revenues greater than government spending for a year. This surplus can reduce the amount of the national debt.

Politics and Fiscal Policy

While we know that changes in taxes and government spending can both be effective in closing recessionary and inflationary gaps, which policy is best to use? It depends on your view of government. Conservatives tend to prefer a smaller role for government and are more likely to call for tax cuts during recessions and spending cuts during inflation. Liberals tend to prefer a larger role for government and more often call for spending increases during recessions and tax increases during inflation. Each policy is effective in achieving the desired economic result, but the political philosophy of those in power tends to guide the policy choices.

Automatic Stabilizers

Automatic stabilizers are government programs that automatically change spending and taxes during economic instability, without requiring government policymakers to pass a new policy. The two primary automatic stabilizers are transfer payments from safety net programs and progressive income taxes. During a recession, as workers lose jobs and incomes fall, households become eligible for government programs such as unemployment benefits, food stamps, and rent subsidies. Government spending automatically rises and works to mitigate the amount by which aggregate demand declines, helping to stabilize the economy. Nations with stronger safety net programs have more effective automatic stabilizers.

Progressive income taxes base the tax rate on household income level. Those with lower incomes pay a lower percentage of their income in taxes, while those with higher incomes pay a larger percentage of their income in taxes. During periods of inflation, as incomes increase, taxpayers can ascend into higher tax brackets. As a result, they pay a higher percentage of their income in taxes, leaving less income available for consumption spending. Therefore, the higher tax rate helps to reduce the effects of inflation by reining in consumer spending. Economies with more strongly progressive tax structures have a more effective tax stabilizer.

In general, when GDP increases, tax revenues increase from all sources—individual income taxes, business taxes, excise taxes, and payroll taxes—because as more jobs are created, incomes rise and consumers are able to buy more products. During periods of recession, tax revenues from all of these sources decline. Transfer payments work in reverse, with government spending for these programs increasing during periods of recession and declining as the economy grows. As a result, the federal budget is affected by economic instability even before fiscal policy is considered. During recessions, a balanced budget tends to go into deficit because tax revenues fall as government spending increases. During economic growth or even inflation, a balanced budget tends to go into surplus because tax revenues rise as government spending declines. But automatic stabilizers alone are usually not powerful enough to deal with significant swings in aggregate demand, so government action is required.

Problems of Fiscal Policy
The recognition lag refers to the time between the initial development of a recessionary or inflationary gap and when it is recognized. It can take months to determine whether a recession or inflation is underway. In December 2008, the National Bureau of Economic Research announced that the U.S. economy had already been in recession for a full year before it was recognized. An administrative lag follows, as Congress takes time, often months, to pass legislation to change taxes or spending to address the identified gap. Finally, an operational lag requires time for the policy to actually take effect, as changes rumble through the system and the multiplier takes effect. This can take yet another six months to a year for fiscal policy to take full effect. These combined lags illustrate how long a recession or inflation can be underway before a fiscal policy solution can take effect. It also points out the importance of automatic stabilizers in helping to reduce the impacts of economic instability.

Another problem with fiscal policy is the political considerations involved in making policy. Voters don't want to hear about tax increases or cuts in their favorite programs, so public officials may hesitate to use contractionary policy when it is warranted. And in order to gain votes at election time, public officials have an incentive to reduce taxes and increase spending for popular programs, even if such actions are contrary to the fiscal policy appropriate for the economic situation. In addition, the government may need to significantly increase spending to deal with a crisis—a natural disaster or a war—even during a time of inflation, exacerbating an inflationary gap. Further, the balanced budget requirements of many state and local governments force them to reduce spending during a recession—which only reduces aggregate demand further, contradicting the federal fiscal policy.

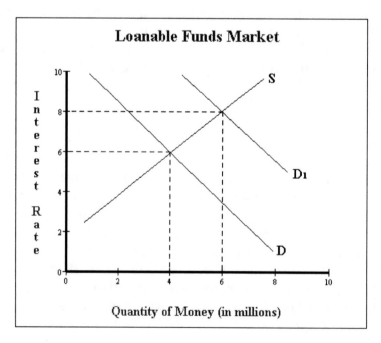

Chapter 30: Fiscal Policy, Deficits, and Debt

Another problem with fiscal policy is the problem of crowding out. When the government uses expansionary fiscal policy to increase spending and reduce taxes, a budget deficit develops. Government must borrow money to finance the deficit. As government demand for money in the loanable funds market increases, interest rates rise. We already know that investment spending is the most volatile of the four sectors—and if interest rates increase, firms can significantly reduce investment spending, crowding other firms out of the loanable funds market. So while government is borrowing money to increase aggregate demand, crowding out reduces the effectiveness of the fiscal policy by offsetting part of that increase in aggregate demand. The higher interest rate can also reduce interest-sensitive consumption spending, such as consumer purchases of homes, cars, and durable goods, further reducing aggregate demand. The crowding out effect, if it occurs at all, tends to occur less during a time of recession, because consumer and investment demand for loans has likely decreased already due to the recession. But if the government increases deficit spending when the economy is at or near full-employment output, crowding out is likely to have a more substantial effect on aggregate demand.

National Debt Concerns

Each year the federal government incurs a budget deficit, it adds to the national debt. In 2008, the U.S. national debt surpassed $10 trillion. As of 2007, interest payments on the debt were the fourth-largest item in the federal budget. Policymakers undertook unprecedented debt in 2008 and 2009 with the stimulus and bailout packages as the economy dramatically deteriorated, so interest payments on the debt will only increase. And those payments do not pay off the debt; they only service the interest on the debt. This significant increase in interest payments leaves policymakers with the difficult decision of raising taxes or cutting spending to make these interest payments—or borrowing even more to pay the interest.

Another concern is the redistribution of income from those with lower incomes to those with higher incomes. Government securities and the interest they earn are disproportionately held by those with higher incomes because of their ability to save. Because the federal income tax system is only slightly progressive, those with lower and middle incomes largely pay the taxes that will pay the interest to the bondholders with higher incomes.

Many people are also concerned about the level of foreign-owned public debt. More than a quarter of the national debt is owned by foreign countries and foreign citizens, and so interest payments on that debt flow out of the U.S. economy. Finally, concerns about the level of crowding out due to extensive borrowing in a full-employment economy may have serious implications for future economic growth. But if the deficit spending is for infrastructure or other capital improvements, overall investment may actually increase.

Multiple-Choice Questions

1. An increase in government spending increases the real GDP by more than the amount of the initial spending because of the
    (A) automatic stabilizers.
    (B) spending multiplier.
    (C) trade deficit.
    (D) aggregate supply.
    (E) national debt.

2. If the economy is operating in the upward-sloping section of the aggregate supply curve, a reduction in personal taxes will cause
    (A) unemployment to increase.
    (B) the price level to decrease.
    (C) aggregate demand to decrease.
    (D) real GDP to increase.
    (E) the budget deficit to decrease.

3. If the country is experiencing significant cyclical unemployment, how would an increase in government spending affect real output, prices, and unemployment?

	Real Output	Price Level	Unemployment
(A)	Increase	Increase	Increase
(B)	Decrease	Decrease	Increase
(C)	Increase	Increase	Decrease
(D)	Decrease	Decrease	Decrease
(E)	Increase	Decrease	Decrease

4. If the government uses a contractionary fiscal policy, it must increase taxes by how much in order to have the same effect as a change in spending?
    (A) by the same amount that it raises spending
    (B) by the full amount of the inflationary GDP gap
    (C) by more than it would reduce spending
    (D) by less than it would increase spending
    (E) by the percentage increase in the inflation rate

5. When the government implements an expansionary fiscal policy to resolve a recessionary gap, it results in a
    (A) budget deficit.
    (B) reduction in interest rates.
    (C) reduction in the national debt.
    (D) budget surplus.
    (E) reduction in real GDP.

6. A situation in which the federal government's taxes are greater than its revenues in one year is
    (A) a budget deficit.

(B)   a budget surplus.
(C)   the national debt.
(D)   a trade deficit.
(E)   a trade surplus.

7.   How does the federal government finance deficits?
        (A)   with higher taxes
        (B)   with imports
        (C)   by lowering spending
        (D)   by the sale of bonds
        (E)   by the sale of stock

8.   According to the Keynesian ratchet effect, once the price level increases due to an increase in aggregate demand,
        (A)   price levels are most effectively reduced by changing taxes.
        (B)   aggregate supply must be decreased to reduce the price level.
        (C)   price levels are most effectively reduced by changing spending.
        (D)   the price level tends not to go back down due to sticky wages.
        (E)   a decrease in aggregate demand will reduce prices to their original levels.

9.   Automatic stabilizers have an advantage over discretionary fiscal policy because automatic stabilizers
        (A)   are directed by the president, while fiscal policy is set by Congress.
        (B)   are stronger than fiscal policy tools.
        (C)   do not add to the national debt.
        (D)   affect the money supply more than they affect discretionary fiscal policy.
        (E)   take effect without requiring action by policymakers.

10.   Crowding out occurs when
        (A)   a product price is set too low, creating a shortage.
        (B)   too many producers are in a market, forcing some firms out of an industry.
        (C)   too many firms request government subsidies in the same budget cycle.
        (D)   government spending is reduced, so programs are eliminated.
        (B)   government borrowing increases interest rates, so firms reduce investment.

11.   Concerns about the size of the national debt include all of the following EXCEPT
        (A)   interest on the debt consuming a larger portion of the national budget.
        (B)   the redistribution of income from those with lower incomes to those with higher incomes.
        (C)   lower interest rates as a result of increased government borrowing.
        (D)   the increase in the level of foreign-owned debt.
        (E)   the impact of crowding out on future economic growth.

Free-Response Question

Assume the economy is operating at less than full-employment output on the upward-sloping portion of the aggregate supply curve and the federal budget is balanced.

(a)   Using a correctly labeled aggregate supply and aggregate demand graph, show the following.
         (i)   real output
         (ii)   price level

(b)   Identify one fiscal policy government could use to return the economy to full-employment output. Explain the following.
         (i)   how that policy works to achieve full-employment output
         (ii)   the effect of the policy on the federal budget
         (iii)   the effect of the policy on the national debt

(c)   On the graph you drew for (a), illustrate the effect of the fiscal policy you identified. Explain the effects of the policy on the following.
         (i)   real output
         (ii)   price level
         (iii)   employment

(d)   Using a correctly labeled money market graph, illustrate the effect of the policy you identified in (b) on the market. Explain the effect on the following.
         (i)   the interest rate
         (ii)   investment

Multiple-Choice Explanations

1.   (B)   The multiplier increases the value of the initial spending as the income is spent and re-spent throughout the circular flow.

2.   (D)   A reduction in taxes leads to an increase in aggregate demand; the other four options result from an increase in taxes.

3.   (C)   An increase in government spending increases aggregate demand, raising real GDP and price level while reducing unemployment.

4.   (C)   Taxes are less effective than spending because consumers will pay part of the tax increase with savings, so consumption will not fall as far as it would if the government decreased spending by the same amount.

5.   (A)   An expansionary fiscal policy creates a budget deficit as taxes are reduced and government spending increases. The additional government borrowing increases interest rates in the loanable funds market and increases the national debt.

6.   (A)   A budget deficit counts overspending in one year; the national debt is the total amount of money the government owes.

7.   (D)   Government sells securities on the open market to borrow money for deficit spending.

8.   (D)   Because workers tend to be hired on contract, firms cannot reduce wages in the short run, leaving wages and prices sticky; therefore, once prices increase, they tend not to decrease again.

9.	(E)	Automatic stabilization programs, such as unemployment benefits or food stamps, go into effect quickly upon the eligibility of households for the programs, avoiding the lag time involved with discretionary fiscal policy.

10.	(E)	Government's increased demand for funds in the loanable funds market raises interest rates, so firms reduce their borrowing, lowering their investment in capital goods.

11.	(C)	Increased government borrowing raises interest rates.

Free Response Explanation
15 points (3 + 4 + 4 + 4)

(a)	3 points:
- 1 point is earned for a correctly labeled aggregate supply and aggregate demand graph.
- 1 point is earned for correctly identifying real output (GDP).
- 1 point is earned for correctly identifying the price level.

(b)	4 points:
- 1 point is earned for identifying either an increase in government spending or a decrease in taxes.
- 1 point is earned for explaining that lower taxes allow consumers and firms more disposable income to increase aggregate demand or that higher government spending directly increases aggregate demand, raising incomes.
- 1 point is earned for stating that the policy would cause a budget deficit.
- 1 point is earned for stating that the deficit would increase the national debt.

(c)	4 points:
- 1 point is earned for showing an increase in aggregate demand.
- 1 point is earned for stating that real output will increase.
- 1 point is earned for stating that the price level will increase.
- 1 point is earned for stating that employment will increase in order to make the additional output.

(d)	4 points:
- 1 point is earned for a correctly labeled loanable funds market graph.
- 1 point is earned for showing an increase in demand for loanable funds.
- 1 point is earned for stating that the interest rate increases due to increased demand.
- 1 point is earned for stating that investment falls because of the higher interest rate firms must pay to borrow.

CHAPTER 31: MONEY AND BANKING

Introduction
While fiscal policy is central to economic stabilization, government officials have a second set of stabilization tools in monetary policy. Money is essential for a modern economy, facilitating the movement of goods and services through the circular flow and serving as the incentive for entrepreneurs and workers. Chapter 31 begins a three-chapter exploration of the role of money in the economy, describing the functions and definitions of money and the structure of the Federal Reserve System. An understanding of these functions and structures paves the way for exploration of how the Federal Reserve uses money to stabilize the economy. Material from Chapter 31 may appear in one or two multiple-choice questions on the AP macroeconomics exam.

The Functions of Money
Money serves three purposes. First, it is a medium of exchange, which means it is used for buying goods and services. It is very difficult, if not impossible, for barter to work in an economy as large as that of the United States. Money facilitates exchange, making the process more efficient. Second, money is a unit of account, making it easier to determine the relative values of goods. Rather than having to remember that eight tomatoes equals one gallon of gas and fifteen gallons of gas equals one sweater, monetary amounts make comparison easier. Finally, money serves as a store of value. You can save money over time and use it for future purchases.

Money is perfectly liquid, meaning it can be spent instantly. Other investments, such as stock or baseball cards or homes, are more illiquid, because it takes time to sell the asset and convert it to cash. Stock can be sold fairly quickly to get spendable money, while it may take weeks or months to sell a home. Liquidity is important, because aggregate demand depends on the ability to purchase goods and services.

Definitions of Money
In general, money is anything that is widely accepted by buyers and sellers as a medium of exchange. However, money can take a variety of forms, including bills, coins, animal teeth, precious metals, or crops—anything buyers and sellers accept. Commodity money is money that has intrinsic value, such as gold coins, corn, or tobacco; it can be used for another purpose and has value for that purpose. Fiat money (or token money) is money that only has value because society accepts that it has value. Federal Reserve Notes used in the United States state "This note is legal tender for all debts, public and private." Fiat money is the common form of currency used in the United States and the world today.

M1 is the most commonly used measure of the money supply. M1 consists of currency (paper money and coins) and demand deposits (checking accounts, including travelers' checks and debit cards which directly draw from your bank account to make purchases). Today, most of M1 consists of currency, but checks can be preferable for transferring large amounts of money owing to their safety and the creation of a receipt when the check is cashed. M1 is perfectly liquid money that can be instantly spent.

Bear in Mind
For decades, demand deposits were a larger proportion of M1 than currency was. In 2002, the relationship reversed, since M1 now consists of currency more than checkable deposits. Older versions of the AP macroeconomics exam refer to the proportions as they existed at that time.

Taking the EEK! Out of Economics
You may have noticed that credit cards, another method of apparently instant payment for goods and services, are not included in the money supply. This is because purchases via credit cards are not money; they are short-term loans from the institution that issued the credit card. The bank makes the payment at the time of purchase, and at the end of the month, you must pay the credit card bill with currency or a check.

M2 is a broader definition of money, including the currency and demand deposits of M1 plus the "near-money" of savings deposits, certificates of deposit (CDs) of less than $100,000, and money market mutual funds. "Near money" is fairly liquid but requires a withdrawal to convert it to cash or a demand deposit.

The Value of Money
Because U.S. currency is fiat money, it has no intrinsic value. As late as the early 20th century, American dollars were "backed" by gold, meaning dollars could be traded in at a financial institution for a specific amount of gold per dollar. This backing was designed to inspire consumer confidence in the value of currency. However, tying the money supply to a precious metal left the money supply susceptible to wide swings in the gold supply. Economists today agree that it is better to be able to change the money supply to meet the needs of the economy. Therefore, the money supply today is not backed, and the money supply is controlled by the Federal Reserve System.

Three things help money to maintain its value today: acceptability, designation as legal tender, and relative scarcity. As long as buyers and sellers accept that a dollar is worth a dollar, that money has value. The government's declaration that money has value, as noted on dollar bills, gives people confidence of that value. The Federal Reserve controls the supply of money in the economy, limiting its availability in order to ensure that it keeps its value.

The purchasing power of money is the amount of goods and services that a specific amount of money will buy. As the consumer price index rises during periods of inflation, the value of the dollar falls, because the same dollars cannot stretch to buy as many products as they could before the inflation. During deflation, the value of the dollar rises and consumers can afford to buy more than before. In order to keep inflation in check, Congress and the president can use fiscal policy while the Federal Reserve can use monetary policy to control the money supply and interest rates on credit.

The Federal Reserve System

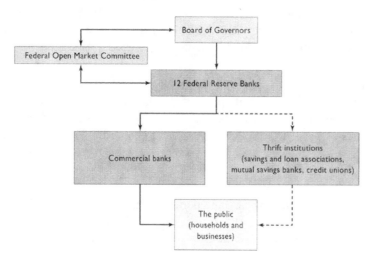

Framework of the Federal Reserve System and its relationship to the public

The Federal Reserve System, also known as "The Fed," is the central banking system for the United States. It controls the country's money supply and monetary policy. The Fed was created in 1913 to address banking crises, runs on banks, and the lack of confidence in the banking system that seriously affected economic performance.

The Board of Governors consists of seven members who are appointed by the president and confirmed by the Senate. Members cannot be fired by the president and serve a non-renewable fourteen-year term in order to insulate the Fed from political pressure. There is significant political pressure to keep interest rates low, in order for consumers to be able to afford to buy homes and cars and for firms to be able to invest in capital. However, increasing the money supply too far can result in inflation. For this reason, the Fed was developed as an independent agency of government. The primary role of the Board of Governors is to control the money supply and run the Federal Reserve System.

The twelve regional Federal Reserve banks throughout the United States serve as "bankers' banks," performing the same functions for banks that your local bank performs for you as a customer. Regional banks allow member banks to deposit cash on account as well as provide loans to member banks. These regional banks implement monetary policy as determined by the Board of Governors. Regional banks are a unique hybrid of private ownership and public control, because the regional banks are actually owned by the member banks of each district, but public officials control the banking system and its policies.

The Federal Open Market Committee (FOMC) consists of the seven members of the Board of Governors, the president of the New York Federal Reserve Bank, and four other regional bank presidents who serve on a rotating basis. The role of the FOMC is to conduct open market operations, or buying and selling government securities (Treasury bonds, bills, and notes) in the market in order to control the money supply and interest rates. Because these open market operations are performed through the New York Federal Reserve, that bank's president is a constant member of the committee.

Member banks consist of the many kinds of financial institutions customers use. While credit unions and savings and loans are regulated by different agencies outside of the Federal Reserve, they are still subject to the same reserve requirements and monetary controls of the Federal Reserve.

Functions of the Federal Reserve
Federal Reserve banks are responsible for a number of functions. They issue new currency and destroy currency that is damaged or worn out. They also set reserve requirements, such as requiring banks to hold a certain percentage of their deposits in cash that cannot be loaned out. Federal Reserve banks loan member banks money that must be repaid with interest, which is known as the discount rate. Reserve banks also supervise bank operations, clear checks through the system, and serve as the official bank of the federal government. But the most important role of the Fed is to control the money supply and interest rates.

Multiple-Choice Questions
1. Which of the following is a function of money?
    I.   A medium of exchange
    II.   A store of value
    III.   A unit of account
    (A)   I only
    (B)   III only
    (C)   I and II only
    (D)   II and III only
    (E)   I, II, and III

2. The kind of currency used in the United States today can be best described as
    (A)   fiat money.
    (B)   intrinsic money.
    (C)   commodity money.
    (D)   state money.
    (E)   federal commodity notes.

3. The largest component of the M1 money supply is
    (A)   demand deposits.
    (B)   travelers' checks.
    (C)   currency.
    (D)   government bonds.
    (E)   savings accounts.

4. U.S. dollars today are backed by
    (A)   gold.
    (B)   silver.
    (C)   government bonds.
    (D)   oil.
    (E)   nothing.

5. The value of money is stabilized primarily by
    (A)   controlling the gold supply.
    (B)   reducing government deficits.
    (C)   increasing taxes.
    (D)   controlling the money supply.
    (E)   reducing interest rates.

6.   During a period of inflation,
      (A)   the purchasing power of money increases by the same rate as inflation.
      (B)   the purchasing power of money decreases.
      (C)   the purchasing power of money remains the same.
      (D)   the change in purchasing power depends on the level of unemployment.
      (E)   purchasing power is based on the level of national debt.

7.   Open market operations consist of
      (A)   the Fed buying and selling stock on the open market.
      (B)   corporations selling stock on the open market.
      (C)   firms selling products to consumers on the open market.
      (D)   the Fed buying and selling government bonds on the open market.
      (E)   firms trading imports and exports on the international open market.

8.   The primary role of the Federal Reserve is to
      (A)   control the money supply.
      (B)   process checks.
      (C)   make loans to member banks.
      (D)   issue new currency.
      (E)   use fiscal policy to stabilize the economy.

Multiple-Choice Explanations
1.   (E)   Money serves all three functions: facilitating exchange, allowing saving, and providing a means to compare values of products.
2.   (A)   Fiat money is money that has no intrinsic value to be used for anything other than currency.
3.   (C)   Currency now comprises more than half of the M1 money supply.
4.   (E)   US currency is no longer backed by gold so that the Federal Reserve can change the money supply to address issues of economic instability.
5.   (D)   By limiting the supply of money in the economy, the Federal Reserve helps money maintains its value.
6.   (B)   Inflation reduces the purchasing power of the dollar, because it takes more dollars to obtain the same amount of goods and services.
7.   (D)   The Federal Reserve buys and sells government bonds in order to change the money supply.
8.   (A)   The Federal Reserve uses the money supply to stabilize the value of money and affect aggregate demand through monetary policy. While the Fed does process checks, make loans to member banks, and issue new currency, its primary role is to control the money supply. Fiscal policy is carried out by Congress.

CHAPTER 32: MONEY CREATION

Introduction
The Federal Reserve System plays a crucial role in the U.S. economy, controlling the money supply and using monetary policy to stabilize the economy. As part of this process, banks create money through the fractional reserve system. Chapter 32 explains the process by which banks increase the money supply and the role of the money multiplier in determining the total increase in the money supply. This knowledge lays the foundation for understanding how monetary policy works. Material from Chapter 32 usually appears in a few multiple-choice questions on the AP macroeconomics exam, as well as occasionally occurring as a complete free-response question on money creation.

The Fractional Reserve System
The U.S. banking system is known as a fractional reserve system, meaning that banks are required to keep a fraction of all checkable deposits in reserve at the bank (or at the Federal Reserve bank) and that the rest of the deposits can be loaned out to other customers. As a result, the reserves at banks are only a fraction of the total money supply.

The banking system creates money by issuing loans. Because the money is loaned and re-loaned, it can create a significantly larger money supply than the original deposit. If the bank retains a large proportion of its deposits, fewer dollars are available to be loaned, so the growth of the money supply will be low. If the fraction of deposits held by the bank is low and the bank keeps loaning large proportions of the subsequent deposits, the money supply can grow rapidly. The ability to change these fractional reserves gives the Federal Reserve considerable flexibility in changing the money supply.

On the other hand, a fractional reserve system carries significant risks for panics and bank runs. If the bank has loaned a significant amount of the original deposits and those deposit-holders return to withdraw those funds, the bank does not have the funds available to repay those funds on demand. The money hasn't disappeared; it will be repaid with interest. But depositors who don't get their money back right away can start a panic, causing other customers to rush to retrieve their funds. The Federal Deposit Insurance Corporation (FDIC) was created to prevent such bank runs by insuring deposits up to $100,000. (That limit was temporarily raised to $250,000 in late 2008 to restore confidence during a serious financial crisis.) When depositors know their accounts are insured by the government, they have confidence that their money is protected and runs are unlikely.

Bank Balance Sheets
Banks perform two primary functions for customers: they provide a safe place for savings, and they loan out money to customers. A bank's balance sheet lists the assets (what the bank owns, the cash on hand, and the money owed to the bank), liabilities (the bank's expenses and debts), and net worth. The balance sheet must remain balanced.

Assets = Liabilities + Net Worth

A new bank is created with $250,000 of stock bought by shareholders, which is a liability for the bank because it must be repaid to the stockholders. From the stock proceeds, $240,000 is spent on property and capital, and $10,000 remains in cash, which are the assets of the bank. The balance sheet is balanced.

Accepting Deposits
Balance Sheet 3: Wahoo Bank

Assets		Liabilities and net worth	
Cash	$110,000	Checkable deposits	$100,000
Property	240,000	Stock shares	250,000

If depositors make $100,000 in deposits into checking accounts, those deposits show up on both sides of the balance sheet—as cash the bank is holding as an asset and as a liability of checkable deposits the bank owes the depositors. However, the economy's money supply has not changed. Remember, M1 consists of currency held by the public and demand deposits at the bank. When the deposits were made, the form of the money changed from currency to checkable deposits, but the quantity of money did not change.

The Reserve Requirement
The reserve requirement (or reserve ratio) is the percentage of checkable deposits that the bank must hold in reserve and cannot loan out. It can hold that reserve as vault cash at the bank or keep it at the regional Federal Reserve Bank. If $100,000 is deposited at the bank and the reserve requirement is 10 percent, the bank is required to hold $10,000 in cash, and it can loan out the other $90,000 to customers. The Federal Reserve determines the reserve requirement.

Actual reserves are the total amount of reserves the bank holds. Excess reserves are the amount of reserves the bank holds beyond the required reserves; these are the funds that can be loaned out to other customers.

Actual Reserves = Required Reserves + Excess Reserves

While it may appear that the purpose of a reserve requirement is to ensure liquidity so that funds will be available when depositors attempt to withdraw their funds, this is not the real purpose of a reserve requirement. The purpose of the reserve requirement is to control the money supply. When a bank makes loans to customers, it increases the money supply; when the loan is repaid, it decreases the money supply. The Federal Reserve can change the reserve requirement, which changes the money supply, to address recession or inflation. The reserve requirement limits how far the money supply can grow in order to prevent significant inflation in the economy.

Government Securities
Banks can also buy and sell government bonds to affect the money supply. If the bank buys bonds from a securities dealer, it increases the money supply because it receives a non-money asset (the bond) and pays with money. If the bank sells bonds, it reduces the money supply by releasing a non-money asset into the economy and taking in money.

Bear in Mind

It is important to note the difference between the change in money supply resulting from a new deposit of cash versus the bank buying securities. A customer deposit causes no change in the money supply because the money is only changing form from currency to a demand deposit, both forms of M1. However, if a bank buys a bond, the money supply does increase. The bank puts money into the economy to buy the bond, while absorbing a non-money asset into its accounts. In answering exam questions, it is important to pay careful attention to the initial action in order to determine whether money is created in that initial action or whether money is created later in the process through loans.

The Federal Funds Market

Banks are like any other firm—they seek profit. Banks make profit by paying a low interest rate on deposits and using those deposits to make loans for which they charge a higher interest rate, or by using those deposits to buy securities, which earn a higher interest rate. So banks have an incentive to loan out as much of their excess reserve as possible. The bank has another objective, though. It has to maintain liquidity for depositors who want to make withdrawals. So it can't loan out so much of the excess reserve that if depositors unexpectedly write a large number of checks at the end of the day, the bank would be left with less than the required reserve. To resolve this issue, banks make overnight loans to each other to ensure they meet their reserve requirements each night. Banks with excess reserves at the end of the day can make overnight loans to banks that need it, charging an interest rate called the federal funds rate.

Multiple-Deposit Expansion

We can see how banks create money through loans by starting with a few assumptions. All of the banks must meet the reserve requirement (10 percent in our example), and the banks start with no excess reserves. Further, we will assume that every time a bank makes a loan, the recipient writes a check for the entire amount, which is fully redeposited in another bank. Finally, we assume that banks will loan out all excess reserves.

	Deposits	Required Reserves	Excess Reserves	Loans	Total Increase in Money Supply
Customer A	$1,000	$100	$900		$ 0
Customer B				$900	$900
Customer C	$900	$90	$810		$900
Customer D				$810	$1,710
Customer E	$810	$81	$729		$1,710

Let's assume Customer A takes $1,000 from under his mattress and deposits it into his checking account at the bank. Did the money supply change? No. The money only changed form, from currency to a checkable deposit. If the bank must hold 10 percent in cash to meet the reserve requirement, it must hold $100 and, therefore, has $900 available in new excess reserves that it can loan to customers.

Customer B takes out a $900 loan to buy a computer from Customer C. At this point, the bank creates $900 in new money. How? Customer A still has his $1,000 in demand deposits at the bank, but now Customer B has a $900 loan from the bank to buy the computer—the $900 has been used twice.

Customer B buys the computer from Customer C, who deposits the $900 in his checking account at a bank. Did this action create more money? No, the money just changed location, from a customer check based on the loan to a new deposit in Customer C's checking account. Of the new $900 deposit, the bank is required to reserve $90 (so banks now hold a total of $190 in required reserves), leaving $810 in excess reserves available for loans.

Customer D comes to the bank to borrow $810, to pay Customer E for car repairs. In creating the loan from the excess reserves, the bank has created another $810 in new money, for a total of $1,710 of new money created by the banking system from the original $1,000 deposit. When Customer E deposits the $810 payment from Customer D, the bank must again keep the 10 percent required reserve ($81) and can again loan the $729 in new excess reserves. This process continues with deposit after deposit and loan after loan.

Important Implications of Money Creation

A few important questions arise from this understanding of the multiple-deposit expansion of the money supply. What happens if depositors try to remove funds that have been loaned? How large will the money supply grow under this system? And why is the reserve requirement important for limiting the growth of the money supply?

First, once the excess reserves have been loaned and reloaned, what if Customer A comes back to the bank and wants to withdraw his $1,000 deposit? It isn't there. Nearly all of it has been loaned out to Customer B. If Customer A can't get his money and makes panicked calls to his friends, Customers C and E, they may rush to their banks to try to get their deposits as well—a classic run on the banks. In modern banking, Customer A is only one of hundreds of thousands of people who have deposits at each bank, and it is extremely unlikely that everyone would show up at once to withdraw their deposits. Even if they did, the FDIC provides government protection of deposits, up to a limit, in case the banks actually collapsed.

The Growth of the Money Supply

An important implication is that with every loan, the money supply keeps growing. How large will it grow? To find out, we need to calculate the money multiplier.

$$\text{Money Multiplier} = \frac{1}{\text{Reserve Requirement}}$$

If the reserve requirement is 10 percent, the money multiplier is 1 / 0.1, or 10. If the reserve requirement is 20 percent, the money multiplier is 1 / 0.2, or 5. The larger the reserve requirement of deposits that the bank must hold, the smaller the multiplier becomes.

Bear in Mind

You cannot use a calculator on the AP economics exams, and you can count on questions that require you to calculate the money multiplier. An easy trick of the trade to calculate the multiplier is to think about the denominator (the reserve requirement) as a fraction of a dollar. For example, if the reserve requirement is 10 percent, the denominator is 0.10—which looks like 10 cents. What must you multiply your dime by to get to a dollar? Ten. Your multiplier is 10. If the reserve requirement is 25 percent, your denominator is 0.25—a quarter. You must multiply a quarter by 4 to get to a dollar, so your multiplier is 4.

Now that we know the multiplier, we can calculate the maximum potential growth of the money supply resulting from an initial deposit.

$$\text{Potential Money Creation} \ = \ \text{Excess Reserves} \ \times \ \text{Money Multiplier}$$

In our earlier example, the initial $1,000 deposit with a 10 percent reserve requirement left an initial $900 in excess reserves. With a money multiplier of 10, the amount of money created by the banking system through loans is $9,000. Added to the $1,000 initial deposit, the total money supply is $10,000. Now we can begin to see the full impact of changes in the multiplier. If the reserve requirement had been 20 percent with a multiplier of 5, the money supply could have grown only by $4,000 for a total of $5,000, because the banks could not have loaned as much. Had the reserve requirement been 50 percent with a multiplier of 2, the money supply could have grown only by $1,000 for a total of $2,000.

The money multiplier is a concept very similar to the spending multiplier and marginal propensity to consume. With the MPC, one person's spending is another person's income, so an initial change in spending eventually leads to a much larger change in real GDP as the money is spent and respent. In the same way, an initial deposit into the banking system is loaned and reloaned, spent and respent, so that an initial deposit into the banking system results in a much larger effect on the money supply.

Limitations on Growth of the Money Supply
Another implication of this multiple-deposit expansion system is the importance of the reserve requirement in controlling the growth of the money supply. Assume for a moment that there was no reserve requirement at all. If banks were free to loan out all deposits made to the bank, how far would the money supply grow? It would grow infinitely. There would be no means to limit the perpetual reloaning of funds, causing massive inflation. Therefore, a reserve requirement is essential for limiting the growth of the money supply and the rate of inflation.

Will the money supply always grow to its potential? Generally not. Remember our opening assumptions—that banks loan out all of their excess reserves and customers redeposit all of their funds at their banks. In reality, consumers hold cash in their wallets and in their homes for purchases, and money not deposited at the bank cannot be used to further expand the money supply. Further, banks may not fully loan funds if they are concerned about meeting their reserve requirement or if customers simply choose not to take out as many loans during an economic downturn. So while we know the maximum potential growth of the money supply, the actual money supply may change less.

Multiple-Choice Questions
1.   A fractional reserve system requires banks to keep a fraction of demand deposits in
    (A)   government securities.
    (B)   loans to customers.
    (C)   vault cash or deposits at a Federal Reserve bank.
    (D)   collateral assets, such as home mortgages.
    (E)   savings accounts or time deposits.

2.   Banks create money in the U.S. monetary system by
        (A)   printing it.
        (B)   making loans.
        (C)   selling government securities.
        (D)   increasing interest rates.
        (E)   increasing the reserve requirement.

3.   If a customer deposits $2,000 and the bank is allowed to loan $1,200 of the deposit, the
        reserve requirement is
        (A)   40 percent.
        (B)   6 percent.
        (C)   167 percent.
        (D)   60 percent.
        (E)   8 percent.

4.   Assume the reserve requirement is 15 percent and a bank initially has no excess reserves.
        If a customer deposits $1,000, how much of that deposit can be loaned?
        (A) $15
        (B) $150
        (C) $7,000
        (D) $850
        (E) $1,015

5.   When a customer deposits $200 cash into his checking account at the bank, the
        money supply
        (A)   increases by $200.
        (B)   decreases by $200 times the multiplier.
        (C)   decreases by $200.
        (D)   increases by $200 times the multiplier.
        (E)   does not change.

6.   The balance sheet below shows the current financial status of Horvath National Bank. If
        the reserve requirement is 20 percent and the bank does not sell any securities, by how
        much could it increase loans?

Assets		Liabilities	
Total Reserves	$35,000	Demand Deposits	$100,000
Loans	$10,000		
Securities	$55,000		

        (A) $0
        (B) $10,000
        (C) $70,000
        (D) $25,000
        (E) $15,000

7.   The federal funds rate is the
        (A)   interest rate banks charge each other for short-term loans.
        (B)   total money supply in the United States.
        (C)   rate of growth of the money supply.
        (D)   percentage of deposits banks must hold in cash.
        (E)   ratio of loans to deposits.

8.   Assume a bank has no excess reserves and the reserve requirement is 20 percent. If a customer deposits $20,000 in currency into his checking account, what is the maximum amount by which banks will increase the money supply through multiple-deposit expansion in the banking system?
       (A) $4,000
       (B) $20,000
       (C) $40,000
       (D) $100,000
       (E) $80,000

9.   If members of the public choose to hold money in currency rather than depositing it into banks, the growth of the money supply will be
       (A)   less than the potential growth of the money supply.
       (B)   infinite.
       (C)   unaffected, because currency is only a different form of M1.
       (D)   determined by the marginal propensity to consume.
       (E)   determined by the reserve requirement.

Free-Response Question
Sandy receives a graduation gift of $1,000 in $100 bills from her grandmother. Sandy deposits the $1,000 into her checking account at the First Federal Bank.
(a)   What is the initial impact of Sandy's deposit on the money supply? Explain.
(b)   If the reserve requirement is 20 percent, calculate the following:
        (i)   the maximum amount First Federal can loan from the initial deposit. Explain how you calculated this amount.
        (ii)   the maximum potential increase in the total money supply as a result of the deposit. Explain how you calculated this amount.
(c)   Identify two reasons why the money supply might not grow to its maximum potential.
(d)   If the reserve requirement were 100 percent, what would be the maximum potential increase in the money supply as a result of Sandy's deposit? Explain.
(e)   If the reserve requirement were 0 percent, explain the following.
        (i)   the maximum potential increase in the money supply as a result of Sandy's deposit
        (ii)   the effect on the purchasing power of the dollar

Multiple-Choice Explanations
1.   (C)   The fractional reserve system means that a percentage of all deposits into checkable accounts must be held in reserve by the bank and not loaned.
2.   (B)   Each time a bank makes a loan from its excess reserves, money is created.
3.   (A)   If the bank is allowed to loan $1,200 of the $2,000 deposit, it must be required to keep $800 of the deposit. 8 / 20 = 40 / 100 = a 40 percent reserve ratio
4.   (D)   The bank is required to hold 15 percent of the $1,000, or $150, in required reserve. The other $850 in excess reserves can be loaned out by the bank.
5.   (E)   When cash is deposited into a checking account, the money supply does not change, because both currency and demand deposits are components of the M1 money supply. The money changed form from cash to checking deposits, but the amount of money did not change.

6.	(E)	Checkable deposits are $100,000, so with a 20 percent reserve requirement, the required reserve is $20,000. Of the $35,000 in actual reserves, $20,000 is required, so the other $15,000 is excess reserves available for loans.

7.	(A)	Banks must sometimes borrow from other banks overnight in order to meet their reserve requirements. The interest rate on these short-term loans is the federal funds rate.

8.	(E)	If the deposit is $20,000 and the reserve requirement is 20 percent, the bank must hold $4,000 in required reserves, leaving $16,000 in excess reserves. The multiplier (1 / Reserve Requirement) is 5 (1 / 0.2). The greatest possible expansion of the money supply is the excess reserve times the multiplier ($16,000 × 5), or $80,000.

9.	(A)	If money is not deposited into the bank, it cannot continue the multiple-deposit expansion, so the money supply will not grow as large as it could have if all of the money had been deposited.

Free Response Explanation
12 points (2 + 4 + 2 + 2 + 2)

(a)	2 points:
- 1 point is earned for stating that Sandy's deposit does not change the money supply.
- 1 point is earned for explaining that currency and demand deposits are just different forms of the M1 money supply, so only the composition of the money supply changed, not the amount of money.

(b)	4 points:
- 1 point is earned for stating that First Federal could loan $800 of the initial deposit.
- 1 point is earned for explaining that the bank has required reserves of $200 (0.20 × $1,000), so excess reserves are $800 ($1,000 – $200).
- 1 point is earned for stating that the money supply will increase by $4,000.
- 1 point is earned for explaining that the multiplier is 5 (1 / 0.2), which is multiplied by the excess reserves of $800 for a total money creation of $4,000.

(c)	2 points:
- 1 point is earned for each of two reasons from the following list:
  - The banks decide to hold some excess reserves and not loan them out.
  - The public holds on to some currency and does not redeposit it at the bank.
  - Consumers are not willing to borrow money from banks.

(d)	2 points:
- 1 point is earned for stating that the maximum increase in the money supply is zero.
- 1 point is earned for explaining that because the bank cannot loan any of the deposit back out, the money supply cannot grow.

(e)	2 points:
- 1 point is earned for stating that the money supply would grow infinitely.
- 1 point is earned for explaining that the purchasing power of the dollar would fall, because inflation resulting from the higher money supply would lower the value of money.

CHAPTER 33: INTEREST RATES AND MONETARY POLICY

Introduction
Changes in the money supply have an important impact on interest rates, aggregate demand, price levels, and employment. The Federal Reserve uses a number of tools to play a central role in determining interest rates and stabilizing the economy. Chapter 33 focuses on the supply and demand for money, the tools of monetary policy and how they are used, and the effects of monetary policy on GDP and economic stabilization. These principles complete the discussion of the role of the money in the macroeconomy. Material from Chapter 33 consistently appears in a significant number of questions in the multiple-choice section of the AP macroeconomics exam, as well as part of a free-response question in nearly every exam.

The Money Market
The interest rate is the price paid for the use of money. There are a number of different interest rates: mortgage interest, auto loan interest, student loan interest, savings account interest, and the interest paid on bonds, among many others. Discussion of "the interest rate" in this context only refers to a general concept rather than a specific interest rate for a particular purpose.

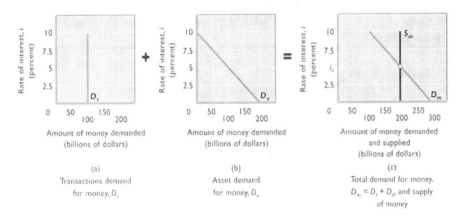

The demand for money, the supply of money, and the equilibrium interest rate

The demand for money is determined by the two reasons people decide to hold money: transactions demand and asset demand. Transactions demand refers to the amount of money people hold as a medium of exchange in order to make purchases. People keep some money in cash from their income in order to pay for gas, groceries, entertainment, and other purchases they make. Transactions demand changes with the amount of nominal GDP, because as output, prices, or incomes increase, consumers need more money to be able to pay for products produced in the economy. Transactions demand is a vertical curve because we assume it is not related to the interest rate.

Asset demand is the amount of money people hold as a store of value, as an asset they can keep to potentially use for future purchases. People can put their savings into stocks, bonds, savings accounts, or a number of other investments that can earn interest or dividends—or they can hold it in cash. Holding assets in cash gives a person immediate liquidity and protects the asset against a potential loss that could occur with stocks or other investments. However, cash earns no return on investment, so people must determine the tradeoffs in deciding what to do with their savings. Asset demand is inversely related to the interest rate, because at a high interest rate, people suffer a higher opportunity cost for holding their savings in cash rather than putting it in a bank; at a lower interest rate, the opportunity cost is lower, so people are more willing to hold a greater quantity of their money in cash. As a result, asset demand is downward sloping.

The total demand for money is the transactions demand plus the asset demand for money—added horizontally. When the nominal GDP increases, consumers want to buy more, so the demand for money increases; a lower nominal GDP reduces demand for money. Since the Federal Reserve determines the money supply, it is a vertical curve. The equilibrium interest rate is determined by the intersection of the demand and supply of money. An increase in the demand for money or a decrease in the money supply will cause interest rates to increase. A decrease in the demand for money or an increase in money supply causes the interest rate to fall. This is a nominal interest rate, incorporating the real interest rate and the expected rate of inflation.

Taking the EEK! Out of Economics
It is important to remember the distinction between the money market and the loanable funds market. Supply in the money market is set by the Federal Reserve and is a vertical curve. Demand is based on how much consumers want to hold in cash. In the loanable funds market, supply is determined by how much people want to save in savings accounts or bonds. Demand comes from consumers, firms, and government borrowing to make purchases. The money market describes the entire money supply in the economy, while the loanable funds market illustrates changes in borrowing in the economy.

The Federal Reserve's Balance Sheet

Assets		Liabilities and Net Worth	
Securities	$713,369	Reserves of commercial banks	$ 11,312
Loans to commercial banks	60,039	Treasury deposits	4,979
All other assets	111,689	Federal Reserve Notes (outstanding)	778,937
		All other liabilities and net worth	89,869
Total	885,097	Total	885,097

Source: Federal Reserve Statistical Release, H.4.1, February 14, 2008. www.federalreserve.gov.

Consolidated balance sheet of the twelve Federal Reserve banks, February 14, 2008 (in millions)

Like commercial banks, the Federal Reserve banks also have balance sheets. Federal Reserve banks have two primary assets: securities and loans to banks. The Federal Reserve buys government securities (Treasury bills, notes, and bonds that finance deficits) in order to expand the money supply. The Fed also makes loans to commercial banks, in order for the banks to loan that money out to customers to further increase the money supply. On the liabilities side of the ledger, the Fed has bank reserves, Treasury deposits, and currency outstanding. Commercial banks leave reserves against their checkable deposits at the Fed. Because the funds are owed to the commercial banks, they are considered liabilities to the Fed. The U.S. Treasury Department also leaves reserves at the Fed to cover checks written by the federal government. The amount of actual currency in use in the economy is also considered a liability of the Fed.

Tools of Monetary Policy
The Federal Reserve has three primary tools by which it can change the money supply: open market operations, the reserve requirement (or ratio), and the discount rate. In addition, the Fed has a new tool it is using in response to the current financial crisis.

Open market operations are the Fed's activities in buying and selling government bonds to commercial banks and the public. When the Fed buys bonds, it creates money in order to pay for the bonds. If the Fed is buying bonds from a commercial bank, the Fed increases its securities on the asset side of the ledger and increases the bank's reserves on account at the Fed on the liabilities side of the ledger. The Fed takes the bond, and the bank has more reserves available to loan out, so the money supply can increase. If the Fed instead buys bonds from the public, it pays with a check, which that person deposits in the bank, increasing that bank's reserves and allowing the bank to loan out more funds. So when the Fed buys bonds, the money supply increases. When the Fed sells bonds, the money supply decreases because the commercial bank reserves that could have been used for loans have been used instead to buy the bonds from the Fed.

The reserve requirement (or reserve ratio) is the percentage of deposits that banks must hold in reserve and cannot loan out. In order to increase the money supply, the Fed reduces the reserve requirement, allowing banks to make more loans with the greater amount of excess reserves. Using the money multiplier (1 / Reserve Requirement), if the reserve requirement is 10 percent, the multiplier is 10. A $1,000 initial deposit in the bank will result in a $10,000 increase in the money supply ($1,000 from the initial deposit and $9,000 from the banking system). But if the reserve requirement is reduced to 5 percent, the multiplier becomes 20, and the same $1,000 deposit results in a $20,000 increase in the money supply ($1,000 from the initial deposit and $19,000 from the banking system). To reduce the money supply, the Fed increases the reserve requirement, requiring the bank to hold on to a higher percentage of checkable deposits and reduce the amount of loans.

The discount rate is the interest rate the Fed charges on loans to commercial banks. In order to increase the money supply, the Fed lowers the discount rate. The lower discount rate encourages commercial banks to borrow from the Fed, which increases the excess reserves available for loans. As more is loaned out, the money supply in the economy increases. In contrast, an increase in the discount rate makes it more expensive for commercial banks to borrow from the Fed, so they borrow less and as a consequence loan out less, reducing the money supply.

Taking the EEK! Out of Economics
Don't get confused by the word "discount," thinking of it as some kind of coupon. Often, students think that if the discount rate is larger, the bank can borrow for a cheaper interest rate. Just the opposite is true. Remember that it is an interest rate, the cost of borrowing money. Also keep in mind that if the Fed is using each of its tools of monetary policy, the reserve requirement and the discount rate would move in the same direction to have the same effect. To increase the money supply, lower the reserve requirement and discount rate; to lower the money supply, raise the reserve requirement and discount rate.

In December 2007, in response to the deepening financial crisis, the Fed created a fourth tool, known as a term auction facility. Every two weeks, banks submit secret bids to borrow from the Fed for a four-week period. Those who offer to pay the highest interest rates are given the loans anonymously, which are repaid with interest. When the Fed wants to increase the money supply, it increases the amount of money offered in the auction.

The Fed also controls the federal funds rate, the interest rate banks charge each other for overnight loans. Banks that are holding too few reserves at the end of the business day to meet their reserve requirement can borrow the excess reserves of other banks overnight, which are repaid with the federal funds rate of interest. The Fed can use open market operations to target the levels of excess reserves in banks, in order to set the desired federal funds rate. The Fed focuses monetary policy on this rate, over which it has a great deal of control. The federal funds rate is closely related to the prime rate, which is the interest rate banks charge their best customers for loans. So the Fed's actions in changing the federal funds rate result in changes in the interest rates faced by consumers and firms across the nation.

Open market operations are the most commonly used tool of the Fed. This tool is the most flexible with the most immediate effects, allowing the Fed to make minor changes in the money supply quickly and easily. The reserve requirement is the most powerful tool of the Fed, because changes in the multiplier have a very powerful effect on the money supply. As a result, the Fed uses this tool very rarely—it has not been changed since 1992. The discount rate is an intermediary tool used during more serious economic downturns.

Expansionary Monetary Policy
To resolve a recession, the Fed uses expansionary monetary policy, or "easy money policy." Expansionary policy is achieved when the Fed lowers the reserve requirement, lowers the discount rate, or buys bonds. When the Fed increases the money supply, interest rates fall. The lower interest rates encourage consumers to borrow to finance spending and entice firms to borrow for capital investment in plant and equipment. This additional spending increases aggregate demand, which increases real output (GDP).

Contractionary Monetary Policy
If inflation is the problem, the Fed uses contractionary monetary policy, or "tight money policy." The Fed can increase the reserve requirement, increase the discount rate, or sell bonds to achieve contractionary policy. By reducing the money supply, the Fed allows interest rates to rise, discouraging firms and consumers from borrowing. The reduction in borrowing leaves firms and consumers with fewer funds to buy products in the economy, lowering aggregate demand and real output (GDP).

Bear in Mind

An understanding of the tools of monetary policy is essential for success on the AP macroeconomics exam. Several multiple-choice questions as well as at least one free-response question will likely be rooted directly in your ability to explain how the Fed should use its tools to address specific economic problems. For the free-response questions, it is also essential for you to be able to explain the changes in each step of the cause-and-effect chain.

Effects of Monetary Policy in the Macroeconomy
The series of four graphs below illustrates how monetary policy works through the linkages among the money, investment, and aggregate demand–aggregate supply markets. An understanding of these relationships is essential.

Figure A represents the money market, with the demand for money representing both the asset and transactions demand for money and the vertical money supply set by the Federal Reserve. The equilibrium real interest rate is determined by the supply and demand for money. When the Fed increases the money supply from S_{m2} to S_{m3}, the real interest rate falls from 8 percent to 6 percent. When the Fed reduces the money supply from S_{m2} to S_{m1}, the real interest rate rises from 8 percent to 10 percent.

Chapter 33: Interest Rates and Monetary Policy

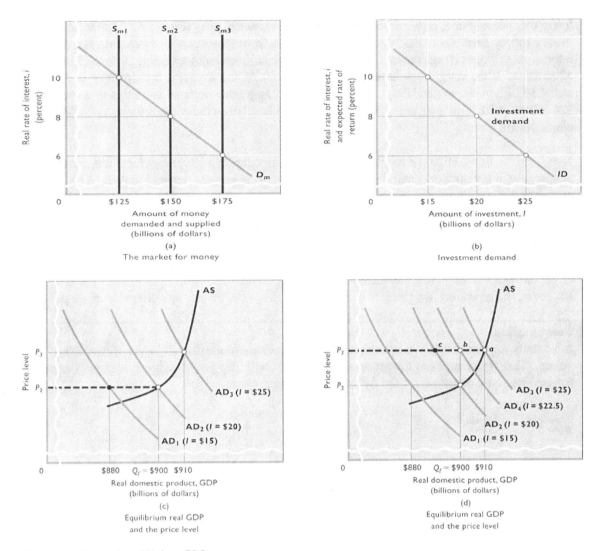

Monetary policy and equilibrium GDP

Figure B represents investment demand of firms, primarily for factory expansion, equipment, and other long-term purchases. Remember, firms borrow for capital investment only if they expect the returns on the investment to be greater than the real interest rate they must borrow to pay for the capital. At high interest rates, firms borrow less for capital investment. At low interest rates, the quantity of money demanded for investment increases. These changes in interest rates also affect consumer borrowing for large purchases such as homes and cars.

Figures C and D illustrate aggregate supply and demand, which determine the price level and the real GDP in the economy. As aggregate demand increases, prices rise and the real GDP increases. As output increases, employment increases because workers must be hired to produce those goods and services. When aggregate demand falls, real GDP falls, and the decrease in output results in a decrease in employment, because fewer workers are needed to produce the lower output. However, remember that prices tend to be downwardly "sticky" with the ratchet effect, so a decrease in aggregate demand tends to result in prices at the same level.

In this example, the economy (Figure C) starts with an equilibrium real GDP of $900 billion and a price level of P_2. If the economy falls into recession, with real GDP dropping by $20 billion, an expansionary monetary policy is appropriate. The Fed would lower the reserve requirement, lower the discount rate, or buy bonds to increase the money supply (Figure A). The increase in money supply from S_{m1} to S_{m2} lowers the interest rate from 10 percent to 8 percent. The lower interest rate (Figure B) results in a $5 billion increase in investment spending, from $15 billion to $20 billion. If the marginal propensity to consume is 0.75, the spending multiplier is 4. As that initial $5 billion is spent and respent in the economy, aggregate demand increases by a total of $20 billion ($5 billion × 4), and the recessionary gap is filled as the economy returns to full employment.

Now, assume instead that the money supply is S_{m3}, resulting in a lower 6 percent interest rate and an increase in investment demand strong enough to push aggregate demand to AD_3. The economy is overstimulated (Figure C), with the increase in aggregate demand causing inflation (AD_3). Therefore, a contractionary monetary policy would be appropriate. In this case, the Fed would increase the reserve requirement or discount rate or sell bonds to reduce the money supply. The increase in the interest rate would reduce the quantity of investment dollars demanded, lowering aggregate demand from AD_3 to AD_4 (Figure D). But notice that, because of the ratchet effect, the price level which was increased by the initial inflation from P_2 to P_3 does not fall. However, the reduction in aggregate demand does reduce the further upward pressure on prices.

Bear in Mind

It is vitally important that you are able to explain the cause-and-effect linkages of monetary policy. This figure explains the process in a way that will help you to achieve stronger scores on the free-response questions on the AP macroeconomics exam.

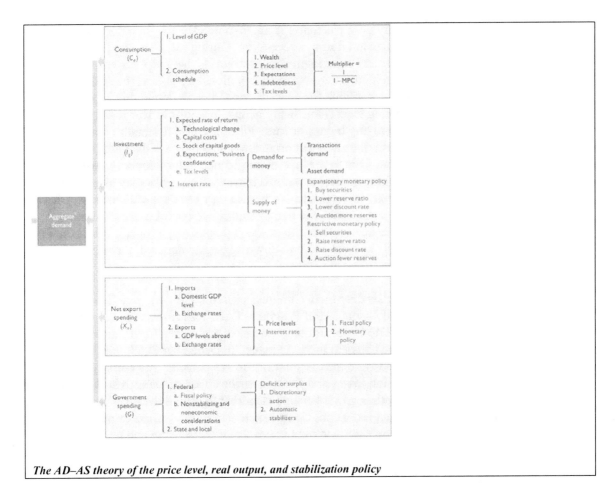

The AD–AS theory of the price level, real output, and stabilization policy

Advantages of Monetary Policy

One primary advantage of monetary policy is it can be made very quickly in a meeting of the Board of Governors, while Congress may take months to pass fiscal policy. A second advantage is the flexibility of monetary policy. The Fed can buy or sell bonds on a daily basis in an attempt to "fine tune" the economy, while fiscal tax and spending measures have much broader effects across the economy. A third important advantage is that members of the Fed are insulated from political pressure, making it easier for them to reduce the money supply and raise interest rates to fight inflation. Members of Congress who must be reelected by their constituents find it much more difficult to raise taxes or lower government spending on popular programs during periods of inflation. Another important difference is that Congress has a wide variety of items on its agenda, and if taxes or spending must be changed to address a more important concern—for example, a decision to go to war—the economic impact is only a secondary concern. The Fed's only concern is the economy, so its policies are determined from that focus.

Problems of Monetary Policy

Remember that fiscal policy faces recognition, administrative, and operational lags before fully taking effect. Monetary policy also encounters problems with the time required to recognize that an economic problem has surfaced, as well as a three to six month lag for the interest rate changes to affect investment, aggregate demand, and real GDP. The Fed, however, avoids the administrative lag of actually making the policy. But even monetary policy requires time to address economic instability.

A more serious problem of monetary policy is that it is much more effective in reducing inflation than it is in stimulating aggregate demand during a recession. During inflation, the Fed can effectively reduce the money supply and raise interest rates to levels that reduce investment and aggregate demand. However, when it comes to expansionary monetary policy, the Fed faces challenges. While it makes reserves available for banks to lend, it can't do anything more than make those reserves available. During recessions, many people lose jobs or fear losing their jobs, so they are less likely to seek loans to buy homes or cars. Firms are also hesitant to borrow during recessions, because revenues fall as they cut production, and they are likely to have excess capacity due to the lower production. Due to the lack of confidence in the economy, even the lower interest rate may not entice firms and consumers to borrow. The banks may also choose not to grant as many loans at the lower interest rates, or people may not deposit their money back into banks. If loans and deposits are not made, the money multiplier cannot take effect to increase the money supply. This has been referred to as the Fed "pushing a rope." While the Fed can effectively use the money supply as a rope to pull down aggregate demand, it cannot as effectively push the rope to increase aggregate demand.

In October 2008, as the financial crisis deepened, Congress passed the Emergency Economic Stabilization Act, with the Troubled Assets Relief Program (TARP) serving as the largest portion of the legislation. The purpose of TARP was to purchase assets and equity from financial institutions in an effort to encourage banks to increase loans. In December 2008, the Fed reduced the federal funds rate to 0–1/4 percent and the discount rate to 1/2 percent. In February 2009, banks still seemed not to be increasing loans, and firms in serious need of loans to survive the economic downturn faced a credit crisis. As it became clear that "pushing the rope" was not effective in addressing the significant recession, Congress created a fiscal stimulus package of more than a half-trillion dollars, expecting increases in government spending and tax cuts would more effectively stimulate aggregate demand and increase output and employment.

Combinations of Fiscal and Monetary Policy
The Federal Reserve and Congress each make policy independent of the other, though members of Congress often invite the chairman of the Federal Reserve Board of Governors to testify about economic conditions and the effects of fiscal and monetary policy in certain conditions. Because the policies are made independently and affect the economy in different ways, it is important to consider how such policies work in combination.

If the Federal Reserve identifies a recessionary gap and reduces the reserve requirement, lowers the discount rate, or buys bonds to increase the money supply, this lowers the interest rate and increases investment so that aggregate demand rises, increasing real GDP, employment, and the price level. If Congress identifies the same recessionary gap and increases government spending and reduces taxes to directly stimulate aggregate demand, then real GDP, employment, and prices will increase. But because Congress must borrow money to finance the deficit created by the expansionary policy, the government's increased demand for money in the loanable funds market pushes the interest rate up, which can crowd out private investment. While expansionary monetary policy reduces interest rates, expansionary fiscal policy increases interest rates, and the effects of monetary policy can be diluted by the crowding out.

If, instead, Congress and the Fed decide to address different economic problems, their policies could have contradictory effects. In the case of stagflation, where high inflation and high unemployment occur simultaneously, the Fed may choose to address the inflation problem because its tools are most effective in addressing inflation. So if the Fed reduces the money supply to increase interest rates, then aggregate demand and employment fall. At the same time, Congress may choose to address the problem of unemployment, because constituents will oppose fiscal anti-inflation measures. So if Congress reduces taxes and raises spending to increase aggregate demand, it must borrow funds, and the increased demand in the loanable funds market will again raise interest rates. In this case, both the fiscal and monetary policies are consistent in increasing interest rates, but the monetary policy works to reduce aggregate demand while the fiscal policy works to increase it.

One last consideration is how these policies affect long-run economic growth. Long-run economic growth results from investment in plant and equipment and increased productivity of workers. Keeping interest rates low is essential to investment, which fuels long-run economic growth. When interest rates are low, firms are more likely to invest in plant and equipment, so the aggregate demand increases in the short run as firms make those purchases. But low interest rates also increase long-run aggregate supply after the firms have finished expansions and installation of equipment, because production increases at a lower cost per unit. Expansionary monetary policies (lower reserve requirements, lower discount rates, and buying bonds) reduce interest rates to promote investment, while contractionary fiscal policies (raising taxes and lowering spending) reduce government borrowing in the loanable funds market, and the combination holds interest rates down to promote long-run economic growth.

Multiple-Choice Questions

1. In the money market,
    (A) the demand for money consists of asset and transactions demand.
    (B) the supply of money is horizontal.
    (C) The interest rate is determined by the demand for money.
    (D) Congress determines the money supply.
    (E) Congress and the Fed jointly determine an appropriate interest rate.

2. The Federal Reserve increases the money supply when it
    (A) buys bonds.
    (B) increases the reserve requirement.
    (C) lowers taxes.
    (D) increases the discount rate.
    (E) increases government spending.

3. The interest rate the Fed charges commercial banks for loans is the
    (A) reserve requirement.
    (B) real interest rate.
    (C) prime rate.
    (D) discount rate.
    (E) federal funds rate.

4. The most commonly used tool of monetary policy is
    (A) the reserve requirement.
    (B) the discount rate.
    (C) open market operations.
    (D) tax rates.
    (E) government spending.

5. If the Federal Reserve sells bonds on the open market,
    (A) the money supply and interest rate both increase.
    (B) the money supply decreases and the interest rate increases.
    (C) the money supply increases and the interest rate does not change.
    (D) the money supply and interest rate both decrease.
    (E) the money supply increases and the interest rate decreases.

6. Expansionary monetary policy is most appropriate when
    (A) the unemployment rate is low.
    (B) The inflation rate is high.
    (C) real GDP is falling.
    (D) the money supply is high.
    (E) interest rates are low.

7. Which of the following policies would be appropriate to resolve a recession?
    (A) increasing the federal funds rate
    (B) the Fed selling bonds to a commercial bank
    (C) increasing the discount rate
    (D) raising the prime rate
    (E) lowering the reserve requirement

8. If the Federal Reserve increases the money supply, how will interest rates, capital investment, and aggregate demand be affected?

	Interest Rates	Investment	Aggregate Demand
(A)	Increase	Increase	Increase
(B)	Decrease	Decrease	Decrease
(C)	Increase	Decrease	Increase
(D)	Decrease	Increase	Increase
(E)	Increase	Decrease	Decrease

9. Which of the following policies would be inappropriate if the Federal Reserve is trying to reduce the inflation rate?
    (A) selling bonds on the open market
    (B) increasing the discount rate
    (C) reducing the federal funds rate
    (D) increasing the reserve requirement
    (E) reducing the money supply

10. How will the Fed's purchase of bonds likely affect real output, employment, and price level?

	Real Output	Employment	Price Level
(A)	Decrease	Decrease	Decrease
(B)	Increase	Increase	Decrease
(C)	Decrease	Decrease	Increase
(D)	Increase	Decrease	Decrease
(E)	Increase	Increase	Increase

11. Which combination of fiscal and monetary policy actions would be most effective in reducing an inflationary gap?
    (A) increasing taxes and decreasing the reserve requirement
    (B) decreasing government spending and the Fed selling bonds

(C)   decreasing taxes and increasing the discount rate

(D)   increasing government spending and decreasing the discount rate

(E)   increasing taxes and the Fed buying bonds

12.   Which of the following policy combinations would be most effective in promoting long-run economic growth?

	Taxes	Reserve Requirement	Fed Action on Bonds
(A)	Increase	Increase	Buy
(B)	Increase	Decrease	Buy
(C)	Decrease	Decrease	Sell
(D)	Decrease	Increase	Sell
(E)	Decrease	Increase	Buy

Free-Response Question

The United States economy is experiencing a significant recession.

(a)   Identify an open market operation the Fed could take to return the economy to full-employment output.

(b)   Using a correctly labeled graph of the money market, illustrate the effect of the open market operation on each of the following.
(i)   the money supply
(ii)   the interest rate

(c)   Explain how the change in interest rate in (b)(ii) affects aggregate demand.

(d)   Using a correctly labeled aggregate demand–aggregate supply graph, illustrate the effect of the change in aggregate demand on the following.
(i)   real output
(ii)   the price level

Multiple-Choice Explanations

1.   (A)   Asset demand is money people hold as savings for future use; transactions demand is the money people hold in order to make purchases.

2.   (A)   When the Fed buys bonds, bank reserves increase, allowing banks to loan out more funds and increase the money supply. Increasing the reserve requirement and discount rate reduce the money supply, and taxes and spending are fiscal policies controlled by Congress rather than the Fed.

3.   (D)   Changes in the discount rate can provide commercial banks the incentive to borrow more or less from the Fed, changing the reserves available for loans.

4.   (C)   Open market operations, the Fed's buying and selling of government bonds, allow the Fed to quickly and easily make minor changes in the money supply.

5.   (B)   By selling bonds, the Fed absorbs money from people or commercial banks, and the lower money supply causes an increase in the interest rate.

6.   (C)   Expansionary monetary policy is appropriate during a recession, when unemployment tends to be high and the inflation rate low. Increasing the money supply lowers interest rates to stimulate spending.

7.   (E)   By lowering the reserve requirement, the Fed increases the excess reserves available for banks to loan, which increases the money supply.

8.   (D)   An increase in the money supply lowers the interest rate, which will lead more firms to borrow for capital investment; capital spending then increases aggregate demand in the economy.

9.   (C)   Reducing the federal funds rate encourages firms to loan more of their excess reserves because it is less expensive for them to take out overnight loans from other

banks. This would increase the money supply, a policy which would exacerbate inflation.

10.   (E)   The Fed's purchase of bonds increases the money supply, reducing interest rates and leading to more capital investment. As aggregate demand increases, real GDP increases, employment increases as workers are hired to make the additional output, and prices rise due to the increase in demand.

11.   (B)   A decrease in government spending directly lowers aggregate demand. The Fed's purchase of bonds reduces the bank reserves available for loans, lowering the money supply and reducing aggregate demand.

12.   (B)   The key to promoting long-run economic growth is low interest rates. If taxes are reduced, government demand for loanable funds is reduced, and interest rates fall. When the Fed reduces the reserve requirement and buys bonds, more reserves are made available for loans, lowering interest rates.

Free-Response Explanation
8 points (1 + 3 + 1 + 3)
(a)   1 point:
  • 1 point is earned for stating that the Fed will purchase bonds.
(b)   3 points:
  • 1 point is earned for a correctly labeled money market graph, with the vertical money supply shifting to the right.
  • 1 point is earned for showing that the money supply will increase.
  • 1 point is earned for showing that the interest rate will decrease.
(c)   1 point:
  • 1 point is earned for explaining that when the interest rate falls, firms increase investment and consumers borrow more to increase interest-sensitive spending. Both factors result in an increase in aggregate demand.
(d)   3 points:
  • 1 point is earned for a correctly labeled aggregate demand–aggregate supply graph, with the aggregate demand curve shifting to the right.
  • 1 point is earned for showing that the real output will increase.
  • 1 point is earned for showing that the price level increases.

CHAPTER 34: FINANCIAL ECONOMICS

Introduction
The information in Chapter 34, while important, is not directly tested on the AP economics exams. The important applications to concepts that may be tested are highlighted below.

- Economic investment is the addition to capital stock by firms—new factories or additions to factories, new equipment, or new replacements for depreciated capital equipment.
- Financial investment, as the term is used by most people, refers instead to buying an asset with the expectation of making a financial gain on the investment (buying stock, commodities, real estate, baseball cards, or famous paintings).
- Present value calculates the current value of money that one expects to receive in the future from an investment.
- Speculation is the act of taking a risk (including the decision to wait to invest until later) on an investment now in hopes of earning a profit in the future.
- Stocks are shares of ownership in corporations; profits are distributed to shareholders as dividends.
- Bonds are loans to corporations or the government that are repaid with interest.
- A mutual fund is a firm that combines the funds of hundreds or thousands of investors. A professional manager diversifies the investment over a variety of stocks and bonds. Professional management and diversity provide the investor some protection from risk in the market.
- Investments with higher risk tend to have a higher expected rate of return, to compensate those who are willing to take the higher risk.
- Changes in the value of stock and bonds create a wealth effect, which can affect aggregate demand in the economy. If investment values rise, consumers increase their demand for products; when investment values fall, aggregate demand falls.
- Changes in Federal Reserve policies that affect interest rates also change aggregate demand. If interest rates rise, firms tend to reduce investment and consumers buy fewer interest-sensitive goods, such as houses and cars. Lower interest rates tend to increase aggregate demand in the short run, as firms buy capital and consumers buy goods. Lower interest rates also increase long-run economic growth, an increase in aggregate supply, as a result of the capital investment.

CHAPTER 35: EXTENDING THE ANALYSIS OF AGGREGATE SUPPLY

Introduction

Our exploration of macroeconomics to this point has focused on measuring economic performance and the policies used to achieve short-run economic stabilization. We now turn to long-run economic growth and differing views on policies affecting aggregate supply. Chapter 35 focuses on aggregate supply, the relationship between inflation and unemployment in the short-run and long-run, and differences among economic theories on aggregate supply. These differences explain much of the debate between schools of economic thought, which will be explored in the next chapter. Material from Chapter 35 frequently appears in several multiple-choice questions, and the AP macroeconomics exam has included free-response questions about the Phillips curve and economic growth.

Short-Run Aggregate Supply

The short-run aggregate supply curve is upward-sloping, with point a_1 representing the price level (P_1) at full-employment output (Q_1). This output also represents the natural rate of unemployment. If the price level increases to P_2, firms are enticed to increase output, because if production costs do not change, firms can increase their profits. In the short run, the firm increases output beyond full-employment output by hiring workers and offering overtime to current workers. So in the short run, real GDP, the price level, and employment all increase as the unemployment rate falls.

Conversely, if the price level falls to P_3 but costs of production do not fall, revenues no longer cover the firm's costs. As the firm loses money, it reduces output and lays off workers. The real GDP falls, prices fall, and employment falls as the unemployment rate increases.

Long-Run Aggregate Supply

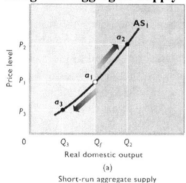
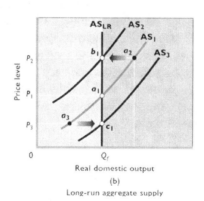

Short-run and long-run aggregate supply

The long-run aggregate supply curve is vertical at full-employment output. This long-run aggregate supply curve develops as a result of long-run adjustments to short-run changes in production. In the short run, an increase in price level to P_2 resulted in a movement from a_1 to a_2 on the aggregate supply curve, with firms increasing output because of increased profit. But this was based on the assumption that the costs of production (notably wages) would not increase. However, in the long run, the increased demand for productive inputs like labor pushes up the cost of those inputs. As a result of the higher costs of production, the aggregate supply curve shifts back to the left (AS_2) until output returns to full-employment output on the long-run aggregate supply curve (at Point b_1).

In the same way, a decrease in the price level leads firms to reduce output and employment because their lower revenues can not cover their costs. However, in the long run, if wages are downwardly flexible, the lower demand for resources leads to lower resource costs, as workers are willing to accept lower wages during a period of high unemployment. The lower cost of production causes the short-run aggregate supply curve to increase (AS_3) until output returns to full-employment output on the long-run aggregate supply curve at point c_1.

Long-Run Equilibrium

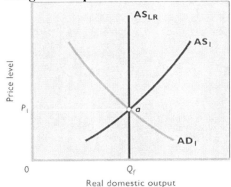

Equilibrium in the extended AD–AS model

Short-run equilibrium occurs at the output where short-run aggregate supply equals aggregate demand. In the short run, this equilibrium can occur at an output greater than full-employment output (a point to the right of point a), illustrating an inflationary gap. A short-run recessionary gap can also occur if equilibrium occurs at a lower output, to the left of point a. Long-run equilibrium occurs at full-employment output where short-run aggregate supply and aggregate demand meet long-run aggregate supply. The economy produces at full-employment output and the natural rate of unemployment is achieved.

Bear in Mind
You may be presented with a graph illustrating short-run equilibrium at a point not on the long-run aggregate supply curve, or you may be asked to draw a graph illustrating the economy producing at less than or greater than full-employment output. An economy producing at less than full-employment GDP must show the vertical long-run aggregate supply (LRAS) curve, with the downward-sloping aggregate demand (AD) curve and the upward-sloping short-run aggregate supply (SRAS) curve crossing to the left of full-employment output. It is important to draw your equilibrium lines illustrating the current output (real GDP) and price level at that point. An economy producing at greater-than-full-employment output would have the vertical LRAS, with SRAS and AD crossing to the right of full-employment output.

Demand-Pull Inflation
Demand-pull inflation results from increased purchases in the economy resulting from an increase in net exports, consumer confidence, investment or government spending, or a number of other factors. It causes an increase in aggregate demand from AD_1 to AD_2, which increases equilibrium from point a to point b and results in a positive GDP gap. In the short run, input prices like wages do not change, so output increases beyond full-employment output to Q_2, while the price level increases to P_2. But in the long run, the increased demand for resources like workers causes nominal wages to increase. This raises the firms' costs of production and results in a leftward shift in the short-run aggregate supply curve, until equilibrium comes to rest at full-employment

output at a higher price level (P_3). In the short run, an increase in aggregate demand causes both output and price level to increase; in the long run, only the price level will increase along the vertical long-run aggregate supply curve.

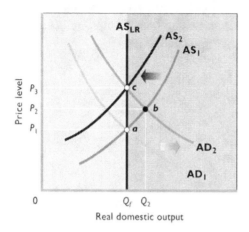

Demand-pull inflation in the extended AD–AS model

Cost-Push Inflation

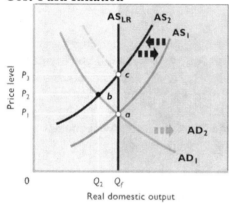

Cost-push inflation in the extended AD–AS model

Cost-push inflation results from an increase in the costs of production, such as resource shortages and supply shocks. Short-run aggregate supply decreases from AS_1 to AS_2, increasing equilibrium from Point a to Point b, resulting in a negative GDP gap. As a result, the price level rises from P_1 to P_2 and output falls to Q_2. But unlike demand-pull inflation, a leftward shift in aggregate supply will not soon return the economy to full-employment output, because this situation *began* with a decrease in aggregate supply. If policymakers decide to use fiscal or monetary policy to increase aggregate demand and restore the economy to full-employment output, it can do so but at the expense of a higher price level of P_3 at point c. Policymakers could instead decide to adopt a hands-off approach, allowing the economy to linger in recession until deep unemployment and significant business failures create serious downward pressure on wages. As the costs of production fall, aggregate supply again increases until the economy returns to point a at full employment with the lower price level. Significant disagreement exists among economists as to whether adopting a hands-off approach is effective or even reasonable during a recession. It requires the assumption that wages and other costs are downwardly flexible and a willingness to allow the economy to experience sustained high unemployment over many months or even years, just waiting for the costs of production—primarily wages—to fall. These questions will be explored further in Chapter 36.

> **Bear in Mind**
> In AP macroeconomics exam questions that may deal with this kind of controversy, the questions will clearly ask you to assume that wages and prices are flexible or to assume that wages and prices are downwardly rigid or that the short-run aggregate supply curve is horizontal or upward-sloping. Watch carefully for the assumptions that are made at the beginning of such questions, as they provide valuable clues and information that are essential to your analysis of the situation.

Ongoing Inflation

While the demand-pull and cost-push models show the effects of a temporary increase in price levels, they do not fully explain the ongoing inflation that occurs in economies. In each case, we assumed that the aggregate demand or supply had shifted by a fixed amount and then there was a response. In reality, the curves remain in motion. Economic growth continues to increase aggregate supply, putting a slight downward pressure on the price level. At the same time, the Federal Reserve continues to increase the money supply to allow for purchases of these products, increasing aggregate demand and putting a slight upward pressure on the price level. Because the increase in aggregate demand is slightly stronger than the increase in aggregate supply, a small but persistent inflation rate results.

Long-Run Economic Growth

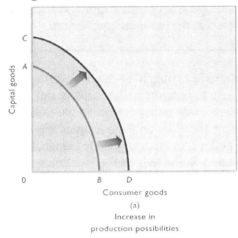
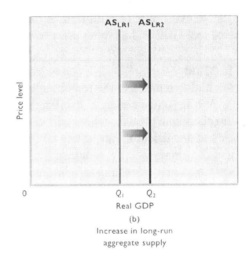

Production possibilities and long-run aggregate supply

Long-run economic growth results from improvements in technology; an increase in the number of land, labor, and capital resources; or more efficient use of resources. An increase in the production possibilities curve allows us to produce more of all products in the economy. In the same way, a rightward shift of the long-run aggregate supply curve demonstrates the economy is capable of producing more products at any price level.

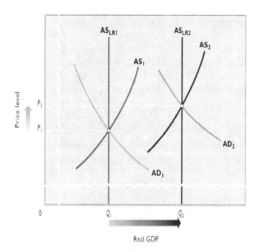

Depicting U.S. growth via the extended AD–AS model

Low interest rates, which allow for increased investment in plant and equipment, are important in promoting long-run economic growth. While such purchases of plant and equipment initially increase short-run aggregate demand, bringing such improvements into operation increases the long-run aggregate supply, shifting it to the right. As firms actually increase output at the lower cost of production, short-run aggregate supply increases. Aggregate demand increases as the Fed injects more money into the money supply. And in the long run, short-run aggregate supply and aggregate demand reach equilibrium at the new, increased long-run aggregate supply, with an increased real GDP and a higher price level than was achieved at the previous equilibrium.

Bear in Mind

It is essential to remember the importance of low interest rates in fueling long-run economic growth. While some economic stabilization policies will help to promote both short-run and long-run economic growth, others will not. Expansionary monetary policy (reducing the reserve requirement and discount rate, along with the Fed purchasing securities on the open market) increases the money supply, reducing interest rates. That policy increases aggregate demand in the short run, while simultaneously increasing aggregate supply in the long run by promoting investment at the lower interest rate. But expansionary fiscal policy (reducing taxes and increasing government spending) may not. While these actions increase aggregate demand in the short run, if the government must borrow money to finance the deficit spending, it can hurt long-run growth. The increased demand in the loanable funds market pushes up interest rates, crowding private investment out of the market. This reduced investment slows long-run economic growth. Targeted tax cuts or subsidies for the purchase of equipment, expansion, or more rapid depreciation of capital may actually promote economic growth by promoting investment. But when questions ask about broader economic policies designed to address a recession or inflation, look for the effect on interest rates to determine the effects on long-run economic growth. Previous multiple-choice and free-response questions have explored this concept, so it is important to clearly understand the implications of such policies in both the short and the long run.

The Phillips Curve

The Phillips curve, named for British economist A.W. Phillips, illustrates the short-run inverse relationship between the inflation rate and the unemployment rate. When the inflation rate is high, the unemployment rate is low; at low rates of unemployment, the inflation rate is high. This short-run relationship results from changes in aggregate demand, assuming aggregate supply is stable. When aggregate demand increases, output increases, so more workers are hired, lowering the unemployment rate. At the same time, the increased demand raises the price level. Thus, when aggregate demand increases, the unemployment rate decreases and the inflation rate increases. In the same way, if aggregate demand falls, output and employment fall, increasing the unemployment rate. At the same time, the rate of inflation falls because of the reduction of upward pressure on prices.

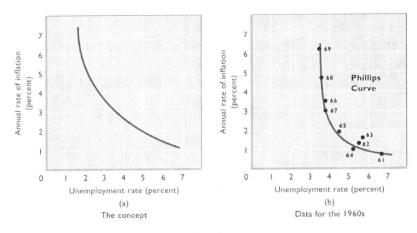

The Phillips curve: concept and empirical data

This stable relationship was the basis for our understanding of the effects of fiscal and monetary policy through the 1960s. When the economy fell into recession, policymakers used expansionary fiscal and monetary policy to reduce the unemployment rate, understanding that the inflation rate would increase as a result of the increase in aggregate demand. During periods of inflation, policymakers used contractionary policies to reduce the inflation rate, with the understanding that the tradeoff would be a higher unemployment rate.

Aggregate Supply Shocks and Stagflation
Events of the 1970s caused a serious revision of the theory after a series of supply shocks struck the U.S. economy. The primary blow was a quadrupling of the price of oil by OPEC, significantly increasing the cost of production for U.S. manufacturers. Major crop shortfalls, a weak dollar, slow productivity growth, and significant wage increases following release of wage and price controls combined to significantly reduce the aggregate supply. As a result, both the inflation rate and the unemployment rate skyrocketed, violating the assumed tradeoff relationship. This new situation, dubbed "stagflation," demonstrated a "hat trick" of bad economic news—a stagnant economy, high inflation, and high unemployment, all at the same time.

In fact, economists discovered that the Phillips curve could move in response to changes in aggregate supply. When aggregate supply was stable, changes in aggregate demand resulted in movement among various points along a stationary Phillips curve, as demonstrated on the following chart by the 1960s data on the lowest Phillips curve. But as aggregate supply fell in the 1970s and 1980s, both the inflation and unemployment rates increased, showing that decreases in aggregate supply cause an outward shift in the Phillips curve. Increases in aggregate supply cause the Phillips curve to shift back inward, as you can see from the data points for the 1990s and since 2000.

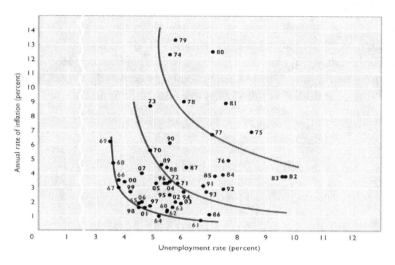

Inflation rates and unemployment rates, 1960–2007

Stagflation created a unique dilemma for policymakers. Understanding the tradeoff between inflation and unemployment, with both at very high levels, any attempt to reduce one would cause the other to become worse. The Federal Reserve acted to significantly reduce the money supply, which successfully reduced inflation but plunged the economy into a severe recession with double-digit unemployment rates in many areas of the country. Eventually, wage reductions in some industries and a lower rate of wage growth in other industries, decreased reliance on oil and a reduction in OPEC's market power, improvements in crop yields and worker productivity, and other factors combined to shift aggregate supply back to the right, lowering both the unemployment and inflation rates.

The Long-Run Phillips Curve

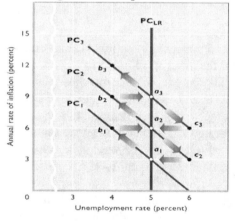

The long-run vertical Phillips curve

The long-run Phillips curve is a vertical curve set at the natural rate of unemployment where there is no cyclical unemployment. This point is often called the natural rate of unemployment or the non-accelerating inflation rate of unemployment (NAIRU). In the long run, there is no tradeoff between inflation and unemployment.

It is, of course, possible for inflation and unemployment rates to change from year to year. In this example, if the natural rate of unemployment is 5 percent, the economy is stable at a 3 percent inflation rate. At the expected 3 percent inflation rate, workers negotiate 3 percent increases in their nominal wages to keep their real wages even with inflation, and banks add the 3 percent expected inflation into nominal interest rates on loans in order to receive dollars in repayment equal to the value of those loaned. But if aggregate demand rose and the inflation rate rose to 6 percent, firms could raise prices without seeing an increase in their resource costs. The higher resulting profit would lead firms to increase output and hire workers, reducing the unemployment rate from point a_1 to point b_1. Higher-than-expected inflation temporarily increases output and reduces unemployment.

However, this point will not remain stable in the long run. Given time, employees will realize their real wages are falling as inflation climbs, and they will renegotiate their contracts to include 6 percent wage increases to retain their purchasing power. As resource costs increase, firms' profits fall and they reduce production, laying off workers until unemployment returns to its natural rate—but inflation remains higher (PC_2 on the new Phillips curve) than it was initially.

The same thing happens in reverse during periods of recession. If the actual inflation rate is lower than the expected inflation rate, profits decrease, firms cut back production and lay off workers, and unemployment temporarily increases. As a result of the layoffs and lower inflationary expectations, workers accept lower wages (or at least lower increases in the wage rates), firms increase production at the lower cost, more workers are hired, and the unemployment rate returns to the natural rate of unemployment.

It is important to note that the natural rate of unemployment can actually shift—and has, in fact, shifted over time in response to changes in the labor force, technology, and economic policy. For example, child labor laws removing children under the age of sixteen from the labor force would have decreased the natural rate of unemployment. The influx of women into the labor force in the 1970s would have increased the natural rate of unemployment as significantly more workers sought jobs throughout the economy. The institution of unemployment benefits would have increased the natural rate of unemployment because workers could afford to take more time in their job search efforts. Improvements in technology and increased job search information in the computer age have likely contributed to another decrease in the NAIRU because unemployed workers can find information about positions more quickly and easily.

Supply-Side Economic Theory
Supply-side economists argue that fiscal and monetary (demand-side) policies only cause inflation and harm incentives to work, save, and invest. Supply-siders promote lower tax rates, arguing that if workers are allowed to keep more of their disposable income, they will increase the number of hours worked—working overtime, postponing retirement, and drawing even more workers into the labor force. Further, supply-siders argue that lowering the tax rate on interest from savings encourages households to increase saving, which increases the funds available for investment. Supply-siders call for lower tax rates for capital income, which would lead to greater investment in capital and equipment, which would in turn increase worker productivity, expanding long-run aggregate supply and spurring economic growth.

The Laffer Curve
The Laffer curve, popularized by American economist Arthur Laffer, illustrates the relationship between the tax rate and tax revenue received by the government. At a 0 percent tax rate, the government receives no revenue. As the tax rate increases, government revenue increases. However, at some theoretical level, the tax rate becomes so high that it serves as a work disincentive. If the government takes 90 percent of a worker's paycheck in taxes, that worker loses the incentive to go to work. This backward bend continues until at a 100 percent tax rate—where the government takes every penny of the worker's paycheck—the government receives

nothing, because no one is willing to work. Throughout the early 1980s, Laffer argued that the United States was on the upper section of the Laffer curve (such as point n) and significant cuts in the marginal income tax rate would result in the double benefit of giving workers a greater incentive to work and significantly increasing the federal government's tax revenues.

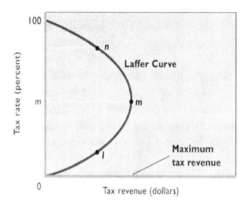

The Laffer curve

Application of Supply-Side Theory

When President Reagan was elected in 1980, supply-side economics (sometimes called "Reaganomics" or "the trickle-down theory" because benefits begin with the wealthy and may eventually trickle down to workers) was put to the test with two major cuts in income tax rates, primarily directed at those with the highest incomes. The tax cuts did result in higher government revenue, but there is general agreement among economists that it did not result from a movement from point n to point m on the Laffer curve; in fact, the consensus among economists is that the U.S. economy is operating in the region below point m, closer to point l on the curve. The tax cuts did not spur an increased work incentive—for many workers it produced no incentive whatsoever, and for some, the extra take-home pay allowed them to work even fewer hours. So what increased the federal revenue when taxes were cut: an increase in aggregate demand, not aggregate supply. As consumers emerged from the deep recession of 1981–1982, they spent the tax cuts on goods and services, increasing real GDP and employment, and tax revenues increased as more workers went back to work and paid income taxes. Empirical evidence from the period shows that saving actually fell as a percentage of personal income, so productivity did not significantly grow and long-run aggregate supply showed little movement. But because government spending grew significantly during the period, the national debt exploded, leading to significantly increased public borrowing.

When President Clinton was elected in 1992, he reversed course, increasing the marginal income tax rates for those with the highest incomes in order to reduce deficits. His work with Congress in holding the line on spending while increasing revenues, paired with significant improvements in technology and productivity in the private sector, led to budget surpluses by the end of his administration.

When President George W. Bush came into office in 2001, he brought supply-side policy back into his administration. He worked with Congress to again significantly cut marginal tax rates, targeting those with the highest incomes. With the help of the Federal Reserve, which significantly reduced interest rates, the economy again expanded, but did it expand as a result of a shift in aggregate supply or in aggregate demand? It seems clear that aggregate demand increased, though a significant increase in oil prices caused a complication by pushing aggregate supply to the left. In addition, massive increases in spending led to unprecedented deficits during the Bush administration, a repeat of the Reagan era.

While mainstream economists today recognize a relationship between tax rates and government revenue, because it is believed that the economy is actually operating on the bottom side of the graph, it is not believed that reducing taxes directly increases government revenue as a result of work incentives. However, the battle of the economists over appropriate economic policy has only begun and will be discussed in detail in Chapter 36.

Multiple-Choice Questions

1.   Which of these situations would cause a decrease in short-run aggregate supply?
        (A)   a decrease in corporate income taxes
        (B)   an increase in the number of available workers in the labor supply
        (C)   an increase in the cost of production
        (D)   a decrease in the money supply
        (E)   an increase in government spending

2.   A favorable supply shock, such as a significant increase in crop output, will cause which of the following effects on real output and the price level?

	Real Output	Price Level
(A)	Increase	Increase
(B)	Increase	Decrease
(C)	Decrease	Increase
(D)	Decrease	Decrease
(E)	No change	Decrease

3.   Long-run economic growth is represented by
        (A)   a rightward shift in the aggregate demand curve.
        (B)   a rightward shift in the upward-sloping aggregate supply curve.
        (C)   a leftward shift in the upward-sloping aggregate supply curve.
        (D)   an upward shift in the aggregate demand curve.
        (E)   a rightward shift in the vertical aggregate supply curve.

4.   Demand-pull inflation is most likely to occur as a result of
        (A)   an increase in interest rates.
        (B)   an increase in consumer incomes.
        (C)   a reduction in the money supply.
        (D)   an increase in the unemployment rate.
        (E)   an increase in the tax rate.

5.   Which of the following factors could result in cost-push inflation?
                I.   An increase in energy costs
                II.   An increase in worker wages
                III.   A decrease in interest rates
        (A)   I only
        (B)   III only
        (C)   I and II only
        (D)   II and III only
        (E)   I, II, and III

6.   Long-run economic growth is illustrated by
                I.   an outward shift of the vertical aggregate supply curve.
                II.   an outward shift of the upward-sloping aggregate supply curve.
                III.   an outward shift of the production possibilities curve.
        (A)   I only
        (B)   II only
        (C)   I and III only
        (D)   II and III only
        (E)   I, II, and III

7.   Each of the following factors promotes long-run economic growth EXCEPT
        (A)   an increase in the quantity of capital stock.
        (B)   an increase in worker productivity.
        (C)   an increase in the labor supply.
        (D)   improvements in technology.
        (E)   an increase in the interest rate.

8.   Which of the following would be the most effective policy combination for resolving a
        recession in the short run, while still promoting long-run economic growth?
                Monetary Policy   *Fiscal Policy*
        (A)   Increase the money supply   Do nothing
        (B)   Reduce the money supply   Reduce government spending
        (C)   Do nothing   Increase government spending
        (D)   Reduce the money supply   Increase taxes
        (E)   Increase the money supply   Reduce taxes

9.   The short-run Phillips curve illustrates the relationship between
        (A)   aggregate supply and aggregate demand.
        (B)   tax rates and government revenue.
        (C)   the money supply and interest rates.
        (D)   inflation and unemployment.
        (E)   interest rates and capital investment.

10.   The long-run Phillips curve illustrates that the natural rate of unemployment
        (A)   is relatively stable.
        (B)   is quite unstable.
        (C)   changes frequently with the level of aggregate demand.
        (D)   changes frequently with the level of aggregate supply.
        (E)   is inversely related to the interest rate.

11.   Stagflation results from
        (A)   an increase in aggregate demand.
        (B)   a decrease in aggregate demand.
        (C)   an increase in aggregate supply.
        (D)   a decrease in aggregate supply.
        (E)   simultaneous decreases in aggregate demand and aggregate supply.

12. According to the Laffer curve, economic growth is best promoted through the increased incentives to work, save, and invest provided by
(A) lower taxes.
(B) lower interest rates.
(C) lower government spending.
(D) lower imports.
(E) lower inflation rates.

Free-Response Questions
1. Assume a nation's economy is operating at less than full employment output.
(a) Draw a correctly labeled aggregate demand–aggregate supply graph showing each of the following.
    (i) long-run aggregate supply
    (ii) current output and price level
(b) Identify an appropriate monetary policy to address the recessionary gap.
(c) Explain the effect of the monetary policy you identified in (b) on each of the following.
    (i) the interest rate
    (ii) aggregate demand
    (iii) long-run aggregate supply

2. Assume a nation's economy is operating at full employment output in year 1.
(a) Draw a correctly labeled short-run Phillips curve and label a point on the curve "Year 1."
(b) Now assume the nation has entered into a recession in year 2. On the same graph you used for year 1, indicate the correct position for a point illustrating the impact of a recession and label that point "Year 2."
(c) Now assume that in year 3 the cost of energy has significantly increased for the nation. Illustrate the change on your graph and label your new point "Year 3."
(d) In year 3, if Congress begins with a balanced budget and addresses the impact of the increased energy costs on the country by lowering taxes, explain the impact of that fiscal policy on the following.
    (i) the unemployment rate
    (ii) the inflation rate
    (iii) the interest rate
    (iv) long-run economic growth

Multiple Choice Explanations
1. (C) An increase in the cost of production reduces supply for firms, decreasing output and increasing the price level.
2. (B) A favorable supply shock shifts the aggregate supply curve to the right, lowering the price level and increasing real GDP.
3. (E) The long-run aggregate supply curve represents full-employment output, and an increase, which shifts the curve to the right, illustrates economic growth.
4. (B) With additional income, consumers increase aggregate demand for products, pushing the price level higher. Higher interest rates, a reduction in the money supply, and an increase in the tax rate would instead work to decrease aggregate demand. An increase in the unemployment rate would result from lower aggregate demand or lower aggregate supply.
5. (C) An increase in the cost of production shifts aggregate supply to the left and causes cost-push inflation. A decrease in interest rates would lead to increased

investment, increasing aggregate demand in the short run and aggregate supply in the long run.

6. (C) The vertical aggregate supply curve is the long-run aggregate supply curve, and a rightward shift indicates long-run economic growth. The production possibilities curve also shifts outward to illustrate that even more of all products can be produced. The upward-sloping aggregate supply curve is the short-run curve which shows short-run changes in aggregate supply but not long-run growth.

7. (E) When interest rates go up, firms invest less in plant and equipment, which reduces long-run economic growth.

8. (A) Increasing the money supply reduces the interest rate, which promotes investment in plant and equipment. Aggregate demand increases in the short run as firms buy the equipment, resolving the recession; aggregate supply increases in the long run as firms put the plant and equipment into operation and increase production at a lower cost. While (E) would also address the recession through lower taxes, the government borrowing required to finance the deficit would push interest rates up, reducing long-run economic growth.

9. (D) The inverse relationship between the inflation rate and the unemployment rate shows that in the short run, if aggregate supply remains stable, then when the inflation rate increases, the unemployment rate decreases.

10. (A) The long-run Phillips curve is vertical at the natural rate of unemployment. While the unemployment rate may increase or decrease in the short run due to changes in aggregate supply and aggregate demand or changes in fiscal and monetary policy, in the long run, it returns to the natural rate of unemployment.

11. (D) A leftward shift in aggregate supply increases the price level while also increasing the unemployment rate.

12. (A) According to supply-siders, a lower tax rate gives workers an incentive to work more and increase both spending and savings, leading to increased investment and long-run economic growth.

Free Response Explanations

1. **10 points** (3 + 1 + 6)
(a) 3 points:
  - 1 point is earned for a correctly labeled aggregate demand–aggregate supply graph.
  - 1 point is earned for including a vertical long-run aggregate supply curve.
  - 1 point is earned for showing current equilibrium (output and price level) to the left of the long-run aggregate supply curve.
(b) 1 point:
  - 1 point is earned for identifying an appropriate monetary policy: the Fed decreasing the reserve requirement or discount rate or purchasing bonds on the open market.
(c) 6 points:
  - 1 point is earned for stating that the interest rate decreases.
  - 1 point is earned for explaining that the monetary policy increases the money supply, causing the interest rate to fall.
  - 1 point is earned for stating that the aggregate demand increases.
  - 1 point is earned for explaining that as interest rates fall, investment and interest-sensitive consumer borrowing and spending increase, raising aggregate demand.
  - 1 point is earned for stating that the long-run aggregate supply increases.
  - 1 point is earned for explaining that the investment in plant and equipment fosters long-run economic growth.

2.	**10 points** (1 + 1 + 2 + 6)
(a)	1 point:
- 1 point is earned for a correctly labeled short-run Phillips curve with a point "Year 1" labeled on the curve.
(b)	1 point:
- 1 point is earned for correctly labeling point "Year 2" on the same short-run Phillips curve, indicating a higher unemployment rate and lower inflation rate than for "Year 1."
(c)	2 points:
- 1 point is earned for drawing a new short-run Phillips curve, shifted out from the origin of the original Phillips curve.
- 1 point is earned for correctly labeling point "Year 3" on the new Phillips curve.
(d)	6 points:
- 1 point is earned for stating that the unemployment rate will decrease.
- 1 point is earned for stating that the inflation rate will increase.
- 1 point is earned for stating that the interest rate will increase.
- 1 point is earned for explaining that the interest rate increases because the government must borrow more money to finance the deficit spending.
- 1 point is earned for stating that long-run economic growth will decrease.
- 1 point is earned for explaining that because the interest rate increased, investment in plant and equipment decreased, reducing the long-run growth rate.

CHAPTER 36: CURRENT ISSUES IN MACRO THEORY AND POLICY

Introduction

What causes economic instability? Will the economy self-correct? Should the government intervene to stabilize the economy, and if so, how? These questions are central to the differences among macroeconomic theories. Chapter 36 introduces some of the most prominent economic theories today and explores the differences among them. This chapter concludes the discussion of domestic macroeconomic theory in preparation for the concluding chapters on the international economy. Material from Chapter 36 tends to appear in a few multiple-choice questions on the AP macroeconomics exam.

What Causes Economic Instability?

The Mainstream (Keynesian) View

The majority of economists believe that the macroeconomy is generally unstable, with most economic instability resulting from unexpected shocks to aggregate demand and supply, as well as wage and price stickiness. The formula for calculating output is GDP = C + I + G + X, representing consumer spending, gross investment of firms, government spending, and net exports. An increase in spending in any one of these four sectors results in a rightward shift of the aggregate demand curve, increasing real output, the price level, or both. Keynesians argue that the investment sector is the most volatile, and because of the multiplier effect, initial changes in investment spending can cause much greater changes in output. An increase in aggregate demand can cause demand-pull inflation, while a decrease in aggregate demand can cause recession. Keynesians also recognize supply shocks as a cause of economic instability, because such shocks significantly increase the cost of production for firms. As aggregate supply shifts to the left, the reduction in output, which increases cost-push inflation, and higher unemployment combine to create stagflation.

The Monetarist View

Monetarism is a school of economic thought developed from the work of American economist Milton Friedman. Monetarists believe that the macroeconomy is generally stable at full-employment output because competitive markets and flexibility in prices and wages promote stability. Monetarists argue that changes in aggregate demand cause changes in wages and prices rather than output and employment. While Keynesians see government as the answer to economic instability, monetarists instead see government intervention as a cause of economic instability. Monetarists argue that minimum wage laws, pro-union legislation giving workers bargaining power to settle multi-year contracts, price floor supports for agricultural products, and similar laws have created the sticky prices and wages central to Keynesian theory. Even more importantly, monetarists argue that government attempts to stabilize the economy—especially through monetary policy—actually exacerbate the strength and duration of business cycles, rather than reducing them.

Monetarists do not view the economy through the Keynesian formula GDP = C + I + G + X but instead focus on the equation of exchange (also known as the quantity theory of money) as central to their theory:

$$M \times V = P \times Q$$

M is the money supply, V is the velocity of money (the number of times a dollar turns over during a year), P is the price level, and Q is the quantity of goods sold during a year. In the equation of exchange, PQ is the nominal GDP. The money supply multiplied by the number of times it turns over in a year equals the value of the output on which it is spent.

Monetarists argue that the velocity is stable and predictable because people tend to hold the same amount of money over time. Therefore, according to monetarists, an increase in the money supply will directly lead to an increase in nominal GDP, which will only cause inflation when the economy is already producing at full-employment output. While higher prices may temporarily cause firms to increase output due to higher profit, once wages and other costs of production begin to rise, firms will return to full-employment output but at the higher price level.

Monetarists view the use of monetary policy as a primary cause of economic instability. Because changes in the money supply and interest rates can run counter to what is appropriate at a particular point in the cycle, can take so long to take effect that they actually exacerbate cycles (for example, a significant increase in the money supply finally taking full effect just as inflation is increasing), or can be ineffective if banks choose not to make loans or customers do not redeposit funds to allow multiple expansion, monetarists oppose the use of monetary policy.

Taking the EEK! Out of Economics

It is important not to confuse monetarism with the similar term "monetary policy." While monetarists and Keynesians both recognize the importance of money to the economy, monetarists oppose government attempts to stabilize the economy—especially those involving monetary policy. Monetary policy is instead associated with Keynesian theory.

The Real Business Cycle View

A third theory claims that economic instability is caused primarily by changes in aggregate supply. According to the Real Business Cycle Theory, changes in aggregate supply, such as a significant increase in production costs or a decline in productivity, cause the long-run aggregate supply curve to shift to the left. With output falling, consumers buy less and the demand for money falls. As aggregate demand falls, output and employment fall but prices do not (because aggregate supply also fell). Conversely, significant increases in the long-run aggregate supply through increased productivity and reduced costs shift aggregate supply to the right and aggregate demand increases with the real output produced, though prices do not rise. As a result, those who adhere to this view of the economy call for no government intervention to stabilize the economy, believing the economy will stabilize itself.

The Coordination Failures View

A fourth theory suggests that instability in the macroeconomy results from a failure of consumers and firms to coordinate information and the problem of expectations resulting from that lack of coordination. A widespread belief that the economy is falling into recession causes firms to cut investment spending to avoid overcapacity. At the same time, consumers reduce spending out of concern their incomes will be reduced due to cuts in hours or layoffs. The actions of people and firms, fearing a recession, causes the very recession they feared: it is a self-fulfilling prophecy. According to this view, if consumers and firms could be convinced to coordinate their efforts to begin making purchases again, aggregate demand would increase and they would all be better off. But the lack of coordination leaves them all in recession.

Will the Economy Self-Correct?
The Neoclassical View
Classical economists believed that the economy was inherently stable, operating at full
employment until some temporary shock created temporary instability. But they believed that in
the long run, the economy would self-correct to full-employment output due to flexible wages
and prices. In the same way, neoclassical economists believe the economy will self-correct over
time. Economists from the neoclassical school of thought tend to be either monetarists or
believers of the Rational Expectations Theory. The Rational Expectations Theory holds that
consumers and firms are knowledgeable about economic conditions and fiscal and monetary
policy. When faced with certain economic conditions, firms and consumers anticipate the
policies Congress and the Fed will undertake and then take action to protect themselves from the
effects of those policies.

For example, during a recession, workers and banks may anticipate that the Fed will increase the
money supply in order to increase aggregate demand. But because such an action can create
inflation in the long run, workers will immediately act to negotiate higher wages to protect real
wages, and banks will add the higher expected inflation rate in determining the nominal interest
rate for loans. The higher wages and interest rates then serve to dampen the growth that would
have occurred as a result of the Fed's action. As a result, adherents of the Rational Expectations
Theory, like monetarists and classical economists, call for the government to avoid engaging in
stabilization policy and instead advocate waiting for the economy to self-correct.

Because the Rational Expectations Theory holds that consumers and firms anticipate government
policy and act even before it is enacted, adjustments occur instantaneously or at least very
quickly. Under this theory, if price and policy changes are anticipated, firms and consumers react
instantly and output does not change. If an unexpected increase in demand for exports increases
aggregate demand for products, firms will increase production based on the extra profit they
anticipate because of the increased price at which they can sell products. But under the Rational
Expectations Theory, even when the initial stimulus was unanticipated, workers almost instantly
recognize prices will increase and begin to demand higher wages, very quickly increasing the cost
of production and dissipating any anticipated profit, so production very quickly returns to full-
employment output.

Monetarists differ from rational expectations theorists in projecting the speed with which such
adjustments will occur. Monetarists believe that people and firms react to changes in the
economy after they have begun to occur rather than anticipating them, so that long-run
adjustments may require two to three years or even longer.

The Mainstream (Keynesian) View
While nearly all economists agree that quick adjustments occur in markets that move very
quickly, such as the stock market and foreign exchange markets, relatively few economists
believe that such adjustments occur quickly across the broader economy. Because empirical
evidence has shown that prices and wages are indeed sticky downward, and because recessionary
and inflationary expectations of consumers and firms may linger for long periods of time, the
economy does not quickly self-adjust. When aggregate demand falls, workers do not readily
accept the lower wages necessary to shift the short-run aggregate supply curve back out and
return the economy to full-employment output. Instead, workers resist a decrease in wages, and
the minimum wage and long-term contracts may even prevent the lowering of wages in many
cases. Firms may also resist lowering wages due to concerns about worker morale, potential
shirking, and increased job turnover as workers leave to seek employment where they can find

higher pay. So, aggregate demand remains lower, with output at less than full-employment output, possibly for a sustained period of time. In the view of mainstream economists today, the economy will not self-adjust—potentially not for years.

Should the Government Intervene to Stabilize the Economy, and If So, How?
The Monetarist View
Monetarists and other neoclassical economists are convinced that government attempts to stabilize the economy instead actually destabilize the economy beyond the effects of the normal business cycle. They point specifically to the problem of monetary policy, concerned that increasing the money supply in an attempt to reduce unemployment will create inflation instead.

Monetarists call for a monetary rule, requiring the Fed to increase the money supply at the rate of average real GDP growth annually, regardless of the state of the economy. Monetarists contend that if the money supply grows at a steady rate, money will be available in the economy in times of recession, while the limit on growth will prevent overstimulation in times of inflation, thereby stabilizing economic growth. In addition, the increase in money supply would reduce interest rates, fueling investment in plant and equipment and further promoting steady annual economic growth.

Monetarists also oppose the use of fiscal policy to stabilize the economy, especially expansionary fiscal policy. Because expansionary policy requires the government to run deficits, the increased demand for money in the loanable funds market forces up interest rates and crowds out private investment—so while government spending may be increasing, it is offset by a decline in spending in the private sector. Further, the increase in interest rates negatively affects long-run economic growth, as firms reduce investment in plant and equipment. Therefore, monetarists and other neoclassical economists oppose the use of fiscal policy to stabilize the economy, and some go so far as to advocate a balanced budget amendment, requiring to federal government to balance its budget every year in an effort to restrict the use of fiscal policy.

The Mainstream (Keynesian) View
Because of the serious harm that can befall firms and consumers in periods of serious recession and inflation, Keynesians see government intervention and stabilization as the answer to swings in the business cycle. Through fiscal policy, consumers and firms respond to incentives in taxes and spending, which directly affect aggregate demand. Through monetary policy, the Federal Reserve changes the money supply and interest rates, affecting aggregate demand more indirectly through interest rate incentives. Further, policies can be developed to promote long-run economic growth that may not result from an economy constrained by monetary rules and balanced budget requirements.

Referring to the equation of exchange, Keynesians note evidence that while the money supply and nominal GDP do correlate over the long run, in the short run velocity actually does become variable. Therefore, a strict monetary rule may not limit changes in aggregate demand and GDP as effectively as monetarists contend it will. If firms significantly increase investment spending because of optimistic expectations for the economy, limitations on the growth of the money supply will not be effective if the velocity is increasing. While the money stock may remain the same, it is turning over faster and faster, creating inflation. But discretionary monetary policy allows the Fed to restrict the growth of the money supply and change interest rates in ways that discourage firms from overinvesting to the extent that they cause inflation. In the same way, business pessimism may reduce investment, and the Fed's failure to act discourages confidence that the economy will emerge soon from a recession. However, the right incentives to invest—

through lower interest rates and the ability to earn a profit on capital investment—can spur an economic recovery.

Keynesians also oppose the requirement of a balanced budget, arguing that such a requirement would significantly worsen economic instability. Because the federal government receives the largest percentage of its revenue from individual income taxes, when unemployment increases during a recession, government revenues fall. A balanced budget amendment would require the government to do one of two things to avoid unconstitutionally falling into a budget deficit: increase taxes or reduce government spending. Either action, or the combination of actions, is precisely the wrong policy to invoke during a recession, as such policies only further reduce aggregate demand—and, as even more workers lose jobs, tax revenues fall further, requiring repeated policy action to lessen the recession. Discretionary fiscal policy allows government to work in a counter-cyclical fashion to try to fill recessionary gaps and reduce inflationary gaps in the short run. Further, Keynesians argue that the problem of crowding out during a recession is likely to be minimal, if it occurs at all. During a recession, business optimism is low and firms are less likely to invest in plant and equipment because of excess capacity and because they are less likely to make a profit on investment. Because firms' demand for loanable funds is already falling due to business conditions, Keynesians argue that increased government demand for loanable funds to finance deficits is not likely to crowd out new investment.

Issue	Mainstream Macroeconomics	New Classical Economics	
		Monetarism	Rational Expectations
View of the private economy	Potentially unstable	Stable in long run at natural rate of unemployment	Stable in long run at natural rate of unemployment
Cause of the observed instability of the private economy	Investment plans unequal to saving plans (changes in AD); AS shocks	Inappropriate monetary policy	Unanticipated AD and AS shocks in the short run
Assumptions about short-run price and wage stickiness	Both prices and wages stuck in the immediate short run; in the short run, wages sticky while prices inflexible downward but flexible upward.	Prices flexible upward and downward in the short run; wages sticky in the short run	Prices and wages flexible both upward and downward in the short run
Appropriate macro policies	Active fiscal and monetary policy	Monetary rule	Monetary rule
How changes in the money supply affect the economy	By changing the interest rate, which changes investment and real GDP	By directly changing AD, which changes GDP	No effect on output because price-level changes are anticipated
View of the velocity of money	Unstable	Stable	No consensus
How fiscal policy affects the economy	Changes AD and GDP via the multiplier process	No effect unless money supply changes	No effect because price-level changes are anticipated
View of cost-push inflation	Possible (AS shock)	Impossible in the long run in the absence of excessive money supply growth	Impossible in the long run in the absence of excessive money supply growth

Summary of alternative macroeconomics views

Keynesians also point to decades of historical use of fiscal and monetary policy to effectively limit periods of inflation and recession, allowing the economy to recover more quickly than would be anticipated if the economy were left alone to self-correct. It is important to note the actions of the Federal Reserve, Congress, and Presidents George W. Bush and Barack Obama in dealing with the worst financial crisis to strike the United States in decades. In 2008, the Federal Reserve moved to reduce key interest rates to the 0–0.25% range, while providing loans to financial institutions facing a solvency crisis. In late 2008, Congress passed a $700 billion bill to bail out financial institutions and later auto manufacturers. In early 2009, Congress passed a fiscal stimulus package of nearly $800 billion in increased spending and tax cuts. The effectiveness of these and other fiscal and monetary measures in reversing the steep slide in aggregate demand will be determined over time. Without question, economists of all theoretical backgrounds will closely examine the situation and policy actions to learn how we can more effectively address changes in our economy.

Multiple-Choice Questions

1.   The economic theory which holds that the economy is generally unstable is
        (A)   classical theory.
        (B)   Keynesian theory.
        (C)   monetarist theory.
        (D)   rational expectations theory.
        (E)   neoclassical theory.

2.   Keynesians argue that the economy does not self-adjust to demand shocks because
        (A)   increased unemployment only lowers wage rates.
        (B)   reductions in demand cause significant deflation in the economy.
        (C)   wages and prices tend to be downwardly sticky.
        (D)   expansionary fiscal policy is unpopular, so consumers do not change their spending in response to fiscal stimuli.
        (E)   firms do not change output in response to reductions in demand.

3.   The monetarist equation of exchange states that the money supply times the velocity equals
        (A)   the inflation rate.
        (B)   the unemployment rate.
        (C)   the federal budget.
        (D)   real GDP.
        (E)   nominal GDP.

4.   According to the quantity theory of money, if the Fed increases the money supply in response to a recession, the policy will result in
        (A)   a reduction in unemployment.
        (B)   a reduction in real output.
        (C)   an increase in interest rates.
        (D)   an increase in the price level.
        (E)   a decrease in the velocity.

5.   Classical economists argue that when the economy experiences supply or demand shocks, it self-corrects through the mechanism of flexible
        (A)   output.
        (B)   employment rates.
        (C)   prices.
        (D)   money supply.
        (E)   tax rates.

6.   Economists who adhere to the Rational Expectations Theory argue that fiscal and monetary policy are ineffective because
        (A)   people anticipate policy changes and act to protect themselves.
        (B)   policymakers take too long to create policy.
        (C)   lower wages during recessions only further reduce aggregate demand.
        (D)   higher interest rates do not reduce inflationary expectations.
        (E)   the policies have contradictory interest rate effects.

7. Monetarists advocate the monetary rule, saying the Federal Reserve should increase the money supply
   (A)   in response to a decrease in aggregate demand.
   (B)   in response to a decrease in aggregate supply.
   (C)   only when Congress simultaneously increases taxes.
   (D)   at a steady rate of average GDP growth.
   (E)   only when fiscal policy has failed to resolve a recession.

8. Monetarists oppose the use of expansionary fiscal policy, claiming that it
   (A)   increases unemployment.
   (B)   reduces interest rates.
   (C)   reduces the money supply.
   (D)   causes deflation.
   (E)   crowds out private investment.

Multiple-Choice Explanations
1. (B)   The other theories hold that the economy is stable at full-employment output, and if any event destabilizes the economy, it self-adjusts.
2. (C)   Prices and wages tend to be downwardly rigid due to long-term contracts, so when demand falls, costs of production do not necessarily follow, leaving the economy producing at less than full-employment output.
3. (E)   Nominal GDP is the P x Q on the right side of the equation, representing the price level and the quantity of output produced.
4. (D)   Monetarists argue that velocity and real output are stable, so any increase in the money supply will only create inflation.
5. (C)   When prices are flexible, wages and costs of production can change, allowing the economy to adjust to shocks.
6. (A)   According to the Rational Expectations Theory, people are fully aware of economic conditions and the fiscal and monetary policies policymakers are likely to undertake. They then take actions to protect themselves from the effects of such policies.
7. (D)   Because monetarists are convinced that increasing the money supply in an attempt to stabilize the economy only causes inflation, they advocate only increasing the money supply by the average rate of increase in the GDP to avoid further destabilizing the economy.
8. (E)   Expansionary fiscal policy requires the government to borrow to finance deficit spending. Increased demand for money in the loanable funds market pushes up interest rates, reducing private investment.

CHAPTER 37: INTERNATIONAL TRADE

Introduction
Opening an economy to international trade brings us full-circle to rediscover many of the concepts from Chapter 1: factors of production, comparative advantage, production possibilities, and gains from trade. Chapter 37 then extends the discussion of international trade, contrasting the gains from trade with the arguments for protectionist trade barriers. Concepts from Chapter 37—particularly production possibilities, absolute and comparative advantage, gains from trade, and supply and demand—are likely to appear in both the multiple-choice and free-response portions of the AP microeconomics exam, while material from throughout the chapter is commonly included in a few multiple-choice questions and a free-response question on the AP macroeconomics exam.

Key Facts
The United States is the largest trading nation in the world in combined imports and exports, though exports are only 12 percent of the total output of the United States. Canada is our most important trading partner in terms of the volume of goods and services traded. Trade deficits occur when imports exceed exports, while a trade surplus is the result of exports exceeding imports. The United States has experienced trade deficits in goods for decades, while we have had a small trade surplus for services. Combined, our net exports result in a trade deficit in the hundreds of billions of dollars per year.

The Economic Basis for Trade
Because land, labor, and capital resources are spread unevenly across the planet, countries and firms must determine which kinds of industry to specialize in to make the most of their available resources. Regions with a great deal of natural resources focus on land-intensive industry, such as wool, cattle, agricultural crops, and mining for metals and minerals. Countries with broad, skilled labor resources are more likely to specialize in labor-intensive industry, such as medicine, financial services, information technology, and entertainment. Nations with large amounts of capital resources tend to concentrate in capital-intensive industry, such as automobiles, electronics, equipment, and chemicals. Countries are not permanently limited by their resources; as countries improve the education and skill levels of their workers or their investment in capital, they are able to broaden their production possibilities. In the circular flow model, imports are a leakage from the flow as money leaves the country, while exports are an injection into the circular flow when foreign firms buy American products.

Production Possibilities
To illustrate the gains from trade, we will return to the production possibilities curve from Chapter 1. We assume that there are only two nations, each nation only makes two products, they have an equal amount of resources and technology, and the opportunity costs associated with making each product are constant as production output changes.

A nation that is able to produce more of a product has an absolute advantage. In the example given below, the United States can produce 30 tons of coffee, while Brazil can only produce 20 tons. The United States can also produce 30 tons of wheat compared to Brazil's 10 tons of wheat. Therefore, the United States has an absolute advantage in the production of both coffee and wheat.

But comparative advantage is the basis for determining specialization. Comparative advantage tells us which country is more efficient in producing each of the goods. We must calculate each country's opportunity cost of producing each product. In the case of the United States, for every additional ton of wheat produced, we must give up producing one ton of coffee. Therefore, 1 ton of wheat equals 1 ton of coffee. In Brazil, for each additional ton of wheat produced, they must give up producing two tons of coffee. Therefore, 1 ton of wheat equals 2 tons of coffee, and 1 ton of coffee equals 1/2 ton of wheat. If both countries were self-sufficient and did not engage in trade, they would have to make a choice between the tradeoffs on the production possibilities curve. But if countries are willing to trade, they can gain from the other countries' efficiencies of production.

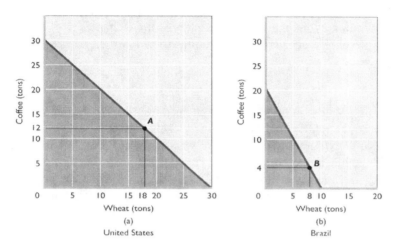

Production possibilities for the United States and Brazil

The Law of Comparative Advantage says that the total output in the world economy will be highest when each country produces the good for which it has the lowest opportunity cost. In this case, to produce a ton of wheat, the United States must give up 1 ton of coffee, while Brazil must give up 2 tons of coffee. Because the United States has the lower opportunity cost, it has the comparative advantage and should produce wheat. At the same time, to produce 1 ton of coffee, the United States has an opportunity cost of 1 ton of wheat, while Brazil's opportunity cost is 1/2 ton of wheat. Because Brazil is the lower-cost producer of coffee, Brazil should specialize in coffee, the United States should specialize in wheat, and the two countries should trade.

The terms of trade are the prices of the products to be traded. For simplicity, we assume a barter economy, with coffee traded for wheat. The terms of trade will always fall between the two countries' opportunity costs, because if either country did not gain from the trade, it would not choose to trade. In this case, the United States is producing each ton of wheat at an opportunity cost of 1 ton of coffee, so it will not accept less than 1 ton of coffee from Brazil in trade for wheat. At the same time, Brazil will not pay more than 2 tons of coffee for a ton of American wheat, because it could have bought its domestic supply of wheat at that price. Therefore, the price of 1 ton of wheat will be between 1–2 tons of coffee, with the final price of wheat determined by supply and demand.

Gains from Trade
If the terms of trade are set at a price of 1 1/2 tons of coffee for 1 ton of wheat, a trading possibilities curve is determined for each of the two countries, showing how much of each product a country can obtain by either producing or trading for the product. As a result, both countries can reach beyond their domestic production possibilities curves to have even more than before the trade. As a result of trade, the United States can gain more coffee than it could

produce domestically, while Brazil could gain more wheat than it could produce domestically given their relative resource constraints: both countries could have more coffee and more wheat than if they depended entirely on domestic production. Therefore, both countries gained from the trade, with the United States moving from A (12 tons of coffee and 15 tons of wheat) to A' (15 tons of coffee and 20 tons of wheat) and Brazil moving from B (4 tons of coffee and 8 tons of wheat) to B' (5 tons of coffee and 10 tons of wheat). While the production possibilities curve can shift out domestically as the result of increases in the amount and quality of resources and technology, we now see that it can also increase as a result of international trade.

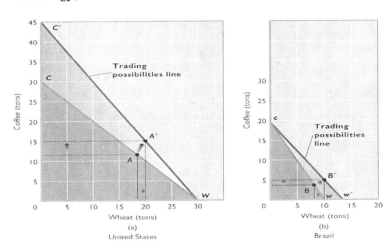

Trading possibilities lines and the gains from trade

The Case for Free Trade

Free trade results in benefits for individual consumers as well as for society as a whole. Because trade relies on comparative advantage, resources are allocated more efficiently. With specialization and trade, resources flow to the lowest-cost producers, and nations and consumers can import products at a lower price than they can produce them domestically. As a result, real income increases, so material well-being also increases for the citizens of nations involved in the trade.

Free trade also deters monopolies by providing competition, which requires domestic firms to use more efficient production methods in order to compete. The competition encourages innovation, further supporting economic growth. In addition, free trade provides a wider variety of goods and services for consumers to choose from, improving the quality of life for consumers.

Free trade also has important political implications. As nations are linked by international trade and multinational corporations, they forge relationships and trade agreements. When faced with political disagreements, such nations are more likely to seek peaceful solutions rather than resorting to war.

Supply and Demand Analysis of Exports and Imports

In a closed economy, domestic supply and demand determine the equilibrium price and quantity. In the figure below, at a price of $1.00 per pound, 100 million pounds of aluminum will be produced and sold within the United States.

The world price is set by supply and demand, as well. If the world price is 75 cents per pound and the United States opens its economy to imported aluminum, the price of aluminum in U.S.

markets will also fall to 75 cents per pound. At the lower price, U.S. consumers increase the quantity demanded to 125 million pounds, but domestic producers are only willing to produce 75 million pounds, leaving a 50 million pound shortage. The United States will import the 50 million pounds of aluminum from other world producers who are willing to sell it at that price. If the world price fell to 50 cents per pound, U.S. producers would reduce production to 50 million pounds as consumers increase their quantity demanded to 150 million pounds, resulting in a 100 million pound domestic shortage that would be imported to meet consumer demand.

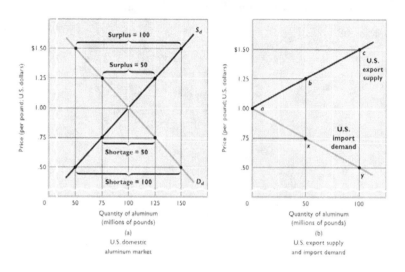

U.S. export supply and import demand

Conversely, if the world price is higher than the U.S. price and the United States opens its borders to trade, domestic firms are willing to produce more, while U.S. consumers demand a lower quantity, resulting in a surplus of products. In this example, at a world price of $1.25 a pound, U.S. firms produce a surplus of 50 million pounds, which they sell as exports in the world market. At the higher price of $1.50 a pound, domestic consumers purchase even less, while U.S. firms produce even more, thus producing a 100-million-pound surplus, which can be exported to other nations. When the world price is higher than the domestic price of products, U.S. firms increase production and export the additional products. When the world price is lower than the domestic price, U.S. firms reduce production and the United States imports additional products.

Trade Barriers
Trade barriers are policies intended to limit the amount of international trade with a country. Tariffs, which are excise taxes on imports, can be collected for two purposes. Revenue tariffs are placed on goods for which there is no domestic industry. Their sole purpose is to earn revenue for the government. Protective tariffs are designed to increase the price of imports in an effort to protect domestic producers from the competition of lower-priced imports. Import quotas limit the number of imports allowed into a country. Non-tariff barriers are licensing requirements, quality controls, consumer safety requirements, or other limitations on imports. "Voluntary" export restrictions are "agreed to" by foreign producers when an importing nation threatens more direct trade barriers (such as a tariff) if the firms don't "voluntarily" reduce exports to that country.

Trade barriers reduce the supply of products within the importing country, increasing the price of the products and reducing the quantity sold. This action results in a number of implications for trade participants. The trade barrier reduces the number of imports sold in the country, hurting the foreign producer. At the same time, the increased price of the product hurts the consumer. Now that the market price is higher, domestic firms are more willing to produce products at the higher price, so both the output and price increases for the firm—which explains why firms lobby Congress so hard for trade barriers to protect them from competition. The other winner from trade barriers can be the government, which collects revenue from the tariffs, fees, and licenses.

But there are other important negative effects of trade barriers. Because less-efficient firms are increasing production while the most efficient producers are reducing production, scarce resources are flowing away from the most efficient producers. Therefore, world output begins to fall. Further, because we are now buying fewer products from other countries, reducing the production and incomes in those countries, foreigners now have less income available to purchase our products, reducing U.S. exports, employment, and GDP. According to McConnell and Brue, numerous studies have shown that the costs of trade barriers to the consumer are substantially greater than the gains to domestic producers and the government. As a result of the shifting of resources to less-efficient producers and the millions of dollars invested in lobbying Congress to create such trade barriers, production becomes more inefficient, output and consumption fall, and the standard of living for consumers falls.

Arguments of Protectionists and Free Traders
Protectionists make a number of arguments in favor of the use of trade barriers. First, protectionists argue that we must protect American industries that produce goods necessary for our national security, so as not to become reliant on foreign firms for our self-defense. Free traders agree that national security is a higher priority than economic efficiency but argue that the self-defense argument is open to abuse by firms who will attempt to argue that they are necessary to self-defense. Free traders propose direct subsidies to domestic producers of items vital to our defense as more effective than trade barriers.

Protectionists also argue that when countries are too specialized in producing a few goods, trade barriers must be used to promote more diverse production of domestic goods. In that way, countries can protect themselves from relying solely on exports in order to finance the imports of products they need. Free traders agree that diversification of an economy is important but note that such a lack of diversity does not exist in the United States and therefore is not a relevant argument in favor of protectionism here.

The infant industry argument states that new domestic firms cannot immediately compete with established, highly efficient foreign firms. So protectionists argue that temporary tariffs should be placed on imports that compete with new domestic firms until those new firms get on their feet and establish efficient production; then the tariffs can be removed to allow competition. Free traders argue that determining which new firms deserve protection is difficult. Further, firms that receive such protection will resist admitting they are prepared to compete, so it is difficult to ever drop the trade barrier. Again, most free traders argue that targeted direct subsidies for protected firms would clearly show which firms are being protected and hold down prices for consumers.

Dumping is the practice of selling a good abroad at a price lower than the firm's cost of production. Firms dumping products may be engaged in price discrimination or attempt to run domestic competitors out of business to become the monopoly producer. Therefore, protectionists argue we should use widespread tariffs to protect U.S. firms from dumping. Free traders argue that what may appear to be dumping by a foreign firm may in fact only be a strong comparative advantage. Dumping is considered an unfair trade practice by the United States and other nations, and when it is discovered, nations impose targeted tariffs to punish the dumping firms and protect domestic industry. Free traders argue that such targeted policy is more effective than widespread barriers in stopping the few instances of dumping that occur.

One of the more popular arguments among protectionists is that trade barriers will save U.S. jobs and firms. They argue that if imports are limited, consumers will buy domestic products instead, increasing domestic output and employment. Free traders point out that while imports may reduce some domestic jobs, others emerge in the transportation and sale of imports. Reducing imports costs these jobs, as well as jobs in the foreign countries where the imports are produced. Lower incomes abroad reduce the demand for U.S. exports, reducing U.S. output and employment in our export industries. Atop this natural progression of events, nations suffering the effects of tariffs are likely to impose retaliatory tariffs, potentially leading to full-scale trade wars. In the long run, trade barriers do not effectively increase domestic employment and instead result in inefficiency and reduced output. While free traders recognize that international trade can reduce output and employment in less efficient domestic industries, the long-run gains to consumers and in output and employment among more efficient producers outweigh those costs. Therefore, most economists support increased international trade.

The final argument of protectionists is that domestic workers and firms must be protected from the low wages paid by firms in foreign countries. Protectionists contend that if U.S. firms are forced to compete with lower-priced imports, U.S. firms will have no choice but to lower prices and the wages of U.S. workers, reducing American standards of living. Free traders argue that U.S. standards of living are in fact increased due to consumers' ability to buy lower-priced imports rather than more expensive domestic products. Further, because U.S. workers are more productive than workers in many other countries, U.S. workers are paid higher wages. But if trade is limited and the United States must allocate resources to produce goods that it produces less efficiently, output and standards of living will fall. Finally, free traders argue that protectionists make the mistake of focusing on the differences in wage per hour, rather than labor cost per unit of output. Because American workers are well-trained and are more likely to use better technology, U.S. productivity is higher, leading to a similar labor cost per unit produced.

The World Trade Organization
The World Trade Organization (WTO) was created in 1993 for the purpose of reducing trade barriers among nations and resolving trade disputes. More than 150 countries had joined the WTO by 2009. While increased trade has increased world output and efficiency and improved the standards of living for workers in producing countries and for consumers, the outsourcing of jobs and the closing of domestic firms results in unemployment and important effects for cities and local governments. While government officials have developed policies to help with the adjustment of workers and communities that have lost jobs and firms, the very real losses associated with trade lead to continued disputes over the wisdom of international trade.

Multiple-Choice Questions
1.   Nations specialize in trade based on their relative levels of
    I.   natural resources.
    II.   labor resources.
    III.   capital resources.
    IV.   technology.
    (A)   I only
    (B)   II and III only
    (C)   III and IV only

(D)   I, II, and IV only
(E)   I, II, III, and IV

Use the data below to answer questions 2 and 3.
Assume that Thailand can produce either 10 tons of fish or 5 units of electronics, while Singapore can produce either 9 tons of fish or 3 units of electronics using the same amount of resources.

2.   Given this data, which of the following statements is correct?
      (A)   Singapore has an absolute and comparative advantage in producing fish.
      (B)   Thailand has an absolute and comparative advantage in producing electronics.
      (C)   Singapore has an absolute advantage in producing fish and a comparative advantage in producing electronics.
      (D)   Thailand has an absolute advantage in producing electronics and a comparative advantage in producing fish.
      (E)   Singapore has an absolute advantage in producing electronics and a comparative advantage in producing fish.

3.   Given this data, how should production occur in order to maximize the efficient use of resources?
      (A)   Thailand should produce both fish and electronics, and Singapore should import both.
      (B)   Thailand should produce fish and import electronics.
      (C)   Both countries would be better off by remaining self-reliant, producing both products for themselves and not trading.
      (D)   Singapore should produce fish and import electronics.
      (E)   Singapore should produce both fish and electronics, and Thailand should import both.

4.   Which of the following serves as an injection into the circular market flow?
      (A)   Exports
      (B)   Quotas
      (C)   Imports
      (D)   Protectionism
      (E)   Dumping of imports

5.   Most economists support international trade for all of the following reasons EXCEPT
      (A)   trade results in a more efficient allocation of resources.
      (B)   production by more efficient producers results in lower product prices.
      (C)   the standard of living generally increases in countries that trade.
      (D)   nations that trade achieve greater economic and political independence.
      (E)   trade provides consumers with a wider variety of products to purchase.

6.   Nations impose trade barriers for the purpose of
      (A)   encouraging exports.
      (B)   increasing productive efficiency.
      (C)   protecting domestic industries.
      (D)   reducing government revenues.
      (E)   increasing employment in export industries.

7.   Each of the following results from a protective tariff on imported wine EXCEPT
      (A)   a higher price for imported wine.
      (B)   an increase in government revenues from the tariff on imported wine.
      (C)   a short-run increase in demand for domestically-produced wine.
      (D)   reduced employment in firms dependent on imported wine.
      (E)   an increase in efficiency among firms producing wine.

8.   Protectionists argue that trade barriers are necessary for all of the following reasons
      EXCEPT
      (A)   temporary tariffs protect infant industries until they are capable of competing
             against more efficient established foreign producers.
      (B)   import quotas help to increase the variety of products available and reduce prices
             for consumers.
      (C)   protection is necessary to ensure the diversity of domestic products.
      (D)   nations have a responsibility to protect industries necessary for national security.
      (E)   protection of domestic industries increases domestic employment and protects
             domestic wages from foreign competition.

Free-Response Questions

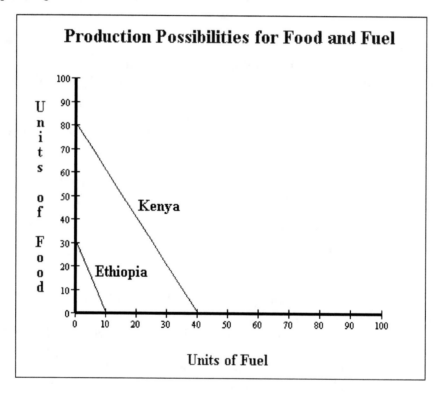

1.   Using the same amounts of resources, Kenya and Ethiopia can produce food and fuel in
      the amounts illustrated in the production possibilities curves above.
(a)   Which country has the absolute advantage in producing food? Explain.
(b)   Which country has the comparative advantage in producing food? Explain.
(c)   If these countries engage in trade, which country will import food? Explain.
(d)   How will the importing country gain from the trade?

2. In an attempt to protect domestic industries from international trade, the United States places a high tariff on the imports of Japanese automobiles. Explain the effect of this trade barrier on each of the following:
(a) the price of Japanese autos for American consumers. Explain.
(b) the output of Japanese auto manufacturers. Explain.
(c) the price of domestically-produced autos for American consumers. Explain.
(d) efficiency of production in the auto industry. Explain.

Multiple-Choice Explanations

1. (E) Firms require land, labor, and capital resources to produce, and the availability of these resources and technology determines production possibilities for each country involved in trade.
2. (B) Thailand has an absolute advantage in producing electronics because it can create 5 units while Singapore can only produce 3 units. Thailand also has a comparative advantage in producing electronics because Thailand's opportunity cost for producing 1 unit of electronics is 2 tons of fish, while Singapore's opportunity cost for producing 1 unit of electronics is 3 tons of fish. Because Thailand has the lower opportunity cost, it holds the comparative advantage.
3. (D) Because Thailand is the more efficient producer of electronics and Singapore is the more efficient producer of fish, they should specialize in the product for which they hold the comparative advantage and trade with each other.
4. (A) When exports are sold, the revenue gained from the sale becomes an injection into the circular market flow of the economy; the purchase of imports is a leakage from the circular market flow.
5. (D) When countries engage in trade, they become more interdependent for goods and services.
6. (C) Countries erect trade barriers with the belief that if consumers cannot purchase imports for lower prices, they will buy domestically-produced products instead.
7. (E) With the trade barrier in place, production at the more efficient foreign firm falls, while production at the less efficient domestic firm increases; therefore, efficiency is reduced.
8. (B) Import quotas reduce the number of imports, reducing the variety of products available to consumers and increasing prices.

Free-Response Explanations

1. **7 points** (2 + 2 + 2 + 1)
(a) 2 points:
  • 1 point is earned for stating that Kenya has the absolute advantage in producing food.
  • 1 point is earned for explaining that Kenya can produce 80 units of food while Ethiopia can only produce 30 units of food.
(b) 2 points:
  • 1 point is earned for stating that Ethiopia has the comparative advantage in producing food.
  • 1 point is earned for explaining that Ethiopia has a lower opportunity cost for producing a unit of food (1/3 unit of fuel) than Kenya does (1/2 unit of fuel).
(c) 2 points:
  • 1 point is earned for identifying Kenya as the importer of food.
  • 1 point is earned for explaining that each country will specialize in the product for which it holds a comparative advantage, so Kenya will produce fuel and import food.

(d)   1 point:
  - 1 point is earned for explaining that Kenya gains from the trade because it can now import food at a lower cost than it can produce it domestically.

2.   **8 points** (2 + 2 + 2 + 2)
(a)   2 points:
  - 1 point is earned for stating that the price for imported Japanese autos increases.
  - 1 point is earned for explaining that the tariff is a tax included in the price of the product, raising the price.
(b)   2 points:
  - 1 point is earned for stating that the output of Japanese autos falls.
  - 1 point is earned for explaining that as American consumers reduce the quantity of Japanese autos demanded at the higher tariff price, Japanese manufacturers reduce their output.
(c)   2 points:
  - 1 point is earned for stating that the price increases for cars produced in the United States.
  - 1 point is earned for stating that demand for domestic autos increases because it is now a lower-priced substitute for the more expensive Japanese autos; increased demand pushes up the price.
(d)   2 points:
  - 1 point is earned for stating that efficiency decreases in auto production.
  - 1 point is earned for explaining that because fewer autos are produced by the more efficient Japanese factories and more autos are produced by the less efficient American producers, overall efficiency in the use of resources declines.

CHAPTER 38: THE BALANCE OF PAYMENTS, EXCHANGE RATES, AND TRADE DEFICITS

Introduction
This study of economics concludes with the examination of how money moves between nations. Changes in the demand for imports, relative inflation and interest rates, and other factors such as tourism, international aid, and speculation can change the relative value of national currencies. Chapter 38 examines the causes and effects of changes in the supply and demand for money in international exchange markets and the effects of such changes on imports and exports, as well as current and capital account balances. Material from Chapter 38 usually appears in several multiple-choice questions and consistently appears in free-response questions on the AP macroeconomics exam.

International Financial Markets
International trade for goods and services or financial assets such as stocks and bonds depends on the exchange of currencies. In order for buyers in one country to purchase products or assets from another country, the buyer must first buy the other nation's currency in the foreign exchange market. If a U.S. firm wants to buy coffee from Brazil, it must buy Brazilian reals to pay for it. If the exchange rate for $1 US were 2.5 Brazilian reals, American importers would have to pay a price of 40 cents per real. If the price of coffee were 1,000 Brazilian reals, U.S. importers would have to pay $400 in U.S. currency ($0.4 \times 1,000$) to buy the reals necessary to buy the coffee.

The Balance of Payments
The balance of payments is the total of all financial transactions that take place between the people of one country and the people of another country. Most of these financial transactions are for the purpose of buying goods, services, or financial assets. But other financial activities are included, such as tourism, the payments of interest and dividends, gifts, loans, and humanitarian aid. The balance of payments is divided into two major categories: the current account and the capital account.

The current account calculates the amount of trade in goods and services. The balance of trade on goods and services is the difference between exports and imports. If exports are greater than imports, the country has a trade surplus; if imports are greater than exports, then the country is experiencing a trade deficit.

The capital account is the inflow of foreign funds for investment in U.S. financial assets, as compared to the outflow of U.S. funds for investment in financial assets of other countries. When capital inflows from other countries exceed capital outflows from the United States, the United States experiences a surplus in the capital account. If our outflows are greater than inflows of funds from other nations into the United States, the United States would experience a capital account deficit.

In the balance of payments, the current and capital accounts must balance; the sum of the accounts must be zero. Countries can only trade products (goods and services) or assets. If one country imports more than it exports, the only way it can make up for that current account deficit is to transfer more assets to the country through a capital account surplus.

Fixed Exchange Rates

From 1879 to 1934, countries used the gold standard to set exchange rates. From 1944 to 1971, the Bretton Woods system set relative values of international currencies in terms of other currencies or gold. If supply or demand for a currency changed, governments intervened in the markets to maintain the fixed exchange rate. Governments could buy or sell currencies or even gold in the market to ensure the currency values remained stable. Countries could also create trade policies such as trade barriers to try to encourage or discourage imports or exports to affect currency values. However, such policies distorted trade and led to reduced efficiency in production, higher prices and fewer choices for consumers, black markets, and international struggles over trade policy. For this reason, few nations today peg their currencies to the value of the U.S. dollar or other currencies.

Flexible Exchange Rates

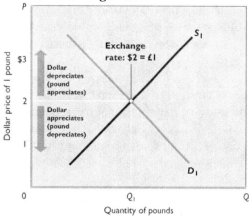

The market for foreign currency (pounds)

Since 1971, exchange rates have been flexible, also known as the "managed float." The relative values of currencies are determined by supply and demand, with occasional interventions by governments and the International Monetary Fund.

When the demand for British pounds increases, the amount of U.S. currency required to buy a British pound increases, and the value of the British pound appreciates. If the demand for British pounds falls, it takes less U.S. currency to buy it, and the value of the British pound depreciates. It is important to recognize that the values of the two nations' currencies change relative to one another. If the British pound is appreciating against the U.S. dollar, the U.S. dollar must be depreciating. This occurs because Americans use U.S. dollars to buy British pounds, changing the relative values of both currencies.

When demand for British pounds increases, Americans must increase the supply of U.S. dollars in the foreign exchange market in order to buy the pounds, simultaneously reducing the value of the dollar. So while the pound appreciates (requiring $2.50 rather than $2.00 to buy the British pound), the dollar depreciates (requiring the British to pay only 0.4 pounds, rather than 0.5 pounds, to buy one U.S. dollar).

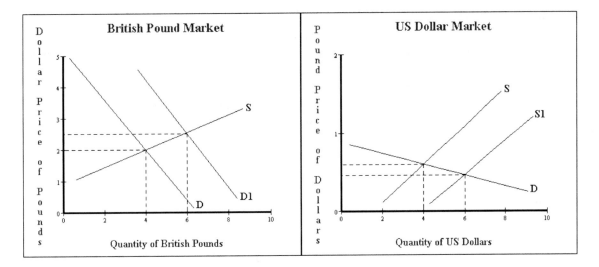

Determinants of Exchange Rates

Several factors can cause a change in the demand for foreign currency. First, a change in consumer tastes affects consumer demand for imports. If a Japanese firm develops a popular new computer game, American consumer demand for the product increases U.S. demand for Japanese yen to pay for the product.

Second, a change in relative incomes changes the demand for currency. If U.S. incomes increase, Americans buy more imports as well as domestic products. The increase in imports increases demand for the foreign currency.

Third, changes in relative inflation rates affect the demand for imports. If prices in the U.S. are increasing relatively more quickly than prices in other countries, consumers will buy more imports as substitutes, increasing their demand for those currencies.

Fourth, changes in relative interest rates are an important factor in determining demand for currency. If Canadian interest rates are higher than interest rates in the U.S., Americans will see Canadian bonds as an attractive investment and increase demand for Canadian dollars.

Fifth, differences in the expected return on investment can affect demand for currency. If U.S. investors expect a greater return on their investment in German stocks, real estate, or other investments, Americans will increase the demand for euros, increasing the supply of dollars in international markets to pay for euros, so the euro will appreciate while the U.S. dollar depreciates.

Finally, speculation contributes to changes in currency values. Speculators invest in currency itself, hoping to make a profit by buying currency at a low price and selling it for a higher price. If American speculators expect the value of the Chilean peso to appreciate, their increased demand for pesos can cause the very appreciation they expected, while the increase in the supply of dollars to pay for the pesos causes the U.S. dollar to depreciate in value.

Bear in Mind

It is important to understand the links between changes in demand for currencies, the relative appreciation/depreciation of currencies, and the effects on imports and exports. Many of the multiple-choice and free-response questions on the AP macroeconomics exam require you to explain those links, causes, and effects.

Flexible Exchange Rates and the Balance of Payments

The effects of changes in exchange rates are important because they can lead to adjustments in deficits or surpluses in the balance of payments. Assume we start with our equilibrium exchange rate, where $2 equals 1 British pound. If consumer tastes change to desire more British imports, an increase in demand for British pounds increases the price of pounds for American consumers. However, because pounds are now more expensive, the prices of British products purchased with those pounds become more expensive. For example, a book worth 10 British pounds in the United Kingdom costs Americans $20 at the original exchange rate. But if it now costs $2.50 to buy 1 British pound, the price of the book has increased to $25. At the higher prices, Americans will begin to reduce the quantity of imports demanded, reducing the demand for British pounds until its value again falls. Where at one point the United States had a deficit in the balance of payments, the change in exchange rates again returned the balance.

From the British side of the same equation, the increasing value of the British pound makes American products seem less expensive, and the quantity demanded increases. As the British demand more U.S. products, the demand for U.S. dollars to pay for those products increases, which increases the value of the dollar. As the price of the dollar increases, American products become more expensive and British citizens demand fewer American imports, bringing their earlier surplus in the balance of payments back into equilibrium. So while currencies may become strong for a number of reasons, the flexibility of the exchange rate eventually reverses the process and leads the balance of payments back to equilibrium.

The flexibility of exchange rates does, however, also cause negative effects. One problem is that the volatility of foreign exchange markets can lead to dramatic swings in the values of currencies within days, causing significant changes in imports and exports. Another problem is that while exchange rates do eventually cycle to balance, currencies can remain strong or weak for years before balance returns. The risks of currency value changes can discourage firms from importing products and investors from making foreign investments, while the same concerns from foreign firms affect export demand from domestic producers.

As a result of this flexibility, changes in currency values can destabilize the domestic economy. Assume the United States has an open economy and begins at full employment output. If the U.S. dollar appreciates, imports increase and exports decrease, creating a trade deficit. The combination of these two actions creates a reduction in net exports, reducing aggregate demand and potentially reducing U.S. output and employment. Conversely, a weak U.S. dollar reduces U.S. demand for imports because of the increase in import prices. But the increase in demand for the substitute American products increases the price of those American products. In addition, the increased foreign demand for American goods due to the cheaper U.S. dollar further increases aggregate demand and the rate of inflation.

The Managed Float

While supply and demand for currency primarily determine the value of currencies today, governments and the International Monetary Fund (IMF) do occasionally intervene to stabilize or alter currency exchange rates. Leaders of the G8 nations (among the largest industrialized nations of the world) meet frequently to discuss economic and trade issues and have also acted to stabilize currency values.

Over the years, the managed float has worked relatively well to stabilize serious international crises that might have caused a fixed exchange rate system to fail. The flexibility of the market allowed it to freely adjust to changes in supply and demand, stabilizing international trade. Critics of the managed float, however, are concerned about the volatility of exchange rates and the continued effects of that volatility on investment and demand for exports. They point to crises that have occurred despite the managed float and the need for the IMF to extend loans to bail out countries victimized by rapid exchange rate changes. While the managed float has not completely eliminated such fluctuations, it has provided the mechanism by which nations can adjust to those changes in exchange rates.

Causes of U.S. Trade Deficits
U.S. trade deficits increased dramatically from 1999 to 2007. The U.S. economy experienced greater growth in that period, and increased incomes allowed consumers to buy more imports than foreign consumers were buying from us. In addition, the United States opened a wide trade deficit with China. Low-priced Chinese products have dramatically increased U.S. demand for imports, but because the Chinese have pegged the yuan to the dollar, the increased demand doesn't raise the price of the yuan and the trade deficit is perpetuated. Further, the significant increase in the price of oil led to a greater U.S. trade deficit with OPEC countries. Finally, the high interest rates and low saving rate of Americans opened a door for those in other countries to invest in American stocks, bonds, and real estate. The concern with current U.S. trade deficits is that they come at the expense of increased borrowing from other nations or the sale of U.S. assets. Foreigners own trillions of dollars more in U.S. assets than Americans own of foreign assets. In order to reverse this trend, Americans would have to reduce imports and increase the sale of exports. An added concern is that this foreign investment provides money for the purchase of capital, which can improve economic growth. Attempts to reduce foreign investment could reduce potential growth.

The Effect of Stabilization Policies on Exchange Rates and International Trade
One final important consideration is how changes in economic stabilization policies can affect exchange rates and international trade. When Congress uses expansionary fiscal policy by reducing taxes and increasing government spending, consumers have more income available to buy imports. At the same time, expansionary fiscal policy requires the government to borrow from the loanable funds market to finance deficit spending, increasing interest rates. The higher interest rates attract foreign investment as a capital inflow, increasing the demand for U.S. dollars and causing them to appreciate. As U.S. dollars appreciate, imports look less expensive, so imports increase; at the same time, the high value of U.S. dollars makes U.S. exports look expensive to foreigners, so exports decrease, increasing the trade deficit.

The Federal Reserve can also use expansionary monetary policy to stimulate economic growth, though its policies will have the opposite effect on capital flows. If the Fed increases the money supply, interest rates fall. Foreigners demand fewer dollars for investment, while Americans demand more foreign currency to invest in other countries that are paying higher interest rates on investment. As a result, a capital outflow develops. The increased demand for foreign currency increases its value, eventually causing imports to fall and exports to increase.

Globalization and International Trade
Changes in supply and demand for currencies and the resulting changes in currency values bring about impacts on production and employment in countries involved in trade. As a result of globalization, the increased interdependence of nations means that we are no longer alone in our achievements—or our problems. As we see the effects of worker strikes, crop failures, or increasing incomes a world away affecting our own economy, we come to realize how important an understanding of economics is for us all.

Multiple Choice Questions

1.   When a nation experiences a trade deficit,
        (A)   imports are greater than exports.
        (B)   the current account is in surplus.
        (C)   the capital account is balanced.
        (D)   the value of the country's currency must be appreciating.
        (E)   exports are greater than imports.

2.   If a country has a current account surplus,
        (A)   the balance of payments must be in surplus.
        (B)   the country is experiencing a trade deficit.
        (C)   the capital account must have a deficit.
        (D)   the federal budget must also be running a surplus.
        (E)   the value of the nation's currency has depreciated.

3.   An increase in American consumers' demand for Mexican chili peppers causes
                I.   the value of the Mexican peso to increase.
                II.   the value of the U.S. dollar to decrease.
                III.   a reduction in the U.S. trade deficit.
        (A)   I only
        (B)   III only
        (C)   II and III only
        (D)   I and II only
        (E)   I, II, and III

4.   Which of the following scenarios could cause the value of the U.S. dollar to increase in
        foreign exchange markets?
        (A)   American consumer tastes change to increase demand for Italian shoes.
        (B)   Foreign incomes increase at a higher rate than U.S. incomes.
        (C)   The U.S. inflation rate is higher than inflation rates in other countries.
        (D)   Speculators act on a belief that the U.S. dollar will depreciate.
        (E)   U.S. interest rates are lower than interest rates in other countries.

5.   When the U.S. dollar appreciates in value,
                I.   imports increase.
                II.   exports increase.
                III.   foreign investment in U.S. bonds increases.
        (A)   I only
        (B)   II only
        (C)   I and III only
        (D)   II and III only
        (E)   I, II, and III

6.   If German citizens increase investment in U.S. bonds,
        (A)   the supply of euros in the foreign exchange market would fall.
        (B)   the international value of the U.S. dollar would fall.
        (C)   the euro would depreciate in foreign exchange markets.
        (D)   German demand for U.S. dollars would decrease.
        (E)   U.S. imports would decrease.

7.   How will an increase in the federal budget deficit affect interest rates, foreign demand for the dollar, and the international value of the dollar?

	Interest Rate	Demand for the Dollar	Value of the Dollar
(A)	Increase	Increase	Increase
(B)	Decrease	Increase	Increase
(C)	Decrease	Decrease	Increase
(D)	Decrease	Decrease	Decrease
(E)	Increase	Decrease	Decrease

8.   If the Federal Reserve increases the money supply, how will interest rates, the international value of the dollar, and imports be affected?

	Interest Rate	Value of the Dollar	Imports
(A)	Increase	Decrease	Increase
(B)	Decrease	Decrease	Decrease
(C)	Increase	Increase	Increase
(D)	Decrease	Increase	Decrease
(E)	Increase	Increase	Decrease

Free-Response Question

Assume the U.S. economy is experiencing a significant recession.

(a)   Identify an appropriate open-market operation the Federal Reserve could use to increase spending in the economy.

(b)   Explain the effects of the Fed's action in (a) on each of the following:
   (i)   the interest rate
   (ii)   capital inflows
   (iii)   capital outflows
   (iv)   the international value of the dollar

(c)   Assuming that the U.S. starts with balanced trade, explain the effects of the change in the international value of the dollar in (b)(iv) on each of the following.
   (i)   U.S. imports
   (ii)   U.S. exports
   (iii)   the U.S. balance of trade

Multiple-Choice Explanations

1.   (A)   Trade deficits occur when a country imports more than it exports in a year.

2.   (C)   The capital account and the current account must add up to zero in order to balance. So if the current account has a surplus, the capital account must be running a deficit.

3.   (D)   The increase in demand for Mexican peppers increases the demand for the peso, increasing its value. To pay for the pesos, Americans increase the supply of dollars in the international market, lowering the value of dollars. An increase in imports would increase the trade deficit, not reduce it.

4.   (B)   A relatively higher increase in foreign incomes will lead foreigners to buy more U.S. exports, and they will increase demand for U.S. dollars to buy those exports, increasing the value of the U.S. dollar.

5.   (A)   When the U.S. dollar increases in value, imports look less expensive because it takes fewer dollars to buy each unit of foreign currency, so U.S. consumers buy more imports. Because U.S. dollars become more expensive to foreigners, they buy fewer exports and invest less in U.S. bonds.

6.   (C)   In order to invest in U.S. bonds, Germans must buy U.S. dollars, paying for them with euros. The increase in the supply of euros in foreign exchange markets would result in a lower value of euros.

7.   (A)   When the federal government runs a budget deficit, it must increase the demand for money in the loanable funds market to finance the deficit, causing an increase in interest rates. The higher interest rate attracts foreign investors, whose demand for dollars to buy bonds increases the value of the U.S. dollar.

8.   (B)   An increase in the money supply lowers interest rates in the money market. As a result, foreign investors reduce investment in U.S. bonds, lowering the demand for dollars and causing the dollar to depreciate in value. When dollars are weak, imports look more expensive, so U.S. consumers buy fewer imports.

Free-Response Explanation
8 points (1 + 4 + 3)

(a)   1 point:
- 1 point is earned for stating that the Fed should buy bonds on the open market.

(b)   4 points (each answer must be connected to an explanation; an assertion of "increase" or "decrease" earns no points):
- 1 point is earned for explaining that the interest rate falls because the money supply has increased.
- 1 point is earned for explaining that capital inflows will decrease because foreigners demand fewer bonds when the rate of interest is lower.
- 1 point is earned for explaining that capital outflows will increase because Americans will see the relatively higher interest rates paid on investments in other countries as a better return on investment.
- 1 point is earned for explaining that the international value of the dollar decreases, because foreign demand for the dollar falls and the supply of U.S. dollars in the foreign exchange market increases.

(c)   3 points (each answer must be connected to an explanation; an assertion of "increase" or "decrease" earns no points):
- 1 point is earned for explaining that U.S. imports decrease because the international value of the dollar fell, making foreign products appear more expensive.
- 1 point is earned for explaining that U.S. exports increase because the lower international value of the dollar makes U.S. products look less expensive for foreign purchasers.
- 1 point is earned for explaining that the United States will develop a trade surplus, because exports will be greater than imports.

MACROECONOMICS PRACTICE TEST 1
Section I
Time: 70 Minutes
60 Questions

Directions: Each of the questions or incomplete statements below is followed by five responses or completions. Select the best one in each case.

1. Scarcity is correctly explained as
    I.   a problem of having limited resources to meet unlimited wants.
    II.   a problem faced only by nations with few resources.
    III.   a problem countries can eliminate by conserving resources.
    (A)   I only
    (B)   II only
    (C)   I and II only
    (D)   II and III only
    (E)   I, II, and III

2. The aggregate demand curve slopes downward, because as the price level rises,
    (A)   the real wealth of consumers increases.
    (B)   interest rates increase due to increased borrowing.
    (C)   the quantity of imports demanded decreases.
    (D)   the real GDP increases.
    (E)   the quantity of exports demanded by other countries increases.

3. If the real interest rate on loans in the United States is 6% and the expected rate of inflation is 2%, the nominal interest rate will be
    (A)   2%.
    (B)   4%.
    (C)   6%.
    (D)   8%.
    (E) -4%.

4. Assume the federal government has a balanced budget when a recessionary gap occurs. Which combination of policy actions will be effective in increasing short-run aggregate demand while still promoting long-run economic growth?
    (A)   Congress lowers taxes and increases government spending.
    (B)   The Fed buys bonds and lowers the discount rate.
    (C)   The Fed buys bonds and Congress increases government spending.
    (D)   The Fed lowers the reserve requirement and Congress lowers taxes.
    (E)   The Fed lowers the federal funds rate and Congress lowers taxes.

5. Classical theory is based on the belief that the economy self-adjusts to negative economic shocks through
    (A)   increases in aggregate demand.
    (B)   flexible output and employment.
    (C)   consumer expectations.
    (D)   flexible prices and wages.
    (E)   higher interest rates.

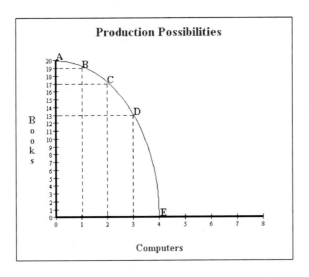

Production Possibilities

Computers

6. If society is currently producing at point B, 19 books and 1 computer, what is the opportunity cost of increasing production to point C?
    (A)   1 book
    (B)   2 books
    (C)   3 books
    (D)   1 computer
    (E)   17 books

7. A worker would be considered structurally unemployed if he lost his job because
            I.   he was replaced by a machine.
            II.   the product he made is no longer purchased by consumers.
            III.   a recession reduced demand for the product he produced.
    (A)   I only
    (B)   III only
    (C)   I and II only
    (D)   II and III only
    (E)   I, II, and III

8. The largest percentage of the M1 money supply consists of
    (A)   demand deposits.
    (B)   savings accounts.
    (C)   tax revenues.
    (D)   government bonds.
    (E)   currency.

9. A fiscal policy appropriate to resolve an inflationary gap is
    (A)   raising the reserve requirement.
    (B)   lowering the tax rate.
    (C)   buying bonds.
    (D)   reducing government spending.
    (E)   increasing the discount rate.

10. Which of the following factors are important to economic growth?
    I.   Improvements in education and training
    II.   Investments in capital equipment
    III.   Improvements in technology
    IV.   Increases in interest rates for loans
    (A)   I and II only
    (B)   III and IV only
    (C)   I, III, and IV only
    (D)   I, II, and III only
    (E)   I, II, III, and IV

11. Using all of its available resources, Kenya can produce 20 tons of coffee or 60 tons of cotton. Uganda can produce 10 tons of coffee or 20 tons of cotton. Which of the following statements is true?
    (A)   Kenya has a comparative advantage in the production of coffee.
    (B)   Uganda can gain by importing cotton.
    (C)   Kenya can gain by importing both coffee and cotton.
    (D)   Uganda has an absolute advantage in the production of cotton.
    (E)   Kenya cannot gain from trade with Uganda under these conditions.

12. A contractionary supply shock, such as a significant increase in resource costs, would cause
    (A)   a decrease in price level.
    (B)   demand-pull inflation.
    (C)   an increase in employment.
    (D)   stagflation.
    (E)   an increase in real GDP.

13. If firms expect a greater percentage return on investment than the current interest rate, what will happen in the loanable funds market and with interest rates?

	Loanable Funds Market	Interest Rate
(A)	Demand increases	Increases
(B)	Demand decreases	Decreases
(C)	Supply increases	Decreases
(D)	Supply decreases	Increases
(E)	Demand decreases	Increases

14. An expansionary fiscal policy will result in
    (A)   a decrease in interest rates.
    (B)   a decrease in real GDP.
    (C)   a decrease in employment.
    (D)   an increase in the price level.
    (E)   an increase in the money supply.

15. Which of the following government policies would promote economic growth?
    (A)   Increasing funding for public education
    (B)   Reducing subsidies for capital investment
    (C)   Increasing sales taxes on industrial equipment
    (D)   Reducing university research grants
    (E)   Increasing per-unit taxes for firms creating negative externalities

16.   Assume tomato soup and saltine crackers are complements and the cost of tomatoes to produce soup increases significantly. Which of the following is the most likely effect on the cracker market?
(A)   An increase in the demand for crackers
(B)   A decrease in the demand for crackers
(C)   An increase in the supply of crackers
(D)   A decrease in the supply of crackers
(E)   A decrease in demand and an increase in supply of crackers

17.   Which of the following would cause an increase in aggregate demand?
(A)   A reduction in consumer wealth
(B)   An increase in imports
(C)   A decrease in investment
(D)   An increase in personal taxes
(E)   A decrease in interest rates

18.   If a customer deposits $500 into his checking account at a bank, and the bank can legally loan $400 of that deposit, the reserve requirement must be
(A)   10%.
(B)   80%.
(C)   90%.
(D)   20%.
(E)   100%.

19.   Crowding out is
(C)   the reduction in capital spending resulting from an increase in government borrowing.
(D)   the increase in foreign investment in U.S. bonds as a result of higher interest rates.
(E)   the required reduction in government spending resulting from lower government revenues.
(F)   the decrease in consumer spending as a result of an increase in taxes.
(G)   the increase in spending that results from an increase in money supply.

20.   The United States initially has a trade balance with imports equal to exports. If Canadian producers reduce their production costs so that prices of Canadian products fall,
        I.   U.S. imports of Canadian products will increase.
        II.   U.S. exports to Canada will increase.
        III.   the U.S. will develop a trade surplus.
(A)   I only
(B)   III only
(C)   II and III only
(D)   I and II only
(E)   I, II, and III

21.   Which of the following represents an injection into the circular market flow?
(A)   Imports
(B)   Saving
(C)   Taxes
(D)   Government spending
(E)   Consumer spending

22.   Significant improvements in technology cause
        (A)   an increase in aggregate supply.
        (B)   a substantial increase in price level.
        (C)   a decrease in real GDP.
        (D)   a decrease in aggregate demand.
        (E)   an increase in money supply.

23.   If a bank has no excess reserves, the reserve requirement is 20%, and a customer deposits
        $10,000, how much of that deposit can the bank loan?
        (A) $8,000
        (B) $20,000
        (C) $2,000
        (D) $5,000
        (E) $50,000

24.   An increase in government deficits will increase
                I.   interest rates in the loanable funds market.
                II.   the national debt.
                III.   the unemployment rate.
        (A)   I only
        (B)   III only
        (C)   I and II only
        (D)   II and III only
        (E)   I, II, and III

25.   Most U.S. economists promote international trade because
        (A)   trade increases the independence of nations.
        (B)   an increase in imports increases the international value of the dollar.
        (C)   the increase in efficiency results in lower prices and greater employment.
        (D)   tariffs are an important source of revenue for the U.S. government.
        (E)   an increase in imports increases the level of real GDP.

26.   The largest sector in U.S. gross domestic product is
        (A)   government spending.
        (B)   consumer purchases.
        (C)   purchases of imports.
        (D)   sales of exports.
        (E)   business spending for capital.

27.   If equilibrium GDP is in the intermediate range of the aggregate supply curve and government
        spending increases, how will the price level, output, and unemployment be affected?

	Price Level	Output	Unemployment
(A)	Increase	Increase	Increase
(B)	Decrease	Decrease	Decrease
(C)	Increase	Decrease	Decrease
(D)	Decrease	Decrease	Increase
(E)	Increase	Increase	Decrease

Assets		Liabilities	
Total Reserves	$25,000	Demand Deposits	$100,000
Loans	$10,000		
Securities	$65,000		

28. First National Bank's balance sheet above reflects its current financial situation. If the reserve requirement is 10% and the bank does not sell any securities, by how much could it increase loans?
    (A) $0
    (B) $10,000
    (C) $90,000
    (D) $15,000
    (E) $5,000

29. The advantage of automatic stabilizers over discretionary fiscal policy is that
    (A) automatic stabilizers cost less than discretionary fiscal policy.
    (B) automatic stabilizers do not require officials to pass new policy.
    (C) discretionary fiscal policy is less effective than automatic stabilizers.
    (D) automatic stabilizers are less likely to add to the national debt.
    (C) discretionary fiscal policy requires coordination between Congress and the Federal Reserve.

30. The use of trade barriers
    (A) increases the number of imports.
    (B) reduces federal government revenues from tariffs.
    (C) increases long-run economic growth.
    (D) increases world output.
    (E) reduces economic efficiency.

31. All of the following activities would be included in calculating GDP EXCEPT
    (A) a firm increasing its inventories in preparation for future demand.
    (B) a father paying his daughter's school tuition.
    (C) a state constructing a new highway.
    (D) a farmer buying seeds to produce a corn crop.
    (E) an investor buying stock in the corporation where he is employed.

32. If investment spending increases by $5 billion and the marginal propensity to consume is 0.75, by how much will real GDP increase?
    (A) $1.25 billion
    (B) $3.75 billion
    (C) $6.67 billion
    (D) $15 billion
    (E) $20 billion

33. If a bank chooses not to fully loan excess reserves, growth of the money supply
    (A) will only be limited by the marginal propensity to save.
    (B) will be infinite.
    (C) will be greater than the expected money supply growth.
    (D) will be less than potential money supply growth.
    (E) will be limited primarily by the federal tax rate.

34. A negative supply shock, such as a significant increase in oil prices, would most likely cause the following effects on output, the price level, and employment:

	Output	Price Level	Employment
(A)	Decrease	Decrease	Decrease
(B)	Increase	Increase	Increase
(C)	Decrease	Increase	Decrease
(D)	Increase	Decrease	Increase
(E)	Decrease	Increase	Increase

35. The international value of U.S. dollars is determined by
    (A) the Federal Reserve Board of Governors.
    (B) the World Trade Organization.
    (C) the supply and demand for currency in foreign exchange markets.
    (D) the current value of gold in commodity markets.
    (E) the rate of inflation in the United States.

40. Real GDP is more accurate than nominal GDP in measuring changes in annual output because real GDP removes the effects of
    (A) price changes.
    (B) unemployment.
    (C) tax rate changes.
    (D) trade barriers.
    (E) externalities.

41. Consumer spending in the economy increases when
    (A) interest rates increase.
    (B) consumer confidence decreases.
    (C) wealth increases.
    (D) the marginal propensity to save increases.
    (E) income tax rates increase.

42. If the Federal Reserve reduces the money supply
    (A) the national debt decreases.
    (B) the inflation rate increases.
    (C) the interest rate increases.
    (D) the unemployment rate decreases.
    (E) real GDP increases.

43. Cost-push inflation is most likely to result from
    (A) an increase in consumer confidence in the economy.
    (B) an increase in the money supply.
    (C) an increase in the cost of raw materials for production.
    (D) an increase in government spending.
    (E) an increase in investment in plant and equipment.

44. When Americans increase demand for imported goods from Mexico,
    (A) the value of the peso depreciates because Mexicans are selling pesos.
    (B) the value of the dollar appreciates because Americans are buying dollars.
    (C) the value of the dollar depreciates because inflation will be higher in the U.S. than in Mexico.

(D)   the value of the peso appreciates because more pesos than dollars are being printed by the government to promote trade.

(E)   the value of the dollar depreciates because Americans are buying pesos.

45.   If the total price of last year's market basket was $500 and the total price of this year's market basket is $600, the consumer price index for this year increased by

(A)   100%.
(B)   83%.
(C)   20%.
(D)   17%.
(E)   10%.

46.   According to classical economists, if spending falls below full-employment output,

(A)   government should increase spending.
(B)   Congress should reduce taxes.
(C)   the Fed should reduce the reserve requirement.
(D)   the Fed should sell bonds.
(E)   the economy will correct itself.

47.   Which action could the Federal Reserve take to increase the money supply?

(A)   Sell securities on the open market
(B)   Reduce taxes
(C)   Increase the reserve requirement
(D)   Increase government spending
(E)   Reduce the discount rate

48.   Long-run economic growth can be illustrated by a rightward shift in the

(A)   downward-sloping aggregate demand curve.
(B)   vertical aggregate supply curve.
(C)   vertical money supply curve.
(D)   vertical Phillips curve.
(E)   downward-sloping Phillips curve.

49.   If the Federal Reserve reduces the money supply, how will interest rates, capital inflows, and the value of the dollar most likely be affected?

	Interest Rate	Capital Inflow	Value of the Dollar
(A)	Decrease	Decrease	Decrease
(B)	Increase	Decrease	Decrease
(C)	Decrease	Increase	Increase
(D)	Decrease	Decrease	Increase
(E)	Increase	Increase	Increase

46.   If Becky's paycheck increases by 3% this year and prices increase by 5%, Becky's real income has

(A)   decreased by 8%.
(B)   decreased by 2%.
(C)   increased by 2%.
(D)   increased by 8%.
(E)   increased by 15%.

47. Keynesian theory holds that
    (A)   prices are sticky, so if aggregate spending falls, unemployment will result.
    (B)   the government should determine output and prices for firms.
    (C)   lower taxes and the sale of bonds by the Fed will correct a recession.
    (D)   the economy naturally remains at full-employment output.
    (E)   output is sticky, so if aggregate spending falls, prices will fall.

48. When the Federal Reserve buys bonds on the open market,
    (A)   the interest rate increases.
    (B)   the money supply decreases.
    (C)   aggregate demand increases.
    (D)   investment decreases.
    (E)   imports decrease.

49. According to the short-run Phillips curve, if Congress reduces taxes in an attempt to lower the unemployment rate, the action will result in
    (A)   a higher inflation rate.
    (B)   a reduction in government revenue.
    (C)   an increase in the money supply.
    (D)   a reduction in exports.
    (E)   an increase in the national debt.

50. How does the appreciation of the U.S. dollar affect imports, exports, and the balance of trade?

	Imports	Exports	Balance of Trade
(A)	Increase	Increase	Balanced
(B)	Decrease	Decrease	Balanced
(C)	Decrease	Increase	Surplus
(D)	Decrease	Increase	Deficit
(E)	Increase	Decrease	Deficit

51. All of the following groups are hurt by unanticipated inflation EXCEPT
    (A)   banks providing student loans.
    (B)   workers earning the minimum wage.
    (C)   savers who earn interest on a certificate of deposit.
    (D)   people who have borrowed money to buy a home.
    (E)   retirees living on fixed pensions.

52. In the Keynesian model, if investment is greater than saving in the short run,
    (A)   unemployment increases.
    (B)   real GDP increases.
    (C)   prices increase.
    (D)   tax rates increase.
    (E)   the value of stock increases.

53. Which policy combination is the most likely to decrease the aggregate demand?

	Taxes	Government Spending	Open Market Operations
(A)	Increase	Increase	Fed buys bonds
(B)	Decrease	Increase	Fed sells bonds
(C)	Increase	Decrease	Fed sells bonds
(D)	Decrease	Decrease	Fed buys bonds
(E)	Increase	Increase	Fed sells bonds

54. Which economic theory advocates use of fiscal and monetary policy to stabilize the economy?
    (A) Classical theory
    (B) Keynesian theory
    (C) Monetarist theory
    (D) Rational expectations theory
    (E) New classical theory

55. If the United States has a capital account surplus, the balance of payments requires a
    (A) current account surplus.
    (B) trade surplus.
    (C) federal budget surplus.
    (D) current account deficit.
    (E) tariff increase.

56. Which of the following people meets the formal definition of unemployed?
    (A) A new college graduate entering the labor force
    (B) A homemaker who has chosen to stay home with her children
    (C) A retired electrical engineer
    (D) A chef who has been out of work so long he has stopped looking for work
    (E) An executive who was fired and now just works part-time delivering pizza

57. If the marginal propensity to consume is 0.8 and the recessionary gap is $10 billion, by how much must government increase spending to reach full-employment output?
    (A) $1 billion
    (B) $5 billion
    (C) $4 billion
    (D) $2 billion
    (E) $1.25 billion

58. If the Federal Reserve increases the money supply, how will interest rates, investment, and real output be affected?

	Interest Rate	Investment	Real Output
(A)	Decrease	Increase	Increase
(B)	Increase	Increase	Decrease
(C)	Decrease	Decrease	Decrease
(D)	Decrease	Decrease	Increase
(E)	Increase	Decrease	Increase

59. The equation of exchange (quantity theory of money) is the foundation of the monetarist argument that increases in the money supply
    (A) are the most effective tool for stimulating aggregate demand.
    (B) reduce inflation but cause higher unemployment.
    (C) cause inflation.
    (D) increase real output.
    (E) increase the velocity of money.

60. An increase in the federal budget deficit is most likely to result in
    (A) depreciation in the international value of the U.S. dollar.
    (B) an increase in capital investment by firms.
    (C) an increase in imports.
    (D) a decrease in interest rates.
    (E) an increase in international demand for the U.S. dollar.

MACROECONOMICS PRACTICE TEST 1
Section II
Planning Time: 10 minutes
Writing Time: 50 minutes

Directions: You have fifty minutes to answer all three of the following questions. It is suggested that you spend approximately half your time on the first question and divide the remaining time equally between the next two questions. In answering the questions, you should emphasize the line of reasoning that generated your results; it is not enough to list the results of your analysis. Include correctly labeled diagrams, if useful or required, in explaining your answers. A correctly labeled diagram must have all axes and curves clearly labeled and must show directional changes. Use a pen with black or dark blue ink.

1. Assume that the United States economy is producing at less than full-employment output and trade is balanced.
(a) Using a correctly labeled aggregate supply and aggregate demand graph, show how current equilibrium output is related to long-run aggregate supply.
(b) Identify an appropriate open market operation the Federal Reserve could take to correct the effects of the recession.
(c) Using a correctly labeled graph of the money market, show how the open market operation you identified in (b) affects the nominal interest rate.
(d) Explain how the interest rate change you identified in (c) affects each of the following in the short run:
    (i)   Aggregate demand
    (ii)   Real output
    (iii) Price level
    (iv)   Capital inflow
(e) Using a correctly labeled graph of the foreign exchange market for the U.S. dollar, show how the interest rate change you identified in (c) affects the international value of the dollar.
(f) Explain how the change in the international value of the dollar you identified in (e) would affect each of the following in the short run:
    (i)   United States imports
    (ii)   United States exports

Consumer spending for food	$100 million
Consumer spending for other goods	$300 million
Firms' capital investment	$200 million
Firms' spending for intermediate goods for production	$ 75 million
Government spending for goods and services	$150 million
Government spending for transfer payments	$ 50 million
Spending for imports	$ 25 million
Sales of exports	$ 40 million

2. The table above indicates the spending for one year in the country of Macroland.
(a) Calculate this year's nominal gross domestic product for Macroland.
(b) Indicate which two items in the table would not be included in the calculation of Macroland's GDP and explain why they are not included.

(c)   If nominal GDP for Macroland this year increased 3%, did the real output
        of products necessarily increase by 3%? Explain.
(d)   If the GDP calculated by the expenditure method increased by 3%, would
        the GDP calculated by the income method necessarily increase by 3%?
        Explain.

3.   The effects of changes in the economy can be illustrated in the Phillips curve.
(a)   Using a correctly labeled short-run Phillips curve, indicate the following:
        (i)   Point A – A point indicating an economy producing at full-employment output.
        (ii)   Point B – A point indicating the change that occurs when this economy is
                suffering from a significant recession.
(b)   Now assume the cost of oil significantly increases. Using a correctly
        labeled aggregate supply and aggregate demand graph, show the effect of
        the increase in oil prices each of the following in the short run:
        (i)   Employment
        (ii)   Price level
(c)   Put a point C on the short-run Phillips curve graph you drew in (a) to
        illustrate the effect of the change in oil prices on the economy.

MACROECONOMICS PRACTICE TEST 1 – KEY
Section I

1.   (A)   Scarcity, a problem faced by all nations, cannot be entirely eliminated because resources are limited and cannot meet all of the desires of people.

2.   (B)   With the interest rate effect, when prices rise, consumers and firms must borrow in order to make the same purchases they did before the increase in price level. The increased demand for money pushes up interest rates.

3.   (D)   Banks add the expected inflation rate to the real interest rate to set the nominal interest rate, so the value of money repaid will equal the value loaned.

4.   (B)   Lower interest rates promote long-run economic growth because firms are more likely to invest in capital. While all of the options increase short-run aggregate demand, the other four options would increase interest rates because the government would have to borrow to finance deficit spending.

5.   (D)   Classical economists believed negative shocks would cause prices and wages to adjust until the economy returned to full-employment output.

6.   (B)   In order to produce 1 more computer, society has to reduce production by 2 books (falling from 19 to 17); the forgone production is the opportunity cost.

7.   (C)   Structural unemployment is the result of a mismatch between a worker's skills and the available jobs: we don't need workers with the skill set this worker has. Demand for labor due to recession is cyclical unemployment.

8.   (E)   M1 consists of currency and demand deposits. Until 2002, demand deposits comprised the majority of M1; now currency does.

9.   (D)   An inflationary gap indicates the economy is producing at greater than full-employment output. A reduction in government spending lowers aggregate demand to bring output back to full-employment output.

10.   (D)   Increases in the quantity and quality of resources and technology promote economic growth. An increased interest rate makes it more expensive for firms to borrow, so firms reduce capital investment, limiting growth.

11.   (B)   Kenya's opportunity cost for producing 1 ton of coffee is 3 tons of cotton. Uganda's opportunity cost for producing 1 ton of coffee is 2 tons of cotton. Uganda has the comparative advantage in producing coffee and can gain from trade because it can import cotton from Kenya at a lower cost than it can produce it domestically.

12.   (D)   Stagflation results from a decrease in the aggregate supply curve, increasing both the price level and unemployment while GDP falls.

13.   (A)   If firms believe that the percentage return on their investment in capital is greater than the interest rate, they will increase their demand for money in the loanable funds market, pushing up the interest rate.

14.   (D)   Expansionary fiscal policy, which consists of higher government spending and lower taxes, increases aggregate demand, which increases real GDP, employment, and the price level.

15.   (A)   Economic growth results from the increase in the quantity and quality of resources and technology. Investing in education improves the quality of labor resources. Increasing investment subsidies, reducing taxes on sales of equipment, and increasing research grants would also promote economic growth.

16.   (B)   Complements are products used together. If the cost of production for soup increases, the price of soup increases. At the higher price, quantity demanded for soup falls, resulting in a decrease in demand for crackers.

17.   (E)   Lower interest rates entice consumers and firms to increase borrowing to buy products, which increases aggregate demand.

Macroeconomics Practice Test 1 Key

18. (D) The reserve requirement is the percentage of the deposit the bank must hold in cash and cannot loan. If the bank must hold $100 of the $500 deposit, the reserve requirement is 20% ($100/$500 = 0.2).

19. (A) The federal government must borrow from the loanable funds market to finance budget deficits. The increase in demand for funds pushes up the interest rate. The higher interest rate crowds firms out of the market, as firms expect less profit from the investment, so capital spending falls.

20. (A) If prices of Canadian products fall, U.S. consumers will increase their imports of Canadian products. U.S. exports will fall as Canadians buy more of their own domestic products at the lower prices. Because imports increase and exports decrease, the U.S. would develop a trade deficit.

21. (D) Government spending increases the money entering the simple circular market flow. Consumer spending is already part of the flow, while imports, saving, and taxes are all leakages from the flow.

22. (A) Improvements in technology allow firms to increase production at a lower cost per unit, increasing the aggregate supply, real GDP, and employment, while prices fall.

23. (A) If the bank must keep 20% of the $10,000 in required reserves, it can loan out the other 80%, and 80% of $10,000 is $8,000.

24. (C) When government increases demand for loanable funds, interest rates rise. An increase in one year's deficit also adds to the national debt. However, an increase in the deficit indicates that spending rose or taxes fell, which would increase the aggregate demand, reducing unemployment.

25. (C) By shifting resources to the lowest-cost producers, more products can be produced and offered at lower prices.

26. (B) The consumer sector of the U.S. GDP accounts for approximately 70% of spending in the U.S. economy.

27. (E) An increase in government spending increases aggregate demand. Moving along the upward-sloping portion of the aggregate supply curve, the price level and output will increase, resulting in greater employment (less unemployment).

28. (D) If the bank has $100,000 in demand deposits with a reserve requirement of 10%, it must hold $10,000 in required reserves. The bank now holds $25,000 in total reserves, so it could increase its loans by $15,000.

29. (B) Automatic stabilizers (programs such as unemployment benefits and food stamps) automatically go into effect during economic downturns as people become eligible for the programs. They do not require Congress to create new economic policy and begin to work more quickly than new programs can be passed through discretionary fiscal policy.

30. (E) Trade barriers restrict imports from more efficient producers, reducing efficiency and world output and harming long-run economic growth.

31. (E) A purchase of stock is a purely financial transaction that does not affect the year's production in the economy, so it is not counted in GDP.

32. (E) If the MPC is 0.75, the MPS is 0.25 and the spending multiplier is 4 (1 / 0.25). An investment spending increase of $5 billion times the multiplier of 4 results in a $20 billion increase in real GDP.

33. (D) If a bank doesn't fully loan its excess reserves, those funds cannot be re-deposited and re-loaned to continue the multiple-deposit expansion of the money supply.

34. (C) A negative supply shock shifts the aggregate supply curve to the left, reducing output and employment and increasing prices.

35.   (C)   The "managed float" allows supply and demand to determine the value of currency. While other factors affect currency supply and demand, the supply and demand mechanism itself determines currency value.

36.   (A)   Because nominal GDP is calculated using the current value of money, increases in nominal GDP include changes in output as well as changes in prices. Real GDP removes the inflation distortion to measure only changes in output.

37.   (C)   When wealth increases, consumers are more willing to make larger purchases, increasing spending. Higher interest rates reduce willingness to borrow, while higher income taxes lower disposable income, and more saving and lower consumer confidence reduce consumer spending.

38.   (C)   When the supply decreases in the money market, the interest rate rises. Higher interest rates reduce aggregate demand, lowering real GDP, employment, and price levels.

39.   (C)   A lower supply or higher cost of resources raises the cost of production, so firms increase prices in the market for consumers.

40.   (E)   When Americans buy pesos in the foreign exchange market, demand for pesos increases and the peso appreciates in value. The supply of dollars increases in the foreign exchange market, causing the dollar to depreciate.

41.   (C)   The $100 increase in prices ($600 – $500) divided by the original price total equals a 20% increase in the CPI ($100 / $500).

42.   (E)   Classical economists believed that flexible wages and prices would allow the economy to self-correct after a shock, so no government intervention was necessary. The other four options are correct policy options according to Keynesian economists.

43.   (E)   A lower discount rate encourages banks to borrow from the Fed, which would increase the reserves available for banks to make loans to consumers, increasing the money supply. (A) and (C) would reduce the money supply, while (B) and (D) are fiscal policies, not monetary policies.

44.   (B)   Long-run economic growth is illustrated by an increase in the vertical long-run aggregate supply curve, shifting it to the right.

45.   (E)   If the Fed reduces the money supply, interest rates increase, attracting foreigners to invest in U.S. bonds. The increased demand for dollars increases the value of the dollar as capital flows into U.S. markets.

46.   (B)   The change in real income is the change in nominal income minus the change in the inflation rate. If wages increase 3% but prices rise 5%, real income decreases by 2% (3% – 5% = – 2%).

47.   (A)   Keynesians believe that output and employment are flexible, while prices are sticky downward. They argue that lower taxes and the Fed's purchase (not sale) of bonds can increase aggregate demand. Classical economists believed that the economy consistently produced at full employment and that prices and wages were flexible.

48.   (C)   When the Fed buys bonds, it makes money available in the money supply to increase aggregate demand for products. The increased money supply raises investment and imports and reduces the interest rate.

49.   (A)   The Phillips curve illustrates the tradeoff between unemployment and inflation. It is important to note on questions like these that while other relationships in answers may also be correct (for example, lower taxes causing an increase in the national debt), the question specifically asked about the Phillips curve, which does not address the national debt.

50.   (E)   When the dollar becomes more valuable, it takes fewer dollars to buy foreign currency. Imports look less expensive, so they increase. At the same time, it takes more

foreign currency to buy dollars, so our exports look more expensive and foreigners buy less. Because imports increase and exports decrease, a trade deficit develops.

51.   (D)   Borrowers gain from unanticipated inflation, because the dollars they repay are worth less than the dollars they initially borrowed.

52.   (B)   If firms spend more for capital investment than consumers are saving (not spending), the result is an increase in aggregate demand and real GDP.

53.   (C)   When taxes increase, firms and consumers have less available income for spending on plant and equipment. A decrease in government spending also directly reduces aggregate demand. When the Fed sells bonds, the money supply decreases, raising interest rates and again lowering aggregate demand.

54.   (B)   Only Keynesian theory advocates government policymaking to affect aggregate demand. The other theories argue government intervention is not necessary because either the economy will self-correct, government intervention will only further destabilize the economy, or policies will be anticipated and counteracted by consumers.

55.   (D)   The balance of payments requires the capital and current accounts to balance (add to zero), so if one is in surplus, the other must be in deficit.

56.   (A)   To be counted as unemployed, one must not have a paying job and have actively looked for work in the past four weeks. Anyone who chooses not to work is not considered unemployed.

57.   (D)   The spending multiplier is 1 / MPS. If the MPC is 0.8, the MPS is 0.2. Therefore, the spending multiplier is 5 (1 / 0.2). In order to increase spending by $10 billion in the economy, government only needs to increase its spending by $2 billion, because that spending times the multiplier is total spending ($2 billion x 5).

58.   (A)   An increase in the supply of money in the money market lowers the interest rate, encouraging firms to increase investment because it now costs less to borrow. Due to increased investment, real output increases.

59.   (C)   The monetarist equation of exchange (MV = PQ) holds that velocity and real output in the economy are stable, so therefore any increase in the money supply will only cause the price level to increase.

60.   (E)   An increase in government borrowing pushes up interest rates, which entice foreigners to buy U.S. dollars to increase U.S. investment, which increases the international value of the dollar.

1.

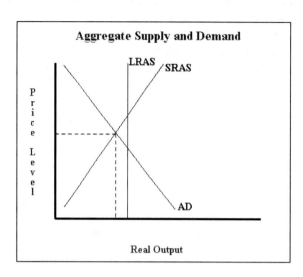

The Federal Reserve could buy bonds in the open market to increase the money supply, in order to increase aggregate demand.

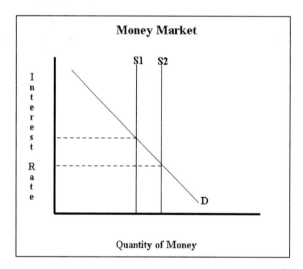

The Fed's purchase of bonds increases the money supply, which decreases the nominal interest rate. Aggregate demand increases because the lower interest rate increases investment by firms in plant and equipment. Real output and the price level increase because of the increase in aggregate demand. Capital inflow decreases because foreigners decrease investment in the United States when the interest rate falls.

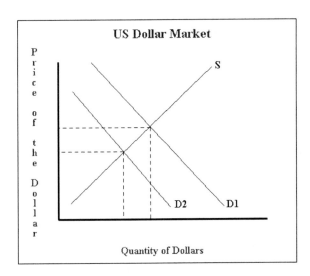

US Dollar Market

The decrease in demand for the dollar from foreign investors decreases the international value of the dollar. U.S. imports would decrease because, with a weak dollar, it takes more dollars to buy foreign currency, making imports look more expensive. U.S. exports would increase because it takes less foreign currency to buy the dollar, so U.S. exports look less expensive to foreigners.

2.   This year's GDP for Macroland is $765 million. Spending for intermediate goods would not be counted in GDP, because only final goods are included; the value of the intermediate goods is counted in the value of the final product. Government transfer payments are also not included in GDP because they are only transfers of money, not production. If nominal GDP increased by 3%, real output would not necessarily have increased by 3%, because some of the increase in nominal GDP could have been caused by inflation. If calculation by the expenditure method showed that GDP increased by 3%, calculation by the income method would also show an increase of 3% in GDP, because spending by one actor in the economy is income to another actor in the economy.

3.

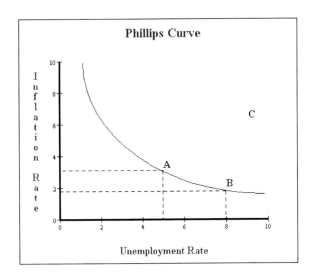

Phillips Curve

When the economy is suffering from a significant recession, the unemployment rate increases and the inflation rate decreases.

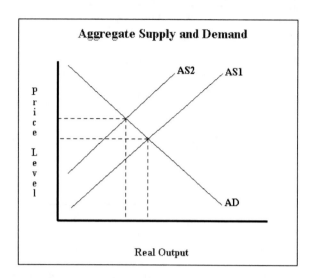

Aggregate Supply and Demand

When the cost of oil significantly increases, the cost of production goes up for firms, so aggregate supply decreases. Employment decreases and the price level goes up. This shifts the short-run Phillips curve to the right, showing higher unemployment and higher inflation.

Sample Essay Rubric

1. **15 points** (3 + 1 + 2 + 4 + 3 + 2)
(a)   3 points:

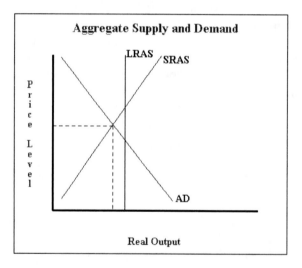

Aggregate Supply and Demand

- 1 point is earned for a correctly labeled AD–AS graph.
- 1 point is earned for a vertical long-run aggregate supply curve.
- 1 point is earned for setting equilibrium output left of long-run aggregate supply.

(b)   1 point:
- 1 point is earned for stating that the Fed should buy bonds.

(c)   2 points:

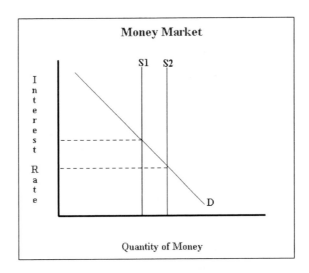

Money Market

- 1 point is earned for a correctly labeled money market graph.
- 1 point is earned for showing an increase in supply, decreasing the interest rate.

(d)   4 points:
- 1 point is earned for explaining that aggregate demand increases because the lower interest rate increases investment.
- 1 point is earned for stating that real output rises because aggregate demand rises.
- 1 point is earned for stating that price level rises because aggregate demand rises.
- 1 point is earned for stating that capital inflow decreases, as foreigners are less likely to invest at the lower interest rate.

(e)   3 points:

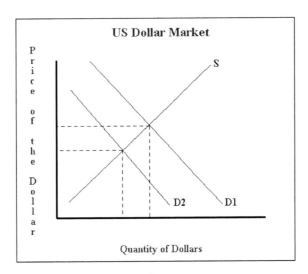

US Dollar Market

- 1 point is earned for a correctly labeled foreign exchange market graph for dollars.
- 1 point is earned for showing a decrease in demand for dollars.
- 1 point is earned for showing that the international value of the dollar decreases.

(f)   2 points:
- 1 point is earned for explaining that imports decrease because it costs more dollars to buy foreign currency, so imports look more expensive.
- 1 point is earned for explaining that exports increase because U.S. dollars now cost less for foreigners, making U.S. exports look less expensive.

2.   **9 points** (1 + 4 + 2 + 2)
(a)   1 point:
- 1 point is earned for stating that the GDP for this year is $765 million ($100 + $300 + $200 + $150 + [$40 − $25]).

(b)   4 points:
- 1 point is earned for stating that spending for intermediate goods is not included.
- 1 point is earned for explaining that the value of the final product (including the intermediate goods) is already counted in GDP.
- 1 point is earned for stating that government transfer payments are not included.
- 1 point is earned for explaining that the simple transfer of money does not create a product (or that it would be counted when it is spent by the recipient).

(c)   2 points:
- 1 point is earned for stating that real output did not necessarily increase by 3%.
- 1 point is earned for explaining that the rate of inflation can affect nominal GDP.

(d)   2 points:
- 1 point is earned for stating that GDP calculated by income must increase 3%.
- 1 point is earned for explaining that GDP calculated by both methods must be equal, because spending by one actor in the economy is income to another actor.

3.   **6 points** (2 + 3 + 1)
(a)   2 points:

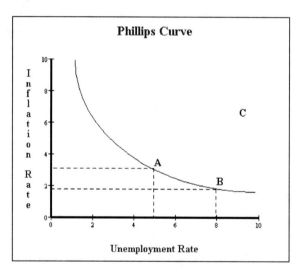

- 1 point is earned for a correctly labeled short-run Phillips curve.
- 1 point is earned for correctly placing points A and B on the curve, with point B lower and to the right of point A, indicating higher unemployment and lower inflation rate.

(b)   3 points:

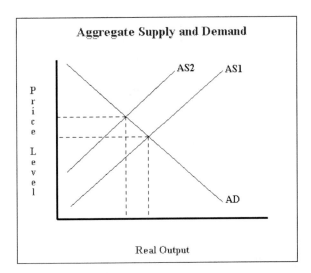

Aggregate Supply and Demand

Price Level

Real Output

- • 1 point is earned for a correctly labeled aggregate supply and aggregate demand graph, with aggregate supply shifted to the left.
- • 1 point is earned for stating that employment decreased.
- • 1 point is earned for stating that the price level increased.

(c)   1 point:
- • 1 point is earned for placing point C on the Phillips curve higher and to the right of point B to illustrate higher inflation and unemployment.

Directions: Each of the questions or incomplete statements below is followed by five responses or completions. Select the best one in each case.

1. Borrowers benefit from unanticipated inflation because
   (A)   it is easier to obtain loans during a period of inflation.
   (B)   increased investment from loans will reduce the inflation rate.
   (C)   increased demand for loans reduces the nominal interest rate.
   (D)   the money repaid is worth less than the money that was borrowed.
   (E)   the Federal Reserve increases the money supply in response to inflation.

2. Classical economists believed that if total spending in the economy was less than full-employment output, the market economy would self-correct because
   (A)   wages and prices are flexible.
   (B)   output and unemployment are flexible.
   (C)   consumers are less likely to buy products during recessions.
   (D)   exports would increase.
   (E)   production possibilities would increase.

3. The fundamental problem of economics is
   (A)   that firms maximize profits by setting prices too high for most consumers.
   (B)   that society's limited resources cannot meet its unlimited wants.
   (C)   that consumers spend their incomes in inefficient ways.
   (D)   that international trade can result in the closing of inefficient firms.
   (E)   the role of government in private sector decision making.

4. The interest rate banks charge each other for overnight loans to meet their reserve requirement is called the
   (A)   discount rate.
   (B)   usury rate.
   (C)   prime rate.
   (D)   mortgage rate.
   (E)   federal funds rate.

5. The federal government finances deficits by
   (A)   raising taxes.
   (B)   lowering spending.
   (C)   selling bonds.
   (D)   buying bonds.
   (E)   lowering the reserve requirement.

6. Proponents of the rational expectations theory argue that the use of fiscal policy to resolve a recession will
   (A)   increase the unemployment rate.
   (B)   increase real output.
   (C)   reduce interest rates.

(D)   be ineffective.

(E)   cause long-run aggregate supply to increase.

7.   Economic growth is illustrated on the production possibilities curve by

(A)   moving from a point under the curve to a point on the curve.

(B)   moving from a point outside of the curve to a point on the curve.

(C)   moving from a point toward the bottom of the curve to a point higher up on the curve.

(D)   an outward shift of the curve.

(E)   an inward shift of the curve.

8.   The unemployment rate underestimates the problem of unemployment because the official unemployment statistic does not count

(A)   people who choose not to work.

(B)   people in prisons, hospitals, and other institutions.

(C)   people who have given up looking for jobs.

(D)   people under the age of sixteen.

(E)   people who have worked and are now retired.

9.   According to Keynesian theory, increasing government spending causes a greater change in GDP than lowering taxes, because

(A)   the government prefers to spend rather than lower taxes.

(B)   consumers support increased spending more than tax cuts.

(C)   consumers save part of tax cuts rather than spending them all.

(D)   the tax multiplier is greater than the spending multiplier.

(E)   government spending is larger portion of GDP than consumer spending.

10.   When the Federal Reserve enacts policy to counteract a recessionary gap, how will that policy affect the money supply and interest rate?

	Money Supply	Interest Rate
(A)	Increase	Increase
(B)	Increase	No change
(C)	Decrease	Decrease
(D)	Decrease	No change
(E)	Increase	Decrease

11.   An increase in deficit spending can cause crowding out of

(A)   imports.

(B)   savings.

(C)   investment.

(D)   incomes.

(E)   exports.

12.   Each of the following factors supports economic growth EXCEPT

(A)   investment in human capital.

(B)   investment in physical capital.

(C)   research and development.

(D)   technological progress.

(E)   a tight money policy.

13. If Malaysia holds a comparative advantage in the production of rubber and Indonesia holds a comparative advantage in the production of wood,
    (A) Malaysia will earn more profit from the sale of rubber than Indonesia will earn from wood.
    (B) Malaysia's government should tax domestic sales of rubber.
    (C) Indonesia can gain by importing rubber and exporting wood.
    (D) Malaysia cannot gain from trade because rubber is more valuable than wood.
    (E) Indonesia can only gain from trade if the price of wood is higher than rubber.

14. Workers laid off during a recession are experiencing
    (A) cyclical unemployment.
    (B) seasonal unemployment.
    (C) frictional unemployment.
    (D) structural unemployment.
    (E) underemployment.

15. The government spending multiplier is equal to the
    (A) tax multiplier.
    (B) consumer spending multiplier.
    (C) marginal propensity to consume.
    (D) marginal propensity to save.
    (E) recessionary gap.

16. The Federal Reserve most frequently changes the money supply through
    (A) the discount rate.
    (B) taxes.
    (C) the reserve requirement.
    (D) the purchase and sale of government securities.
    (E) government spending.

17. An appropriate fiscal policy to counteract a recessionary gap is to
    (A) increase taxes.
    (B) increase the reserve requirement.
    (C) reduce the discount rate.
    (D) buy bonds.
    (E) increase government spending.

18. If Econland's real GDP last year was $8 billion and this year's real GDP is $10 billion, what was the rate of Econland's economic growth this year?
    (A) 2%
    (B) 18%
    (C) 20%
    (D) 25%
    (E) 80%

19. If household incomes rise and cars are normal goods, what would be expected to occur in the market for cars?
    (A) The price and quantity of cars will fall.
    (B) The price and quantity of cars will rise.
    (C) The price of cars will rise, but the quantity produced will fall.

(D)   The price of cars will fall, but the quantity produced will rise.
(E)   The price of cars will rise, but the quantity produced will not change.

20.   The natural rate of unemployment (or full-employment) is achieved when
        (A)   the unemployment rate falls to zero.
        (B)   there is no frictional unemployment.
        (C)   only structural unemployment exists.
        (D)   employers cannot find suitable employees.
        (E)   cyclical unemployment is eliminated.

21.   If the economy experiences a $1,000 recessionary gap and the marginal propensity to consume is 0.75, by how much should government increase spending to restore the economy to full-employment output?
        (A) $200
        (B) $250
        (C) $750
        (D) $1,000
        (E) $400

22.   All of the following policies could resolve inflation EXCEPT
        (A)   increasing the money supply.
        (B)   increasing taxes.
        (C)   increasing the reserve requirement.
        (D)   increasing the discount rate.
        (E)   decreasing government spending.

23.   Short-run aggregate supply would increase as a result of
        (A)   a reduction in the cost of productive resources.
        (B)   a reduction in the number of available workers.
        (C)   an increase in the marginal tax rate.
        (D)   an increase in wages.
        (E)   a reduction in the money supply.

24.   International trade generally results in
                I.   lower production and employment for less efficient firms.
                II. a more efficient allocation of resources.
                III. an increase in the standard of living among nations that trade.
                IV. higher prices and employment for importing countries.
        (A)   I only
        (B)   II and III only
        (C)   I and IV only
        (D)   I, II, and III only
        (E)   I, II, III, and IV

25.   Gross domestic product is the
        (A)   sum of consumer, government, and business spending in one year.
        (B)   total dollar value of all products produced in a country in one year.
        (C)   an accounting of all of the money that transfers between countries.
        (D)   value of all products produced by a nation's firms and citizens in one year.
        (E)   quantity of products produced by a nation in one year.

26. Each of the following factors would increase aggregate demand EXCEPT
    (A)   an increase in consumer wealth.
    (B)   an increase in government spending.
    (C)   an increase in personal income taxes.
    (D)   an increase in exports.
    (E)   an increase in investment by firms.

27. If the nominal interest rate on loans in the United States is 7% and the inflation rate is 4%, what is the real interest rate?
    (A)   − 3%
    (B)   3%
    (C)   4%
    (D)   7%
    (E)   11%

28. Demand-pull inflation can be caused by
    I.   an increase in the money supply.
    II. an increase in consumer incomes.
    III. a reduction in the cost of production.
    (A)   I only.
    (B)   III only.
    (C)   I and II only.
    (D)   II and III only.
    (E)   I, II, and III.

29. Which of the following policy combinations would be consistent in reducing a recessionary gap?

	Taxes	Discount Rate	Open Market Operations
(A)	Increase	Increase	Fed buys bonds
(B)	Decrease	Increase	Fed buys bonds
(C)	Increase	Decrease	Fed sells bonds
(D)	Decrease	Decrease	Fed buys bonds
(E)	Increase	Increase	Fed sells bonds

30. If the United States placed an import quota on cars from Japan,
    (A)   the demand for Japanese yen would increase.
    (B)   the quantity of cars imported from Japan would increase.
    (C)   U.S. demand for U.S.-produced cars would increase in the short run.
    (D)   the value of the Japanese yen would appreciate.
    (E)   Japanese demand for U.S.-produced cars would increase.

31. Which of these statements correctly describes the circular market flow?
    I.   Firms sell final products in the resource market.
    II. Households sell labor services in the resource market.
    III. Households buy final products from firms in the product market.
    IV. Firms buy the factors of production in the resource market.
    (A)   II only
    (B)   I and IV only
    (C)   II and III only
    (D)   II, III, and IV only
    (E)   I, II, III, and IV

32.   Stagflation would most likely result from
        (A)   a decrease in workers' wages.
        (B)   an increase in the money supply.
        (C)   a reduction in the reserve requirement.
        (D)   an increase in the cost of energy.
        (E)   a decrease in government spending.

33.   If households choose to increase their savings in banks, rather than holding their savings in
        cash, the effect in the loanable funds market is that
        (A)   fewer funds will be available for firms to borrow.
        (B)   demand for loanable funds will increase.
        (C)   the supply of loanable funds will decrease.
        (D)   the government will restrict the number of available loans.
        (E)   interest rates will decrease.

34.   If the Federal Reserve increases the money supply, how will aggregate demand, real output,
        and the price level be affected?

	Aggregate Demand	Real Output	Price Level
(A)	Increase	Increase	Increase
(B)	Decrease	Decrease	No change
(C)	Increase	Decrease	Decrease
(D)	Decrease	Increase	No change
(E)	Increase	Decrease	Increase

35.   The long-run Phillips curve illustrates that, while short-run changes in aggregate
        supply and aggregate demand may affect output, the price level, and employment,
        the natural rate of
        (A)   inflation is relatively stable.
        (B)   unemployment is relatively stable.
        (C)   real output is very unstable.
        (D)   economic growth is relatively stable.
        (E)   real wage increase is very unstable.

36.   An increase in U.S. demand for Russian products would cause
        (A)   the value of the Russian ruble to appreciate.
        (B)   the value of the U.S. dollar to appreciate.
        (C)   the demand for rubles in the foreign exchange market to decrease.
        (D)   the supply of U.S. dollars in the foreign exchange market to decrease.
        (E)   the price of Russian products to decrease.

37.   Which of the following actions would be included in the calculation of GDP?
        (A)   A retired steelworker receiving a Social Security check
        (B)   A teenager buying illegal drugs
        (C)   A father preparing his family's dinner at home
        (D)   A bakery buying flour from a wheat mill to make bread
        (E)   A condominium complex building four new condos

38. A short-run increase in aggregate supply would result in higher
    (A)   real GDP.
    (B)   unemployment.
    (C)   price levels.
    (D)   tax revenues.
    (E)   imports.

39. Open market operations are
    (A)   corporate sales of stock in the stock market.
    (B)   purchases and sales of government securities by the Federal Reserve.
    (C)   the voluntary exchange of goods in the product market.
    (D)   markets which operate without government regulation.
    (E)   sales of imports and exports in markets free of trade barriers.

40. Assume the federal government has a balanced budget when an inflationary gap occurs.
    Which combination of policy actions will be effective in reducing short-run aggregate demand
    while still promoting long-run economic growth?
    (A)   The Fed selling bonds and increasing the discount rate
    (B)   Congress increasing taxes and reducing government spending
    (C)   The Fed increasing the reserve requirement and Congress raising taxes
    (D)   The Fed selling bonds and Congress reducing government spending
    (E)   The Fed increasing the federal funds rate and Congress raising taxes

41. Long-run economic growth results from increases in
                I.   the quantity of land, labor, and capital resources.
                II. interest rates.
                III. technology.
                IV. investment in human capital.
    (A)   I only
    (B)   II and III only
    (C)   I, II, and III only
    (D)   I, III, and IV only
    (E)   I, II, III, and IV

42. U.S. demand for euros would be most likely to increase if
    (A)   interest rates in the U.S. are higher than Italian interest rates.
    (B)   the inflation rate in the U.S. is higher than the Italian inflation rate.
    (C)   speculators in the foreign exchange market expect the euro value to fall.
    (D)   Italian incomes are rising more quickly than U.S. incomes.
    (E)   U.S. demand for Italian clothing significantly decreases.

43. If nominal GDP increased by 5% and prices increased by 3% this year,
    (A)   real GDP increased by 8%.
    (B)   real GDP increased by 2%.
    (C)   real GDP decreased by 2%.
    (D)   real GDP increased by 1.67%.
    (E)   real GDP increased by 0.6%.

44. If the aggregate supply curve is horizontal and investment decreases, how will the price level, output, and employment be affected?

	Price Level	Output	Employment
(A)	Increase	Increase	Increase
(B)	Decrease	Decrease	Decrease
(C)	No change	Decrease	Decrease
(D)	Decrease	No change	No change
(E)	Increase	Decrease	Decrease

45. Assume the reserve requirement is 10% and a bank initially has no excess reserves. If a customer deposits $1,000, how much of that deposit can be loaned?
    (A) $900
    (B) $100
    (C) $1,100
    (D) $10,000
    (E) $10,100

46. If the economy is operating in the upward-sloping range of the aggregate supply curve, a decrease in personal taxes will cause a decrease in
    (A) the real GDP.
    (B) the price level.
    (C) the national debt.
    (D) aggregate demand.
    (E) unemployment.

47. Keynesian economists argue that the economy will not automatically self-adjust to changes in aggregate demand because of
    (A) crowding out.
    (B) fiscal policy.
    (C) sticky prices and wages.
    (D) inflexible output.
    (E) budget deficits.

48. An increase in the federal budget deficit is likely to affect interest rates, capital inflows, and the value of the dollar in which of the following ways?

	Interest Rate	Capital Inflow	Value of the Dollar
(A)	Decrease	Decrease	Increase
(B)	Increase	Increase	Decrease
(C)	Decrease	Decrease	Decrease
(D)	Decrease	Increase	Increase
(E)	Increase	Increase	Increase

49. The primary measure of inflation in the United States economy is the
    (A) real GDP.
    (B) disposable Income.
    (C) gross domestic product.
    (D) consumer price index.
    (E) real income.

50.   When the marginal propensity to save increases,
       (A)   the spending multiplier decreases.
       (B)   federal tax revenues increase.
       (C)   required reserves increase.
       (D)   the inflation rate increases.
       (E)   the unemployment rate decreases.

51.   If the reserve requirement is 25% and a consumer deposits $400 at the bank, how will the
       bank's liabilities and excess reserves change?

	Liabilities	Excess Reserves
(A)	Increase $400	Increase $400
(B)	Increase $300	Increase $1,200
(C)	Increase $1,600	Increase $1,600
(D)	Increase $400	Increase $300
(E)	Increase $300	Increase $300

52.   Which of the following policies is most likely to create an inflationary gap?
       (A)   Tax rates are significantly reduced.
       (B)   Government spending is significantly reduced.
       (C)   The Federal Reserve sells bonds on the open market.
       (D)   Firms reduce investment.
       (E)   Consumer confidence in economic growth is low.

53.   Monetarists oppose the use of monetary policy because they argue it creates
       (A)   greater economic instability and inflation.
       (B)   higher interest rates and greater investment.
       (C)   higher unemployment and reduced output.
       (D)   increased trade deficits.
       (E)   greater federal budget deficits.

54.   An increase in the reserve requirement
               I.   increases the interest rate.
               II.   increases the money supply.
               III. results in increased foreign investment in U.S. bonds.
       (A)   I only
       (B)   II only
       (C)   I and III only
       (D)   II and III only
       (E)   I, II, and III

55.   Rafi's disposable income is $10,000 and his average propensity to consume is 0.9. If his
       disposable income increases by $500 and his marginal propensity to consume is 0.6, how
       much will Rafi save in total?
       (A) $10,500
       (B) $9,600
       (C) $9,300
       (D) $1,400
       (E) $1,200

56.   If the value of the U.S. dollar appreciates in foreign exchange markets,
       (A)   U.S. demand for imports decreases.
       (B)   foreign investment in U.S. bonds increases.
       (C)   U.S. exports to other countries decrease.
       (D)   foreign demand for U.S. products increases.
       (E)   U.S. investment in foreign markets decreases.

57.   Assume a bank's excess reserves are fully loaned and a customer deposits new reserves of
       $10,000 from outside the banking system. If the reserve requirement is 20%, what is the
       maximum amount by which the money supply could increase if that deposit is fully loaned
       throughout the banking system?
       (A) $2,000
       (B) $20,000
       (C) $50,000
       (D) $5,000
       (E) $8,000

58.   A federal budget deficit is
       (A)   government spending greater than revenues in one year.
       (B)   financed by reducing taxes.
       (C)   government revenues greater than spending in one year.
       (D)   increased by the use of contractionary fiscal policy.
       (E)   the total amount the government owes bondholders.

59.   Monetarists are critical of the use of fiscal policy, claiming that expansionary fiscal policy
       (A)   decreases the inflation rate.
       (B)   increases the unemployment rate.
       (C)   creates budget surpluses.
       (D)   reduces the interest rate.
       (E)   crowds out private investment.

60.   The balance of payments requires a nation with a current account deficit to have
       (A)   a capital account surplus.
       (B)   a trade surplus.
       (C)   an appreciating currency.
       (D)   a budget surplus.
       (E)   a recessionary gap.

MACROECONOMICS PRACTICE TEST 2
Section II
Planning Time: 10 minutes
Writing Time: 50 minutes

Directions: You have fifty minutes to answer all three of the following questions. <u>It is suggested that you spend approximately half your time on the first question and divide the remaining time equally between the next two questions.</u> In answering the questions, you should emphasize the line of reasoning that generated your results; it is not enough to list the results of your analysis. Include correctly labeled diagrams, if useful or required, in explaining your answers. A correctly labeled diagram must have all axes and curves clearly labeled and must show directional changes. <u>Use a pen with black or dark blue ink</u>.

1.   Assume that a nation's economy is producing at full-employment output on the upward-sloping section of the short-run aggregate supply curve and that the nation has a balanced budget.

(a)   Now assume a crisis in consumer confidence causes consumers to significantly reduce spending. Using a correctly labeled aggregate supply and aggregate demand graph, show and explain the short-run effect of this reduced consumer spending on each of the following:
- (i)   Real output
- (ii)   Price level
- (iii)   Employment

(b)   Identify an appropriate fiscal policy the government could take to address the reduction in consumer spending.

(c)   Using a correctly labeled graph of the loanable funds market, show the effect of the fiscal policy you identified in (b) on the interest rate.

(d)   Explain the effect of the interest rate change you identified in (c) on each of the following:
- (i)   Firms' investment in plant and equipment
- (ii)   Short-run aggregate demand
- (iii)   Long-run economic growth

(e)   Using a correctly labeled graph of the short-run Phillips curve, label two points.
- (i)   Point A shows a point on the curve before the fiscal policy in (b) is enacted.
- (ii)   Point B shows a point on the curve after the fiscal policy in (b) has fully taken effect.

2.   The money supply plays an important role in economic performance.

(a)   If Brett deposits $500 cash in his checking account at the bank, what is the effect of that action on the money supply? Explain.

(b)   If the reserve requirement is 25%, calculate each of the following:
- (ii)   The maximum amount of Brett's deposit the bank is allowed to loan out to other customers
- (iii)   The maximum amount of increase in the money supply as a result of the deposit in (a) if it is fully loaned

(c)   Identify two factors that could cause the money supply to increase by less than the maximum amount you identified in (b)(ii) and explain why they limit the growth of the money supply.

(d)   Explain how an increase in the money supply affects each of the following in the short run:
- (i)   Aggregate demand
- (ii)   Real output and price level

3.   Assume that using equal amounts of resources, the United States can produce 100 tons of coffee or 300 tons of cotton, while Brazil can produce 50 tons of coffee or 200 tons of cotton.

(a)   Identify which country has the comparative advantage in producing coffee. Explain how you determined your answer.

(b)   Assume the two countries specialize and trade, agreeing on the price of 3.5 tons of cotton for 1 ton of coffee.

   (i)   Which country will import coffee? Explain.
   (ii)   How do consumers in the importing country gain from trade?
   (iii) How is world output affected by specialization and trade?

(c)   Now assume that incomes rise in Brazil and Brazilians increase their imports of products from the United States.

   (i)   Using a correctly illustrated foreign exchange market for the U.S. dollar, show the effect of an increase in Brazilian purchases from the United States.
   (ii)   Explain the effect of the change in (c)(i) on the international value of the dollar.

MACROECONOMICS PRACTICE TEST 2 – KEY
Section I

1.   (D)   Because the purchasing power of the dollar decreases with inflation, borrowers repay loans with dollars that are worth less than they were when the money was originally borrowed.

2.   (A)   Classical economists believed that the economy would self-correct from temporary shocks because wages and prices would fall to reduce the cost of production.

3.   (B)   The fundamental problem of economics is scarcity, which requires actors in the economy to make choices.

4.   (E)   The discount rate is what the Fed charges commercial banks for loans. The usury rate is the highest interest rate allowed by law, while the prime rate is the lowest interest rate that banks charge their best customers. The mortgage rate is the interest rate banks charge for home mortgages.

5.   (C)   The federal government must sell government bonds (borrow money) to finance deficit spending.

6.   (D)   Proponents of the rational expectations theory argue that people will anticipate the policies government will enact to counteract a recession and will act to protect themselves in ways that render the policy ineffective.

7.   (D)   Moving from one point to another point on the production possibilities curve does not indicate any change in economic growth.

8.   (C)   The official unemployment statistic includes people who are not working but are actively looking for work. Because discouraged workers are not actively looking for work, they are not counted as unemployed, even though they want jobs.

9.   (C)   When the government spends money in the economy, the entire amount of that spending goes directly into demand for products. But when the government cuts taxes, consumers tend to save part of the money, so a tax cut does not have the same impact that government spending does.

10.   (E)   To counteract a recessionary gap, the Fed would increase the money supply, shifting the money supply to the right and lowering interest rates.

11.   (C)   When the government increases demand for money in the loanable funds market to finance deficits, interest rates increase, crowding firms out of the market which reduces investment in plant and equipment.

12.   (E)   Increases in the amount and quality of resources and technology promote economic growth. But a tight money policy increases interest rates, so firms are less likely to invest in capital, which can limit economic growth.

13.   (C)   If Indonesia holds a comparative advantage in the production of wood rather than rubber, Indonesia can import rubber for a lower cost than it can produce it domestically; therefore, it can gain from trade with Malaysia, which is a more efficient producer of rubber.

14.   (A)   When the economy is in the contraction phase of the business cycle, real GDP falls and, as output falls, employment falls.

15.   (B)   The government spending multiplier equals the consumer spending multiplier because spending from either source increases GDP by the same amount. The tax multiplier is lower than the government spending multiplier because consumers save part of any tax cut and draw part of any tax increase from savings.

16.   (D)   The Fed most frequently uses open market operations to change the money supply because it can be used to make small changes, "fine tuning" the money supply to adjust to economic changes.

Macroeconomics Practice Test 2 Key

17. (E) An increase in government spending increases aggregate demand to counteract a recessionary gap. While a reduction in the discount rate and the Fed buying bonds would be appropriate policies for counteracting a recession, they are monetary policies, not fiscal policies.

18. (D) The rate of economic growth is this year's real GDP minus last year's divided by last year's real GDP ($2 billion / $8 billion = 0.25, or 25%).

19. (B) An increase in incomes causes demand to increase, raising both price and quantity produced.

20. (E) When cyclical unemployment is zero, the economy is operating at full-employment output. It is impossible to reduce the entire unemployment rate to zero because frictional unemployment always exists.

21. (B) If MPC is 0.75, the MPS is 0.25. The multiplier is 1 / MPS (1 / 0.25 = 4). In order to restore the economy to full-employment output, the government must increase its spending by $250 which, when multiplied by the multiplier of 4, fills the $1,000 recessionary gap.

22. (A) Increasing the money supply lowers the purchasing power of the dollar, increasing the negative effects of inflation. The other four options reduce aggregate demand to reduce inflationary pressure.

23. (A) When the cost of production decreases, supply increases, increasing real GDP and lowering the price level.

24. (D) International trade relies on comparative advantage, with more efficient firms increasing production and less efficient firms reducing production. As a result, resources are allocated more efficiently and prices fall, so consumer standards of living increase.

25. (B) (A) did not include net exports, (C) is the balance of payments, and (D) is gross national product.

26. (C) An increase in personal income taxes would reduce disposable income for consumers, reducing their aggregate demand.

27. (B) Banks add the expected inflation rate to the real interest rate to determine the nominal interest rate. In this case 7% – 4% = 3% real interest rate.

28. (C) An increase in the money supply and higher incomes can both induce more consumer spending, leading to demand-pull inflation. A reduction in the cost of production would increase aggregate supply, which would reduce prices.

29. (D) Lower taxes increase disposable income, promoting an increase in aggregate demand. A decrease in the discount rate encourages banks to borrow from the Fed and, combined with the Fed buying bonds, the money supply increases, also promoting an increase in aggregate demand.

30. (C) If the United States limited imports of Japanese cars, demand for U.S. cars as a substitute would increase in the short run. Consumers would buy fewer Japanese cars, so demand for the yen would decrease, causing the yen to depreciate. Because Japanese incomes would fall due to fewer exports, their ability to demand U.S.-produced cars would decrease.

31. (D) Firms sell their final products to households in the product market.

32. (D) Stagflation is caused by a decrease in aggregate supply, which can be caused by an increase in the cost of production.

33. (E) In the loanable funds market, the supply of funds is provided by the savings of consumers. When saving increases, the supply of funds increases, lowering the interest rate.

34. (A) When the Fed increases the money supply, interest rates fall, promoting interest-sensitive consumer spending and the investment spending of firms. Aggregate demand increases, which causes real output and the price level to increase.

35. (B) The long-run Phillips curve is vertical at the natural unemployment rate. Changes in the business cycle affect short-run unemployment rates, but the natural unemployment rate tends to remain stable.

36. (A) When U.S. demand for Russian imports increases, buyers increase the demand for rubles to pay for the goods, increasing the value of the ruble in the foreign exchange market.

37. (E) Government transfer payments, the underground economy, home production, and intermediate goods are not counted in calculating GDP.

38. (A) An increase in the short-run aggregate supply curve increases real GDP and employment while reducing the price level.

39. (B) The Fed's actions in buying and selling bonds in the open market are the primary ways the Fed changes the money supply.

40. (B) All of the policy actions will help to reduce the inflationary gap. But long-run economic growth is promoted by a lower interest rate that encourages investment. With a budget surplus, Congress does not need to borrow from the loanable funds market, holding interest rates down. The Fed options to reduce the money supply all increase interest rates.

41. (D) Increases in the quantity and quality of resources and technology promote long-run economic growth. But higher interest rates discourage firms from investing in capital, limiting long-run economic growth.

42. (B) If U.S. inflation rates are higher than Italian inflation rates, Italian imports will look relatively less expensive to U.S. consumers, who will buy more of them as substitutes for domestically-produced goods. Demand for euros increases in order to buy the imports.

43. (B) The increase in nominal GDP is the increase in real GDP plus the increase in prices, in this case, 5% = 3% + 2%.

44. (C) If the aggregate supply curve is horizontal, a decrease in aggregate demand has no effect on the price level but output and employment fall.

45. (A) The bank must hold $100 of the deposit in required reserves, so $900 of the deposit can be loaned.

46. (E) Lower taxes increase disposable income, increasing aggregate demand, which increases the real GDP, employment, and price level.

47. (C) Keynesian economists argue that because wages and prices are sticky downward, the economy will not automatically adjust to economic shocks.

48. (E) Government borrowing to finance deficits pushes up interest rates in the loanable funds market. The higher interest rates attract foreign investment, so capital inflow increases. Because foreigners must buy dollars in the foreign exchange market in order to buy the bonds, the dollar appreciates in value.

49. (D) The consumer price index measures the prices of thousands of items purchased by the typical urban consumer.

50. (A) The spending multiplier formula is 1 / MPS. So when the percentage of income saved increases, the percentage of income spent decreases, and the multiplier becomes smaller.

51. (D) The bank's liabilities increase by the amount of the deposit, because the deposit represents money the bank owes its depositors. If the reserve requirement is 25%, the bank must hold $100 of the $400 deposit in cash, and the remaining $300 is excess reserves the bank can loan.

52. (A) A significant reduction in tax rates increases disposable income so that aggregate demand increases and can create an inflationary gap. The other options all reduce aggregate demand.

53. (A) Monetarists use the equation of exchange (or quantity theory of money) to explain that increases in the money supply only increase inflation. They argue that because of lags in creating and implementing fiscal and monetary policy, such policies only make the economy more unstable.

54. (C) An increase in the reserve requirement reduces the money supply, increasing the interest rate and attracting foreign investment in U.S. bonds.

55. (E) Rafi saves $1,000 of his original income ($10,000 x 0.1) and $200 of his additional income ($500 x 0.4), so he saves $1,200 altogether.

56. (C) When the international value of the dollar appreciates, it takes more foreign currency for foreigners to buy U.S. dollars. Therefore, U.S. products look more expensive to them, and the demand for U.S. exports decreases.

57. (C) The money multiplier is 1 / Reserve Requirement, or 1 / 0.2 = 5. With a deposit of $10,000, the bank's 20% reserve requirement allows it to loan $8,000. The initial loan times the multiplier is $8,000 x 5, or $40,000. So the initial deposit will cause a maximum $50,000 increase in the money supply – $10,000 from the original deposit (because it came from outside the banking system) and $40,000 from the multiple-deposit expansion in the banking system.

58. (A) The deficit is financed by selling bonds, and contractionary fiscal policy would reduce deficits. (C) is a budget surplus, and (E) is the national debt.

59. (E) Monetarists criticize the use of expansionary fiscal policy, because when Congress increases spending and reduces taxes, the resulting deficit forces government to increase borrowing to finance the deficit. The increasing interest rate makes it more expensive for firms to borrow to purchase capital, so they are crowded out of the market.

60. (A) The balance of payments requires that the capital and current accounts add up to zero. So if the current account has a deficit, the capital account must have a surplus.

MACROECONOMICS PRACTICE TEST 2 – KEY
Section II – Sample Essays

1.

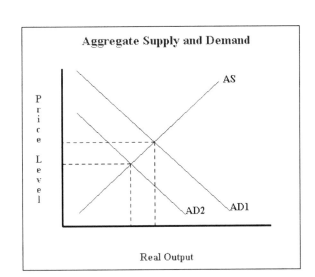

When consumer confidence falls, aggregate demand decreases, lowering real output and the price level. Because fewer products are produced, employment decreases. In order to increase aggregate demand again, the government could increase its spending.

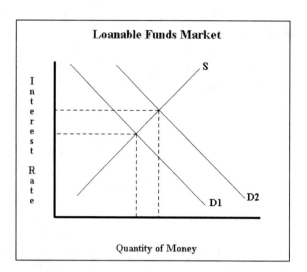

Loanable Funds Market

The increased government spending causes a deficit, requiring government to demand more money in the loanable funds market. As a result, the interest rate increases. Because the interest rate increased, firms are less willing to borrow, so they are crowded out of the market and their investment in plant and equipment decreases. Short-run aggregate demand falls because of the decrease in investment. Long-run economic growth is also limited, because firms are not investing in plant and equipment for growth.

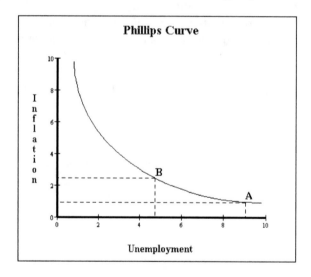

Phillips Curve

Before the fiscal policy is put in place, unemployment is high and inflation is low. After government spending causes the aggregate demand to increase, the unemployment rate goes down and prices go up.

2.   Brett's deposit of cash into his checking account at the bank does not change the money supply. Currency and checking accounts are both counted as part of the M1 money supply, so while the money changed form from currency to demand deposits, the money supply did not change. If the reserve requirement is 25%, the bank could loan out $375 of Brett's deposit. The maximum amount by which the money supply could increase as a result of the multiple deposit expansion is $1,500, because the initial loan ($375) times the multiplier (1 / .25 = 4) is $1,500.

The money supply may not grow by the full $1,500, though. If banks decide to keep their excess reserves and not loan them out, or if consumers decide not to re-deposit their money back into the bank, the money will not be fully re-loaned, and the money supply will not grow by as much as it could. An increase in the money supply lowers interest rates, so firms are more willing to borrow for investment spending and consumers are willing to borrow for interest-sensitive spending for items like houses and cars. So, aggregate demand increases, which increases real output and the price level.

3.   The United States has the comparative advantage in producing coffee, because it has the lower opportunity cost for production. The U.S. has to give up producing 3 tons of cotton for every ton of coffee it produces, while Brazil has to give up 4 tons of cotton for every ton of coffee it produces. If the countries agree to trade at a price of 3.5 tons of cotton for each ton of coffee, Brazil will import coffee because the U.S. can produce it at a lower cost than Brazil can. Consumers in Brazil gain from the trade because they can buy the imported American coffee at a lower price than they can buy their domestically-produced coffee. World output increases as a result of specialization and trade, because the more efficient producers are producing each product.

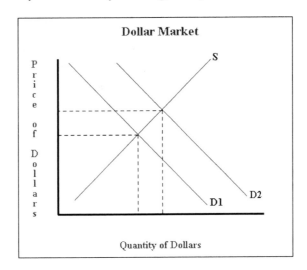

If Brazilian incomes increase and consumers buy more imports from the United States, the demand for the U.S. dollar increases, which increases the international value of the dollar (it appreciates).

Sample Essay Rubric

1.   **14 points** (5 + 1 + 3 + 3 + 2)
(a)   5 points:

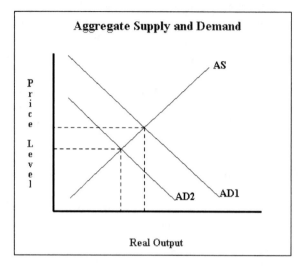

- 1 point is earned for a correctly labeled aggregate supply and aggregate demand graph.
- 1 point is earned for showing a decrease in aggregate demand.
- 1 point is earned for stating that real output decreases.
- 1 point is earned for stating that the price level decreases.
- 1 point is earned for stating that employment decreases.

(b)   1 point:
- 1 point is earned for stating an appropriate fiscal policy: either an increase in government spending or a decrease in taxes.

(c)   3 points:

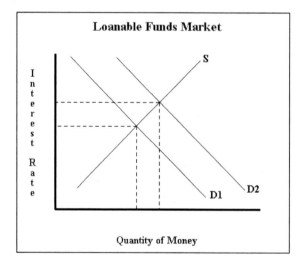

- 1 point is earned for a correctly labeled graph of the loanable funds market.
- 1 point is earned for showing an increase in demand for loanable funds.
- 1 point is earned for stating that the interest rate increases.

(d)   3 points:

- 1 point is earned for explaining that firms' investment decreases, because the higher interest rate increases the cost of borrowing.
- 1 point is earned for explaining that short-run aggregate demand decreases, because the reduced investment by firms lowers aggregate demand.
- 1 point is earned for explaining that long-run economic growth is limited, because firms are reducing investment in plant and equipment, which would have promoted long-run growth.

(e)   2 points:

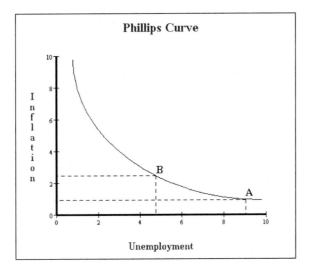

- 1 point is earned for a correctly labeled Phillips curve graph.
- 1 point is earned for placing two points on the curve. Point A must be located lower and to the right of point B, showing higher unemployment and lower inflation.

2.   **8 points** (2 + 2 + 2 + 2)

(a)   2 points:
- 1 point is earned for stating that this action did not change the money supply.
- 1 point is earned for explaining that currency and demand deposits are both part of M1, so the money supply did not change, only its composition changed.

(b)   2 points:
- 1 point is earned for stating that the bank could loan out $375 of Brett's deposit. It must hold $125 to meet the 25% reserve requirement and can loan the rest.
- 1 point is earned for stating that the maximum increase in the money supply as a result of the deposit is $1,500. The multiplier is 1 / Reserve Requirement (1 / 0.25 = 4). The initial loan times the multiplier is $1,500 ($375 x 4 = $1,500).

(c)   2 points:
- 1 point each is earned for identifying two factors that could limit the growth of the money supply. Correct answers include the following:
  - Banks decide not to loan out all of the available funds, so the deposits don't fully expand.
  - Consumers decide not to borrow all of the available funds, so money is not spent again to continue the expansion of the money supply.
  - Households do not redeposit money in the bank, so banks cannot loan it out to continue the expansion.

(d)   2 points:

- 1 point is earned for stating that aggregate demand increases.
- 1 point is earned for stating that both real output and price level increase.

3.   **8 points** (2 + 4 + 2)

(a)   2 points:
- 1 point is earned for stating that the United States has the comparative advantage in producing coffee.
- 1 point is earned for explaining that the U.S. has the lower opportunity cost for producing coffee. The U.S. opportunity cost for 1 ton of coffee is 3 tons of cotton, while Brazil's opportunity cost is 4 tons of cotton.

(b)   4 points:
- 1 point is earned for stating that Brazil will import coffee.
- 1 point is earned for explaining that the United States can produce at a lower cost than Brazil can.
- 1 point is earned for explaining that Brazilian consumers gain because the price of imported American coffee is lower than the price of domestic Brazilian coffee.
- 1 point is earned for explaining that world output increases because the most efficient producers are specializing in producing each product.

(c)   2 points:

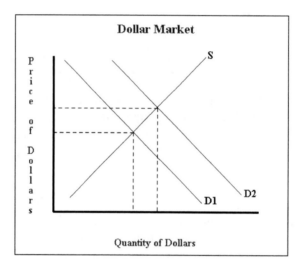

- 1 point is earned for a correctly labeled foreign exchange market graph for the U.S. dollar, showing demand for dollars increasing.
- 1 point is earned for stating that the international value of the dollar increases.

MICROECONOMICS PRACTICE TEST 1
Section I
Time: 70 Minutes
60 Questions

Directions: Each of the questions or incomplete statements below is followed by five responses or completions. Select the best one in each case.

1. Opportunity cost is defined as
   (A) the monetary cost of producing one more unit of a product.
   (B) the most valuable alternative one gives up as the result of a decision.
   (C) the revenue a firm receives from selling one more product.
   (D) the monetary cost of hiring one more worker.
   (E) the benefit one receives from making one choice rather than another.

2. Unlike firms in other market structures, an oligopolist making price and output decisions must be concerned with
   (A) the quality of its products.
   (B) achieving productive efficiency.
   (C) the cost of labor resources.
   (D) the actions of its rivals.
   (E) achieving allocative efficiency.

3. Each of the following would cause demand for large cars to decrease EXCEPT
   (A) the price of gas increasing.
   (B) consumer incomes decreasing.
   (C) the price of small cars decreasing.
   (D) the cost of producing large cars increasing.
   (E) pickup trucks becoming very popular among consumers.

Quantity	Total Cost
0	10
1	18
2	24
3	30
4	42

4. According to the chart above, the average variable cost of producing 4 units is
   (A) $42.00.
   (B) $10.50.
   (C) $12.00.
   (D) $3.00.
   (E) $8.00.

5. If the government places a price floor below the equilibrium price, the result is
   (A) a decrease in price.
   (B) an increase in quantity sold.
   (C) a shortage.
   (D) a surplus.
   (E) no effect.

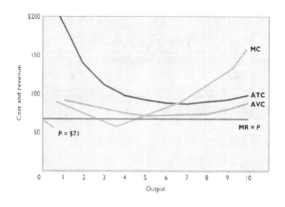

6.   A firm's costs and revenues are depicted above. In the short run, this firm should
      (A)   maximize productive efficiency by producing where MC = ATC.
      (B)   maximize profit by producing where MC = MR.
      (C)   maximize allocative efficiency by producing where MC = AVC.
      (D)   minimize loss by producing where MC = AVC.
      (E)   shut down.

7.   The government has the greatest amount of decision-making power in
      (A)   laissez faire economies.
      (B)   market economies.
      (C)   mixed economies.
      (D)   command economies.
      (E)   traditional economies.

8.   Which of the following situations is the best example of the Law of Demand?
      (A)   A coal miner uses his pay raise to buy a new stereo system.
      (B)   A corporation uses additional profits to invest in new capital.
      (C)   When the price of computers goes down, a student buys a computer.
      (D)   When the government raises income taxes, people buy fewer cars.
      (E)   A mother buys the brand of cereal for which her children have been asking.

9.   When the wage rises by 2%, the quantity of workers hired falls by 4%. Therefore, the demand
      for labor is
      (A)   perfectly elastic.
      (B)   relatively elastic.
      (C)   unit elastic.
      (D)   relatively inelastic.
      (E)   perfectly inelastic.

10.   The perfectly competitive firm's short-run supply curve is, for the portion above the average
      variable cost curve, the firm's
      (A)   average total cost curve.
      (B)   marginal cost curve.
      (C)   marginal revenue curve.
      (D)   average fixed cost curve.
      (E)   average revenue curve.

11. Compared to monopolies, perfectly competitive firms and industries in long-run equilibrium achieve all of the following EXCEPT

   (A) lower prices.
   (B) higher levels of output.
   (C) productive efficiency.
   (D) allocative efficiency.
   (E) long-run economic profit.

12. If TU = total utility, MU = marginal utility, and P = price, in order to maximize utility, a consumer should purchase the mix of hamburgers and hot dogs where

   (A) the MU of hamburgers equals the MU of hot dogs.
   (B) the MU equals the TU of hamburgers, and the MU equals the TU of hot dogs.
   (C) the TU of hamburgers equals the TU of hot dogs.
   (D) the MU / P of hamburgers equals the MU / P of hot dogs.
   (E) the TU / P of hamburgers equals the TU / P of hot dogs.

13. For the range of output where long-run average total cost decreases, a firm finds

   (A) economies of scale.
   (B) diseconomies of scale.
   (C) economic profit.
   (D) allocative efficiency.
   (E) normal profit.

14. A country can increase its production possibilities by

   (A) producing more of its highest-priced products.
   (B) reducing imports and relying on domestic production.
   (C) investing in the development of new technology.
   (D) producing only those products for which it has an absolute advantage.
   (E) reducing its spending for education and training.

15. Which of the following is the best example of perfectly inelastic demand?

   (A) When the price of insulin rises, diabetics buy the same quantity of insulin.
   (B) When more farmers produce corn, the price of corn falls.
   (C) When consumer incomes rise, consumers buy significantly more rice.
   (D) When the population increases, the demand for houses increases.
   (E) When the cost of production increases, car manufacturers raise prices.

16. Assume a perfectly competitive industry is initially in long-run equilibrium. How will lower per-unit variable costs in the industry affect each of the following?

	Short-Run Firm Output	Short-Run Profit	Long-Run Firm Movement
(A)	Increase	Increase	Enter
(B)	Decrease	Decrease	Exit
(C)	Increase	Decrease	Exit
(D)	Decrease	Increase	Enter
(E)	Decrease	Increase	Exit

17.   If tie-dye T-shirts are sold in a competitive market and become a popular fad at the same time that improvements in technology increase the productivity of tie-dye T-shirt factory workers, one can be sure that
(A)   the equilibrium price of tie-dye T-shirts in the market will increase.
(B)   some tie-dye T-shirt producers will leave the industry.
(C)   the equilibrium quantity of tie-dye T-shirts in the market will increase.
(D)   the equilibrium price of tie-dye T-shirts in the market will decrease.
(E)   the equilibrium price and quantity of tie-dye T-shirts in the market will both decrease.

Questions 18–19 refer to the graph below, which shows the costs and revenues for a profit-maximizing monopoly firm.

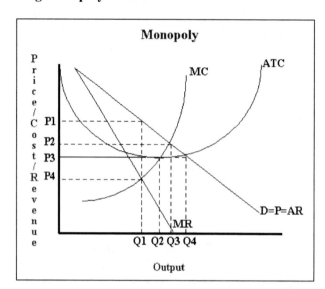

18.   This monopoly maximizes profit at the following output and price:
         Output   Price
(A)   Q1   P1
(B)   Q2   P3
(C)   Q3   P2
(D)   Q4   P3
(E)   Q1   P4

19.   If the government wanted to encourage the firm to produce the socially optimal output, it would set a price ceiling at the price where
(A)   MR = ATC.
(B)   MR = MC.
(C)   MC = ATC.
(D)   MC = D.
(E)   ATC = D.

20.   As Nikki eats candy bars, she gains less and less satisfaction from each additional candy bar she consumes. This situation describes the concept of
(A)   diminishing marginal utility.
(B)   diminishing returns.
(C)   economies of scale.

(D)   comparative advantage.

(E)   elasticity of demand.

21. Firms tend to heavily advertise product differentiation in which of these markets?

(A)   Monopolistic competition and oligopoly

(B)   Monopoly and monopolistic competition

(C)   Monopoly and perfect competition

(D)   Oligopoly and monopoly

(E)   Monopolistic competition and perfect competition

22. If cookies and milk are complements and the price of milk significantly increases, one would expect

(A)   the quantity demanded of milk would increase.

(B)   the supply curve for milk would shift to the right.

(C)   the demand curve for cookies would shift to the left.

(D)   the quantity demanded of cookies would fall.

(E)   the demand curves for both milk and cookies would shift to the left.

23. A profit-maximizing, perfectly competitive industry in long-run equilibrium exhibits which of these features?

      I.   Allocative efficiency

      II. Productive efficiency

      III. Firms earning economic profit

      IV. Firms earning normal profit

(A)   II only

(B)   III only

(C)   I, III, and IV only

(D)   I, II, and IV only

(E)   I, II, III, and IV

24. If the market for cigarettes is initially in equilibrium, with a relatively inelastic demand and elastic supply, and a state places an excise tax on sales of cigarettes,

(A)   the quantity of cigarettes sold will fall to zero.

(B)   consumers will pay most of the tax burden.

(C)   producers will pay most of the tax burden.

(D)   the firm must absorb the entire tax burden to remain in business.

(E)   the quantity of cigarettes sold will increase.

25. Because the supply is perfectly inelastic, economic rent is paid for

(A)   land.

(B)   labor.

(C)   capital.

(D)   entrepreneurship.

(E)   interest.

26. All of these are characteristics of a perfectly competitive market EXCEPT

(A)   a large number of firms.

(B)   no significant barriers to entry or exit.

(C)   identical products.

(D)   long-run economic profit.

(E)   price-taking individual firms.

27.	If the equilibrium wage for unskilled workers is $8 per hour and the state sets a minimum wage of $9 per hour, all of the following are likely effects EXCEPT
(A)	the quantity of workers willing to work increasing.
(B)	the quantity of workers demanded decreasing.
(C)	the number of workers hired decreasing.
(D)	unemployment resulting.
(E)	the wage rate decreasing in the long run.

28.	At a local restaurant, Judy can prepare 4 sandwiches or 8 bowls of soup in ten minutes, while Janet can prepare 2 sandwiches or 6 bowls of soup in ten minutes. Which of the following statements is correct?
(A)	Judy has a comparative advantage in producing sandwiches, while Janet has a comparative advantage in producing soup.
(B)	Judy has a comparative advantage in producing soup, while Janet has a comparative advantage in producing sandwiches.
(C)	Janet has an absolute advantage in producing both sandwiches and soup.
(D)	Judy has a comparative advantage in producing both sandwiches and soup.
(E)	Janet has an absolute advantage in producing soup, while Judy has a comparative advantage in producing sandwiches.

29.	The marginal cost curve
(A)	increases slightly and then falls.
(B)	equals average total cost at the lowest point on the ATC curve.
(C)	is the sum of the average fixed cost and average variable cost curves.
(D)	is inversely related to the average total cost curve.
(E)	equals the average total cost curve at the peak of the marginal cost curve.

30.	If a competitive market experiences a long-run surplus, the cause must be
(A)	an increase in supply.
(B)	a decrease in demand.
(C)	an effective price floor.
(D)	an increase in the price of a substitute.
(E)	a reduction in consumer incomes.

31.	A natural monopoly, such as an electric company, produces at greater efficiency with one large firm rather than several smaller electric companies because of
(A)	lower wages.
(B)	higher profit.
(C)	economies of scale.
(D)	government subsidies.
(E)	increased competition.

32.	If the government drafts soldiers for war, significantly decreasing the supply of labor in a perfectly competitive civilian labor market, how would you expect the wage and quantity of workers employed in civilian work to change?

	Number of Workers Employed	Wage
(A)	Increase	Increase
(B)	Increase	Decrease
(C)	Decrease	Increase
(D)	Decrease	Decrease
(E)	No change	No change

33. An increase in demand in a perfectly competitive market causes the individual firm to experience a short-run increase in
     (A) marginal revenue.
     (B) average total cost.
     (C) average fixed cost.
     (D) average variable cost.
     (E) normal profit.

34. Characteristics of public goods include which of the following?
       I.   Those who do not pay cannot be excluded from obtaining them
       II. Long-run surpluses result in the market
       III. The tendency to produce negative externalities
       IV. One consumer's use of the good does not interfere with another consumer's use of the same good
     (A) II only
     (B) II and III
     (C) I and IV
     (D) I, II, and IV
     (E) I, II, III, and IV

35. When a lipstick producer raised the price of its product, the firm's total revenue fell. Assuming all else was equal, this reaction indicates that
     (A) the supply of lipstick is perfectly inelastic.
     (B) the demand for lipstick is price elastic.
     (C) the demand for lipstick is unit elastic.
     (D) the supply of lipstick is income elastic.
     (E) the demand for lipstick is income inelastic.

Questions 36–37 are based on the payoff matrix below.

		Chris's Wine Producing Strategy	
		Red Wine	White Wine
Jeri's Wine Producing Strategy	Red Wine	$1000, $700	$700, $600
	White Wine	$800, $900	$600, $800

The payoff matrix above shows the profits per day that can be earned by two firms in an oligopolistic industry producing red and white wine. They must grow the grapes for their wine each year and cannot change the crop during the growing season. The first number in each cell shows the profit Jeri's Winery can earn, and the second number in each cell shows the profit Chris's Winery can earn.

36. Which of the following statements about this industry is correct?
       I.   Jeri's dominant strategy is to produce red wine.
       II. Chris has no dominant strategy.
       III. If Jeri produces white wine, she would gain a greater profit if Chris produces red wine than if Chris produces white wine.
     (A) II only
     (B) III only
     (C) I and II only
     (D) I and III only
     (E) I, II, and III

37.   If each of the firms chose its production strategy without knowing the other firm's decision in advance, what amount of profit would each firm earn?

	Jeri's Profit	Chris's Profit
(A)	$1,000	$700
(B)	$800	$900
(C)	$700	$600
(D)	$600	$800
(E)	$1,000	$900

38.   A monopoly may engage in price discrimination for the purpose of
(A)   increasing its efficiency.
(B)   reducing its average total cost.
(C)   reducing its output.
(D)   increasing its price.
(E)   increasing its total revenue.

39.   The concept of derived demand shows that as the demand for a product goes up,
(A)   the price of the product goes up.
(B)   the government's tax revenue goes up.
(C)   the quantity of the product sold goes down.
(D)   the demand for public goods goes up.
(E)   the demand for labor to make the product goes up.

40.   Which combination of policies would most effectively promote income equality?
(A)   Progressive income taxes and reduced spending for rent subsidies
(B)   Proportional income taxes and increased spending for highways
(C)   Regressive income taxes and increased spending for education
(D)   Proportional income taxes and reduced spending for national defense
(E)   Progressive income taxes and increased spending for food stamps

41.   In the short run, if the marginal product of the next worker hired is greater than the average product of the workers at the plant,
(A)   wages must be increasing.
(B)   the average total cost must be increasing.
(C)   the average product must be increasing.
(D)   product demand must be increasing.
(E)   the average fixed cost must be increasing.

42.   In long-run equilibrium, a monopolistically competitive firm incurs
(A)   economic profit because of barriers to entry.
(B)   no economic profit because competitors enter when profits occur.
(C)   economic losses because it has no control over its price or costs.
(D)   economic profit because of patents or other barriers to entry.
(E)   economic losses because competition forces the firm to lower price.

43.   An example of a public good is
(A)   a city bus.
(B)   a road.
(C)   gasoline.
(D)   a movie.
(E)   a corporation's stock.

44. A reduction in interest rates causes
    (A)   a reduction in firms' investment in worker training.
    (B)   consumers to put money into savings accounts rather than holding cash.
    (C)   an increase in firms' investment in plant and equipment.
    (D)   a reduction in firms' spending for research and development.
    (E)   a reduction in economic growth and employment.

45. Which of the following factors contributes to a downward-sloping demand curve?
    I.   The income effect
    II. The substitution effect
    III. Diminishing marginal utility
    (A)   I only
    (B)   III only
    (C)   I and II only
    (D)   II and III only
    (E)   I, II, and III

Questions 46–47 refer to the table below, which shows the daily total product of a firm operating in perfectly competitive product and labor markets.

Number of Workers	Total Product
1	10
2	18
3	24
4	28
5	30

46. What is the marginal product of the fourth worker?
    (A)   4 products
    (B)   28 products
    (C)   18 products
    (D)   2 products
    (E)   7 products

47. If the firm sells its products for $10 each and the wage the firm must pay workers is $60 per day, how many workers should the firm hire to maximize profit?
    (A)   1 worker
    (B)   2 workers
    (C)   3 workers
    (D)   4 workers
    (E)   5 workers

48. Using equivalent amounts of resources and technology, India can produce 10 pounds of spices or 5 pounds of tea per hour. Using the same amount of resources, Pakistan can produce 9 pounds of spices or 3 pounds of tea per hour. Given this information, which of the following statements is true?
    (A)   Pakistan has an absolute advantage in the production of spices.
    (B)   Pakistan should specialize in the production of tea.
    (C)   Both nations benefit if they trade and the price of 1 pound of tea is set at 4 pounds of spices.
    (D)   India has a comparative advantage in the production of tea.
    (E)   India has an absolute disadvantage in the production of tea.

49. Positive externalities result when
    (A) the marginal social cost is greater than the marginal social benefit.
    (B) the marginal private cost is greater than the marginal social cost.
    (C) the marginal social benefit is greater than the marginal private benefit.
    (D) the marginal private cost is greater than the marginal private benefit.
    (E) the marginal private benefit is greater than the marginal private cost.

50. The distribution of household income in a country is measured by the
    (A) Laffer curve.
    (B) supply curve.
    (C) marginal revenue curve.
    (D) Lorenz curve.
    (E) total revenue curve.

51. In a perfectly competitive market, a firm is producing at an output where the product price is $10 and the marginal cost of producing the next product is $8. In order to increase profit, the firm should
    (A) produce the next product.
    (B) reduce the product price.
    (C) keep production at the current output.
    (D) increase the product price.
    (E) reduce the output.

52. Which government action is appropriate to address a negative externality?
    (A) A noise ordinance limiting how loudly outdoor restaurants can play music
    (B) A subsidy for a manufacturing plant that hires disabled workers
    (C) A fine placed on firms that move their operations out of state
    (D) An excise tax placed on the sale of gasoline
    (E) A state providing public education

53. At the monopoly firm's profit-maximizing quantity of output, all of the following statements are true EXCEPT
    (A) the marginal revenue equals the marginal cost.
    (B) the marginal revenue is lower than the price.
    (C) the average total cost is lower than the price.
    (D) the marginal cost is lower than the price.
    (E) the average total cost equals the marginal cost.

54. Which of the following combinations of labor and capital represents a least-cost combination of output for a particular firm?

	Marginal Product of Labor	Price of Labor	Marginal Product of Capital	Price of Capital
(A)	10	$5	20	$20
(B)	5	$1	10	$1
(C)	7	$3	3	$7
(D)	6	$2	12	$6
(E)	8	$4	14	$7

55. Government officials justify the regulation of monopolies, arguing that, compared to competitive firms, unregulated monopolies
    (A) hire more workers at higher wages.
    (B) raise prices and lower output.
    (C) pay more tax revenues.
    (D) engage in extensive advertising.
    (E) extensively export their products.

56. Collusive agreements among oligopolistic firms often fail because
    (A) collusive behavior is illegal in all countries.
    (B) collusion requires firms to produce at productive efficiency.
    (C) each firm recognizes it can increase its profit if it is the only one to cheat.
    (D) the entry of competitors eliminates economic profit and firms shut down.
    (E) consumers avoid purchasing products that involve collusive agreements.

57. Each of the following situations would increase the supply of chicken EXCEPT
    (A) the cost of chicken feed decreasing.
    (B) a new vaccine reducing the incidence of disease among chickens.
    (C) technology improving the efficiency of chicken processing.
    (D) the government granting a subsidy to chicken producers.
    (E) the wages of poultry processing workers increasing.

58. When a monopolistically competitive firm is in long-run equilibrium, at the profit-maximizing output,
    I. marginal revenue equals marginal cost.
    II. average total cost equals the price.
    III. average total cost is at its minimum.
    (A) I only
    (B) II only
    (C) II and III only
    (D) I and II only
    (E) I, II, and III

59. An economic activity resulting in costs to others outside of a transaction is
    (A) a negative externality.
    (B) diminishing returns.
    (C) a public good.
    (D) a positive externality.
    (E) diminishing marginal utility.

60. An increase in wages, a variable cost, will result in all of the following for the profit-maximizing firm in the short run EXCEPT
    (A) an increase in the average total cost.
    (B) an increase in the average fixed cost.
    (C) an increase in the marginal cost.
    (D) an increase in the average variable cost.
    (E) an upward shift in the average variable cost curve.

MICROECONOMICS PRACTICE TEST 1
Section II
Planning Time: 10 Minutes
Writing Time: 50 Minutes

Directions: You have fifty minutes to answer all three of the following questions. <u>It is suggested that you spend approximately half your time on the first question and divide the remaining time equally between the next two questions.</u> In answering the questions, you should emphasize the line of reasoning that generated your results; it is not enough to list the results of your analysis. Include correctly labeled diagrams, if useful or required, in explaining your answers. A correctly labeled diagram must have all axes and curves clearly labeled and must show directional changes. <u>Use a pen with black or dark blue ink</u>.

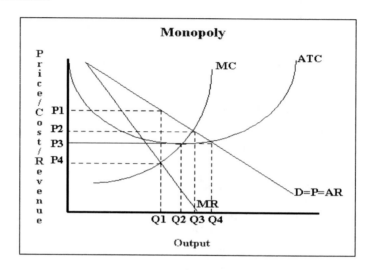

1.   The graph above shows the cost and revenue curves for a profit-maximizing monopoly.
(a)   Using the labels on the graph, identify each of the following:
        (i)   The profit-maximizing output – state the rule for finding the profit-maximizing output.
        (ii)   The price at the profit-maximizing output
        (iii)   The area of economic profit or loss
(b)   Using the labels on the graph, identify the output at which the firm reaches productive efficiency. Explain.
(c)   Explain why the unregulated monopoly does not produce at productive or allocative efficiency.
(d)   Assume government regulators place an effective price ceiling to require the firm to produce at allocative efficiency. Using the labels on the graph, identify each of the following:
        (i)   The quantity of output at which the firm reaches allocative efficiency
        (ii)   The price set by government regulators
        (iii)   The area of economic profit or loss at that output
(e)   Assume this firm hires workers in a perfectly competitive labor market. Draw a correctly labeled labor market graph for the industry and this firm.
        (i)   Identify the wage and the firm's profit-maximizing quantity of labor.
        (ii)   Illustrate the change in the firm's labor market graph as a result of the new output determined in (d)(i).
        (iii)   Explain the effect of the new output on the quantity of workers employed by the firm.
        (iv)   Explain the effect of the new output on the wage the firm pays workers.

2. Two jewelry companies, Juan's Wonders and Mei-Ling's Marvels, sell class rings to high school students across the country. These two are the dominant firms in the industry. They must set their prices for the year in the summer before the beginning of each school year and cannot change them during the year. Each firm must decide whether to adopt a high-price strategy (setting a high price in the hope of maximizing per-unit profit) or a low-price strategy (setting a lower price in the hope that the increase in the number of rings sold will increase total profit). The payoff matrix is below, with the first number in each cell indicating Mei-Ling's profit per day and the second number in the cell indicating Juan's profit per day.

		Juan's Pricing Strategy	
		High-Price Strategy	Low-Price Strategy
Mei-Ling's Pricing Strategy	High-Price Strategy	$5,000, $3,000	$3,000, $4,000
	Low-Price Strategy	$4,000, $2,000	$1,000, $1,000

(a) If Mei-Ling chooses a high-price strategy, which price strategy is best for Juan?

(b) If Mei-Ling chooses a low-price strategy, which price strategy is best for Juan?

(c) Identify the dominant strategy (if any) for Mei-Ling.

(d) Identify the dominant strategy (if any) for Juan.

(e) If both firms know the information in the payoff matrix and do not collude, how much will Juan earn in profit per day?

(f) Now assume these firms successfully collude, with both firms agreeing to a high-price strategy. Would this relationship likely remain stable? Explain.

3. The table below shows the total utility Rosemary gains from consuming music CDs and movie DVDs.

Quantity of CDs	Total Utility of CDs	Quantity of DVDs	Total Utility of DVDs
0	0	0	0
1	120	1	300
2	220	2	500
3	260	3	600
4	280	4	660

Assume the price of a CD is $10 and the price of a DVD is $20. Rosemary will spend her entire income of $60 on CDs and DVDs.

(a) Determine the marginal utility of the third CD.

(b) Use marginal utility per dollar spent for CDs and DVDs to answer the following:

   (i) Explain whether Rosemary will purchase a CD or a DVD first and your reasoning.

   (ii) Identify the utility-maximizing quantity of CDs and DVDs Rosemary will purchase.

   (iii) State the mathematical equation for utility maximization.

   (iv) Use the equation to show Rosemary has maximized her utility by purchasing that combination of goods.

   (v) Identify the total utility Rosemary gains from this total purchase.

(c) If Rosemary's income increases by $20, will she purchase one more DVD or two more CDs to maximize her utility? Explain your reasoning.

MICROECONOMICS PRACTICE TEST 1 – KEY
Section I

1.   (B)   Opportunity cost represents the choice not taken; (A) is marginal cost, (C) is marginal revenue, and (D) is marginal resource cost.

2.   (D)   The response of rivals can significantly affect the quantity sold and revenue for the oligopolist. Perfectly competitive and monopolistically competitive firms are too small a part of the industry for other firms' decisions to affect them, and a monopoly is the only firm in its industry.

3.   (D)   A higher cost of production would reduce supply, not demand. Gas is a complement, so as price increases, consumers buy fewer large cars. Cars are normal goods, so as incomes fall, demand for cars falls. Small cars and pickup trucks are substitutes for large cars, so a lower price for small cars or popularity among pickup trucks reduces demand for large cars.

4.   (E)   The total cost of 4 units is $42.00. The fixed cost (total cost at 0 output) is $10.00, so the remaining variable cost is $32.00. Average variable cost is variable cost divided by output ($32.00 / 4).

5.   (E)   Market equilibrium remains at rest unless something occurs to change the equilibrium. A price floor above the equilibrium price would be effective in raising the price and causing a surplus. But if the price floor is lower than equilibrium, it has no effect on the market.

6.   (E)   At the loss-minimizing output where MC = MR, the firm's revenue is lower than its average variable cost. There is no point where the firm can cover its variable cost of production, so it would minimize loss by shutting down.

7.   (D)   Command economies are defined as economies in which the government owns/operates most firms or makes significant output and price decisions.

8.   (C)   The Law of Demand states that as the price of a product decreases, consumers buy more; at higher prices, consumers buy less of the product.

9.   (B)   The elasticity of demand for labor is the percentage change in the quantity of workers divided by the percentage change in the wage. Because the quantity of workers changed by more than the wage (E > 1), demand for workers is relatively elastic.

10.   (B)   The firm maximizes profit where marginal cost equals marginal revenue. Because the firm is a price-taker, it must accept the MR set in the industry and set output wherever MC = MR. So marginal cost is supply.

11.   (E)   Perfectly competitive firms do not achieve long-run economic profit because the industry lacks barriers to entry and profit draws competitors into the industry, increasing supply until economic profit falls to zero.

12.   (D)   Consumers maximize their utility by buying products such that the marginal utility per dollar spent for the last hamburger equals the marginal utility per dollar spent for the last hot dog. If the MU / P of hot dogs is higher than the MU / P of hamburgers, the consumer would be better off consuming more hot dogs and fewer hamburgers.

13.   (A)   Diseconomies of scale occur where long-run ATC rises. Profit and allocative efficiency cannot be determined by the ATC curve alone.

14.   (C)   Increases in resources and technology shift the production possibilities curve outward. Producing more of one product or another only changes the point of production on the existing curve. Reducing imports from countries with a comparative advantage or reducing productivity through less education reduces production possibilities.

15.   (A)   When demand is perfectly inelastic, consumers do not respond at all to a change in the price of a product. (B) and (E) indicate shifts in supply, while (C) and (D) indicate shifts in demand.

16. (A) Lower variable costs reduce marginal cost, so MC = MR at higher output. Lower ATC, with no change in price, allows the firm to earn short-run economic profit. In the long run, profit draws firms into the industry.

17. (C) When both demand and supply increase, both factors increase quantity, so the quantity will definitely increase. However, the effect on price cannot be determined without more specific information, because it depends on the relative changes in supply and demand. All other things equal, one would expect the increasing revenues and lower costs to cause firms to experience a short-run profit, causing firms to enter, not leave.

18. (A) Monopolies maximize profit at the output where MC equals MR, and then set the price on the demand curve at that output.

19. (D) The socially optimal output is allocative efficiency, where the marginal cost equals the marginal benefit to society (the demand curve).

20. (A) Diminishing marginal utility occurs as a consumer's wants are satisfied with consumption; (B) refers to reduced output from each additional unit of labor, (C) refers to a lower ATC as output increases; (D) refers to a country's ability to produce more efficiently than another country; (E) refers to consumer sensitivity to price changes.

21. (A) Monopolistically competitive and oligopolistic firms attract customers by focusing on the appealing differences of their products. Products of perfectly competitive firms are identical and monopolists are sole producers, so neither has product differentiation to advertise.

22. (C) Consumers respond to higher prices by buying less, so if the quantity demanded for milk falls (moving along the milk demand curve), demand for the complement cookies would fall as well (shifting demand leftward).

23. (D) Economic profit would draw firms into the industry until the economic profit returned to zero. Normal profit continues in the long run because it is necessary to pay the entrepreneur to remain with the firm.

24. (B) If demand is relatively inelastic, consumers will slightly decrease the quantity demanded, but the firm can pass on most of the tax to the customers without losing significant sales.

25. (A) Economic rent is paid when a resource is provided whether there is demand or not and when an increased price cannot bring about an increased quantity of the resource. The quantity of labor, capital, and entrepreneurship supplied increase when the price paid for them increases.

26. (D) In perfectly competitive markets, economic profit draws new firms into the industry, so long-run economic profit cannot continue.

27. (E) The minimum wage prevents the wage from falling any lower than the legal wage. An effective minimum wage increases the quantity of workers supplied and reduces the quantity demanded, creating unemployment.

28. (A) Judy has an absolute advantage in producing both sandwiches and soup, because she produces a greater quantity of each. Judy's opportunity cost for producing each sandwich is 2 bowls of soup, while Janet's opportunity cost is 3 bowls of soup; with the lower opportunity cost, Judy has the comparative advantage in producing sandwiches. Janet has the lower opportunity cost and the comparative advantage in producing soup.

29. (B) When marginal cost is lower than ATC, it pulls ATC down. When MC is higher, it pulls ATC up. So MC and ATC are equal at the lowest point on ATC. MC falls slightly before rising. ATC = AFC + AVC.

30. (C) When an event disturbs competitive markets, they automatically adjust back toward equilibrium. The only factor listed that could prevent an adjustment to equilibrium is an effective price floor.

31. (C) Economies of scale occur when average total cost falls over a large range of output, so one large firm produces at a lower ATC. If the same output were produced by several smaller firms with higher ATCs, efficiency would be reduced.

32. (C) If industry labor supply shifts to the left, the wage increases, transferring as a higher marginal resource cost to the individual firm. At the higher wage, MRC = MRP at a lower quantity of workers, so the firm will employ fewer workers.

33. (A) Because the perfectly competitive firm is a price-taker, an increase in industry demand raises the price, transferring higher marginal revenue to the firm. This does not change any cost, and although the firm may experience a short-run economic profit, it does not affect normal profit.

34. (C) Non-excludability and non-rival consumption are defining characteristics of public goods. Long-run surpluses and negative externalities are not generally associated with public goods.

35. (B) With price elastic demand, the percentage change in quantity demanded is greater than the percentage change in price. Because consumers were so sensitive to the price rise, the quantity demanded fell significantly, resulting in less revenue for the firm. Income elasticity is consumer sensitivity to a change in income, which did not occur in this case.

36. (D) Jeri's dominant strategy is to produce red wine, because she gains more profit from doing so whether Chris chooses to produce red (because $1,000 > $800) or white (because $700 > $600). Chris's dominant strategy is to produce red wine, because he gains more profit from doing so whether Jeri chooses to produce red (because $700 > $600) or white (because $900 > $800). If Jeri produced white wine, she would earn $800 if Chris produced red wine and $600 if he produced white wine.

37. (A) Chris and Jeri both use their dominant strategies to produce red wine. On the matrix, it shows Jeri's profit as $1,000 and Chris's profit as $700.

38. (E) The monopoly can raise the price for consumers with inelastic demand, because the quantity sold falls by a small amount, increasing total revenue. The firm can then lower the price for consumers with elastic demand, and because the percentage increase in quantity sold is greater than the percentage decrease in price, the firm again increases its total revenue.

39. (E) The demand for labor is derived from the demand for the product. (A) refers to a shift in product demand, and (C) refers to the Law of Demand.

40. (E) Progressive income taxes charge those with higher incomes a higher tax rate, reducing the disposable income of those with higher incomes. Increased spending for food stamps increases available funds for those with lower incomes. In combination, the policies help equalize incomes.

41. (C) If the next worker's production is higher than the average production, it will pull up the average production; therefore, average product must be increasing.

42. (B) Monopolistic competitors face few barriers to entry, so when firms earn short-run profit, competitors enter until economic profit falls to zero.

43. (B) Public goods have characteristics of non-rival consumption and difficulty excluding those who have not paid for the good.

44. (C) Because firms often borrow to finance investment in plant and equipment, a lower interest rate lowers the full cost of the investment.

45. (E) All three factors contribute to consumers buying a greater quantity of products when the price falls.

46. (A) Marginal product is the increase in production from hiring the next worker (28 − 24 = 4).

47.	(C)	The marginal product of the third worker is 6 products, which can each be sold for $10, so the marginal revenue product of the third worker is $60. The wage (marginal resource cost) is $60, and the firm maximizes profit when it hires where MRC = MRP.

48.	(D)	India has an absolute advantage in producing both spices and tea. India has a comparative advantage in producing tea, giving up 2 pounds of spices to produce 1 pound of tea, while Pakistan's opportunity cost is 3 pounds of spices. So India should specialize in producing tea. The price of tea must fall between 2–3 pounds of spices for both nations to benefit.

49.	(C)	When the marginal benefit to society is greater than the marginal private benefit, the consumer does not take the benefits to others into account when making a purchase decision, so the product is under-produced.

50.	(D)	The Lorenz curve measures the percentage of income that is distributed among the five quintiles of households in the country to determine the degree of income inequality.

51.	(A)	As long as the marginal revenue (price) is greater than the marginal cost, the firm should produce the product. To maximize profit, the firm should continue to produce until marginal cost equals marginal revenue.

52.	(A)	An outdoor restaurant playing loud music imposes costs on residents who live near the restaurant. A noise ordinance is an appropriate remedy to require the firm to reduce the costs it imposes on others.

53.	(E)	The monopoly restricts output in order to raise the price and maximize profit. Therefore, productive efficiency (where MC = ATC) occurs at a higher output than the profit-maximizing output.

54.	(E)	Least-cost production occurs where the marginal product divided by the price of labor equals the marginal product divided by the price of capital (8 / $4 = 14 / $7).

55.	(B)	To maximize profit, monopolies restrict output and raise prices. Regulators can limit the market price or subsidize the firm's costs to increase production and lower prices.

56.	(C)	Firms have an incentive to cheat on collusive agreements if they can increase their profits by cheating. While many countries have made collusion illegal, it is still legal in many places. Competitors rarely enter oligopolistic markets due to barriers to entry.

57.	(E)	A wage increase raises the cost of production for the firm, decreasing the supply of the product. The other options reduce the cost of production.

58.	(D)	In long-run equilibrium, the monopolistically competitive firm maximizes profit where MC = MR and sets its price on the demand curve. Average total cost is tangential to the demand curve at the price point but reaches its minimum (crossing marginal cost) at a higher output.

59.	(A)	A negative externality imposes costs on outsiders, while a positive externality extends benefits to others not involved in the transaction.

60.	(B)	Fixed costs do not change with the amount of output. A change in variable cost does not affect the fixed cost.

MICROECONOMICS PRACTICE TEST 1 – KEY
Section II – Sample Essays

1. The profit-maximizing output is Q1. The profit-maximizing rule is that the firm should produce where marginal revenue equals marginal cost. The price is P1, set on the demand curve at the profit-maximizing output. The area of economic profit is (P1 – P3) × Q1. This firm achieves productive efficiency at the output Q2, where the marginal cost equals average total cost. At that point, the firm produces at the lowest average total cost. Monopolies do not produce at productive or allocative efficiency because they maximize profit by reducing output and increasing the price. Regulators would set a price ceiling to achieve allocative efficiency at the output Q3 and at the price P2. The firm's area of profit at that output is (P2 – P3) × Q3.

    In order to increase output, the firm's demand for labor increases and more workers are hired. But the wage will not change because, in a perfectly competitive labor market, the individual firm is such a small part of the industry, changes at the firm do not affect wages in the industry.

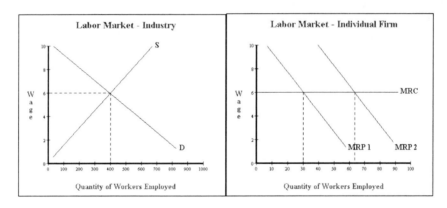

2. If Mei-Ling chooses a high price strategy, Juan's best strategy is a low-price strategy, because his daily profit would be $4,000 rather than $3,000. If Mei-Ling chooses a low price strategy, Juan's best strategy is a high-price strategy, because his daily profit would be $2,000 rather than $1,000. Mei-Ling's dominant strategy is a high-price strategy, because she always makes a higher profit with this strategy, regardless of Juan's strategy. Juan does not have a dominant strategy, because his profit-maximizing strategy depends on the strategy Mei-Ling chooses. Juan will earn $4,000 profit per day, because Mei-Ling's dominant strategy is a high-price strategy, and based on that, Juan will choose a low-price strategy to make the most profit. If the firms collude, the relationship is not likely to remain stable. Juan has an incentive to cheat on the agreement because he can earn more profit by using a low-price strategy.

3.   This table includes MU and MU / Dollar calculations for CDs and DVDs.

Q of CDs	TU of CDs	MU of CDs	MU / Dollar of CDs	Q of DVDs	TU of DVDs	MU of DVDs	MU / Dollar of DVDs
0	0	--	--	0	0	--	--
1	120	120	12	1	300	300	15
2	220	100	10	2	500	200	10
3	260	40	4	3	600	100	5
4	280	20	2	4	660	60	3

The marginal utility of the third CD is 40 utils (260 – 220 = 40). Rosemary will buy a DVD first because the 15 utils per dollar she gains from the DVD is greater than the 12 utils per dollar she gains from the first CD. Rosemary will maximize her utility if she buys 2 CDs and 2 DVDs. The formula for utility maximization is $MU_{CD} / P_{CD} = MU_{DVD} / P_{DVD}$, where MU = marginal utility and P = price. In this case, the marginal utility per dollar of her last CD (100 / $10) equals the marginal utility per dollar of her last DVD (200 / $20). Rosemary's total utility from the purchase is 720 utils: 220 from the CDs and 500 from the DVDs. Rosemary will buy 1 more DVD, because she gains 100 units of utility from the DVD, while the two additional CDs will only bring her 60 units of utility.

Sample Essay Rubric

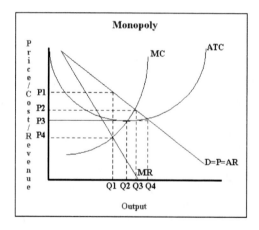

1.   **15 points** (4 + 2 + 1 + 3 + 5)
(a)   4 points:
- 1 point is earned for identifying the profit-maximizing output as Q1.
- 1 point is earned for stating that the rule for finding profit-maximizing output is to produce where the marginal cost = marginal revenue.
- 1 point is earned for identifying the price at the profit-maximizing output as P1.
- 1 point is earned for identifying the area of economic profit as (P1 – P3) x Q1.

(b)   2 points:
- 1 point is earned for identifying the output at productive efficiency as Q2.
- 1 point is earned for stating that this is the point of least-cost production, or where the marginal cost crosses the average total cost at its lowest point.

(c)   1 point:

- 1 point is earned for explaining that the monopolist can maximize profit by restricting output and charging a higher price, so it has an incentive to maximize profit rather than achieve efficiency.

(d)   3 points:
- 1 point is earned for identifying the output at allocative efficiency as Q3.
- 1 point is earned for identifying the price set by government regulators as P2.
- 1 point is earned for identifying the area of economic profit as (P2 – P3) x Q3.

(e)   5 points:
- 1 point is earned for a correctly labeled side-by-side graph of a perfectly competitive labor market for the industry and firm, with the wage set in the industry and represented as the marginal resource cost for the individual firm.
- 1 point is earned for identifying the profit-maximizing quantity of labor at the point where the marginal revenue product equals the marginal resource cost.
- 1 point is earned for showing a rightward shift in the firm's MRP (demand) curve.
- 1 point is earned for explaining that the firm increases the quantity of workers employed to produce the additional output.
- 1 point is earned for explaining that the wage does not change because the firm is a wage-taker that cannot affect the wage set in the industry.

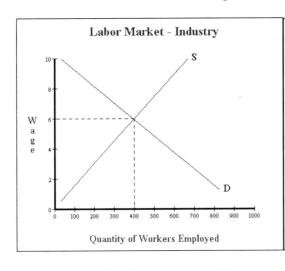 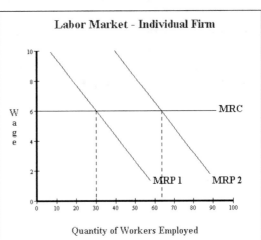

2.   **7 points** (1 + 1 + 1 + 1 + 1 + 2)

(a)   1 point:
- 1 point is earned for stating that Juan's best strategy is a low-price strategy.

(b)   1 point:
- 1 point is earned for stating that Juan's best strategy is a high-price strategy.

(c)   1 point:
- 1 point is earned for identifying a high-price strategy as Mei-Ling's dominant strategy.

(d)   1 point:
- 1 point is earned for stating that Juan does not have a dominant strategy.

(e)   1 point:
- 1 point is earned for stating that Juan will earn $4,000 profit per day.

(f)   2 points:
- 1 point is earned for stating that the relationship is not likely to remain stable.
- 1 point is earned for explaining that Juan has an incentive to cheat on the agreement because he can earn a higher profit if uses a low-price strategy.

3.   Calculations of marginal utility and MU / P necessary to answer the free response

Q of CDs	TU of CDs	MU of CDs	MU / Dollar of CDs	Q of DVDs	TU of DVDs	MU of DVDs	MU / Dollar of DVDs
0	0	--	--	0	0	--	--
1	120	120	12	1	300	300	15
2	220	100	10	2	500	200	10
3	260	40	4	3	600	100	5
4	280	20	2	4	660	60	3

8 points (1 + 5 + 2)

(a)   1 point:
- 1 point is earned for stating that the marginal utility of the third CD is 40 utils.

(b)   5 points:
- 1 point is earned for explaining that Rosemary would buy a DVD first because she gains 15 utils per dollar, while a CD only provides 12 utils per dollar.
- 1 point is earned for stating that Rosemary will maximize her utility by buying 2 CDs and 2 DVDs.
- 1 point is earned for stating the mathematical formula $MU_{CD} / P_{CD} = MU_{DVD} / P_{DVD}$, where MU = marginal utility and P = price.
- 1 point is earned for showing the mathematical formula $100 / \$10 = 200 / \$20$.
- 1 point is earned for stating that Rosemary's total utility from this purchase is 720 utils (220 from 2 CDs and 500 from 2 DVDs).

(c)   2 points:
- 1 point is earned for stating that Rosemary will buy 1 more DVD.
- 1 point is earned for stating that Rosemary's total utility will increase by 100 utils if she buys the DVD but only 60 utils if she buys the two CDs.

Directions: Each of the questions or incomplete statements below is followed by five responses or completions. Select the best one in each case.

1. In a market economy, economic decisions are made primarily by
    (A) the government.
    (B) custom and tradition.
    (C) a panel of leading national economists.
    (D) firms and consumers.
    (E) the Secretary of the Treasury and the Chairman of the Federal Reserve.

2. An effective price ceiling placed below the equilibrium price results in
    (A) a higher price.
    (B) a shortage.
    (C) an increase in supply.
    (D) no effect.
    (E) a surplus.

3. Economies of scale occur when
    (A) the long-run average total cost falls as output increases.
    (B) the marginal cost is greater than the average total cost.
    (C) the average fixed cost is equal to the marginal cost.
    (D) the total cost falls as output increases.
    (E) the average variable cost is greater than the marginal cost.

4. The Law of Demand can be explained by
    I.   the substitution effect.
    II. the income effect.
    III. diminishing returns.
    IV. diminishing marginal utility.
    (A) III only
    (B) I and II only
    (C) I, III, and IV only
    (D) I, II, and IV only
    (E) I, II, III, and IV

5. Profit-maximizing, perfectly competitive firms in long-run equilibrium produce
    (A) where marginal revenue is greater than marginal cost.
    (B) at both productive and allocative efficiency.
    (C) at an output that sustains long-run economic profit.
    (D) at the output where marginal cost is at its minimum.
    (E) where the marginal cost equals the average variable cost.

6.	The largest proportion of national income is paid as
	(A)	wages to labor.
	(B)	profit to corporations and proprietors.
	(C)	interest to banks and loan institutions.
	(D)	economic rent to landowners.
	(E)	taxes to government.

7.	Which situation would cause demand for movie theater tickets to increase?
	(A)	The price of DVD rentals decreases.
	(B)	The income of consumers increases.
	(C)	The cost of producing films decreases.
	(D)	The price of movie theater popcorn significantly increases.
	(E)	The number of movie studios producing films decreases.

8.	Marginal product tends to increase with the first workers hired because
	(A)	firms hire the highest-quality workers first, and workers hired later tend to be less productive.
	(B)	the firm can charge a higher price with a lower output.
	(C)	workers begin to specialize and use equipment more efficiently.
	(D)	firms find it more profitable to train workers as more workers are hired.
	(E)	the marginal cost rises starting with the first worker hired.

9.	Assume a perfectly competitive market is in long-run equilibrium. If a population increase raises product demand, how will each of the following be affected in the short run for the individual firm?

	Price	*Profit*	*Output*
(A)	Increase	Increase	Increase
(B)	Decrease	Decrease	Decrease
(C)	Increase	Increase	Decrease
(D)	Decrease	Decrease	Increase
(E)	Increase	Decrease	Decrease

10.	In order to achieve socially efficient output for a monopoly, a government agency would establish a price ceiling at the point where
	(A)	marginal revenue equals average total cost.
	(B)	marginal revenue equals marginal cost.
	(C)	marginal revenue equals price.
	(D)	marginal cost equals demand.
	(E)	marginal cost equals average total cost.

11.	In which market structure are firms mutually interdependent?
	(A)	Perfect competition
	(B)	Monopolistic competition
	(C)	Oligopoly
	(D)	Monopoly
	(E)	Natural monopoly

12.	If the demand increases for bricklayers in a perfectly competitive labor market,
	(A)	the wages of bricklayers will increase.
	(B)	the number of workers who choose to become bricklayers will decrease.

(C)   the wages of architects will increase.
(D)   the quantity of bricklayers hired will decrease.
(E)   the supply of bricklayers will decrease.

13.   If a pencil producer's total revenue increases when it lowers the price of pencils,
(A)   the demand for pencils is price elastic.
(B)   the supply of pencils is price inelastic.
(C)   the demand for pencils is cross-price inelastic.
(D)   the demand for pencils is income inelastic.
(E)   the demand for pencils is price inelastic.

14.   In the short run, if a firm's marginal cost is higher than the average total cost,
(A)   the marginal cost curve is falling.
(B)   the average total cost curve is falling.
(C)   the average total cost curve is rising.
(D)   the average total cost curve is at its lowest point.
(E)   the marginal cost curve is at its highest point.

15.   In a competitive grape soda market, which of the following combinations could result in both a higher price and a lower quantity of soda sold?

	Supply	*Demand*
(A)	Increase	Increase
(B)	Increase	Decrease
(C)	No change	Increase
(D)	Decrease	Increase
(E)	Increase	No change

16.   As more units of a variable resource are added to a fixed amount of capital, after some point, marginal output begins to fall, according to
(A)   the Law of Demand.
(B)   the Law of Supply.
(C)   the Law of Diminishing Marginal Utility.
(D)   the Law of Diminishing Returns.
(E)   the Law of Comparative Advantage.

17.   The market for public goods fails because
(A)   consumers only have a demand for private goods.
(B)   of the free-rider problem.
(C)   negative externalities affect too many people.
(D)   firms earn too much profit and provide too few goods.
(E)   economic profit in the industry falls to zero in the long run.

18.   Why must a purely competitive firm's marginal revenue equal the product price?
(A)   The firm maximizes profit by raising the product price.
(B)   As a price taker, the firm must sell each product at the same price.
(C)   As a price maker, the firm increases the product price by restricting output.
(D)   The government establishes a price ceiling for the product.
(E)   Lower product demand increases the product price.

19.   An increase in the fixed cost of production at a particular output causes
        (A)   an increase in the average total cost.
        (B)   an increase in the average variable cost.
        (C)   an increase in the marginal cost.
        (D)   an increase in the marginal product.
        (E)   an increase in the marginal revenue.

Questions 20–21 refer to the table below, which shows the total utility Brian gains from consuming peanuts and jelly beans.

Quantity of Peanuts	Total Utility from 1 cup of Peanuts	Quantity of Jelly Beans	Total Utility from 1 cup of Jelly Beans
0	0	0	0
1 cup	5	1 cup	11
2 cups	9	2 cup	19
3 cups	12	3 cup	26
4 cups	14	4 cup	30

20.   What is the marginal utility of the third cup of peanuts Brian consumes?
        (A)   3 units of utility
        (B)   9 units of utility
        (C)   12 units of utility
        (D)   2 units of utility
        (E)   14 units of utility

21.   If the price of peanuts is $1 per cup and the price of jelly beans is $2 per cup, and Brian wants to maximize his utility, what should he purchase first?
        (A)   1 cup of peanuts, because peanuts produce a lower total utility
        (B)   1 cup of peanuts, because the price of peanuts is lower
        (C)   1 cup of peanuts, because the marginal utility per dollar for peanuts is lower than the marginal utility per dollar of jelly beans
        (D)   1 cup of jelly beans, because the marginal utility per dollar for jelly beans is higher than the marginal utility per dollar of peanuts
        (E)   1 cup of jelly beans, because jelly beans produce a higher total utility

22.   Each of the following is an example of a factor of production EXCEPT
        (A)   a food service worker.
        (B)   a tree used to create pencils.
        (C)   an entrepreneur using her abilities to develop a new business.
        (D)   a car used to drive a barber to work.
        (E)   a computer used by researchers at a pharmaceutical company.

23.   In a perfectly competitive market, the demand curves have the following slopes:

	Industry	*Individual Firm*
(A)	Downward sloping	Downward sloping
(B)	Horizontal	Horizontal
(C)	Upward sloping	Upward sloping
(D)	Horizontal	Downward sloping
(E)	Downward sloping	Horizontal

24. The monopolistically competitive firm is similar to the perfectly competitive firm, because in long-run equilibrium, both firms
    (A) maximize profit where marginal cost equals marginal revenue.
    (B) achieve both productive and allocative efficiency.
    (C) are able to sustain economic profit in the long run.
    (D) have significant barriers to entry of other firms into the industry.
    (E) are price-takers.

25. The market fails for positive externalities because
    (A) the product is overproduced, given the social costs and benefits.
    (B) the subsidy for production is set too high.
    (C) society wants government to eliminate the spillover benefits.
    (D) the marginal tax rate for the product is set too low.
    (E) the product is under-produced, given the social costs and benefits.

26. Which of the following is an example of derived demand?
    (A) When the price of strawberries falls, the quantity demanded rises.
    (B) When the demand for cars increases, the demand for car workers increases.
    (C) When the price of donuts falls, the demand for muffins decreases.
    (D) When the demand for cookies increases, the demand for milk increases.
    (E) When the supply of gold increases, the demand for gold rings increases.

27. When wheat is harvested, the straw can be used for animal bedding. Both wheat and straw are sold in competitive markets. If the supply of wheat increases,
    (A) the price of wheat increases.
    (B) the price of straw increases.
    (C) the demand for wheat increases.
    (D) the supply of straw decreases.
    (E) the price of straw decreases.

28. Monopolies differ from perfectly competitive firms because monopolies
    (A) face a perfectly elastic demand curve for their product.
    (B) determine the price of the products they sell.
    (C) achieve productive efficiency.
    (D) cannot sustain long-run profit.
    (E) produce where marginal cost equals marginal revenue.

29. If the "Big Three" firms in an industry are able to collude to restrict output,
    (A) each of the three firms will produce at its minimum average total cost.
    (B) profits of the three firms will be lower than if the firms did not collude.
    (C) competitors will be able to overcome the barriers to entry into the industry.
    (D) product prices will be higher than if the firms did not collude.
    (E) each of the three firms will produce at the socially optimal output.

30. The table below shows the number of hours required for Country A and Country B to produce one television or one radio.

	Televisions	Radios
Country A	10 hours	2 hours
Country B	8 hours	2 hours

Which of the following statements is true?
- (A) Country A has a comparative advantage in producing televisions and should export televisions to Country B.
- (B) Country B has an absolute advantage in producing both televisions and radios and cannot gain from trade with Country A.
- (C) Country B has a comparative advantage in producing televisions and should import radios.
- (D) Country B has a comparative disadvantage in both televisions and radios and should erect trade barriers to protect domestic industries.
- (E) Country A has a comparative advantage in producing radios and should import radios.

31. The difference between the price a consumer is willing to pay and market price is
- (A) producer surplus.
- (B) profit.
- (C) average total cost.
- (D) elasticity.
- (E) consumer surplus.

32. If generic peanut butter is an inferior good, a decline in consumer income causes
- (A) the price of generic peanut butter to go down.
- (B) the demand for name-brand peanut butter to go up.
- (C) the supply of generic peanut butter to go up.
- (D) the demand for generic peanut butter to go up.
- (E) the price of bread to go down.

33. If the marginal revenue product for hiring the next worker is higher than the wage of that worker, in order to maximize its profit, the firm should
- (A) hire the worker.
- (B) not hire the worker.
- (C) hire the worker only if it reduces the cost of capital.
- (D) lay off one worker.
- (E) reduce its product price.

34. A monopolistically competitive firm generally chooses an output that results in excess capacity because
- (A) the firm must anticipate its competitors' responses to its output decisions.
- (B) the firm maximizes profit at an output less than allocative efficiency.
- (C) the firm finds it difficult to anticipate consumer tastes and desires.
- (D) the firm is more focused on achieving efficiency at the lower output.
- (E) the firm's average total cost of production is minimized at the same point where profit is maximized.

35. If the government imposes a lump sum tax on a single firm in a monopolistically competitive industry, what are the short-run effects for the firm?

	Output	Price	Profit/Loss
(A)	Decrease	Increase	Short-run profit
(B)	Decrease	Decrease	Short-run loss
(C)	No change	Increase	No change
(D)	Increase	No change	Short-run profit
(E)	No change	No change	Short-run loss

36. Each of the following is an example of a public good EXCEPT
   (A) a city street.
   (B) national defense.
   (C) a lighthouse.
   (D) a city park.
   (E) a professional football stadium.

37. If the demand for Product A increases because the price of Product B increases,
   (A) Products A and B are complements.
   (B) Products A and B are substitutes.
   (C) Products A and B are inferior goods.
   (D) Product A is a normal good and Product B is an inferior good.
   (E) demand for Product A is elastic, while demand for Product B is inelastic.

38. At a particular output, a perfectly competitive firm's marginal cost and average total cost are lower than the price. To maximize profit, the firm should
   (A) increase output.
   (B) decrease output.
   (C) remain at the same level of output.
   (D) shut down.
   (E) raise the product price.

39. Monopolies do not produce at an allocatively efficient level of output because
   (A) they over-allocate resources to produce too many products.
   (B) they lower prices in order to sell more products.
   (C) they produce at the lowest average total cost rather than where marginal cost equals marginal revenue.
   (D) they reduce output in order to increase the price.
   (E) they produce at an output where the price is equal to demand.

40. If the government places an excise tax on a product with relatively elastic supply and demand, which of the following effects will occur?
   I.   The price of the product will increase.
   II. The quantity of the product sold will increase.
   III. A deadweight loss will develop.
   (A) I only
   (B) II only
   (C) I and III only
   (D) I and II only
   (E) I, II, and III

41. As illustrated by the production possibilities curve, if a society's resources are fully employed,
    (A) more of one good can only be made by producing less of another.
    (B) an increase in the number and quality of resources causes the curve to shift inward.
    (C) any attempt to increase production will only cause unemployment.
    (D) the country must make a decision to produce only the product for which it has an absolute advantage.
    (E) a change in economic system from a market economy to a command economy is the best way to increase future production.

42. The "invisible hand" that serves as an incentive for firms in the market system is
    (A) the threat of government punishment for failing to meet production quotas.
    (B) the self-interest of earning profit.
    (C) the satisfaction of knowing customers are pleased with products.
    (D) the production of public goods.
    (E) the promise of government subsidies for producing high-quality products.

43. If the firms in a perfectly competitive industry merged to form a monopoly and the costs of production did not change,
    (A) the price would fall.
    (B) the industry output would fall.
    (C) the monopoly would produce at productive efficiency.
    (D) the firm would achieve allocative efficiency.
    (E) the marginal cost would fall.

44. The United States federal government primarily redistributes income through
    (A) externalities and public goods.
    (B) marginal utility and diminishing returns.
    (C) progressive taxes and safety net programs.
    (D) regressive taxes and public goods.
    (E) import tariffs and voluntary export restrictions.

Questions 45–46 are based on the payoff matrix below.

		Zack's Bike Shop Strategy	
Catrina's		High Price	Low Price
Bike Shop	High Price	$200, $200	$150, $250
Strategy	Low Price	$250, $150	$100, $100

The payoff matrix above shows the profits per day that can be earned by two bike shops in an oligopolistic industry. The first number in each cell shows Catrina's profit, and the second number in each cell shows Zack's profit.

45. If neither firm knows the other firm's strategy and the firms do not collude, what will each firm's profit be?

	Catrina's Profit	*Zack's Profit*
(A)	$200	$200
(B)	$250	$150
(C)	$150	$250
(D)	$100	$100
(E)	$200	$150

46.   If the firms collude, which of the following statements is correct?
       I. Both Zack and Catrina should choose a high-price strategy if they are confident both
           firms will maintain their agreement.
       II. Both Zack and Catrina would earn $200 profit per day.
       III. Both Zack and Catrina have an incentive to cheat on their collusive agreement
       (A) I only
       (B) III only
       (C) I and II only
       (D) II and III only
       (E) I, II, and III

47.   A movie theater that charges $10 per ticket for adults and $5 per ticket for children and senior
       citizens is engaging in
       (A) allocative efficiency.
       (B) diminishing marginal returns.
       (C) comparative advantage.
       (D) economic profit.
       (E) price discrimination.

48.   If the supply of authentic 1960 "John Kennedy for President" campaign buttons is
       fixed and the buttons become a new fad, what would occur in the market?

	Price	Quantity
(A)	Increase	Increase
(B)	Decrease	Decrease
(C)	No change	Increase
(D)	Increase	No change
(E)	Decrease	No change

49.   Which government policy would be appropriate to resolve a negative externality?
       (A) Grant the firm a per-unit subsidy
       (B) Set a price ceiling for the product
       (C) Charge the firm a per-unit tax on production
       (D) Place a tariff on exports
       (E) Establish a minimum wage for workers in the industry

50.   If a firm's average total cost is higher than the price at the loss-minimizing output, the firm
       should remain in operation in the short run as long as
       (A) the firm is earning a profit.
       (B) the price is higher than the marginal cost.
       (C) the price is higher than the average variable cost.
       (D) the marginal cost is equal to the average variable cost.
       (E) the average total cost is greater than the marginal cost.

51.   The change in the firm's revenue that results from hiring one more resource is
       (A) marginal cost.
       (B) marginal revenue.
       (C) marginal product.
       (D) marginal revenue product.
       (E) marginal utility.

Questions 52–53 refer to the graph below, which shows the costs and revenues for a profit-maximizing firm in a perfectly competitive industry.

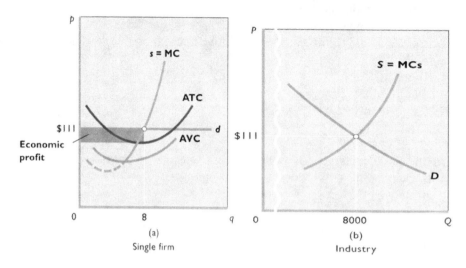

(a)
Single firm

(b)
Industry

52.   The dark shaded area on the graph for the individual firm represents
       (A)   economic profit.
       (B)   the area of loss.
       (C)   normal profit.
       (D)   diminishing returns.
       (E)   marginal utility.

53.   How will long-run equilibrium be achieved in this industry?
       (A)   Firms will exit the industry.
       (B)   The government will institute a price ceiling.
       (C)   Firms will seek lower-cost methods of production.
       (D)   Firms will enter the industry.
       (E)   Government subsidies will lower the production costs of firms.

54.   An increase in labor productivity from worker training results in
       (A)   an increase in labor demand.
       (B)   a decrease in labor demand.
       (C)   an increase in labor supply.
       (D)   a decrease in labor supply.
       (E)   a decrease in wages.

55.   Which statement correctly describes the relationship of costs and revenues for the monopoly producing at profit-maximizing output?
       (A)   The average total cost is higher than the price.
       (B)   The marginal cost is higher than the marginal revenue.
       (C)   The average variable cost is higher than the average total cost.
       (D)   The marginal revenue is higher than the marginal cost.
       (E)   The price is higher than the marginal revenue.

56. If a firm uses only labor and capital to produce its output; the marginal product of labor is MPL and price of labor is PL; and the marginal product of capital is MPK and the price of capital is PK, the least-cost rule for hiring labor is
    (A) MPL + MPK = PL + PK
    (B) MPL x PL = MPK x PK
    (C) MPL – PL = MPK – PK
    (D) MPL / PL = MPK / PK
    (E) MPL + PL = MPK + PK

57. Antitrust legislation is designed to promote
    (A) mergers of firms in order to achieve economies of scale.
    (B) the equality of incomes.
    (C) improvements in technology and productivity.
    (D) profit maximization.
    (E) increased competition in markets.

58. If consumer incomes decrease and demand for cars is relatively elastic,
    (A) the demand for auto assembly workers will decrease.
    (B) the supply of auto assembly workers will increase.
    (C) the wages of auto assembly workers will increase.
    (D) the demand for cars will increase.
    (E) the demand for gasoline will increase.

59. Which of these factors explain the inequality in the distribution of U.S. incomes?
    I.   Education and training
    II. Minimum wage laws
    III. Ability levels and talents
    IV. Discrimination
    (A) I only
    (B) II and III only
    (C) I, III, and IV
    (D) I, II, and IV
    (E) I, II, III, and IV

60. A subsidy is an appropriate action for government to take when
    (A) a firm is producing a product that generates negative externalities.
    (B) consumers are struggling to afford computers because prices are rising more quickly than wages.
    (C) a firm is producing a product that generates positive externalities.
    (D) wages are rising in response to an increase in demand for labor.
    (E) a firm is increasing production due to higher product demand.

MICROECONOMICS PRACTICE TEST 2
Section II
Planning Time: 10 Minutes
Writing Time: 50 Minutes

Directions: You have fifty minutes to answer all three of the following questions. <u>It is suggested that you spend approximately half your time on the first question and divide the remaining time equally between the next two questions.</u> In answering the questions, you should emphasize the line of reasoning that generated your results; it is not enough to list the results of your analysis. Include correctly labeled diagrams, if useful or required, in explaining your answers. A correctly labeled diagram must have all axes and curves clearly labeled and must show directional changes. <u>Use a pen with black or dark blue ink.</u>

1. Maggiori Farms produces raspberries in a perfectly competitive domestic industry with a closed economy.

(a) Draw correctly labeled, side-by-side graphs for the raspberry industry and for Maggiori Farms in long-run equilibrium. Show the following:
   (i)   Price and output in the industry
   (ii) Price and output for Maggiori Farms

(b) Now assume the government opens the economy to imported raspberries, which sell at a world price significantly lower than the domestic price. Draw new correctly labeled, side-by-side graphs for the domestic raspberry industry and show the following short-run effects of opening trade on the domestic raspberry industry:
   (i)   The change in domestic industry supply and/or demand. Explain.
   (ii)   The price and quantity of raspberries in the domestic industry
   (iii) The price and quantity of raspberries produced by Maggiori Farms
   (iv)   State whether Maggiori Farms is experiencing a profit or a loss.

(c) State the rule for determining whether Maggiori Farms should continue producing in the short run.

(d) Explain how the following will change in the long run for the domestic raspberry industry:
   (i)   The number of domestic firms producing raspberries
   (ii)   The reasoning for the change in the number of domestic firms
   (iii) Domestic output of raspberries

2. Herman's Hoops is a profit-maximizing producer of basketballs. It can sell every ball it produces in the market for $10 each, and it can hire all of the labor it needs for $100 per worker per day. The table below shows the short-run production function for Herman's Hoops.

Number of Workers	Total Product Per Day
0	0
1	9
2	23
3	35
4	46
5	52
6	54
7	51

(a)   Calculate the marginal product of the sixth worker.
(b)   Calculate the marginal revenue product of the third worker.
(c)   State the rule for determining the profit-maximizing quantity of labor to hire.
(d)   How many workers should Herman's Hoops hire to maximize profit?
(e)   Explain why Herman's Hoops would not hire the seventh worker.
(f)   If the firm's fixed cost is $20 per day and labor is the firm's only variable cost, what will be the firm's short-run daily profit if it hires 4 workers?
(g)   Assume the industry wage increases to $120 per day. How many workers will Herman's Hoops hire to maximize profit at the higher wage?

3.   The graph below shows the price and quantity of textbooks produced by an unregulated firm. During the production process, this firm creates significant air and water pollution for city residents.

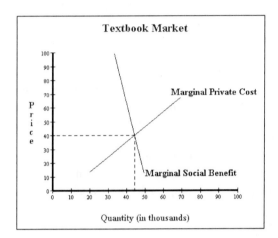

(a)   Identify the term that explains this scenario.
(b)   Redraw this graph and include a curve to show where the marginal social cost is located.
(c)   Use marginal benefit and marginal cost analysis to explain how this firm is misallocating resources.
(d)   Now assume the government regulates this industry and imposes a $10 per book tax on production in an effort to promote socially optimal output. Explain the effect of the tax on each of the following for the firm:
        (i)   Marginal private cost
        (ii)   Output
        (iii)   Given the elasticity of demand illustrated in this market, will the firm or the consumer pay the larger burden of the tax? Explain.
(e)   Explain another policy, other than a tax, that the government could take to correct this market failure.

MICROECONOMICS PRACTICE TEST 2 – KEY
Section I

1.   (D)   Most decisions in a market economy are made by firms and consumers through the forces of supply and demand.

2.   (B)   When the price is held below equilibrium, the quantity demanded rises as the quantity supplied falls, creating a shortage.

3.   (A)   Long-run average total cost consists of the minimum average total cost points at the different plant sizes. With economies of scale, long-run ATC falls as plant size increases, showing greater efficiency with a larger plant.

4.   (D)   The substitution effect, the income effect, and diminishing marginal utility all lead consumers to buy more at lower prices. Diminishing returns refers to the decrease in marginal output per worker as more workers are hired.

5.   (B)   In the long run, firms in perfect competition produce at minimum average total cost and where industry supply equals demand. Firms produce where marginal revenue equals marginal cost to maximize profit but earn no long-run economic profit because such profit draws in competitors.

6.   (A)   Approximately 70% of national income is in the form of workers' wages.

7.   (B)   When income increases, demand for normal goods increases. If the price of DVDs (a substitute) decreases or the price of popcorn (a complement) increases, demand would fall. A lower cost of production would increase supply, while fewer film studios would reduce supply.

8.   (C)   As specialization increases efficiency, marginal product rises and marginal cost falls for the first workers hired. As more workers are hired, marginal product begins to fall (and marginal cost to rise) as specialization wears off and workers begin to overwhelm the capital.

9.   (A)   An increase in demand raises the price in the industry, which transfers to an increase in marginal revenue (price) for the firm. Output increases because MR = MC at an increased output, and because the price is now higher than the ATC, the firm enjoys a short-run economic profit.

10.   (D)   The output where marginal cost equals demand is the point of allocative efficiency and is socially efficient. MC = MR is the profit-maximizing output, and MC = ATC is productive efficiency.

11.   (C)   In an oligopoly, the effects of a firm's decisions depend on the decisions of rivals. In perfect and monopolistic competition, each firm is such a small part of the market that one firm's decisions do not affect other firms. Monopolies are the only firms in their industries.

12.   (A)   An increase in demand raises the wage and quantity hired.

13.   (A)   When demand is elastic, a small percentage decrease in price causes a larger percentage increase in quantity demanded, so total revenue rises.

14.   (C)   When the marginal cost is higher than average total cost, MC pulls ATC up, so the ATC curve is rising.

15.   (D)   Potential double-shift questions can be solved by process of elimination. (A) and (E) both require an increase in quantity. (B) requires the price to fall. (C) is wrong because increased demand raises the price, but it also raises the quantity demanded. The only option left is (D), which definitely results in a higher price, though quantity could increase or decrease.

16.   (D)   The Law of Demand says that at a lower price, consumers buy more. The Law of Supply says that at a higher price, producers increase the quantity supplied. The Law of Diminishing Marginal Utility says that the more of a good a consumer gets, the less

364   Microeconomics Practice Test 2 Key

utility he gets from each additional unit. The Law of Comparative Advantage says that mutually beneficial trade can occur if countries produce what they are most efficient at producing and then trade.

17. (B) Public goods are those desired by consumers, but because non-payers cannot be excluded, the free-rider problem makes it impossible for private firms to profit from producing the good. Because the market fails and the product would be under-produced, government instead provides the good.

18. (B) The perfectly competitive firm is such a small part of the industry that it has no control over price, so it must accept the market price. The firm cannot sell more by lowering the price, and if it tries to raise the price, the quantity demanded drops to zero as consumers simply buy a substitute.

19. (A) Because fixed cost is a component of the total cost, an increase in fixed cost must cause average total cost to increase. Fixed cost is not a component of the other costs or revenues.

20. (A) The total utility increases from 9 to 12, so marginal utility is 3 units.

21. (D) To maximize utility, Brian should purchase the item that maximizes marginal utility per dollar spent. The first cup of peanuts brings 5 utils per dollar, while the first cup of jelly beans brings 5.5 utils per dollar (11 / $2), so Brian would be better off purchasing jelly beans first.

22. (D) Land, labor, capital, and entrepreneurship used as a resource are factors of production. The car, in this context, is not a factor of production. If the car were being used in production, such as a realtor driving clients to view homes for sale, it would be considered a factor of production.

23. (E) Industry demand is downward sloping as a result of the Law of Demand. The price-taking firm must accept the industry price, which does not change with the firm's output; therefore, the firm's demand is horizontal.

24. (A) MC = MR is the profit-maximizing rule for firms in every market structure. Perfectly competitive firms achieve productive and allocative efficiency and are price takers; monopolistically competitive firms are not. Neither firm sustains long-run economic profit or has significant barriers to entry.

25. (E) Positive externalities extend spillover benefits to others outside of a transaction. Because consumers do not consider all of the social benefits of the product, it is under-produced.

26. (B) Derived demand is the concept that when demand for a product increases, the demand for workers to produce the product increases.

27. (E) Because wheat and straw are produced together, when the supply of wheat increases, the supply of straw also increases, decreasing the price of straw.

28. (B) Monopolies are price makers, while perfectly competitive firms are price takers. (A), (C), and (D) are characteristics of perfectly competitive firms, not monopolies. Both kinds of firms produce where MC = MR.

29. (D) By restricting output, the firms can raise the product price. The firms in this oligopoly will still remain productively and allocatively inefficient, and competitors still face the same barriers to entry into the industry.

30. (C) Country B has a comparative advantage in TVs, because Country B's opportunity cost for producing a TV is 4 radios, while Country A's is 5 radios. Country A has a comparative advantage in radios. Therefore, Country B should produce TVs and export them to Country A while importing radios. Country B has the absolute advantage in producing TVs, and neither country has an absolute advantage in producing radios.

31. (E) Consumer surplus is the triangle to the left of equilibrium above price.

32. (D) When income falls, demand for inferior goods increases, as consumers substitute inferior goods for the normal goods they would have bought with a higher income.

33. (A) The firm increases profit when it hires all workers who bring in a higher marginal revenue product than the wage it costs to hire them. Profit is maximized when the firm hires the number of workers where MRP equals wage.

34. (B) Monopolistically competitive firms maximize profit where MC equals MR.

35. (E) A lump-sum tax affects fixed and total costs but not marginal or variable costs or the firm's revenue. The marginal revenue and marginal cost do not change, so the firm still produces at the same output and price. But now that ATC has increased, the firm produces at a loss in the short run.

36. (E) One of the defining characteristics of a public good is the inability to exclude those who refuse to pay for the product. It is relatively easy to prevent a non-payer from entering a professional football stadium.

37. (B) If the products were complements, a price increase in B would cause demand for A to fall.

38. (A) The firm is earning a profit, because Price is greater than ATC. To maximize profit, the firm should keep producing until MC equals MR (the price).

39. (D) Monopolies maximize profit where MC equals MR and produce at that lower output, under-allocating resources, rather than producing at efficiency.

40. (C) An excise tax reduces supply, raising the price and lowering the quantity sold. A deadweight loss develops in the triangle to the left of equilibrium between the supply and demand curves, representing the loss of producer and consumer surplus as a result of the tax.

41. (A) The production possibilities curve illustrates choices society must make in the production of goods because of scarce resources. Points inside the curve represent unemployment, while increases in the number and quality of resources and improvements in technology shift the curve out.

42. (B) The profit motive draws firms into industry in a market economy.

43. (B) The monopoly does not achieve productive or allocative efficiency. The output of the industry would fall as the firm restricts output in order to raise the price and maximize profit.

44. (C) Progressive taxes charge those with higher incomes a higher tax rate, and the government redistributes those funds to those with lower incomes via transfer payments such as welfare, food stamps, and rent subsidies.

45. (D) Neither firm has a dominant strategy, so its profit depends on the decision of the other firm. If each firm chooses a low-price strategy in an attempt to achieve the highest profit ($250), the firms each earn $100 profit.

46. (E) Each of the firms would earn $200 profit if it could be sure the other firm would stay with the high-price strategy. If only one firm cheats, its profit would rise to $250 while the other firm's profit would fall to $150, and if both cheated, their profit would fall to $100. So each has an incentive to cheat to increase its profit but only if the other firm does not.

47. (E) Price discrimination is charging customers different prices for a product when the differences cannot be justified by differences in production cost.

48. (D) A fixed supply is perfectly inelastic, so the quantity cannot change. An increase in demand for the campaign buttons pushes the price upward.

49. (C) A negative externality produces spillover costs, so the product is over-produced. A per-unit tax on production causes the firm to reabsorb its costs of production, leading to a more efficient output.

50.   (C)   If the firm's price covers the variable cost of producing additional units, the firm should keep producing in the short run because any additional revenues can be put toward the fixed cost. But if the firm cannot even cover its variable cost, it should shut down because it will lose more money by remaining in operation than if it shut down.

51.   (D)   Marginal cost is the increase in total cost from producing one more unit. Marginal revenue is the increase in total revenue from selling one more unit. Marginal product is the increase in total product from hiring one more worker. Marginal utility is the increase in total utility gained from consuming one more product.

52.   (A)   The difference between price and average total cost is profit per unit; multiplied by the output, it is the total profit.

53.   (D)   Short-run profit draws new firms into the industry. As firms enter, industry supply increases, lowering the price until at the MR = MC output, the price again equals average total cost.

54.   (A)   When the marginal product of labor increases, the marginal revenue product also increases, increasing the demand for labor.

55.   (E)   Imperfectly competitive firms have prices higher than marginal revenue because the firm must lower the price in order to sell additional units, and that price cut must apply to all of the units sold, not just the last unit.

56.   (D)   To find the least-cost combination of labor and capital, the firm must hire each until the marginal product per dollar of labor equals the marginal product per dollar of capital.

57.   (E)   Antitrust legislation is designed to limit the market power of monopolies and other combinations in order to increase competition in markets.

58.   (A)   As incomes fall, consumer demand for cars falls, resulting in a lower price for cars and a lower marginal revenue product for auto workers. Because MRP is the demand curve for labor, demand for labor falls.

59.   (C)   Minimum wage laws help reduce the inequality of income distribution.

60.   (C)   Products producing positive externalities are under-produced because not all of the benefits are considered. A subsidy encourages production.

MICROECONOMICS PRACTICE TEST 2 – KEY
Section II – Sample Essays

1.

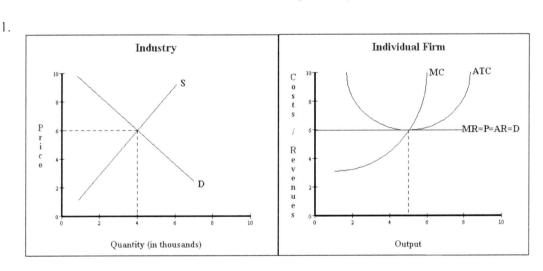

In the industry, the equilibrium price is $6 and quantity is 4,000. For Maggiori Farms, the price is also $6 because it is a price taker from the industry. The firm's quantity is 5, set where the marginal revenue equals marginal cost.

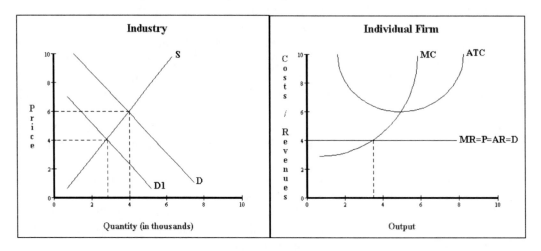

If the country begins to import lower-priced raspberries, demand for domestic raspberries falls because consumers prefer the cheaper substitute. The lower demand reduces the price and quantity of raspberries sold in the domestic industry. At Maggiori Farms, the price falls because the firm must accept the price set in the industry. At the lower price, MC = MR at a lower output, so output falls. Maggiori Farms is now producing at a loss, because the price is lower than the average total cost. Maggiori Farms should only continue to produce in the short run if the price is greater than or equal to the average variable cost. In the long run, the number of domestic firms producing raspberries will fall, because firms experiencing long-run economic losses exit the industry. As a result, the domestic output of raspberries decreases.

2.   This table includes marginal product and marginal revenue product calculations.

Number of Workers	Total Product Per Day	Marginal Product	Marginal Revenue Product
0	0	--	
1	9	9	$90
2	23	14	$140
3	35	12	$120
4	46	11	$110
5	52	6	$60
6	54	2	$20
7	51	-3	$-30

The marginal product of the sixth worker is 2 basketballs (54 − 52). The marginal revenue product of the third worker is $120 (12 × $10). The firm maximizes profit by hiring workers where the marginal revenue product equals the wage (marginal resource cost). Herman's Hoops should hire four workers, because the MRP is $110 and the wage is $110. The fifth worker's MRP is lower than the wage, so the firm would not hire that worker. This firm would not hire the seventh worker because the marginal product of that worker is negative. The firm's short-run daily profit would be $40. The four workers produce 46 balls for a total revenue of $460 (46 × $10). The total cost is the $20 fixed cost plus $400 for the workers (4 × $100). The profit is $40 ($460 − $420 = $40).

If the wage increases to $120, the firm will only hire three workers, because that is where MRP equals MRC.

3.   This situation describes a negative externality. The marginal social cost is higher than the marginal private cost because the firm does not accept all of the costs of production.

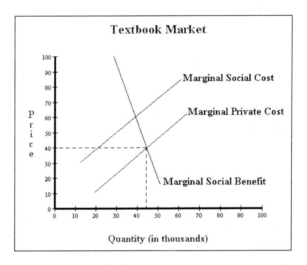

The firm is over-allocating resources to production because it produces where the marginal social cost is greater than the marginal social benefit. If the government placed a $10 tax on book production, the marginal private cost would increase and output would decrease. The consumer would pay the larger burden of the tax because demand is relatively inelastic, so the firm can pass on most of the tax increase to the customer. Government could correct this market failure by setting pollution limitations and fining firms that violate those pollution restrictions.

Sample Essay Rubric

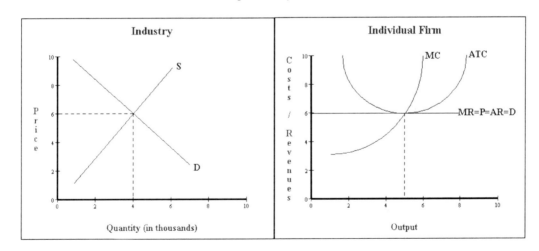

1.   **15 points** (4 + 7 + 1 + 3)
(a)   4 points:
   - 1 point is earned for a correctly labeled graph of the raspberry industry with equilibrium price and quantity correctly indicated.
   - 1 point is earned for showing that the price for Maggiori Farms is the industry price.
   - 1 point is earned for showing Maggiori Farms' output where MC equals MR.
   - 1 point is earned for showing ATC at a minimum where MC equals MR.
(b)   7 points:
   - 1 point is earned for showing a decrease in demand in the industry.
   - 1 point is earned for explaining that demand for domestic raspberries falls because consumers instead demand a greater quantity of the lower-priced import substitute.
   - 1 point is earned for showing that the industry price of domestic raspberries will fall.
   - 1 point is earned for showing that the quantity of domestic raspberries produced in the industry will fall.
   - 1 point is earned for showing that the price at Maggiori Farms falls, which is connected to the decrease in the industry price.
   - 1 point is earned for showing that the quantity produced at Maggiori Farms falls, with the firm producing where MC equals MR.
   - 1 point is earned for stating that Maggiori Farms is experiencing a loss.
(c)   1 point:
   - 1 point is earned for stating the rule that as long as price is equal to or greater than the average variable cost, the firm should continue to produce in the short run.
(d)   3 points:
   - 1 point is earned for stating that the number of domestic firms will decrease.
   - 1 point is earned for explaining that economic losses will lead some firms to leave the industry in the long run.
   - 1 point is earned for stating that the domestic output of raspberries will decrease in the long run.

2.   **7 points** (1 + 1 + 1 + 1 + 1 + 1 + 1)
(a)   1 point:
   - 1 point is earned for stating that the marginal product of the sixth worker is 2 balls.
(b)   1 point:
   - 1 point is earned for stating that the marginal revenue product of the third worker is $120.
(c)   1 point:
   - 1 point is earned for stating the profit-maximizing rule that the firm should hire labor where the marginal revenue product equals the marginal resource cost (wage).
(d)   1 point:
   - 1 point is earned for stating that Herman's Hoops should hire four workers (although MRP > MRC, the firm would not hire the fifth worker because MRC > MRP, so the firm stops hiring with the fourth worker).
(e)   1 point:
   - 1 point is earned for explaining that the seventh worker brings negative returns, decreasing the firm's output.
(f)   1 point:
   - 1 point is earned for stating that the firm's short-run daily profit would be $40. The total revenue (46 balls × $10) minus total cost ($20 fixed + $400 variable) equals $40.

(g)   1 point:
    • 1 point is earned for stating that the firm would hire three workers.

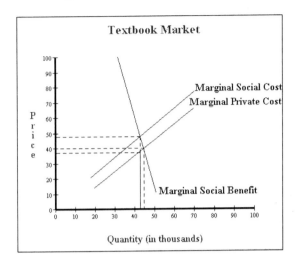

3.   **8 points** (1 + 1 + 1 + 4 + 1)
(a)   1 point:
    • 1 point is earned for identifying this scenario as a negative externality.
(b)   1 point:
    • 1 point is earned for drawing the marginal social cost higher and to the left of the marginal private cost curve.
(c)   1 point:
    • 1 point is earned for explaining that the firm over-allocates resources because the firm produces where the marginal social cost is greater than the marginal social benefit.
(d)   4 points:
    • 1 point is earned for stating that the marginal private cost increases.
    • 1 point is earned for stating that the output decreases.
    • 1 point is earned for stating that the consumer pays the larger burden of the tax. (An answer that the consumer pays all of the tax is incorrect, because demand is not perfectly inelastic.)
    • 1 point is earned for explaining that because demand is relatively inelastic, the firm is able to shift the incidence of most of the tax to the consumer.
(e)   1 point:
    • 1 point is earned for stating another policy which would be effective in reducing output. Correct answers include: restricting output of the product, restricting the pollution level, fining firms that violate pollution restrictions, lawsuits against the firm, requiring the firm to install devices to reduce pollution emission, selling pollution permits, or creating cap and trade programs.